British Tradition and Interior Design

British Tradition and Interior Design

Town and Country Living in the British Isles

Claudia Piras and Bernhard Roetzel
with photographs by Rupert Tenison

KÖNEMANN

© 2000 Könemann Verlagsgesellschaft mbH
Bonner Strasse 126, D-50968 Cologne

Publishing and Art Direction: Peter Feierabend
Project Manager: Birgit Gropp
Assistant: Ruth Mader
Layout: Stephanie Weischer
Photographic Assistant: Francesca Hanbury-Tenison
Picture Editor: Mitra Nadjafi
Production: Mark Voges
Repro Studio: Niemann + Steggemann, Oldenburg

Original Title: Traditional Style. Wohnkultur auf den Britischen Inseln

© 2001 for this English edition
Könemann Verlagsgesellschaft mbH
Bonner Strasse 126, D – 50968 Cologne

Translation from German: Harriet Horsfield, Karen Waloschek, Martin Pearce,
Patricia Cooke, Phil Goddard in association with First Edition Translation Ltd.,
Cambridge, UK
Editing: Andrew Mikolajski in association with First Edition Translation Ltd.
Typesetting: The Write Idea, Cambridge, UK, in association with
First Edition Translation Ltd.
Project Management: Béatrice Hunt and Gabriela Hallas for First Edition Translation Ltd.
Project Coordination: Nadja Bremse-Koob and Isobel Kerr
Production: Mark Voges
Printing and Binding: Mateu Cromo Artes Gráficas, Madrid

Printed in Spain

ISBN 3-8290-4851-3

10 9 8 7 6 5 4 3 2 1

CONTENTS

Foreword

The English house, the English garden, the elegant English style. Anything labeled "English" has been for centuries a seal of excellence, a sign of quality, a guarantee of exquisite taste. England influenced the stylistic and cultural leitmotifs of entire epochs. Anyone with any sense of style took pains to live and reside in the English way. However, enthusiasm for all things English was probably most widespread in the 19th and early 20th centuries. The Victorian and Edwardian years witnessed a prospering Empire with about a quarter of the world's population subjects of its majesty. Those who did not belong to it still saw mighty England as a yardstick. The embodiment of a successful Sunday was an English picnic, ladies in long skirts played the new fashionable sport of tennis, and a nanny attended to the children's upbringing. Furniture from English workshops or their imitations adorned the living rooms of the European neighbors, and marmalade and fine china by Spode or Wedgwood appeared on breakfast tables south of the English Channel.

For many tourists who visit the British Isles everything is "English" regardless of whether it is actually Scottish, Welsh, or Irish. Others strive for greater clarity and are well aware of the difference between the English, the Scots, the Welsh, and the Irish. However, it is interesting to note how these differences are defined. Thus the English stand for the Royal family, afternoon tea, and chintz sofas, the Scots for tartan and whisky, the Welsh for leeks and beautiful scenery, and the Irish for conviviality, Guinness, and folk music. On the other hand this classification is a source of great amusement on the part of the English, Scots, Welsh, and Irish, for nowhere do they better understand the humorous use of clichés, at the same time employing them as the perfect marketing tool, than in the British Isles.

We are speaking of the British Isles in a geographical and not a political sense. The British Isles are inhabited by the British and the Irish, that is by the population of the United Kingdom of Great Britain and Northern Ireland and the population of the Republic of Ireland. The name "Great Britain" includes England, Scotland, and Wales, while "United Kingdom" refers to Great Britain and Northern Ireland. The British Isles is the politically neutral and geographically correct term for the group of islands which consists of the two large islands of Great Britain and Ireland, as well as numerous smaller islands such as the Isle of Man, the Isle of Wight, the Hebrides, the Shetland Islands, the Orkneys, and a few others.

British Tradition and Interior Design traces the roots and also the currently visible features of a world of homes and lifestyles often closely interwoven with the historical fate of the British Isles. In this volume we shall deal primarily with the regions of Great Britain and Ireland which belong to the United Kingdom. The Republic of Ireland is also represented through isolated examples which reflect the common cultural development of a time in which the countries were subject to a common crown. The Tudor castles, the Baroque palaces, the great country houses of the landed gentry, the cabinet-maker's art of the 18th century, the craft revival of the Arts and Crafts Movement, the Colonial style of the 19th century, all contribute to make up what is now the modern British home, whose charm lies above all in the uncopyable mixture of old and new, tradition and innovation, and sometimes even art and bric-a-brac.

The Authors

Even slightly older pieces of furniture are treated with respect in the British Isles:
this elderly armchair stands in Burghley House in Cambridgeshire.

THE BASIC PRINCIPLES OF
BRITISH STYLE

THE INHERITED LOOK

"Show me how you live, and I'll tell you who you are." Nowhere in the world can this saying be more deceptive than in the British Isles. We are dealing with a region where anyone who can afford it can copy a lifestyle that is difficult to distinguish from the original it is imitating. Not everyone has parents who can bequeath them a country house full of antiques, but if you have enough money at your disposal you can easily make up for this shortcoming – that's what real estate brokers, antiques dealers, and interior designers are there for, after all. They help you find an old house and furnish it in such a way that it looks as if the new owner had inherited it from his ancestors complete with all the furniture. This is achieved by skillfully mixing old and new, as well as old and old. So for example the living room is not furnished entirely in Early Georgian style, but rather in a conglomerate of Early Georgian, Edwardian, and Late Victorian.

Purity of style would betray the fact that an ambitious interior designer, and not time, had assembled the furniture, and this is exactly what should be avoided. The art of the interior decorator consists in producing that stylistic diversity that is typical of genuinely inherited interiors. Perfection in matching the furniture would be detrimental to comfort; collisions between colors, designs, and style are inevitable. Houses in uniform style are only to be expected of designers, artists, photogra-

In spite of the expense traditionally incurred in furnishing both historic and new houses, too great and too obvious a degree of perfection is taboo. For this reason one often finds a detail which mars perfection, like a tilted lampshade which does not really match the lamp stand. But this effect is deliberate, for the interior should never ever look like a furniture showroom. Moreover, old and slightly dilapidated things fit in with the propensity for the inherited look.

phers, fashion makers, and other professional aesthetes. The predilection for the old is not only prevalent among the rich: students, booksellers, and pensioners beautify their homes with finds from flea markets, auctions, or their favorite charity shops. What the Hepplewhite bureau is to the millionaire, the Victorian vase from Oxfam is to the less well-heeled. Crucial to a convincing inherited look are signs of use, which should on no account be repaired.

Thus an armchair with completely threadbare upholstery stands in the entrance hall under the Rubens, and it never occurred to anyone to have it recovered. The more worn out, the better – this impression is created when, considering the state of some of the upholstered furniture on offer in the antique shops' windows. What does it matter if the stuffing is sticking out of a chair's arm, as long as you can feel that you are sitting on an heirloom inherited from your great-grandfather. The inherited look also dictates that you should not be overly careful with new pieces of furniture. Splashes of tea or red wine cause as little consternation as dog and cat hairs. If after ten years the new sofa looks as though it has been in use for twice as long, you have, as it were, quite by chance produced an antique. Nevertheless, should the proud owners eventually find themselves in the predicament of having to have a piece of furniture refurbished, they can fall back on an army of specialists who will repair or restore every detail true to the original. Naturally, they proceed in such a way that the operation cannot subsequently be detected, for a genuinely old and inherited piece should not look like a replica of itself. As a result of their many years of experience the restorers and conservers often have an astonishing knowledge of the epochs of art history, elements of style, and materials. Their clientele appreciates this and has no qualms about entrusting their family heirlooms to them.

In London there are streets devoted entirely to antique shops. Here you can find simply everything for the stylish house. It is then up to you whether or not you will claim later that the pieces bought there were inherited from your great-aunt.

Things that in other countries pass for worn or threadbare are considered patinated or venerable with age in the British Isles. "I know the carpet is old, but it still serves its purpose," that might be the commentary to the floor covering shown below.

Above: Many British interiors have been put together over years or even decades and naturally consist of furniture and ornaments from very different epochs. But the mixture of styles is intentional as it shows that family traditions are valued and inheritance is given its due honor. But the most important thing in the living room is comfort: heavy armchairs as well as sofas, thick carpets, the upholstered stool, and naturally the arrangement of the group around the indispensable fireplace.

Left: Covered, permanent flea markets can be found all over the British Isles. At these often very large trading posts one can acquire art, kitsch, furniture, and decorative knick-knacks to suit every taste and every pocket. Anyone with a little knowledge can occasionally even pick up genuine antiques at knock-down prices.

British interiors present not only a rich accumulation of furniture and ornaments, but also a great variety of patterns and colors. The trick is to combine all the elements so as to produce a harmonious whole. If this is not successful, however, it does not cause a serious problem to many of the inhabitants of the British Isles.

In any case, they would only rarely abandon an original favorite piece simply because the color did not fit in. Thus originality clearly ranks higher on the value scale of interior decoration than a perfect match of color and design.

A MIXTURE OF PATTERNS

A mixture of patterns is typical of the British style of decoration, and in spite of the attendant design problems it has gained a hold in the homes of the British Isles. It is actually easier to furnish a room or even a whole apartment in a single color scheme and decorative style, for example by painting the walls white, laying a gray carpet, and buying only black furniture. Anyone examining the interior of a British house, on the other hand, will usually find a combination of very different patterns, colors, and materials: wallpaper, floor coverings, soft furnishing fabrics, curtains, lampshades, sofa cushions, all in the most varied colors and designs. In addition, there will usually be yet more dabs of color, perhaps a plaid throw spread over the sofa, a tablecloth on a side table, or vases and bowls of the most differing designs.

The faint-hearted are easily intimidated by this menacing flood of patterns and step back from their intention to furnish in the British style. In fact it is not a simple matter to combine colors, patterns, and different materials with skill. Not because of the existence of a long list of arcane rules, but because of an almost complete absence of them. No one anywhere has ever laid down which chintz cushions match a rose-patterned sofa. Each person has to find that out for themselves, and of course there are decorators willing and able to help. What many fail to appreciate, however, is the fact that chance often has a hand in the creation of an interior. It may be because the carpet is an heirloom which was only acquired after the purchase of the rest of the furniture. Or it may be because the suite was picked up for a good price at an auction, or simply because the householder took a fancy to an armchair and bought it without thinking about the wallpaper. Skillful pattern-mixing calls for a little taste, but above all courage and self-confidence.

When furnishing a house or apartment one should always keep in mind the principle of the inherited look. All too perfectly matching patterns suggest that you have bought everything yourself; with inherited furniture you have no influence over the covering fabrics or the veneer. There are, however, rooms which are so obviously new that it would be ridiculous to produce the impression of an inherited mixture of patterns – for example in a newly opened hotel. Here the task of the interior designer is to harmonize different patterns with each other. The showrooms of many big furniture stores present a similarly interesting field

The English style of furnishing is distinguished not only by a great variety of furniture and decorative pieces, but also by the combination of the most varied patterns and materials. Here a striped wallpaper was chosen to go with a diamond-patterned carpet, and the window is dressed with both floral and geometric designs.

of study. The interiors on display are completely artificial but in the ideal case give the impression of an actual living room.

There is only one way to train your feeling for color: look and try. Periodicals, books, catalogs – all are valuable sources of inspiration. There is hardly a color combination which cannot look good, even if theoretically it breaks one of the many rules of color. And it is the same with the combination of patterns: theories abound, but basically anything goes, as long as you like it.

To begin with it is simplest to combine single-colored and patterned surfaces, picking up the color of the single-colored surface in the patterned item. The next step is the combination of large patterns with smaller ones. The more the patterns differ in their dimensions, the easier it is to combine them. Thus, it is completely unproblematic to put a cushion with small checks on a sofa with broad stripes. The more similar the patterns are in form, rhythm, and color, the more flair is required for their combination. Only practice can help here. You can borrow fabric samples from interior design shops and experiment. The mixture of patterns and colors is successful when a harmonious whole is produced that puts together in the detail things which do not match at all. Even in a hotel lounge we occasionally find incongruities of this type, certainly not the result of a meeting of heirlooms from different sources, but producing this impression all the same. But since the hotel guests are supposed to feel at home, they will also find here those chance combinations which they recognize from their own living room.

The proverbial coziness of traditional British homes is due in part to the creation of small harmoniously decorated islands. Here the flower pattern on the floor-length tablecloth is picked up by the bouquet of flowers and the delicate garland on the lampshade. The arrangement harmonizes with the color of the adjacent sofa.

Upholstered furniture does not necessarily have to be covered in matching fabric. The individual pieces do not even have to be of the same style. Here an opulent floral two-seater with fringing stands harmoniously next to a more sober yellow armchair which fits in with the basic color of the living room.

Tapestries are artistic pictorial textiles made from wool, silk, or mixed fibers. They are used as wall hangings or decorative fabrics.

Embroideries are woven fabrics painstakingly decorated by hand with various motifs.

A velvet cover gives furniture a particularly fine and noble appearance, at the same time being a very tactile choice.

FABRICS

TAPESTRY

When decorative fabrics for the British house are mentioned, tapestries are always first in line. These hand-woven wall hangings, originally from Arras, Bruges, Brussels, and Tournai, were widespread throughout the whole of Europe in the 14th, 15th, and 16th centuries and extremely popular in Great Britain since the 15th century. Unfortunately only a few early examples have been preserved, since these wool and silk hangings were naturally less durable than the houses for which they were made. The oldest known English tapestry was made prior to 1588 in Barchester by William Hicks for the Earl of Leicester, and this work of art can be admired today in the Victoria & Albert Museum in London. From 1620 onward the Mortlake Tapestry Works began to produce outstanding woven tapestries with the help of Flemish workers. However, in the 18th century tapestries fell out of fashion and only experienced a revival in the second half of the 19th century as a result of the Arts and Crafts Movement. Since that time tapestry work-shops have used threads dyed with artificial and not plant-based dyes. For this reason the colors are now more durable but also gaudier. Tapestries today are either used in the original sense as wall hangings or for furniture coverings, curtains, and cushion covers.

EMBROIDERY

The layman easily confuses woven and embroidered fabrics. In contrast to woven tapestries, the motifs in embroidery are worked by hand, stitch by stitch. Embroidery is a traditional technique which is pursued both as a hobby and professionally. The industrial embroidery factories employed mainly men until well into the 19th century, and even among those who embroidered for pleasure women were not necessarily in the majority. All types of fabric were embroidered – linen, cotton, or even silk, according to whether it would be used for a chair cover or a bed curtain. In old British houses embroideries from the 18th century can still be found today, and in spite of their inestimable value they are often put to everyday use. Of similar value are the works of the 19th century which were created during the Arts and Crafts Movement. They were designed as tapestries, wall hangings, and covering fabrics. Since the beginning of the 20th century embroidery has also been carried out by machine, but this has in no way harmed the popularity of hand-embroidered goods.

VELVET

Velvet is one of the most noble fabrics and indeed an armchair covered with red velvet always looks like a royal throne. This is not a chance association. Velvet was for a long time only within the reach of monarchs and princes – it only gained access to the houses of normal mortals through its mass production from cotton in the industrial age. With velvet you can create interesting and sometimes positively dramatic accents in every room. Fabric dealers distinguish between warp velvet and filling velvet. Velvet is also known as velours. It is manufactured by using a pile warp in addition to the ground warp. During weaving the pile warp yarns are laid over rods so that loops form. Later the rods are pulled out and the loops can either be left as they are (uncut velvet) or cut (cut velvet). With filling velvet the pile is woven directly into the warp as a weft or filling. Then the weaver cuts the pile, then brushes and shears it to the desired length. Ribbed velvet and corduroy are also produced in this way. The origins of velvet lie in the Near East, but during the Renaissance Italy became the main producer. A distinction was made between Genoese and Milanese velvet and velvet from Lucca, Modena, and Venice according to which city the fabric was woven in. Today these designations refer to a particular style of fabric which can be produced everywhere. Genoese velvet, for example, is a patterned textile with different pile lengths. Originally velvet was woven from silk, but later they used less valuable fibers such as cotton, wool, or linen. Today there are also velvets made from synthetic fibers. The rise of velvet to a popular upholstery fabric began in the 19th century when the demand for soft furnishing grew. The patterned types are more suitable as covering fabrics than the single-colored and smooth types which show signs of wear more readily. An interesting alternative to velvet is chenille, in which the pile-forming threads do not need to be cut since the pile is formed by the chenille yarn.

Pure silk is still one of the most sumptuous textiles that can be used in interior decoration.

Damask fabrics are equally patterned on both the right and wrong sides and therefore are well suited for free-hanging decorations such as curtains.

Jacquards are richly patterned, usually heavy, hardwearing fabrics made from cotton, wool, silk, or blends.

SILK

Today silk is no longer the most expensive decorative fabric. But if you add "high-quality," then this material is in fact one of the most sumptuous to be used as curtaining or covering fabric. For this noble fabric we are indebted to the silk moth whose caterpillars spin silken threads during pupation. Silk production depends on the breeding of silkworms and the Chinese were the first to master this art. Byzantine monks also brought a knowledge of silkworm culture to Europe. Spain and Italy were quick to specialize in the production of this coveted cloth. Because of its high price, silk at that time was used exclusively in the church and the royal courts. But the real "Land of Silk" is France; in the middle of the 17th century it assumed the leading role in silk production until printed cotton and muslin began to gain in popularity in the 18th century. However, no other fabric could displace silk from the fine reception rooms and cabinets of state. Yet the aristocratic nature of this material can be tempered if it is woven into patterns. Today silk is used as curtaining for windows and fourposter beds, as covering fabric for furniture and for tablecloths, lampshades, cushion covers, and quilted bedspreads.

JACQUARD

In the year 1802 the Frenchman Joseph-Marie Jacquard invented a weaving loom, in which yarn control could be "programmed" to produce the most varied patterns using perforated cards. A single worker was sufficient to operate this loom. In addition it was virtually impossible to make a mistake in the weaving. In memory of this momentous invention, fabrics with woven multi-colored patterns and structures are called Jacquards. Early Jacquard patterns were floral motifs in cotton or woolen fabrics. Using the new method, carpets and tapestries, formerly handwoven, could also be produced with considerably more profit. In 1810 Jacquard adapted his invention for silk weaving and thus made possible the more economical production of silk fabrics. William Morris applied the French technique in his workshops in Merton from 1881 onwards and in this way implemented his designs for decorative and covering fabrics. Thanks to the Jacquard method, structured fabrics were also possible in which the pattern stood out three-dimensionally and had a distinctive feel. Like real Jacquard fabrics they are very suitable for curtains and coverings since they hang well on account of their weight, are hard-

wearing, and show marks less because of the pattern. A special place among woven fabrics is reserved for brocade. The artistic and extremely rich interweaving of different colored, as well as gold or silver threads, produces the impression of filigree embroidery. Brocade is especially suitable as upholstery fabric for delicate 18th-century furniture.

DAMASK

Damask or English damask does not refer to a fabric, but a style of weaving which basically produces a Jacquard fabric in which different patterns are produced using single-colored threads. The name damask recalls the origins of this technique, supposedly in Damascus. Damask silk is said to have been produced there since the 12th century. In Europe damask has been manufactured since the 16th century from both silk and wool. We find the material in many British interiors of the 18th century as upholstery fabric or silk wallpaper. In Belgium white damask linen has been woven since the 18th century, much in demand as table linen. Today the more economical cotton is mainly used for this purpose. High-quality damask silk is reserved for side chairs, that is chairs which serve a mainly decorative purpose. Only very hardwearing cotton mixtures are suitable for covering well-used sofas and armchairs. Damask is equally popular for curtains, provided the size of the pattern is right for that of the window.

PRINTED COTTON AND CHINTZ

There is no other fabric so "English" as chintz. Yet this classic among cotton fabrics is actually an Indian invention, as its name betrays, for chintz comes from the Hindi *chint*, which means colored. In the 17th century the first multi-colored printed fabrics reached England via the East India Company and caused a stir there with their opulent colors and patterns. True, printed fabrics were already known in Europe, but these were mainly simple stripes and could not hold their ground in comparison with the Indian imports. On the wishes of their European trading partners the Indians matched the design of their chintzes to the English taste and produced goods in the style of fine embroideries. The fabric manufacturers of Europe now felt the pressure of competition and worked feverishly to improve their production methods. But this was not easy since the Indians were ahead of them, not only in printing techniques, but also in the matter of dyes and fixing. The technique of printing with copper plates, used since 1752, could be used to produce intricate filigree single-color designs known as *toile de jouy*. But it was not until the introduction of roller printing that the precise and rapid printing of different colors became possible. This technique held sway until the middle of the 19th century. By this time mineral dyes were used instead of plant-based dyes, which added brighter and more vibrant shades to the palette. Besides the still very popular flower designs, pictorial motifs were also printed, such as cock fights, hunting scenes, landscapes, or battle scenes.

Nowadays cotton fabrics are mostly printed by the screen printing process, which is even more precise, faster, and more economical. The name chintz is no longer used for all colored printed cottons, only for those with a shiny finish. The smooth surface of these so-called glazed cottons resists dust penetration and thus the colors retain their luminosity. Chintz is not very robust and is often used for loose covers, which can easily be taken off, cleaned and, if necessary, repaired.

WOOL

Sheep's wool has been used for fabric production literally since ancient times, as demonstrated by finds from the neolithic period. In the Middle Ages the processing of wool was already very advanced and the choice of colors and designs correspondingly large. Woolen fabrics were used predominantly for the production of clothing; painted woolen fabrics, which represented an affordable alternative to woven tapestries, served as decoration for the house. Wool was also the original material for every kind of woven fabric such as damask, velvet, and Jacquard. When wool is mentioned today in connection with decorative fabrics for the house, it is less likely that these types are meant. Many traditional British woolen fabrics are best known from menswear, but tweed is not only for sports jackets, it is also popular as upholstery fabric for armchairs or as cushion material. Another example is Scottish tartan, used for trousers and kilts as well as for curtains, cushions, and covers. Tweeds and tartans are just right for an English country house, tartans especially for Scottish houses. In addition to these two classics, other fabrics from the sample books of gentlemen's tailors keep coming into fashion, for example Prince of Wales check, serge, or even pinstripes. Like all woolen fabrics they are ideally suited as upholstery fabrics, cushion covers, or curtains and lend a room a very British and often masculine air.

LINEN

Linen is not only the oldest fabric of plant origin known to man, it is also a decorative and covering fabric rich with tradition. In antiquity the Egyptians spun the fibers of the flax plant into yarn and wove it into linen. For hundreds of years linen was the most important material in Europe for clothing and household textiles. It was not until the 18th century that cotton replaced this robust fabric in the home, since it could be produced in larger quantities and more cheaply. However, linen continued to be popular as bed curtains or covers to protect expensive upholstery. In view of the extremely high price of silk chair covers, loose covers made from flax fibers were the everyday attire of much upholstered furniture.

In the 19th century the adherents of the Arts and Crafts Movement gave linen a new lease of life as a decorative fabric and used it for curtains, bedspreads, table cloths, and upholstered furniture. The wonderfully faded linen fabrics of this epoch are among the most beautiful fabrics ever produced by British textile design. With their matt surfaces they harmonize beautifully with antique carpets and old furniture, but also go well with a mixture of old and new styles. Above all, when linen is printed with plant-based dyes in sympathetic natural tones it has a warmer and often more elegant effect than the shiny surface of many chintzes. Since pure linen is more expensive than cotton or synthetics, linen blends are often offered today.

PAISLEY

The Paisley design was named after the Scottish industrial town of Paisley, situated seven and a half miles (12 kilometers) to the west of Glasgow in the Strathclyde region. In Victorian times, high-quality Jacquard looms were operated there by expert weavers. The characteristic Paisley motif, a leaf with a tapering and slightly curved end, was originally an Indian invention. Like many ideas from the subcontinent, it found its way to Great Britain during the colonial period. Queen Victoria loved Paisleys and the appropriately embroidered cashmere shawl became a veritable fashion trend. But few could afford the Indian original, so the Scottish

Printing of colors and motifs on fabrics represents an economical alternative to embroidery and woven designs.

Woolen fabrics, familiar from the clothing industry, can also be applied successfully in interior decoration.

Linen is usually thought of as a workaday textile, but at the same time there are many buyers who will pay high prices for antique linen – the best types come from Belgium.

weavers set to work and imitated the pattern using the Jacquard method. In the town of Paisley weavers were particularly skilled in the manufacture of the finest woolen cloth, which they now decorated with this modern design. Only the initiated could tell the difference between a hand embroidered Paisley and one woven on the weaving loom, since the Jacquard process produced a prominent motif. Traditional Paisleys of English or Scottish origin are made of wool and have predominantly red color schemes. Today Paisleys are often simply printed and therefore come in all possible colors (including dark colors). Richly patterned Paisley fabrics have the advantage that when used as upholstery coverings, throws, or sofa cushions they show small marks and smudges much less than lighter-colored fabrics.

QUILTING AND PATCHWORK

Quilting and patchwork are two traditional ways of using fabric. In quilting, an invention of the American settlers, particularly the Amish, two layers of fabric are stitched together in a particular way. Between the two layers of fabric there is a wadding of various degrees of thickness or just air – either will make a quilt. This is all there is to a quilt, which is especially warm and therefore ideal for cold nights. According to what you could or would pay for a quilt, it was made of silk or the cheaper cotton. Like quilting, patchwork is not a type of fabric but a sewing technique. Pieces of fabric of different types and colors are sewn together to make a design. Patchwork is an apt name for the technique since it literally uses patches. Originally patchwork was a way of using up remnants of fabric. Later the technique was employed for its own sake and fabrics were bought expressly for the purpose of forming decorative patterns. A distinction is made between the appliqué method, in which the fabric pieces are sewn on to a backing fabric, and the intarsia method, in which the fabric remnants are stitched directly to each other. In addition patchwork can be subdivided into those types in which regular patterns are produced and crazy patchwork, formed from all kinds of fabrics and designs. Today quilts and patchworks are found mainly as bed covers or throws in the bedroom, perhaps not of a very elegant house, but wherever unaffected coziness is allowed.

LACE AND MUSLIN

The technique of lace-making developed simultaneously in Italy and Flanders in the 15th century. The products of this handicraft were considered valuable status symbols for centuries. At first only small parts, such as a collar or a cuff, would be made of lace, but new techniques soon made it possible to produce larger pieces. Thus Queen Elizabeth I of England is said to have possessed about 3,000 lace garments, and Napoleon's wife was presented with a lace dress by the city of Brussels, which had taken 600 women ten months to make. From the 19th century onward there were machines which produced fine nets on to which lace designs were embroidered by hand. But in 1813 this stage was taken over by a machine developed in Nottingham. Because of its high price lace had only isolated uses as a household textile, perhaps a little cover for an occasional table, a decorative edging for bed linen or, if you could afford it, a whole curtain or blind. Muslin, at that time no less costly, was introduced from India in the 17th century. It was not until the end of the 18th century that the requisite fine yarn could be spun in England and woven into the gauzy material which quickly caused a fashion wave. Clothes, curtains, tablecloths, suddenly everything had to be made from this filmy fabric. Today lace and the finest muslin are also produced in synthetic fibers. Although these fabrics can be no more than an economical substitute for the original, many decorators prefer these hardwearing and easycare alternatives, particularly if they are for pieces such as curtains or bedspreads which will receive a lot of wear.

The lively, decorative Paisley designs with their harmonious colors can be printed or woven.

Quilts and patchworks were originally meant to use up fabric remnants, but today real works of art are produced using this technique – here a quilt in appliqué.

Delicate lace and fine muslin have only limited use as decorative materials but can make fine accents.

Rarities – Silk Fabric from England

Since 1903 the Sudbury-based Gainsborough Silk Weaving Company has been weaving the finest furnishing fabrics from silk, wool, cotton, and linen for a select clientele throughout the world. This English weaving company has earned its good reputation not only through its, in the best sense of the word, old-fashioned perception of quality, but also through its high level of expertise in matters of historical weaving designs. More than 1,000 designs are stored in the archive, ready to serve as a reference or an inspiration to customers. This factory with 50 employees produces not only reproductions but also exclusive original creations. When homeowners wish to cover their dining chairs with silk bearing a pattern formed from the entwined initial letters of their names, they know they will be in good hands at Gainsborough's. For every imaginable design will be converted into a fabric, even for the relatively small minimum order of 30 yards (about 27 meters). The Queen also appreciates the extraordinary specialized knowledge of the firm, as indicated by the royal warrant. For that reason her staff turned to the specialists in the county of Suffolk in complete confidence when seeking to restore the furniture in Windsor Castle following the devastating fire of 1992.

Above: At the Gainsborough Silk Weaving Company yarn from China is dyed in house. Designs are then produced using threads in different shades.
Below: The model room offers an insight into the possible ways of using and combining the different fabric designs.

After dyeing the yarn is wound onto bobbins for later use as warp or weft. The warp thread is stretched lengthwise in the weaving loom, and the weft thread is woven across it horizontally.

In the early years of the 19th century the Frenchman Joseph-Marie Jacquard invented a machine with which complicated designs could be woven in large webs of cloth.

Although fabrics from worsted and carded yarns, such as tweed, are much more typical in Great Britain, you will also find choice silk fabrics here.

Typically British – Horsehair

As early as 1760 Thomas Chippendale was covering his seating for the library, drawing room, and dining room with costly horsehair fabrics, and some 30 years later George Hepplewhite praised this type of fabric as the only correct choice for covering mahogany chairs. This durable, elegantly shiny, and therefore easycare fabric also enjoyed great popularity in England during the reign of Queen Victoria.

Up until the end of the First World War this fabric, much in demand, was produced almost everywhere throughout the island kingdom by small to medium-sized factories. Nowadays horsehair is a rarity – not because better wall and upholstery coverings are available, but because the raw material has become scarce and its processing is labor-intensive and therefore too expensive. Worldwide there is only one horsehair weaver who weaves the horsehair in the traditional way on historical looms in order to produce fabrics in classical or modern designs and colors.

The small factory, situated in rural Somerset, is called John Boyd Textiles and was founded in 1837. There have not been many changes in the production techniques over the years, but nowadays the hair comes mainly from China, where they still use horses in agriculture. To prevent the horses' tails becoming caught in the plough or other implements the farmers cut them off and sell them to Somerset. The raw material is either black, gray, mixed, or white. Black hair is re-dyed dark so that it becomes deep black; gray-brown hair is used as it is. White hair is very rare and the producers of horsehair fabrics have to fight over it with the

violin bow makers and the manufacturers of English judicial wigs. This expensive raw material is bleached and then, if it is to be used for furnishing fabric, dyed in bright colors.

On the weaving loom the carefully combed hairs are used as the weft threads. The warp is fine cotton or silk. This is the reason why horsehair fabrics are relatively narrow: the natural length of the raw material dictates the width. To further embellish the finished product, colorful embroidery is sometimes applied. Family coats of arms, flowers, and small bees are particularly popular.

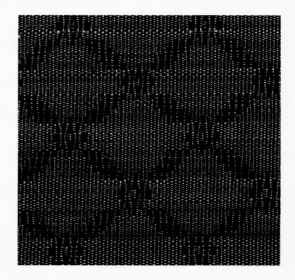

Fabrics with horsehair were extremely popular in the Victorian era as economical, hard-wearing upholstery fabrics. Today these fabrics are considered expensive specialties at the upper end of the price scale.

In the 19th century horsehair fabrics were manufactured in various weaves, but black was the most usual color. It is only in recent years that colored and richly embroidered types have come into fashion.

SYMMETRY

Symmetry is one of the most important principles for the arrangement of surfaces and rooms. In a room the symmetrical arrangement of the furniture begins with the establishment of one or more central points around which everything is then grouped symmetrically. In Great Britain this central point is ideally the fireplace, which has usually already been positioned in such a way that the walls, windows and doors form a symmetrical arrangement. Seating, side tables, lamps, pictures, rugs, mirrors, clocks, and all the other decorative objects are arranged accordingly.

Where there is no fireplace, another central point is created, for example, by a narrow table or a sideboard. The main thing is to have a focus for the sofa and the armchairs. The desire for symmetry is also pursued in the detail. Lamps, vases, pictures, mirrors, and candles are all preferably bought in pairs so that zones of symmetry can be created all over the room.

Desk and sideboard are both decorated with two lamps, two vases stand on the mantelpiece and to the right and left of it hang two pictures in the same style and with the same frames. Side tables also stand in pairs, arranged to the right and left of the sofa. Also for reasons of symmetry single objects are always placed in the middle. A mantel clock takes its place in the middle of the mantelpiece,

The decorative scheme of this typically British arrangement of fireplace, matching mantelpiece, and framed mirror hanging above it shows perfect symmetry. The mantel clock stands exactly in the middle of the mantelpiece and is flanked by two identical goblets, placed level with the mirror frame.

a single painting or a mirror hangs exactly in the center above the sideboard or the fireplace.

Smaller single objects can be placed away from the middle and then balanced with another object. But you should not attempt to find something as similar as possible. This jars on the eye of the observer. It is better to create an optical counterweight. If there is a single bust on the right-hand side of a narrow sideboard, a crystal vase with flowers can be placed on the left-hand side. The flowers occupy a greater area than the small bust, but that is allowed since they are much lighter in substance than the bronze or china object.

Symmetry is by no means an end in itself but helps to organize the room and direct attention in a particular direction. If we hang a picture above the fireplace it is because our glance falls on this part of the room first when we enter it. If wall surfaces need to be organized, once again the arrangement of pictures can help to fix focal points. A niche can be created on the long side of a room beneath a group of symmetrically arranged pictures, where you can sit at a small table to write letters and such like.

Symmetry is also found in British houses for practical reasons. Two sofas placed opposite each other invite conversation. Two armchairs arranged to the right and left of a little table silently but quite unmistakably prompt two visitors coming from the bar with a drink in their hand, to sit down. Symmetry automatically leads the visitor in a British house to the place where he or she will feel most comfortable – to the fireplace, to an armchair, or to a card table – and directs attention toward the decorative objects or their partner in conversation. Symmetrical room designs are, however, also popular for another reason. The paired or central arrangement of furniture and objects constantly lends a room a certain gravity, an important aspect since the British house is also always at the service of hospitality. Visitors should notice that their hosts are people who live in an appropriate environment and, conversely, guests love to be received in rooms which meet their own discriminating taste. They say an Englishman's home is his castle and with this in mind, living and dining rooms nearly always have the feel of the throne room.

Symmetry is one of the unwritten rules of all interiors in the British style. Alongside the inherited look and the mixing of patterns it is the third element of the trinity. Even with the biggest muddle, if you take a second look you will see that the law of symmetry prevails: here the big plate in the middle of the upper shelf defines the center. The hanging cups are also arranged symmetrically, as is the collection of china dogs and the plates, jugs, and boxes on the lower shelf.

The pictures above this inviting sofa have a strictly symmetrical arrangement. The large painting in the middle is framed optically by two smaller works of art on each side, each pair in identical frames. Even the arrangement of the sofa cushions conforms to the criteria of symmetry. The scheme is disrupted however by the lighting: a small table lamp provides light on the left side, while on the right, because of the adjacent door, there would hardly be room for a side table.

The secret of symmetry is focus. Therefore it is crucial first of all to determine the all-important middle point of the room. In interiors of the classical British style this is not difficult – here it is almost always the fireplace. The living room in the picture appears very symmetrical, for the structural lines of the room focus attention completely on the fireplace. Thus it is not so noticeable that the arrangement and style of the chairs and the position of the occasional table and lamp are asymmetrical.

Scrupulously observed symmetry is an outstanding stylistic device for emphasizing an unusual object. On this sideboard nothing competes with the large figurine for the place of honor. But rules are made to be broken – what's in the casket on the right?

If someone rejects symmetry as a basis for room design, it is generally because he finds the central and paired positioning of furniture and ornaments boring. It would actually do this mantelpiece good if at least one element could deviate from the rigid scheme.

Wood

Even if textiles have a high value in our modern homes, wood plays and has always played a larger role in providing a functional, safe, comfortable, and sometimes even elegant home.

Wood is present in every corner of the house, in the actual construction and in the furniture. Beams, roofs, window frames, and doors are all made of wood. Tables, chairs, benches, trunks, bedsteads, cupboards, wainscoting, and much more besides would be unthinkable without this versatile raw material. Even if plastics and metal are in competition with wood at the present time, the natural character of this primary material is unsurpassed.

If we classify British wooden furniture according to the date of its manufacture we can identify three main epochs: the oak period, the walnut period, and the mahogany period. However, this does not mean, of course, that no other types of wood were known or worked during those times.

The oak period spans the years between 1500 and 1660. This includes the late Middle Ages, the Renaissance, the Tudor and Stuart periods, and the epoch of Puritanism. The furniture of this style was characterized by dark wood and the pieces are correspondingly weighty and bulky. At the same time there were also exuberant carvings and interesting architectural elements which gave new impulses to furniture making.

The walnut period lasted from 1660 to 1720. It begins with the Restoration and ends with the Queen Anne style. The introduction of new materials had become necessary for various reasons including the devastating Great Fire of London in 1666. Veneering techniques, marquetry, wood turning and carving, and a distinct partiality for ornamentation ensured the great attractiveness of the new, lighter furniture.

The mahogany period spans a scant 200 years from 1720 to 1914. This stylistically exceedingly rich and varied period includes the Georgian, Regency, Victorian, and Edwardian eras. Of course oak and walnut did not suddenly disappear, but walnut had indeed become very scarce in Europe by the beginning of the 18th century. Imported walnut was almost as expensive as mahogany, and the latter was much easier to work, durable, resistant to pests, and looked simply exquisite. The new material inspired cabinet-makers such as Chippendale, Hepplewhite, and Sheraton to those aesthetic achievements which we view today as the epitome of British furniture-making.

It is not always easy to identify types of wood and when considering the purchase of an expensive antique the layman should seek the advice of an expert. Wood is a living material which changes constantly. A particular type of wood can appear darker or lighter according to its place of origin and will exhibit different and perhaps even atypical graining depending on the age of the tree from which the wood came. The storage conditions, both of the unworked wood and the finished piece of furniture, also affect its appearance, as do its previous position and the care the wood has received. Pieces of furniture which have stood by a light window for a long time eventually become faded. This can produce an aesthetically interesting effect, but equally can cause real damage. Light colored woods can be stained dark to give the impression of a more expensive type of wood – a classic mahogany red does not always prove that you are dealing with real mahogany. Certain polishes and care remedies can also contain stains which tamper with the appearance.

The oak, widespread all over the northern hemisphere, has heavy, durable, and very hard wood. While it was the material for all fine furniture in the 17th century, in later times it was used mainly for invisible load-bearing parts and rustic pieces.

Walnut comes from either the walnut tree or the black walnut tree. Because of its beautiful markings it has been used since the 17th century mainly as veneering. The wood shrinks little, polishes excellently, and is considered very valuable.

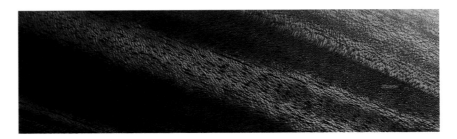

Mahogany has been imported from India, the Caribbean, and South America since the 18th century. The reddish-brown wood with its high luster supplied the original material for the finest and best that British cabinet-making has ever produced.

The wood of the ash, native to Asia Minor and large parts of Europe, has lively graining and is therefore especially suited to inlay work. The initially light color of this wood can with age develop a very beautiful patina. A material for rustic furniture.

The yew, native to Great Britain, provides hard, durable wood and is suited to the manufacture of furniture which will be well used. In the 18th century it was also used for marquetry. Today we usually only find it as a veneer on pressed chipboard.

Rosewood comes from India and Brazil. The hard, heavy wood is singularly grained. It was a fashionable wood in the Regency and the Victorian period. Later the importance of this Indian import declined.

Birch as a genus is widespread over the whole of the northern hemisphere. Its wood is very hard, it can be stained very easily, and with appropriate treatment it makes a convincing imitation mahogany. An ideal material for solid pieces.

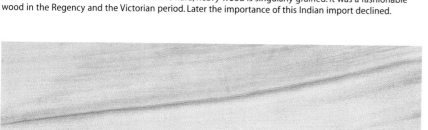

Chestnut is a wood native to Great Britain. A distinction is made between the light colored wood of the horse chestnut and the somewhat darker and more durable wood of the sweet chestnut. In spite of its typical spiraling grain chestnut was used where few other types of wood were available.

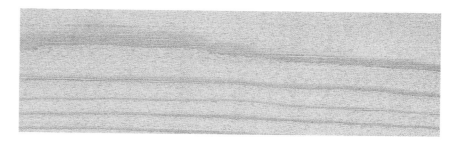

The many species of pine and other conifers (deal) are usually used either for shelves or interior constructions which are then further finished with paint, varnish, or veneer. Untreated conifer wood is used for rustic furniture.

The wood of the many species of cherry displays a soft, warm red tone. This attractively grained material, which unfortunately is not very strong and is also susceptible to pests, was used for inlays as well as for both fine and rustic furniture.

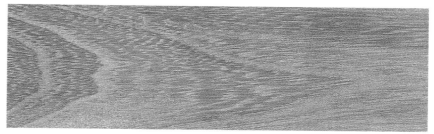

The English elm is native to Great Britain. If the surface is treated properly it develops a beautiful patina. Unfortunately it is soon attacked by pests. Elm was popular for chairs, tables, and trunks in the country.

Cedar wood comes from North America and the West Indies. Because of its pest-repelling odor – which is, however, pleasant to the human nose – it was used to make linen chests. Cedar wood blocks are still used to deter moths today.

Ebony is an extremely expensive, heavy, very dark wood from the tropics. Because of its high price it was almost never used for solid pieces, but rather as a veneer and for small inlays.

Beech occurs all over Europe. This heavy, hard, resistant material comes into its own especially in the frames of armchairs and sofas. It can be oiled or polished, but unfortunately is susceptible to fungal attack and becomes black if it comes into contact with moisture.

The European sycamore is a typical wood for English furniture. Its fine lively graining makes it ideal for marquetry and inlay work but it can also be used for solid items. A popular material since Tudor times.

"My Home is My Castle"

The British and their houses is a subject of positively inexhaustible variety. For, unlike on the continent, tastes here are truly very varied. If one person considers the practical semi-detached house to be heaven on earth, another can only be comfortable in masonry at least 300 years old. The reasons for this are often not so much depending on the taste of the individual, but rather on what he or she does, represents, or wants to represent in life. The newly rich, whether they have earned their fortune on the stock exchange, in films, television, or through music, will often take pains to conceal the novelty of their wealth. What could be better suited to this than an old house?

Those with less money but a lot of imagination, creativity, or education also like to demonstrate this through their choice of dwelling. But the author, artist, or composer would not choose the yuppie's country house or the investment banker's elegant town address, but rather the converted floor of an old cotton mill or a lighthouse with a sea view. To say nothing of the diverse forms of interior decoration: Neo-Gothic, Victorian, modern, or all of these together! And just as variable as the people are the lifestyles we encounter in their houses. Work can be one of the activities taking place there. All those to whom this applies, for whom life and work are one and the same, can consider themselves fortunate. And when this activity, often a passion or vocation, can be carried out within one's own four walls, or at the very least within four pleasant walls, then not much else stands in the way of a Briton's happiness – whether headmaster, restorer, castle owner, bat researcher, artist, or journalist.

Jeremy Nichols, headmaster of Stowe School, in the Neo-Gothic library of the Buckinghamshire boarding school. When he is not busy teaching he goes for a drive in his old Bentley.

Lucian Thynne and his dog Bisou live in London when they are not checking out locations for shooting films. Quite the country gentleman, this nephew of the Marquess of Bath enjoys shooting and fishing in his free time.

Michael Cunningham, the restorer, combines home and workplace. In the workshop of his house in the former London borough of Fulham he removes dust, soot, and dirt from paintings and drawings, and has brought to light many an unexpected treasure in the process.

Carol Arnold creates real works of art from wool and silk with her embroidery needle, without leaving the comfort of her own fireside. She also owns a significant collection of valuable old embroidery.

Sir Jack Leslie is master of his family's ancestral seat, Castle Leslie in County Monaghan in the Republic of Ireland. When he is not devoting himself to the upkeep of his castle, he is researching the behavior of the bat or improvising on the grand piano.

Journalist and author John Morgan lived in the legendary Albany, London's most elegant apartment house. When he went out – very reluctantly – at most it was for a cup of tea at Claridge's.

In Llangoed Hall in Brecon, a country hotel in Wales, visitors can feel as though they own a country house for a couple of days.

COUNTRY LIFE

THE MYTH OF BRITISH COUNTRY LIFE

Whenever the talk is of British country life, two concepts are always mentioned: the landed gentry and country sports. Both are important to explain why the idea of country living still prevails as part of the British national myth. Landed gentry means the land-owning lower echelons of the blue-blooded – baronet, knight, and dame. This minor aristocracy also includes the squires, landowners who do not necessarily have an imposing family tree. For a long time the landed gentry, along with the true aristocracy, was the only layer of the population with the right to vote and provided more than half the Members of Parliament in the House of Commons until the beginning of the 19th century. This group still numbers several thousand members who live in the country in the traditional way and manage their estates.

At the close of the 19th century well-to-do members of the middle classes who wanted to rival the nobility began to acquire elegant country seats, without however concerning themselves with agriculture. The reason for this was a crisis in the agricultural market which led to the sale of many country seats. This fashion continued into the Edwardian era, that brief period between 1901 and 1914, often romantically glorified today. The houses built in these years were designed exclusively for their owners' pleasure, and they did not only belong to Britons, but also to rich Americans and other foreigners who either were property owners in their right or had married into British aristocratic families. Instead of profuse Victorian adornment they now prized light, welcoming rooms. Small wonder that the predilection for antiques developed in this epoch. People gathered in their elegant country domiciles from Friday to Sunday to recuperate from the stress and strains of city life. Large staffs had to maintain the vast country seats permanently, even if guests only came once a week. The Edwardian country house is the archetypal British country house, especially since it calls to mind the epoch of the greatest prosperity and authority in Britain's history.

This expansive lifestyle came to an abrupt end with the outbreak of the First World War, and since that time properties of this size have never been built again. The end of the Second World War brought lean years for the British: the population had to live with rationing and restrictions. The socialist government under Prime Minister Clement Attlee introduced a high death duty, which almost ruined many landowners, after death duty had already been increased in 1919. Many had no other recourse than to open their houses to the public, so that at least a fraction of the running costs could be defrayed from entrance fees and donations. In the 1960s and 70s the situation was reversed. Rising land prices made many landowners rich overnight. In addition, there were more prosperous people again who could afford to take a rundown property under their wing. Anyone who thought they were anyone became the owner of a country house.

Rock stars, film actors, entrepreneurs – all discovered the exclusive charm of country life and wanted to lead the leisured existence of the landed gentry. Their favorite pastimes were country sports – hunting, shooting, and fishing. Hunting refers to fox hunting, shooting corresponds to hunting as it is known in continental Europe, and fishing means the high art of fly fishing.

Opposite page: For many inhabitants of the British Isles a weekend in the country includes a shooting party with friends, relatives, and business partners, as here at Cabilla Manor, Cornwall.

Right: Reading in the shade of a tree is one of the joys of a garden for which home owners are envied. Those who live in apartments, however, can be consoled by the knowledge that they do not have to mow the lawn.

Many a stressed banker at the weekend exchanges his pinstripes for overalls and rubber boots, called Wellington boots in Britain, to find rest and relaxation working in the barn or in the field.

These sports have been a noble tradition since the Middle Ages and are still carried on today from the country houses. Many premises serve the sole purpose of accommodating shooting guests. The landed gentry and their country sports provide the main turnover of many trades which have specialized in the supply of clothing and equipment. Tailors and clothing manufacturers, bespoke shoemakers and shoe factories, saddlers, farriers and hat makers, gunsmiths, and hunting requisites shops all subsist on the fact that genuine and would-be country gentlemen want to enjoy the British country life properly fitted out. But a large portion of the country life cake also goes to real estate brokers, interior designers, furniture dealers, and antique shops. They help those who can afford it to realize their dream of life in the country. And each has his own version of this dream. The retired couple would like to buy a little cottage, a modest little house in the country in which to spend their twilight years, the successful entrepreneur wants to show that he has made it, the artist seeks inspiration, the businessman is looking for a good investment. The hunting enthusiast wants to pursue his passion in peace, the nature lover seeks rest far from the city – British country life offers everyone what he wants from it.

CASTLES AND CASTLE OWNERS

Probably the best known English saying about homes and houses runs "An Englishman's home is his castle." This creed is also cited outside the United Kingdom whenever the discussion turns to British houses. To feel comfortable and safe in one's house is a basic human need. We want to be able to withdraw inside our own four walls and behind those walls, cut off from the outside world, we want to be ourselves, and in the most pleasant and comfortable way possible. To that extent the sense of the saying seems clear. But what about those people who turn it round and say quite consciously not "My home is my castle" but "My castle is my home"? And who, with eyes wide open, move into half ruined, scarcely habitable castles of archaic dimensions, which swallow up enormous sums on maintenance?

The British passion for castles is difficult to explain. It is certain, however, that it is rooted in history. Even when peaceful times dawned with the accession of Henry VII to the throne at the end of the 15th century, and fortified ramparts began to lose their strategic military and defensive significance, Britons carried on building castles regardless. There are even buildings which look like castles and could have come straight from the Middle Ages, which were actually built in the 18th, 19th, and 20th centuries. The 19th century in particular witnessed a wave of romanticism for castles, reflected not only in architecture, but also in painting. Castles and castle ruins like Cilgerran Castle in Pembrokeshire in Wales inspired numerous artists, including William Turner. And today tourist attractions such as Warwick Castle in Warwickshire, Lindisfarne Castle and Alnwick Castle in Northumberland, Bodiam Castle in East Sussex, Leeds Castle in Kent and also smaller castles like Scotney Castle in Kent and Glamis Castle in Scotland attract thousands of visitors every year, by no means all of them foreign tourists.

But to be a castle enthusiast and to visit an interesting example of the genre occasionally is one thing, to live in one is another. After all, living in a fortified castle is even less necessary today than it was in the 18th century, unless you are a particularly cautious individual and seek protection from burglars or curious glances behind strong walls. There are of course other reasons for settling on a fortress as a place of residence – a decided sense of the Romantic, or noble birth. Thus in the United Kingdom there is a sizeable group of castle owners, both male and female, who have either acquired their unusual domicile out of pure enthusiasm or have quite simply inherited it. A good example of a typical "family castle" which is passed from generation to generation is Glamis Castle, for 600 years the seat of the Bowes Lyon family. In 1372 King Robert II of Scotland handed Glamis to Sir Robert Lyon as a fiefdom and four years later the new lord of the castle married the monarch's daughter.

Lovers of Shakespeare frequently associate Cawdor Castle with the Thane of Cawdor from the play Macbeth. Incorrectly, since the historical Macbeth died in 1052, and the castle in Nairnshire in Scotland was not built until the 14th century. This fact, however, should not deter Shakespeare lovers from imagining the romantic castle as the scene of dreadful tragedies.

However, the fame of Glamis Castle extended beyond the Scottish border in its capacity as the parental home of Queen Elizabeth the Queen Mother. She was not born at the castle, since her father only inherited the splendid estate along with the title of the Earl of Strathmore when she was four years old. But Queen Elizabeth's second daughter, Princess Margaret Rose, came into the world at Glamis in 1930.

Since 1972 the 17th Earl of Strathmore and Kinghorne has been the master of Glamis. When they married, his wife was well aware that one day her husband would inherit the castle, but at first she could not raise any particular enthusiasm for the prospect. But the initial skepticism was soon forgotten and today the Countess is proving to be an ardent custodian of the property. Like most of the old ancestral seats in Great Britain, whether castle, country house, or palace, Glamis houses an extensive collection of valuable furniture and works of art, and almost every piece has an association with the long family history.

Turning to those people who have acquired an old fortress from a sense of pure Romanticism, these "voluntary" castle owners sometimes also have their own aristocratic family tree and a room groaning with antiques. First and foremost their unusual place of residence is the fulfillment of a long-cherished dream. A good example of this is Fordel Castle in Fife. The politician and lawyer Nicholas Fairbairn acquired the comparatively small 14th-century structure at the end of the 1960s for a trifle, and then spent 20 years of love, devotion, and physical labor restoring it. The effort was worth it and his wife Samantha, who organizes Scottish tours for foreign visitors, regularly invites her guests to dine at Fordel Castle.

Another castle owner by choice is the Scottish businessman and banker Angus Grossart, master of Pitcullo to the north east of Fife since 1978. It took several years of searching before Grossart finally found the object of his dreams – then the laborious renovations were destroyed, half-finished, by a serious fire. But the impassioned collector of Scottish antiques did not think of giving up, and from then on indefatigably devoted every minute of his limited free time to this unique project. Today Pitcullo is a comfortable family home.

Opposite page: In the far north of England, in the wildly romantic border region between England and Scotland, Bamburgh Castle stands right on the shore of the North Sea. The dwelling tower of this fortified structure was built in the 12th century.

Scotney Castle in Kent was built at the end of the 14th century and remains the image of a medieval fortified structure. Today it is a popular destination for excursions mainly because of its gardens.

Glamis Castle is generally considered the perfect example of a Scottish castle. Admittedly, only the core of the building complex is of medieval origin, the larger part of the magnificent building bearing witness to later generations of the Strathmore family's fondness for building.

A fortified tower was built on the River Tweed in Scotland in the 14th century. Its remains are the oldest part of Neidpath Castle near Peebles.

Opposite page: Alnwick Castle in Northumberland was the seat of the de Vescy family until the early 14th century and in the possession of the Percy family from the 14th to the 17th century. Today the Duke of Northumberland lives in part of the castle, which is also used as a military museum.

THE DEVELOPMENT OF CASTLE BUILDING

With the invasion of the Normans in 1066, early military architecture in England changed fundamentally with the introduction of the motte and bailey castle. If there was no natural elevation present, an artificial hill (Norman: motte) was constructed on which a wooden defensive tower was placed. Constructing the hill automatically created a ditch which also served as defense. A palisade or wall was then erected round the fortified tower at a distance from it, thus creating an enclosure, the bailey. The advantage of this method of building was that it was very quick. William the Conqueror is said to have built his first castle in England within two weeks, and that for the main part with unskilled workers.

Thus the main component of the Norman castle is a strongly protected tower, which was also used for living in. The corners mostly take the form of wall towers. If the main tower was not constructed around an inner courtyard, the "Great Hall", the main room of the castle, was situated in the center of the ground floor. There was also always a castle chapel. The White Tower in London was one of the first stone buildings William had built. Its purpose was to intimidate the Anglo-Saxon population and defend London from the east. This truly imposing building – the White Tower with its four towers still overtops the rest of the castle today – was also his residence: it had four stories and walls almost four yards thick at the base. The light colored stone from which it was built was specially imported from Caen in France.

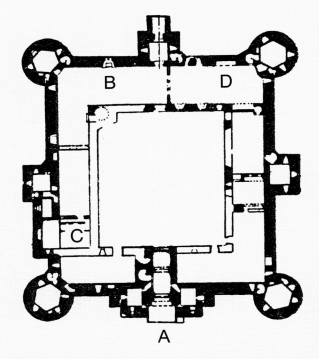

Bodiam Castle in Sussex was built in 1386–1388 by Sir Edward Dalyngrigge as a defense against the French. Its unusual symmetrical layout with four round corner towers and three square side towers was already old-fashioned by the time of building. A bridge over the wide moat leads to the entrance (A) in the fortified turreted gate house. The living quarters, today in ruins, lay on two stories around a central courtyard: on the left opposite the entrance, the L-shaped great hall (B) in which the family ate and celebrated and where gatherings were held. A small chapel (C) was situated to the left of the entrance and jutted out slightly from the wall. The family rooms lay to the left of the entrance on the east side, and the servants and guards lived in the west wing close to the kitchen (D). While the outer walls had no windows, the rooms must have been illuminated by high windows on the courtyard side.

Opposite page: Warwick Castle is one of the most important tourist attractions in central England. William the Conqueror built a wooden fort here in the 11th century, this was later replaced by a massive castle. Today a branch of Madame Tussaud's, the London waxworks, displays figures in the historical rooms.

Right: About three and a half miles to the south east of Maidstone in Kent lies Leeds Castle, the fame of which extends beyond England. Every year more than half a million tourists visit this castle built on two islands. The attraction of the fortress is further enhanced by the events which are held regularly within its historic walls.

The 14th and 15th centuries were a turbulent time, marked first by the Hundred Years War with France and then by the Wars of the Roses, in which the Houses of York and Lancaster fought for the succession to the throne. So it is not surprising that many castles were either built or enlarged at this time. Older models, still made of wood, were replaced by stone buildings, like Leeds Castle. They were now proper castles with single or double walls armed with battlements and embrasures. Alongside these complex, "extended" constructions there were, however, also castles which were planned and built in a single campaign, like Bodiam Castle in Sussex. With the accession of Henry VII to the throne at the end of the 15th century more peaceful times dawned, in which many castles were turned into respectable palaces. In the north of England and Scotland, however, most of them remained heavily fortified for a while longer, since armed disputes continued to erupt here.

Below: Lindisfarne Castle in Northumberland served as a fortress in the Tudor period. In 1902–1903 the architect Edwin Lutyens converted it into a private house. The charm of the castle is increased by the fact that it can only be reached by visitors, both invited and uninvited, at low tide.

Tartans

The catchword Scotland immediately brings to mind men in tartan skirts and the question as to what the gallant whisky drinkers wear under this colorful outfit. This question has been posed (and has remained largely unanswered) since the Middle Ages, for already at that time Scottish warriors were wearing an early forerunner of the article of clothing that is so well known today. This consisted of not much more than a knee-length mantle or cloak gathered into pleats with a belt. Pictorial representations of men attired in this way on graves in Argyll and on the Scottish islands indicate that this costume, known as "leine croich", was worn until the early 17th century. In the same period the "belted plaid", a kind of belted blanket, appeared. This garment, also known as "feileadh breacan" or "feileadh mor", in English "the great kilt", may be considered the direct predecessor of the modern kilt. Putting it on was a somewhat complicated procedure. First the belt was laid on the ground, inner side up, and the big blanket was spread over it. The material was distributed in such a way that the length of a skirt showed below the belt. The Scot then sat or lay on the blanket and put the belt on so that the blanket fell into even pleats. Next the whole thing was wrapped around the hips. The fabric hanging over the belt was either draped decoratively or worn around the shoulders and head for protection. To form the kilt of today, the blanket merely had to be shortened, thus leaving just the skirt. It is presumed that this development took place in the middle of the 18th century. In order to simplify putting on vis-à-vis the traditional lying-down method, the short kilt was soon offered ready-pleated and the complicated gathering of the blanket was abandoned. This "patent kilt" could be put on just like a normal woman's skirt. Since that time there have been no real changes in the kilt. Only its length varies slightly – just as in women's fashion.

The Scots are not the only ones to view the skirt as men's clothing. In other parts of the world also men traditionally wrap a piece of cloth around their hips. It is the checked pattern which makes the skirt Scottish, and this again is quite a recent invention. It is probable that tartans – the correct term for the Scottish check pattern – only came into use

Originally the sporran, worn in front of the kilt, was a practical mini-rucksack. Today it serves a mainly decorative purpose. Nevertheless this little fur-covered pouch is part of the outfit of a Highlander in full dress.

The formal version of the highland dress, worn for special occasions and in the evening, cannot disavow its military origin.

at the close of the 18th century. Some time later the tartans were used for the purpose we recognize today: as the distinguishing mark or uniform of a particular clan. It cannot be assumed that the fabric manufacturers had this idea, but they were certainly not averse to the notion that each clan should have its own tartan.

The precarious historical basis for the linking of patterns and clans is apparent from the fact that many color combinations can be associated with several clans. An attempt is made to deal with this by introducing subtle nuances into the colors and patterns. Thus the tartans of the Lamont and Forbes families only differ in that the white lines in the uppermost checks of the Forbes tartan are outlined almost invisibly in black. What makes matters even more difficult is the fact that tartans are not laid down according to any standardized code. Further, they are only described by such imprecise adjectives as red, green, blue, and yellow. But what is red – light red, dark red, burgundy, or tomato red? Thus the patterns, apparently laid down so unambiguously, are reproduced from weaver to weaver as they see fit with consequent variations. In spite of all the uncertainties, since the 19th century there have been numerous and, in part, very honorable attempts to catalogue the tartans. But something is not quite right when, for the 100 or so recognized clans, there are fully 2,000 tartans.

Tartans cannot be defined with scientific exactness. This is due to the fact that the various designs have never been described with reference to a uniform color scale. Thus there are no standard examples of the various tartans in the form of binding weave- or color-samples. Every weaving mill that tries its hand at one of the numerous designs simply increases the existing number of variations on the theme. But this does not detract from the charm of the colorful tartans or diminish the seriousness with which each family insists on its exclusive right to wear them.

Left: Dancing displays are among the high points of any Highland gathering. The often very difficult sequences of steps and figures in dances such as "The Highland Fling," "The Reel," and "The Sword Dance" make great demands on the girls, but they are assured of the public's good will even if they make a false step.

Below: The Highland Games provide a good opportunity to fit yourself out with authentic clothing in the Scottish style. Sales stands for pullovers, kilts, caps, and shawls with the Scottish look belong quite naturally at the Highland Games in Inverness.

The Braemar Gathering

Since the Victorian era the Braemar Gathering has been the best known and most prestigious of the Highland Gatherings held each year in Scotland and the New World. Its renown is due in no small part to Queen Victoria, who took over the patronage of the Braemar Highland Society, the event's organizer, in 1866. But Braemar is not the oldest Highland Gathering: A similar test of strength was held as early as 1314 in the village of Ceres and this gathering, culminating in a horse race, has been held every year ever since.

On a Saturday in September a great number of musicians, costume groups, folk dancers, and sportsmen gather in Braemar under the gaze of about 20,000 spectators to celebrate Scottish national culture with music, dancing, and spectacular exhibitions and contests.

Anything unwieldy and heavy is thrown – granite balls, tree trunks, and hammers. Added to this are such disciplines as stone lifting and the inevitable tug-o'-war.

The motive for this picturesque event has not always been merely to keep customs alive. In the year 1817 the Scottish sports festival served charitable purposes. The organizer at that time was the Braemar Wrights Friendly Society, an association of local craftsmen. The games were used to collect money for widows, orphans, the sick, and the old. It was not until 1826 that the charitable organization also began to be concerned with Scottish national identity. Queen Victoria first took part in the Braemar Gathering in 1848. At that time it was still held at Invercauld House before Braemar Castle was made the venue for two years. The monarch thus established a tradition of royal visits which still continues today. The regular attendance of blue-blooded spectators is also connected with the fact that the Royal family is usually staying in the vicinity at the time of the games anyway, in Balmoral Castle.

Since 1906 the festival of sport, music, and national dress has had a fixed address. It was in that year that the Duke of Fife gave the Braemar Gathering a new home in the Princess Royal and Duke of Fife Memorial Park. The park was named after Princess Louise, who was the daughter of the Prince of Wales and granddaughter of Queen Victoria, and her husband the Duke of Argyll. He was made Duke of Fife in 1889 and it is in this capacity that he has remained in the memory of the many friends of the Braemar Gathering.

Among the sporting competitions at the Highland Games, next to the tug-of-war, throwing the weight is one of the main attractions. The athletes, naturally, have to wear traditional Highland dress, which does not make the contest any easier in this or the other disciplines. There is usually also something for the children, they can for example compete under the singularly difficult conditions of the sack race.

Anyone who has been to the Highland Games and seen the Scots hurling tree trunks through the air will perhaps no longer consign the tales of Gaelic heroes to the realm of fantasy. The more than five yard long caber, as the unwieldy piece of timber is called, weighing fully 130 lbs (60 kg), must first be balanced vertically and then, after a short run, tossed into the air.

THE PALACE

In the *Concise Oxford Dictionary* the word "palace" is defined as the official residence of a sovereign, archbishop or bishop, or as a "stately mansion; spacious building for entertainment, refreshment, etc." This description applies fairly exactly to Hampton Court Palace, which was originally a bishop's palace and then, until the death of Queen Caroline in 1737, served as the residence of several English heads of state, ending with George II. In 1838 Queen Victoria opened the state rooms, the gardens, and Bushy Park to the public; today the whole palace is accessible.

The present Royal family lives in various houses and palaces. But undoubtedly their best known residence is Buckingham Palace. It was originally neither a palace nor a royal residence, but the house of the Duke of Buckingham. In 1762 King George III bought Buckingham House for 28,000 pounds, gave it to his wife Charlotte – which led to the renaming of the mansion as Queen's House – and had it extended by William Chambers. In 1825 the architect John Nash was commissioned by King George IV to convert the house into a palace. Nash could already look back on a very successful career when he began the alterations. The 73-year-old architect had made his name both with the design of country houses and with important urban projects. The vision of an elegant garden city around Regent's Park can be attributed to him, and the plan for Regent's Street, which still today has a decisive impact on the townscape in London's West End, is his work.

The remodeling of Queen's House, however, progressed less auspiciously. In 1830 before the alterations were finished the King died and Nash lost the commission after five years work. His colleagues Edward Blore and Thomas Cubitt completed the plan in 1837 after a further two years work, but William IV, who succeeded to the throne after George IV, did not live to see the inauguration of the new residence in 1837 any more than his predecessor had done.

Queen Victoria was the first monarch to move into the new palace 12 years after building had begun. She was to use it as her residence for the rest of her life – just like all British crowned heads ever since. Thus the Queen also lives there when she is in London. The hoisted flag signals that the monarch is at home. But there is probably not a single royal resident who particularly appreciates staying in this building. Beginning with Victoria, who gladly withdrew to Windsor Castle, Balmoral Castle, or Sandringham, other Royals also have loved and still love the smaller

Although royal in size, Blenheim Palace near Oxford was built for a mere duke in 1705, namely John Duke of Marlborough. With this magnificent building Queen Anne thanked her general for his successes in the War of the Spanish Succession. Probably the best-known scion of the family is the politician and author Winston Churchill, who was born in Blenheim Palace.

Left: In August and September the Queen of England deigns to open Buckingham Palace to the nation and tourists. Although the visit is not exactly cheap the visitors come in hoards every year. Apparently they want to see what formerly was reserved for the eyes of crowned state guests, diplomats, and courtiers.

main   rooms

drawing
room

hall

gallery

working yard

great courtyard

working yard

N

While palaces like Hampton Court Palace are repeatedly extended and altered by their occupants over the centuries, Blenheim Palace was built in a relatively short time to one uniform design. Both palaces are constructed around an inner courtyard, but the great courtyard at Blenheim is open at the front and only closed off by decorative railings. On the outer sides of both main buildings there are the galleries and windows of fine living and reception rooms. At Blenheim the two side wings house the working buildings (kitchen and stables). The main part of the palace is accessible from a central entrance hall with side staircases. Unlike Hampton Court, where the various rulers favored different parts of the building as their living quarters, the main and subsidiary rooms are quite clearly differentiated here.

country seats far more than the fine, but not very cozy London palace. King George VI called it "the icebox", Edward VIII complained about the "dank musty smell", and Mark Phillips, Princess Anne's former husband, remarked that he found it difficult to relax in Buckingham Palace. Actually the palace is too much of a state building to provide a pleasant home for its inhabitants.

According to the definition in the *Oxford Dictionary*, a palace is the domicile of a king, bishop, or archbishop, but not all the palaces in Great Britain were or are inhabited only by those of the highest rank. An example of this is Blenheim Palace, originally built neither for a king nor a prince of the church. Blenheim Palace was, rather, a thank you from Queen Anne to the First Duke of Marlborough for his victories in the War of the Spanish Succession. His new domicile was christened Blenheim Palace to commemorate the decisive battle of Blenheim in 1704. The building works on the palace designed by the architects

Vanbrugh and Hawksmoor lasted from 1705 to 1724. When you face a building like Blenheim, it is difficult to draw an exact boundary between royal palaces and other stately homes, for the old established families of Great Britain have always had houses which, from their size and historical significance, would be fit for a king. Thus many of the palaces used by the Queen and her family only appear splendid when compared with a normal family house; other town and country properties make them seem almost modest. It's one of the characteristics of the residences of Great Britain that no distinction can be made between royal houses and those of the "lesser" nobility.

Hampton Court Palace, built in the 16th century and extended in the 17th century, gives a good impression of the splendor of the English court in the Tudor period. The south-western front was designed by Sir Christopher Wren in the English Baroque style.

St James's Palace became the main residence of the English monarch in 1698 after the palace in Whitehall was burnt down. Today it is the official residence of the Prince of Wales.

From Castle to Palace

The palace developed from the castle as an elegant residential and state building. With the end of the Wars of the Roses in the late 15th century, comfort and a display of power, not defense, were the main functions of the ruler's residence. Gate houses like the one at Hampton Court Palace, or corner towers – as at Blenheim Palace – still suggest a potentially armed stronghold, although they would hardly be able to perform a defensive function. Entrances frequently situated in inner courtyards are also the remains of castle architecture.

In the Baroque period the entrance side of the courtyard was preferably left open, so as to form a three-sided great courtyard. It served less to control access than as a place for the occupants and their guests to assemble and parade. Usually the open side was closed off by decorative iron railings or a row of pillars. Behind the central main building there was often a garden with an ornamentation reflecting the building.

Besides these complex rambling constructions the Baroque style also gave birth to compact palaces formed in a single block without side wings or inner courtyards worth mentioning.

Left: The English Royal family acquired Kensington Palace in the year 1689. Since 1760 it has not been lived in by the monarch himself, but by members of his family.

Opposite page: Chatsworth in Derbyshire is sometimes unjustly referred to as a house; with 175 rooms, palace would be a more appropriate term for the seat of the Duke and Duchess of Devonshire. It is not the biggest house in England, but probably one of the grandest.

The Alfriston Clergy House, acquired in 1896, was the National Trust's first historical building. Today it is one of the more than 164 houses belonging to this organization devoted to the protection of historical buildings and the landscape.

THE NATIONAL TRUST

The National Trust can look back on a history of just over 100 years. The inaugural meeting took place on July 16th, 1894 in Grosvenor House in London with the three founders, Octavia Hill, Sir Robert Hunter, and Canon Hardwicke Rawnsley as the main speakers. Six months later, on January 12th, 1895 "The National Trust for Places of Historic Interest or Natural Beauty," to give it its full name, was officially registered. The main concerns of the three founders were the effects of industrialization and unrestricted access to land. The National Trust, as a representative of the nation, would buy tracts of land and buildings threatened with disfigurement or destruction and would act as custodians to protect them and make them accessible to all.

In February 1895 the first piece of land was entrusted to the organization. It was about 18 hectares (45 acres) of cliffland in Dinas Oleu near Barmouth in Wales. The first historical building was acquired in 1896, when the National Trust bought the 14th-century clergy house in Alfriston, Sussex for ten pounds. Three years later the first nature reserve was added, two acres of land at Wicken Fen in Cambridgeshire. In 1907 a law was passed that allowed the National Trust to declare its properties inalienable – that is, not transferable to another party. This means that

neither land nor houses can be sold again once they have been transferred to the National Trust, unless Parliament consents to it according to a precisely laid down procedure.

In 1931 the National Trust for Scotland was founded, and three years later the first complete village passed into the hands of the organization. In 1937 the "Country House Scheme" began, based on the National Trust Act of 1907. The central idea of this scheme was to make British country houses accessible to the public, being as they are, part of the cultural heritage. Of course, a private house can only be opened with the consent of the owner, but since many owners found themselves in great financial difficulties during these years, the offer of tax exemption on their buildings was an inducement. In the 1960s, however, this was no longer enough, since maintenance costs had risen rapidly. Finally, a new financial solution was decided which has safeguarded the upkeep of the many houses and lands of the National Trust until today.

The National Trust even continued its work during the Second World War and in 1939 it took the first industrial buildings into its care. Those responsible were quick to recognize the relevance of this special architecture for the cultural and architectural history of Great Britain. In the meantime many of these buildings, brought together under the heading of "Industrial Heritage," are among the most popular National Trust properties for outings. "Industrial Heritage" is a far-reaching concept, including as it does a locomotive and a lighthouse and also the first house in the British Isles to have electricity. The "Country House Scheme" bore its first major fruits in 1940. The Eleventh Marquess of Lothian bequeathed his property, Blickling Hall, together with 4,760 acres of land to the National Trust. In 1945, the year the war ended, the National Trust celebrated its 50th birthday. In memory of those fallen in the war, from 1946 the State made over to the Trust various properties which had been transferred to the State by the heirs of those who did not return from the war for the purposes of settling death duties. In 1948 the National Trust began to concern itself with gardens which were worthy of preservation, even if they did not belong to an historic building. For this purpose the Gardens Fund was set up in conjunction with the Royal Horticultural Society. About 160 gardens had come into the hands of the organization by 1994. 1948 was also the year in which the members formed clubs and took part in the work of the National Trust.

1965 saw the beginning of the most ambitious project to date, the "Neptune Appeal." Its aim was to acquire the largest possible sections of undeveloped coastline in England, of which only 900 miles remained. As of 1994, 18 million pounds had been collected and the National Trust has since then been able to rescue 550 miles of coastline.

When the association celebrated its 75th birthday in 1970, it already had 226,200 members. Only 11 years later a million people had signed up with the National Trust. By this time the organization was a very well-established component of British life, thanks not least to the more than 268 shops, restaurants, and tea rooms it maintains. In October 1997 the Trust had exactly 2,558,563 members. The total area of protected land

In the National Trust shops the interested visitor can purchase not only literature about the work of the organization and the houses and places of natural beauty in its care, but also nice accessories for house and garden and also gifts. In the Christmas period many members use the mail order service for stress-free Christmas shopping.

amounts to 244,133 acres. Properties accessible to the public comprise 164 houses, 19 castles, 47 factories, 49 churches and chapels, nine prehistoric and Roman ruins, 13 farms, 114 other buildings, 160 gardens, and 73 landscape and wildlife parks.

The National Trust has long been the embodiment of a cultured weekend. Using the annually up-dated handbook sent to each member, you can plan an outing near or far and according to your taste and whim you can visit a grand stately home, a medieval castle, or the comfortable home of an author. Anyone wishing to take children or elderly people along with them can find out from the description of the attraction whether or not there is a playground or a cafeteria. And so as to avoid reproachful looks from your dog, you can also learn whether or not boisterous retrievers and young labradors are welcome on the property.

Visitor numbers show how popular the properties of the National Trust are with the British and their foreign guests. In the 1996/1997 season, for example, visitors numbered 11,624,587. That the largest private organization in the world is an English association for the preservation of historical buildings and natural beauty shows how highly the heritage of old houses, romantic gardens, and enchanting landscapes is valued in the island kingdom.

Blickling Hall fell to the National Trust under the "Country House Scheme." The former owner, the Eleventh Marquess of Lothian, bequeathed the property to this organization committed to preserving historical buildings and gardens, in 1940.

Above: Hilltop, Beatrix Potter's Lake District home, is an extremely popular destination for outings, especially as the children's author wrote many of her famous works here. The cottage, built in the 17th century, appears in many illustrations to her stories after 1905.

Right: The novelist and poet Thomas Hardy lived in Max Gate in Dorchester from 1885 until his death in 1928. In this house, which he designed himself, he wrote *Tess of the D'Urbervilles* and *The Mayor of Casterbridge* as well as much of his poetry and other works.

Below: Old Soar Manor. The remains of the home of a knight from the late 13th century gives some idea of how a noble gentleman of that period would have lived. A chapel is also preserved.

Mompession House near Salisbury. The house will perhaps appear familiar to film fans, since it featured in the award-winning film *Sense and Sensibility*. Besides exceptionally beautiful stuccowork the house, which dates from the 18th century, also possesses a collection of 18th-century drinking glasses.

Wordsworth House. The poet William Wordsworth was born in 1770 in this Georgian town house in Cockermouth, Cumbria. The rooms are partly furnished in the style of the 18th century. Some of the poet's personal belongings are also on display.

Right: Bateman's, Sussex. The National Trust owns several houses that belonged to famous authors, including that of Rudyard Kipling, the famous balladeer and creator of the *Jungle Books*. The author spent the last 34 years of his life in Bateman's and wrote some of his best-known works there.

Far right: Mr Straw's House, Worksop in Nottinghamshire. This Edwardian semi-detached house, number 7 Blyth Grove, is a time capsule from the 1920s and 30s. The owners left the house, both inside and outside, exactly as it was when their parents bequeathed it to them in the 30s.

Above: Clouds Hill, Dorset. The film *Lawrence of Arabia* from 1962 with Peter O'Toole in the title role was a fine memorial to T.E. Lawrence, the adventurer and soldier. After acquiring the cottage in 1925, Lawrence often withdrew to Clouds Hill to write.

Right: Chartwell, Kent. Winston Churchill's house is ranked by the National Trust as a memorial to the statesman and author. It was here that the legendary officer, journalist, and politician penned the works which earned him the Nobel Prize for literature in 1953.

THE BIG COUNTRY HOUSE

The country house is perhaps the most British of all forms of housing. There is probably scarcely another country in which large, and splendidly furnished country houses are so abundant. But extensive estates and sonorous titles are not necessarily associated with properties of this kind. From the late Middle Ages onward it was accepted in Great Britain that anyone who could afford it bought himself a country seat. The ascent of the middle classes into the lower nobility was, at least from the 18th century onward, easier to accomplish than on the continent. Prosperous commoners who wanted to be accepted as quickly as possible by their blue-blooded neighbors married off their daughters into the often impoverished noble families.

In the 17th and 18th centuries numerous new branches of industry appeared, and with them ways of making money. The new prosperous middle class layer was enthusiastic about country life, they wanted to imitate the lifestyle of the aristocratic estate owners, and could now afford it too. With the beginning of industrialization the country house began to lose its original function as a farm or estate house, although into the second half of the 19th century extensive lands still generally belonged to properties of this type.

In any case this land often no longer played any role as a source of income for the new owner, but rather it was soon considered an expensive "extra." For this reason rich members of the middle classes took to acquiring mansions without land which was of no use to them. Many big country houses of this time, therefore, stand on comparatively small plots of land.

The date of building of a country house gives only limited information about the person and purpose for which it was built. From the 17th century onward the landed gentry were inclined to shuttle between London, the country house, and various watering places, and residences of aristocratic families with whom they were friendly, so that country houses frequently served the purpose of pure pleasure. However, the rapid development of agriculture from about 1750 led to a sweeping increase in yields, with the result that many country houses lay in the middle of vast cultivated lands. All the same, it is practically impossible to tell from a house of 1750 whether it was built by a count or the owner of a cotton mill. The interior too, with comparable resources, would hardly differ. Like the social climber of today, the middle classes of the past showed the greatest aptitude when it came to adopting the lifestyle of the upper classes. The highest recognition, namely recognition at court, however, often only came to the "money aristocracy" in the Victorian era. Thus, during his long wait for the throne, Queen Victoria's eldest son surrounded himself with an illustrious entourage of rich merchants, entrepreneurs, bankers, and actors and cared little whether or not this was suitable. However much his German cousin, Emperor Wilhelm II, poured scorn on the fact that Bertie went sailing with his grocer – meaning by this the millionaire Thomas Lipton – it did not trouble the

This Tudor house, Owlpen Manor in Gloucestershire, was built and altered between 1464 and 1616. Apart from a few small modifications in the early 18th century it has not been changed since. Norman Jewson, the Arts and Crafts architect, rescued the house in 1925 and also redesigned the garden.

Prince of Wales. And it did His Majesty no harm when he attended a synagogue on the occasion of a Rothschild wedding. In order to penetrate the Prince of Wales' circle, however, it was necessary to have a suitable residence, and so his friends and would-be friends built or bought themselves houses which would be worthy of a king and, in contrast to earlier times, they actually had the chance to entertain the heir to the throne.

From the end of the 19th century until the outbreak of the First World War practical considerations finally began to be taken into account in house buying, due to the crisis in agriculture which began in 1880. You did not need extensive estates which were expensive to maintain if you were only going to the country for the occasional weekend. The main thing was to have enough rooms for the entertainment and accommodation of the guests and perhaps a pretty but not too enormous garden. It was also important for the house to be in an accessible position near to the capital so as to be able to arrive there promptly on Friday evening. Those who had made it in the Edwardian era made ever more frequent use of the motor car.

The First World War put an end to these jolly activities and several of the large mansions became deserted. Many of the former domestic servants changed to other professions and without housemaids, pages, gardeners, cooks, housekeepers, and butlers the colossal houses could hardly be kept alive.

In addition there were financial problems in the form of death duty, increased in 1919, which became due as soon as the owner of a property died. If his younger brothers who had succeeded him then fell in the war one after the other, death duty was due again each time, and this brought even very rich families to the brink of ruin. Thus, after the First World

Elton Hall situated near Peterborough has been in the possession of the Proby family since the 16th century. The oldest parts of the property, the gate house and the chapel, date from the 15th century. The library contains a prayer book which belonged to Henry VIII.

War many of the big country houses were simply closed, abandoned and occasionally even pulled down.

Anyone who had successfully struggled through the interwar years faced a new threatening fiasco after the Second World War – hardly anyone could pay the death duties and the horrendous maintenance costs. The last chance for many house owners was to open their homes to the public. Anyone who was not comfortable with this thought had to move into a small annex and sell the rest of the property for less than it was worth – or hand it over to the National Trust. It was not until 1970 that some of the old families came into money again and were able to renovate their houses or re-acquire them. The reasons for this sudden prosperity lay in the increased price of land and consequent re-evaluation of the estate, or possibly an inheritance or even a successful auction sale of the valuable antiques collection. Most of the country houses teemed with works of art and in view of the record prices on the relevant markets it is understandable that many could not resist the temptation of parting with the Rubens from the dining room or the Van Dyck from the drawing room to raise a little ready money.

Today the country house is witnessing auspicious times similar to those before the First World War. There is a new generation of house buyers who have made their fortune with computer software, successful television production companies, and in the service sector and who want to own a prestigious property.

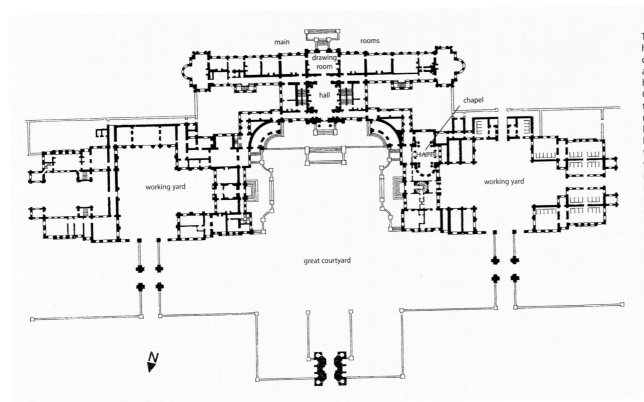

main rooms

drawing room

hall

chapel

CHAPEL

working yard

working yard

great courtyard

N

The interchangeability of the concepts "country house," "palace," and "castle" becomes clear in a comparison of the ground plans of Castle Howard and Blenheim Palace (see page 41): in this country house in North Yorkshire belonging to Lord Carlisle, which was built between 1699 and 1712, the kitchen and stable yards, together with the main building, also form a great courtyard. In fact, both Blenheim and Castle Howard were designed by the same architect, Sir John Vanbrugh. Typical of the great houses is the imposing entrance hall, which leads on to the drawing room, the center piece of the house. Magnificently furnished waiting, reception, and guest rooms lead off from it to right and left. These fine rooms lay on the *piano nobile*, the main or "noble" floor. The family's private rooms were mostly situated upstairs, the staff lived below stairs, just like in a castle.

THE GOLDEN AGE OF THE COUNTRY HOUSE

A country house was originally the dwelling of a noble family. It was surrounded by parkland or garden and no longer served any defensive purpose. After Henry VII came to power in 1485 the property and power situation in England was relatively stable, and so it became possible to move out of the sturdy but rather inhospitable castles, or to convert them into comfortable residences. For this reason the architectural boundaries between the palace and the big country house are fluid: great country houses such as Castle Howard are equal in splendor and architecture to palaces such as Blenheim Palace or Chatsworth. The 18th century represented the golden age of country house building. Countless houses were built or remodeled at enormous expense in order to conform to the very latest standards of comfort and taste, as for example Saltram House and Osterley Park.

The "Grand Tour," the obligatory tour of Italy undertaken by the young aristocrats, new editions of treatises on architecture from the Renaissance, and the publication of views of places of antiquity aroused among the noble and the cultured an enthusiasm for everything Classical. Their country seats reflected this: porticoes, Greek, Etruscan, and Roman columns, triangular or semicircular pediments over windows and doors, circular entrance halls, and domed rooms appeared everywhere. But there are also examples of country houses such as Knole and Owlpen Manor that managed to preserve their medieval or early Renaissance character.

Castle Howard in North Yorkshire is a country house with a palatial construction, as the ground plan above clearly shows. Lord Carlisle, the owner of the property, had the enormous house surrounded by extensive parklands which are among the most unusual in England.

Groombridge Place, Kent. This red brick mansion is surrounded by a moat, since it replaced a Norman castle. After the coronation of Charles II in 1660 the owner, lawyer, and scholar Philip Packer had the old house pulled down; he had the present building built in 1674.

The golden age of the country house came to an end with the beginning of the Victorian period in the 1830s. Many aristocratic families whose wealth had dwindled away were even forced to open their homes to the paying public. Big private building contracts became more unusual. Instead, the public purse became an important builder, commissioning buildings for use as museums, government buildings, and universities. Port Lympne was one of the last big country houses to be built, around the time of the First World War.

Above: Osterley Park, Greater London. In 1761 the architect Robert Adam was commissioned to remodel the Elizabethan manor house. He not only added a magnificent Ionic portico to the facade, but also altered the interior rooms.

Right: Knole, Kent. Although for a time the property of the Crown, Knole was no royal palace, but the residence of the Archbishop of Canterbury. With its 365 rooms, 52 staircases, and 12 entrances it is one of the largest houses in England.

Above: Saltram House, Devon. The old Tudor house was remodeled in the 1740s for the Parker family. Robert Adam designed the drawing room, library, and dining room in 1768–1782 for John Parker, who is described as a slovenly but jovial landowner. In spite of his uncultured appearance he was a sensitive connoisseur whose friends and advisers included the artist Sir Joshua Reynolds.

Left: The west facade of Petworth as it is today reflects the taste of the sixth Duke of Somerset. He had the house remodeled at the end of the 17th century to make it more comfortable and more elegant.

Opposite page: Lyme Park, Cheshire. Lyme Park acquired its present form in the early 18th century from the Italian architect Giacomo Leoni. Peter Legh, the head of the family at that time, entrusted the alterations to the architect. The interior of the house, however, remained intact.

THE SMALLER COUNTRY HOUSE

The smaller country house, on a larger scale than a rustic cottage and radiating a friendlier atmosphere than a castle or a palatial mansion, provides a quite particular ambience for its occupants. By smaller country houses we mean buildings which from the beginning, while grand, were of reasonable proportions, either from reasons of comfort or because they were only intended to accommodate a few occupants. There are also houses which were not originally conceived as the country seat of a person of rank, but as farm houses or perhaps as the domicile of a prosperous craftsman or trader, which were remodeled in the grand style at a later date. In addition, there is a further group of country houses built between the end of the 19th century and the outbreak of the First World War, which were about on the same scale as a villa in town. These well laid out country houses, frequently standing in a plot of land which ended at the garden fence, were ideal places for a pleasant weekend or a peaceful retirement.

An example of a smaller country house of this type is Chartwell, the home of Winston Churchill. He spotted it in 1922 while driving past and immediately fell in love with the property, at that time quite dilapidated. A doctor from the neighborhood is said to have told him that the previous owner used to put an umbrella up in bed because the roof leaked. But Churchill was not deterred by a leaky roof, especially as an unexpected inheritance provided the means necessary to buy the house. The origins of Chartwell lie in the Middle Ages, but as with so many other old properties, it had been altered several times. Churchill charged the architect Philip Tilden with the renovation of the building. It is said that Mrs Churchill never had any great affection for Chartwell, however, probably mainly because the renovation swallowed up large sums of money. These considerations were obviously of secondary importance to her husband, for he loved the house for the rest of his life. It was just far enough away from London to afford rest and relaxation but still near enough for him to be in the city quickly. In fact it is only a mere 25 miles from Hyde Park Corner.

Properties planned from the outset as more modest country houses are scaled-down copies of larger structures, they simply have fewer rooms than the originals. Therefore, the changing fashions which can be traced in the large houses are also reflected in the smaller models.

But whether large or small the architect was regularly faced with a fundamental question at the planning stage, which could be answered differently according to the opinion and taste of the time: should the arrangement of the rooms follow the outer symmetry of the house, or should the outside of the building reflect the form and arrangement of the interior rooms. Up to around 1500, a country house was for the most part a single building, but in the Tudor period buildings were combined in such a way as to take account of the trend for unity and symmetry. During the late 18th century and particularly in the 19th century the functions of the different parts of the building were frequently separated again, to produce a stronger sense of differentiation. This culminated in a strict separation of the spheres of male and female, masters and servants in the time of Queen Victoria. Naturally, for smaller buildings compromises had to be made.

And it is just these compromises and their "habitability" that make smaller houses particularly attractive to today's taste, for they often have a layout, tailor-made for a family without staff or with few employees. If a "smaller" house of this type could previously accommodate a couple of guests as well as the family and the servants, it would be considered almost gigantic by today's standards. But such a big house can offer the perfect solution to anyone wanting to use it as their place of work as well as their home. There is then enough room for the living and bedrooms as

From the beginning of the 16th century until 1850 Melbourn Bury in Cambridgeshire belonged to the bishops of Ely. This elegant country house lies in an extensive landscaped garden with a lake and today is used as a hotel.

well as two or three offices. Anyone who has more than three children, or a parent living with them, or who would like to employ an au pair and have weekend guests would not find such a house too big.

This must have been Prince Charles' experience with his private country seat Highgrove House, which he bought in 1980 for about a million pounds. The house, built in the Georgian style, is the ideal size for the needs of a young family. The ground floor comprises entrance hall, living room, dining room, study, library, and billiard room. On the second floor there are four suites of bedrooms and the nursery wing – the rooms for the children and their attendant. On the third floor there are five more bedrooms and two bathrooms. Anyone who considers this big should keep in mind that the purpose of a country house is largely to entertain and accommodate guests.

Even if smaller country houses are no longer surrounded by land in the sense of extensive estates, their gardens are still mostly worth mentioning. This makes them naturally all the more attractive to the garden-loving British and many of the more modest country houses, which have often stood empty for decades, are once again being sold to young families, and sometimes even rented – a peculiarity in a nation of house owners. Anyone who needs room, finds it, even if the size of the property causes certain difficulties to start with. It is obviously considerably more expensive to furnish seven rooms than to furnish two. Many occupants solve this problem by furnishing the house over several years. But there are also many young people in England who inherit such a large collection of furniture that they need an enormous house to put it in.

Right: Constable Burton Hall, Yorkshire. This Georgian villa owes its existence to an enormous mistake: in 1762 Sir Marmaduke Wyvill commissioned the architect John Carr to remodel his Elizabethan ancestral home; when he came to check on progress five months later, Carr had pulled the building down. The vast late Palladian building then cost almost ten times the original estimate.

Below: Pinfold Stud in Hales, Shropshire dates from the 18th century and is a good example of a Georgian country house such as was often occupied by tenant farmers. It is situated on the 3,000 acre estate of the Hall family and today is part of their stud farm.

Above: Anglesey Abbey is situated in Cambridgeshire. Originally built in the 12th century as a small monastery, it eventually came into the possession of a rich entrepreneur in 1926. In 1966 he bequeathed the house and his art collection to the State.

The Palladian Movement or Palladianism in Country House Architecture

Besides the palatial country houses of the powerful landed gentry, other smaller mansions were built between 1500 and 1830 which were often no less splendid than the big ones. They are often stylistically even more avant-garde than the bigger houses, since the building project was easier to oversee and could be completed within one generation or style epoch. One of the most important of these architectural styles for country houses was the Palladian movement, or Palladianism.

Until the end of the 16th century the English aristocracy in general had no particular connection with Catholic Italy. If they wanted to see something of the world they traveled to France, Holland, or Germany. At home they clung to the late Gothic Tudor style. A great and persistent change came about when in 1613 to 1614 the English architect Inigo Jones went to Italy to study the ruins of antiquity and their influence on the works of the Renaissance architect Andrea Palladio. As chief court architect he realized his vision of a rigorous, unadorned, Classical building style, particularly in the royal residences. The influence of Palladianism, as the style was called, which broke radically with the manneristic English late Gothic style, lasted from that time until well into the 19th century.

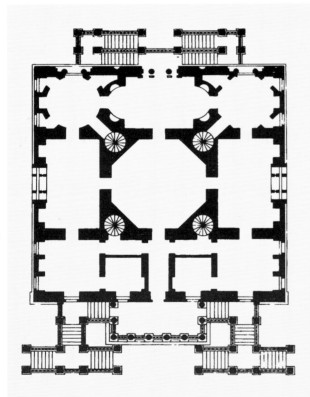

This country house has a square ground plan, the center of which forms a domed octagon. A portico emphasizes the main entrance. The lower ground floor originally housed the library, and on the first floor there is a series of state rooms designed by Robert Adam. Around the octagonal drawing room lie the gallery and the red, green, and blue velvet rooms. The staircases do not form theatrical stairwells as in other houses, but are spiral staircases, hidden in the corners of the central octagon. Both the exterior and interior of this small country villa had a strong influence on the subsequent style of English country houses.

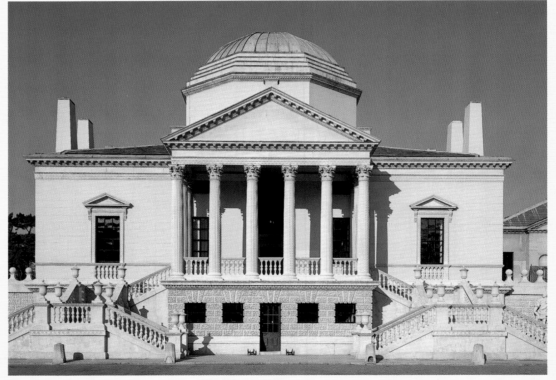

Chiswick House was built between 1725 and 1729 as a villa for the Third Earl of Burlington, who had discovered for himself the architecture of the Renaissance on his Italian journeys. So he, with the help of the architect Colen Campbell, produced the design for his "Temple of the Arts" himself, mainly based on Andrea Palladio's famous Villa Rotonda near Vicenza. Burlington wanted his villa mainly to house his art and book collections and to entertain guests; at any rate, there were also bedrooms.

Opposite page: Farnborough Hall in Warwickshire was remodeled in the Italian style by its owner William Holbech in 1745 on his return from a 15-year journey around the Italian peninsula.

By the 18th century the Italian journey, the so-called "Grand Tour", had become obligatory for the young nobility. New editions of architectural treatises from antiquity and the Renaissance, such as the "Ten Books on Architecture" by Vitruvius and those by the architect Palladio were published, and drawings of remote sites in Dalmatia and Greece and the like appeared. This all rekindled the enthusiasm for everything classical among the rich, the noble, and the cultured. The influential amateur architect Lord Burlington, who produced an example of "Neo-Palladianism" with his country villa in Chiswick, played a major role in the spread of the classical Italian style. In the process, however, he made himself unpopular with the painter and engraver William Hogarth and his friends, among them the poet Alexander Pope, who were trying at this time to establish an independent "English school" in art. This gave rise to a hail of lampoons and caricatures of Burlington and his followers, such as the architect William Kent. Palladianism was indeed very widespread and supported by men of importance, but Hogarth's taunts demonstrated that it was by no means the universally accepted style of the 18th century.

The "reviewed Palladianism" was less bound by the writings of the ancient and Renaissance architects than had been the case in the 17th century. Robert Adam, the Scottish architect, furniture designer, and interior decorator, who with his brothers James and John developed the characteristic Adam style between 1760 and 1790, did not worry about the servile observance of prescribed proportions; he was of the opinion that the proportions of a column depended less on Vitruvius's treatise than on its position in the room. From his archaeological research he was familiar with the interiors of Etruscan, Roman, and Pompeiian houses and tried to transpose these styles into his interior designs. Thus the walls would be covered with intricate, often gilded ornaments made from flat pieces of stucco, producing a cheerful, lively effect, which would perhaps seem rather gaudy today.

Above: Ebberston Lodge in Yorkshire is so small that it would fit into the hall of a big country house. Colen Campbell designed the tiny Palladian house in 1718.

THE RUSTIC COTTAGE

Between 1200 and 1700 many half-timbered houses were built in Great Britain, particularly in the well-wooded West and South. From the different window styles of these houses in East Sussex one can see that during their long use they have been repeatedly renovated and adapted to the needs of their occupants.

Besides the fine country house, the cottage is the British house *par excellence*. Much more than the large-scale mansion, it symbolizes a British place of residence that unites all classes and is suitable for almost all social groups. A cottage can be the home of an author, an officer of the guard, a stock broker and his family, a teacher, a clergyman, a professor, or an actress. The cottage is a special manifestation of a group of buildings which can be brought together under the term "vernacular architecture." This term describes smaller houses in a variety of building styles, built between the middle of the 14th century and the beginning of the 19th century. "Vernacular" means native or peculiar to popular taste, and the architecture is marked by a strong regional character.

Originally cottages were simple farmhouses. When a modern owner, on the other hand, speaks proudly of his cottage, it is often an understatement, for it is frequently not the modest house of a simple man but a gem, furnished in the best manner possible. Thus for example there are many farms, which were constantly enlarged over the generations until the 18th century, when they ended up as grand estates. Besides farmers, craftsmen and merchants also commissioned such houses. The size and construction of the buildings varied quite substantially according to the monetary resources at their disposal. Even the employees of the big local landowners built themselves often quite remarkable houses in the immediate vicinity of their employer's country seat, and these houses also fall into the category of "vernacular architecture." What makes these smaller houses so interesting is their variety, both in their absolute number and in their variation according to region and time of building.

Vernacular houses are also always a reflection of what nature has provided as building materials in a particular region in the form of wood and stone. In the county of Lancashire or in West Yorkshire, for example, there are houses built from the local millstone grit, a type of sandstone. In Somerset there is locally extracted limestone and in Warwickshire and East Sussex you can admire half-timbered houses. These romantic medieval facades with their characteristic visible timbers were generally favored in the south and east of England, the West Midlands, the eastern part of Wales and the flat regions of Yorkshire and Lancashire. It was not until the turn of the 18th century that people changed over to building with bricks here. In the mountainous, relatively unwooded regions of the west and north of England and in large parts of Scotland and Wales stone was the most usual building material.

As mentioned earlier, the last vernacular houses were built toward the end of the 19th century. The industrial revolution now made it possible to deliver building materials relatively easily over great distances. Thus the builder had a much wider choice of material to fall back on, which as paradoxical as it sounds, has resulted in greater uniformity in architecture. Houses in a regional style are relatively expensive on the real estate market and it is the dream of many a Briton to find an old vernacular house, renovate it, and furnish it in authentic historical style. The fulfillment of this dream sometimes drags on for years and begins with scouring the relevant advertising journals and endless trips around the country. This time is considered an important phase of life, the eventual end of which is almost to be regretted. As so often, the dream of the cottage can be summed up by the saying "To travel hopefully is better than to arrive."

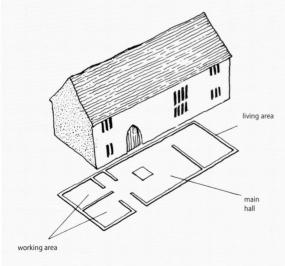

living area

main hall

working area

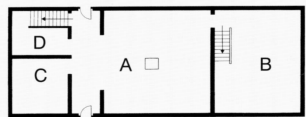

What we call cottages today were originally the huts of farm laborers or small farmhouses. In the Middle Ages, just as in the castle, there was a hall in the center of the rural cottage which occupied the whole height of the building. Here there would also be the fireplace, open until the middle of the 16th century, the smoke from which could usually only escape through cracks in the roof. To right and left of the hall (A) were separate living (B) and working (C, D) rooms, sometimes also animal stables. Soon they put joists in the side rooms to make additional lower rooms. The handling of milk and other foodstuffs took place in a small room in the coolest part of the house on the ground floor between the two heated rooms.

The second half of the 16th century brought an important innovation: the fireplace with a chimney to conduct smoke away. Now another floor could be inserted over the whole area of the house to build a continuous second story. This gave the occupants more space and comfort. More rooms were now created which could be used for particular activities, either work-related, such as a weaving room or a dairy, or a private retreat for individual members of the family, a custom which was gradually coming into use.

From "Cottage" to "Cottage Ornée"

While the simple rural population lived in shacks, which often consisted of only two rooms (stable and living area), from the 15th century more impressive country houses also developed. Usually there was a central hall, which was separated quite early from the master and mistress's rooms. From the late 16th century the division between the ruling and serving classes deepened. A distinction was made between the hall and the great chamber, reserved for important visitors; in addition there would be a drawing chamber near the bedrooms and a gallery, an impressive connecting passage. These rooms were often arranged in a double sequence around the hall: one for displays of pomp, the second for important guests. Country houses of the Tudor period were frequently arranged symmetrically around a courtyard. From 1600 onward further rooms were added which the guests had to cross before they met their host in the privacy of his cabinet. How far the guest was allowed to advance was a sign of the importance accorded to him. From the 18th century onward the increasingly powerful and mobile city-based nobility shuttled from London to Bath, from there to their country seat or to that of other members of the aristocracy with whom they were friendly, and then back again. Within this upper echelon, so fond of traveling, hierarchies played a lesser role,

and so suites of rooms were laid out running around a central staircase on the upper floor. At the same time experiments were being made with heating and sanitary appliances. English Palladianism with its puristic, neoclassical style and mighty porticos now became predominant. But already the first hints of Gothicism, which was to assert itself at the turn of the 19th century, were beginning to give notice.

From the late 18th century the landed gentry took to building the *cottages ornées*, a house which looked just like an old farmhouse. This glorified view of country life came of age at the end of the 19th century with the propensity of the upper middle classes for buying or copying old houses and then fitting them out with all the comforts of town. The driving force behind this aspiration was the magazine *Country Life*, which appeared from about 1890 and whose significance for the 20th century and its relationship with the country cottage should not be underestimated. Since the Edwardian period country houses have been of more modest proportions and embody the dream of seclusion and traditional rural life. This dream has lasted until the present day: indeed new houses are built, but the British still prefer old bricks and mortar.

The geological nature of the region determines the materials for vernacular architecture. Where there are occurrences of a particular type of stone or earth these lend the local architecture a distinctive character. If there is useable clay you will find a building tradition of cob or brick houses.

Above: Two chimneys on the gable ends of the house make possible a central entrance and the division of the living area into several rooms on each floor.

Opposite page, above: Stone was used as a building material wherever it occurred in sufficient quantities, as for example here at the Trekkener Mill in Cornwall.

Opposite page, bottom left: Typical regions for brick houses were the Thames Valley and East Anglia with their rich clay deposits.

Opposite page, bottom right: Thatched roofs from straw or reed are typical for a rural cottage, the walls of which are made of half-timbered work or stone according to region.

Left: Until the beginning of the 18th century half-timbered houses like these in Warwick were built all over England.

Above: It was not until the 19th century that bricks replaced the regional building materials such as wood and natural stone.

HOUSE BUYING IN GREAT BRITAIN

It could all be so simple: you find a nice house, sign a couple of documents, give notice that you are leaving your old home, pack up bag and baggage, and move house. But changing apartment or house only works like that in the very rarest of cases. Apart from the physical exertions involved in the concentrated packing of valuable china or dismantling of oak furniture that weighs a ton, any number of errands and even more telephone calls await the prospective house-mover. There will be discussions with the bank and the legal adviser, viewing appointments will have to be coordinated with journey times, especially if you are moving a long way, the gas and electricity supply will need to be cut off in the old house and connected in the new one, friends and acquaintances will want to know your new address, and on top of all this, there is your sensitive Labrador who will have to be found a place in a kennel because removal day will be much too stressful for him.

In spite of all the misery and trouble connected with house buying and moving, every year in the British Isles a great many people fulfil their dream of a house of their own or a bigger house. As soon as it is certain that they need a new abode, the search is on. In Great Britain no less than in other countries you can call on the assistance of a broker. Together with the client, the real estate specialist will draw up an exact profile of the wishes and requirements for the new home and then will submit suitable properties for consideration. If you would like to spare this expense you can look around on your own account.

One important question is: What is the best time to put your old, still occupied, house on the market? Is it better to acquire the new house first and then sell the old one, or do you advertise the old house as soon as you start looking for a new one? At the end of the day, after all, no one wants to end up with two houses or, even worse, no house at all. For reasons of safety it is usually preferable to sort out the new acquisition first and then to finalize the sale of the old house.

As soon as a house has been shortlisted, viewing appointments have to be arranged. It is important not to let yourself be overly influenced by the first impression, although this naturally often makes the difference between spontaneous sympathy and antipathy. It is much better to be guided by a critical inspection of the building. A roof that now looks romantically warped can collapse completely in two years and entail very high costs.

Antiquated water pipes may fit in very well with the age of the house, but they will be troublesome to all occupants if night-time visits to the bathroom have to be avoided because of the noise. Viewing on a warm summer's day can conceal the fact that the masonry is damp and unpleasantly cold from September to April. And what about the energy supply? Further you have to negotiate with the present owner to find out what they are going to leave in the house and what they will take with them. Is the splendid Aga oven staying? What about the carpets? Can we buy the lighting made specially for the library? Often quite considerable extra charges accrue for apparent trifles, and you should always plan for these in good time.

Buying a house requires large sums of money but very few prospective buyers have enough capital at their disposal to be able to pay for their new property outright. Consequently the road usually leads to the bank. A real estate mortgage is taken out on the future home. Those considering moving house should consult the various mortgage providers before even beginning to look at houses to find out what amount of mortgage would be available to them and which offers the most favorable terms. In most cases this narrows the choice from the outset since you do not even need to consider houses which are unattainable, saving time, money, and nerves.

In order to be sure of the legal side of house buying and selling it is recommended that you employ a solicitor or licensed conveyancer to deal with the arrangements. While legally qualified, solicitors should not be confused with barristers. Solicitors are mainly engaged in preparing lawsuits and giving legal advice. Barristers are entitled to appear in the higher courts as counsel for the defense or prosecution. The conveyancer also carries out notarial tasks as does the solicitor occasionally, and both solicitor and conveyancer can overcome all the hurdles when dealing with the transfer of property rights. When buyer and vendor have agreed about the price and other conditions, the house buyer will usually want to sell his old house. A broker can help here too.

Most British people are garden lovers, so the terraced or semi-detached house with a patch of green at the back is at the top of the list for house-hunters, particularly city dwellers. It is, however, only really desirable if the style of the new housing displays elements of British vernacular architecture, like for example half-timbered work and brick.

In contrast to many other countries in northern and central Europe, people in the British Isles would rather own their homes than live in rented accommodation. Therefore setting up home for yourself or moving house usually involves the purchase of real estate. Some people rely on what the broker has to offer, others prefer to search in person.

Anyone who wants competent assistance with house hunting should apply to a serious real estate broker, such as London-based Marcus Kemp. A certified specialist with a thorough knowledge of the real estate market will usually be able to offer you the first properties after a very short time. The broker's preliminary selection, made on the basis of a profile provided by the customer, saves a lot of time. If a contract is agreed, the broker claims commission.

If one of the properties is shortlisted the broker will arrange a viewing appointment for the client and will accompany him or her. If the client is seriously interested in the property, at least one further appointment should be arranged, as the first impression of a strange house or apartment can be deceptive. Also to be recommended are viewings at different times of day to check out lighting conditions, noise levels, etc.

A structural survey is not only recommended for older houses. New houses also can have serious defects due to work carried out incorrectly, bad planning, or plain negligence. To that extent it is money well spent to employ a local architect, structural engineer, or some other specialist to carry out a structural survey. The survey should provide detailed information about the state of the roof, masonry, foundations, windows, floors, plumbing, electrical and gas appliances, chimneys, garden, drainage, and paths, and it will mercilessly inform the interested party if mold, rot, or woodworm are infesting the object of desire.

If the prospective buyer intends to extend or alter the property after purchase, it is essential to find out whether it has listed status before any contracts are signed. The Department of the Environment lists all buildings of special historical value, and works on such houses require official consent. The same is true of "conservation areas," which are also given special protection. If the building stands within one of these areas no building works can be carried out under any circumstances without official approval. Trees in the front garden are equally unassailable. Anyone looking for really old bricks and mortar would sometimes do better to embrace the idea of converting an old school, a redundant church, a defunct railway station, or an abandoned warehouse into a dwelling house. With luck a building of this type will not be listed. Local education authorities, diocesan offices, the British Rail Property Board, and various local firms are all able to assist in the search for a suitable property.

However great their enthusiasm, prospective buyers should never forget that a house only belongs to them once all the contracts have been signed. The fact that a first offer has been accepted by the vendor does not signify by any means that the transaction will come about. Perhaps the real estate broker receives an offer which is £5,000 above the negotiated price. He will try to persuade the first buyer to match this. Or perhaps the vendor himself is pressed for time because he can move into his new home more quickly than expected. He may then declare a contract race, that is he will sell to the first person to have all the necessary papers ready and be in a position to complete the contract with his solicitor. In addition there is also always the possibility that the potential buyer will already have paid broker's fees, advertising charges for his old house, the fee for the survey on his new house, solicitor's or notary's costs, and have made several trips to view the property, when the owners suddenly decide that they really do not want to sell after all.

The Business of the Lease

Anyone wanting to buy a house in Great Britain can raise a loan at any bank or one of the many building societies established for this purpose. In actual fact the lender buys the property and owns it until the loan is paid back with interest. The procedure for repaying this mortgage, as the loan is called, differs considerably from bank to bank. Usually the rates correspond to a monthly rent, so that buying and renting differ mainly in the fact that in the first case the house belongs to you entirely once the term of the mortgage is over. With buying also there is always the possibility of reselling and buying a better house, and in fact many home owners make a good profit by skillful trading-up. Occasionally, however, falling real estate prices can ruin the buyer before the house belongs to him entirely.

After paying off the mortgage in many cases, however, you still only own the house. The plot of land on which it stands stays in the possession of the landowner, often a member of one of the great aristocratic families. You lease the land from the landlord or landlady as leasehold. In the 18th and 19th centuries a piece of land, along with the buildings on it, reverted to the landlord or his family on the expiry of the lease – a profitable enterprise for the aristocratic landowners. If a lease that a buyer has taken over from the previous owner of a house only has a few years left on it, there is increasingly the possibility of acquiring the plot as freehold property, that is with unrestricted tenure. The sale of freehold property is becoming more and more common today.

Floorboards are planed individually before laying.

The wall is only plastered between the joists, the wooden struts remain visible, which preserves the character of the span ceiling.

The vertical sections are first packed with wattle and daub and then plastered.

The irregular timberwork of an old house does not exactly ease the task, but has a lot of charm for all that.

Water pipes must be checked and if necessary repaired to prevent them from disappearing beneath the plaster.

The last layer of plaster is applied carefully, since the unevenness of the old wall is supposed to remain visible.

The structure of the half-timbered work can be incorporated into the decoration of the house and lends atmosphere to the interior.

It is better to repair windows than to replace them, since new windows seldom fit in with the character of the old house.

How to Renovate a House in the Authentic Style

Renovating an old house is a lot of work and also requires an expert knowledge of the history of architecture and questions of style. Anyone who is not an expert or a knowledgeable amateur in this field should make sure they receive specialist help, especially since there are often a number of regulations to take into account with old buildings.

The front door is an important element. It dominates the whole entrance area and therefore it is especially important to proceed with care here. If the original door is beyond restoration it is usually due to inadequate painting. Many people forget that a door has six surfaces which all need to be painted. Since modern doors seldom look really authentic, a door from a house that is being demolished would fit the bill. Many have also had a fair measure of success in repairing doors. This is often the best solution when no suitable replacement can be found.

Internal doors can stick or fit badly for a variety of reasons. Typical causes are expansion of the joints, warping due to various temperature and moisture conditions on both sides of the door, rotting through dampness, weakness of the hinges due to age, or even movement of the walls. With internal doors also a fresh coat of paint is preferable to replacing them completely. The door furniture is frequently a critical subject. At best you should look for second-hand or salvaged items, or have new ones made to the original design by a specialist.

Almost more attention should be devoted to the windows than to the doors. Under no circumstances should you simply exchange old windows for new ones, since they never fit in with the character of the house as well as the originals. For that reason damage should be repaired if possible. A good specialist can undetectably replace the individual wooden parts of an old window. With sash windows the movable parts can be replaced easily without spoiling the overall effect. With all wooden windows regular repainting is the best provision against deterioration. This is also true for shutters.

Moisture is the biggest enemy for timber frames and other exposed wooden parts, especially if it can penetrate deep into the joints where it will not dry out again. Thanks to protective impregnations and coatings rain, snow, and fog cannot harm the timber. But care must be taken to ensure that moisture originating in the house can dry out and not become trapped inside.

Damage to supporting walls can be very expensive, and also dangerous. It is best to leave the diagnosis to an expert in this case. The causes of weakness in such walls are many and varied. Sometimes pests destroy the wood, in other cases underground drilling can literally undermine the foundations of the wall. The original state of the wall should serve as a guide to its final treatment. Thus, according to the age of the house and the style of its architecture, the wall could have been bare plaster or wallpapered. If you are lucky, fragments of the first wallpaper will still be present. There are specialist firms which will produce a new wallpaper from a small snippet of the original.

Paving tiles can also be reproduced to old designs if you need to exchange broken ones. Old paving tiles should be taken up occasionally so that they can be cleaned and then re-laid. Should this be impossible you can buy contemporary, stylistically correct replacements quite cheaply from demolished houses.

Stucco is an important decorative element in house interiors. It is very difficult to restore it authentically, so this work should be left to the experts. The removal of layers of paint which have been added over the years can often bring to light astonishing details. The decorative plaster underneath can be much finer than was first thought. Completely decayed stucco has to be replaced, but some corners will perhaps be worse affected than others. In this case you should get together with a stuccoworker and discuss the possibility of partial restoration. The important thing is to ensure that the new sections fit in stylistically and do not look too new.

Wooden floors, like doors and windows, should as far as possible remain in their original condition. Partial repairs are best here also. If old floorboards are polished their subsequent treatment should be in keeping with the age of the house. Shiny surfaces would, for example, be out of place in a house built before the middle of the 18th century.

In houses with more than one floor, woodwork on the stairs and staircases can be repaired by a carpenter. If a staircase has to be completely renovated you should try to retain at least a couple of old pieces, such as the knob at the end of the banister rail, or something similar. The antique pieces can usually be easily incorporated into the new construction.

Replacing piping is an expensive procedure. It is often more sensible to leave the broken pipes in place and lay new ones in another position. The removal of old pipes usually causes a lot of damage. In some cases it can be more convenient to run the new piping through the old ducts. Sanitary appliances make a big contribution to the character of a house. Owners of old houses should reflect on the fact that there were hardly any fitted bathrooms in the past. Besides, many houses had no bathroom at all or only one in the corridor.

It is absolutely essential to have electrical fittings tested for safety by a specialist. If they are to be restored in authentic style, there are firms which will supply the appropriate materials.

External metal parts such as balcony railings or window decorations will usually need to have the rust removed. Then they should be repainted in keeping with the style of the house. But don't forget rust protection, it's worth the trouble. Damage to cast iron can be welded. Guttering must constantly be kept clear and frequently checked for damaged parts. At the end of the day it fulfills an important function, carrying potentially damaging moisture away from the house. However, if possible the old guttering should be retained since it is an important architectural detail. Simply replacing it with a plastic replica is justifiably considered to be lacking in style. But such a solution is acceptable, if need be, in places where it cannot be seen.

All in all, there is a lot to consider when renovating an old house. The points raised here are only a small part of the relevant aspects. They show that restoring an historic building is often more difficult than building a new one, quite apart from the costs incurred. Nevertheless countless home-owners in Britain take on this challenge. They prefer the character and charm of an historic building to any, ever so perfect, new one.

Architectural Salvage Yards, a Gold Mine for the House

If you are looking for a part for your old car you can look around the scrap yard. There you will often find quite usable parts, even if the cars they belonged to are long gone. Architectural salvage yards or reclamation yards, the specialist outlets for historic building supplies, operate on the same principle. They are a veritable goldmine for all those enthusiasts who would like to renovate their old houses in authentic style.

The purchase of a completely run-down historic house and its restoration over many years is one of those things that becomes your life's work. It fits in with the British sporting spirit to undertake almost superhuman exertions in order to rescue this piece of the national cultural heritage. It is easy to buy a new house, but to rescue a moldering pile is considered a positively heroic act. Thus a whole genre of magazines is devoted to this subject, and the readers love reports about how some enthusiast or other has by patient meticulous work restored every detail of an architectural gem to its original state.

But back to the comparison between scrap yard and architectural salvage yard: while going to the scrap metal yard sometimes carries the whiff of stinginess about it, the intention of repairing your house with the remains of another building is not considered at all dishonorable. On the contrary, the re-use of good old materials is very much in keeping with the British sense of economy and nostalgia.

In other European countries the re-use of old bath tubs, windows, doors, and guttering would be unthinkable. Even professed environmentalists live in brand-new custom-built houses, the energy loss of which is close to zero thanks to the most modern building, heating, and insulation techniques. In Great Britain, on the other hand, it is believed that everything was better in the past. A Victorian bathtub has fundamentally more value than its present-day counterpart and besides it is less expensive. Moreover, it fits much better stylistically into an old bathroom. There is simply no reason not to fall back on the alternative from the architectural spare parts store.

Architectural salvage yards display building materials rescued from old houses in hangars and open-air yards, as here at Drummond's.

PRINCE CHARLES AND AGRICULTURE

It is remarkable that Prince Charles, the future King of a country that has hit the headlines as the country of origin of mad cow disease, has been making well-founded contributions to the debate about nature conservation for the last 30 years. His interest in ecology, landscape protection, and agriculture has, indeed, given him the reputation of being a green eccentric with certain sections of the public, but this does not bother him. On the contrary, if possible he puts the theories he advocates into practice, in the first instance in the garden of Highgrove, his country house. Here he gave up using artificial fertilizers and pesticides in 1980 and has since created a delightful natural garden full of flowers and butterflies.

This commitment on the part of the heir to the throne was extremely suspect to many Britons. They would have preferred it if his concern for nature had been confined to hunting. A future king who talks to his flowers simply did not fit in with their idea of a sovereign. Admittedly the British have also always had a soft spot for eccentricity, and so the Prince's passion for ecology could simply be regarded as a fad.

The garden experiments, however, did not satisfy the environmentally friendly prince and so he decided to use the Home Farm of the Duchy of Cornwall to experiment on a larger scale. The farm lies in the neighborhood of Highgrove House, near Tetbury in Gloucestershire, which the Prince acquired in 1980. The Home Farm was originally situated in Stoke Climsland in Cornwall, but in 1984 it was leased to Cornwall County Council, which needed it for educational purposes. As an interim solution the Prince farmed in Wales, until he decided to acquire land in the vicinity of his country seat in 1985. In 1986 he began to convert to organic methods on parts of the Home Farm. He stopped using artificial fertilizers and pesticides and this proved so successful that he changed over to organic methods for the whole farm in 1990.

A year later sheep-rearing was organized according to holistic principles and two years after that the same principles were applied to the dairy herd. The animals are kept as naturally as possible and not constantly pumped full of prophylactic vaccines, worming cures, and antibiotics, but

only treated when necessary and then with selected medications. Homeopathic and herbal remedies are also used. Thanks to these measures, which strengthened the natural resistance of the animals, the veterinarian's costs were halved.

The Prince's experiments with natural agriculture have also proved successful from an economic point of view. The milk from the Home Farm is sold through a cooperative and made into yogurt and cheese. Beef and lamb are retailed through controlled butcher's shops, wheat and oats are sold to the independent firm Duchy Originals, which makes them into cereal products sold internationally under the same name. Rye is sold wholesale to manufacturers of organic bread, beans are used as natural cattle feed.

The Home Farm is not only exemplary on account of its methods of cultivation but also as regards landscape and nature conservation. So, for example, the wooded areas were reforested, six miles of hedge were planted, the old stone walls were repaired and ponds were dug. All the fields are edged by a two to three yard (two to three meter) wide green strip. Where it borders on a field it serves as a barrier against weeds, between field and hedge or stone wall it is home to small animals and insects. In addition, the Prince of Wales makes the gardens of Highgrove and the land of the Home Farm available for research projects, for example to ascertain to what extent organic agriculture affects the population

The livestock on the Home Farm includes not only cows and bullocks, but also rare breeds of pigs and sheep. The meat from the animals, reared according to organic principles, is extremely palatable and very much in demand with the consumer. It is sold locally by selected butchers.

The Prince of Wales moved his Home Farm near his country seat, Highgrove in Gloucestershire, in 1985. The buildings and land of the former Home Farm in Cornwall were leased to Cornwall County Council which set up an agricultural college where prospective agronomists have been learning about their future profession, including the practical side, since 1984.

of birds, butterflies, and other insects. Of the many projects with which the heir to the throne is involved, the Home Farm is undoubtedly one of his favorites. Not least because over the last 20 years it has demonstrated that he was correct in his commitment to organic agriculture, long before meat scandals about hormone-injected calves and poisoned cattle proved him right.

Not all foodstuffs marketed under the Duchy Originals label are products of the Home Farm. Only meat, milk, and cereals actually come from Cornwall. However, every product that aspires to this prestigious brandname must originate from strictly organic cultivation.

Above: Originally the Home Farm of the Duchy of Cornwall was in Stoke Climsland. Since 1984 it has been used as an agricultural college.

Below, right: The stables at the former Home Farm in Cornwall offer enough places for the agriculture students' horses.

The Man who was James Herriot

There is probably hardly another 20th-century author who has formed such an enduring picture of England as the veterinarian and author Alf Wight. He published his vet stories between 1970 and 1992 under the pseudonym James Herriot and by the time of his death in 1995 he had sold about 50 million books worldwide. According to estimates by his biographer Graham Lord, Alf Wight earned about £40 million during his life, mostly from his books. A remarkable sum, especially as the veterinarian only published his first book at the age of 54.

The BBC television series based on his works was also a worldwide success and boosted the sale of his books even more. The first episode of *All Creatures Great and Small* was broadcast in Great Britain on January 8, 1978, and was followed by 40 further installments in the next five years. Week by week an average of 13 million viewers sat in front of the television when the exploits of James, Siegfried, Helen, and Tristan were screened. The series was also shown in the USA and there each episode had about 37 million viewers. Altogether *All Creatures Great and Small* was sold to 42 countries. Fans all over the world watched captivated as the good vet helped sick animals and rubbed along with their more or less eccentric but always thoroughly English owners. Dogs, cats, afternoon tea, a whisky by the fire, English breakfast, red-faced farmers, and

The television version of the witty and touching stories about the veterinarians' practice in the wild romantic scenery of the Yorkshire Dales aroused worldwide interest in the region to the north of Bradford. Other tourist regions can only dream of such an effective advertising campaign.

The Yorkshire Dales National Park offers ramblers and nature lovers a host of possibilities. But fans of the successful vet stories also get their money's worth. If you want to see where the outdoor shots of Darrowby, the fictitious site of the vets' practice, were filmed, you have to visit the village of Askrigg in Wensleydale. There to this day James Herriot fans try to recognize scenes from *All Creatures Great and Small*.

bumpy cobblestones – the world could not get enough of an England that was free from crime and environmental pollution. Even though the first series is set at a time of international economic crisis, there is no sign of the Depression.

The English House in Literature, Film, and Television

Above: Dyrham Park in South Gloucestershire appears in the film *The Remains of the Day*, based on the original novel by Kazuo Ishiguro. It represented the exterior of Darlington Hall, the house in which the employer of the butler played by Anthony Hopkins conducted his amateur foreign policy. Dyrham Park was built between 1691 and 1710 for William Blathwayt, the Secretary of State and Secretary of State for War of King William III. The architect William Talman designed the building in a style which was conservative for those times. Since Blathwayt's descendants left the property almost unchanged, Dyrham Park together with its interior decorations has been preserved, as it were, in a time capsule until modern times.

Above: The ball scene in the film version of the novel *Emma* by Jane Austen was filmed in Claydon House. The property, situated in Buckinghamshire, is considered to be one of the most unusual historic buildings in England. Claydon House was the seat of the Verney family, one of the old influential families of England which has produced a number of great personalities. In the 15th century a Verney was Lord Mayor of London, in the 17th century the family provided a marshal of England, and Ralph, the second Earl of Verney, went down in history as a dilettante and spendthrift. He wanted to remodel Claydon House in the grand style, but this ruined him before the building works were completed. The beginnings of the alterations which remain give a good impression of how splendid Claydon House would have looked if only there had been enough money.

Right: In the film version of Jane Austen's novel *Sense and Sensibility* from 1995 we see four different historic English houses. Compton Castle was chosen for the exterior of Mr. Willoughby's home. The property, situated in Devon, was the seat of the Gilbert family from the 15th century onward, a family whose offspring includes among others Sir Humphrey Gilbert, the stepbrother of Sir Walter Raleigh. Sir Humphrey set out in 1583 with the intention of discovering the sea route to China, but actually landed in Newfoundland and founded the first English colony in North America, in St John's Harbour. Unfortunately, he was not able to receive the gratitude of his countrymen, for his ship sank on the homeward voyage to England.

The English House – Model for German Modern Design

In 1896 the German Emperor Wilhelm II sent Hermann Muthesius, the architect of the *Preußisches Entwurfsbüro* (Prussian Design Bureau), to London to acquire "technical information." His brief was to study the the English Arts and Crafts Movement founded by William Morris, John Ruskin, and Norman Shaw, and to assess its applicability in Germany. Up until 1903 Muthesius published reports and essays from England as well as the book *Stilarchitektur und Baukunst* (Period Architecture and Building Design). In this he criticized academic historicism which worked with past architectural forms but was devoid of all feeling, and on the other, inveighed against the mawkish *Jugendstil* (*art nouveau*) with its addiction to harmony. In contrast to this he characterized as exemplary the English house with its simple comfort and connection with nature. After his return to Berlin in 1903 he published perhaps his best known work: *Das englische Haus. Entwicklung, Bedingungen, Anlage, Aufbau, Einrichtung und Innenraum* (The English House. Development, Conditions, Planning, Building, Furnishing and Interior).

This three-volume presentation of the history of English house construction with an emphasis on the latest examples was intended, on the one hand, as a kind of textbook for architects, and, on the other, for interested property owners. Written in a graphic style it describes all aspects of architecture with their geographical, historical, social, and legal conditions and even makes reference to building laws. Many illustrations, both photographs and technical drawings, elucidate his ideas. Alongside these often radical reports Muthesius presents clear considerations of the advantages and disadvantages of the architectural solutions described. Sometimes he wonders whether it would be sensible to introduce a certain feature into Germany, or whether it owed too much to the sometimes bizarre and eccentric character of the English.

As an independant architect Hermann Muthesius (1861–1927) exerted a great influence on German residential architecture. He was a co-founder of the *Deutscher Werkbund* (German Association of Craftsmen).

In general, however, there was a lot to learn from the modern English house built according to the principles of the Reform Movement, as Muthesius writes in his introduction: "English housing conditions are of increasing interest today when so many people are beginning to experience a longing to constantly growing restlessness of life with the peacful refuge of his own home. … The Englishman lives, purely and simply, in a way that he believes to be wholesometo the inner man and agreeable to his family and so that he can enjoy life to the full and develop his individuality". Of hide-bound historicism and extravagant *art nouveau* there was "Thank heaven, no trace. Everything exudes simplicity, plainnes, rusticity." In the sphere of town planning, Muthesius was inspired by the English garden cities, suburbs of large cities which were planned in close connection with nature and had generous gardens. After his return he was commissioned by the government with reforming the Prussian polytechnics and technical schools according to the English model. Since he was also working as an architect, his insights and ideas became very influential. Once the first "Reform House" had been built in Berlin-Zehlendorf in 1904 he became for a time the most sought-after architect of the upper middle classes. Moreover, Muthesius collaborated with the foundation of garden cities. In the technical schools he advocated the rejection of imitations of style and "bogus splendor." This upset the factory owners and traders who were producing and distributing objects such as these which denied their industrial origin. Heated public debate about the "correct" style led in 1907 to the foundation of the "Deutscher Werkbund" which brought together reforming artists, industrialists, and dilettantes. Muthesius was one of its authoritative leaders until the First World War.

With his villa Freudenberg, built in Berlin-Zehlendorf in 1904, Muthesius created the first German example of Reform architecture according to the English model. The photograph shows the present state of the villa. The original lattice windows have been replaced by modern windows.

The four photographs show interiors of Villa Freudenberg designed by Hermann Muthesius in Berlin-Zehlendorf. Muthesius planned his country houses as homes entirely arranged for the daily life of the family, but some rooms also offer the possibility of "elegant conviviality" in larger circles. Here the music room with its various seating groups provides room for company. The fireplace with the symmetrically arranged porcelain figures and the painting as the central focal point above the mantelpiece produces a typically British effect.

Like the other main living rooms, the nursery is also on the first floor, at garden level. In keeping with the English model, the big window admits a lot of light into the room and at the same time offers the enticement of a stimulating glimpse of nature. The proportions of the furniture are adapted to the needs of the child: a low table is surrounded by benches, ideal for casual sitting, the cupboard can be opened at three different heights, one of which is accessible to even the smallest child. The practical lozenge-shaped decoration, the only architectural ornamentation, is perhaps a little severe.

As in the English country house, the entrance hall, occupying more than one floor, is the highest room in the house. A gallery gives access to the rooms on the upper floor. Its parapet is decorated with quite simple ornamentation reminiscent of the geometric style of the Arts and Crafts Movement.

The dining room is light and airy since the patterned wallpaper does not reach up to the ceiling. The fireplace with its light-colored surround and the loose arrangement of several small lights over the dining table sustain this comfortable effect.

Guests at Durbins – the Bloomsbury Group

Durbins in Surrey is a "reformed" English house *par excellence*. The gigantic windows in the warm brick facade admit light and air into the property of the English artist and art historian Roger Eliot Fry and his wife. It was hoped that country life and pleasant cheerful architecture would dispel Helen Fry's depression, but these conditions were not so easy to find. So, to end the long search for the right house, Fry finally took up his pencil himself and produced a design so perfect in transparency, light, and openness that it would have satisfied Hermann Muthesius. Under a mansard roof, living areas on five levels are skillfully fitted into the three stories in an open plan design. In the center lies the two-story living room with windows almost as high as the walls, which seem to have the effect of bringing the garden inside the house. Viewed from the outside they are the most striking feature of this remarkable mixture of the modern and architectural history produced by Roger Fry, the novice architect, in 1909.

The members of the Bloomsbury Group, a circle of publishers, poets, artists, and intellectuals, were welcome guests at Durbins, Roger Fry's "Reform House," on account of their liberal and open attitudes.

From left to right Jimmy Doggart, Frances Marshall, Alec Penrose, Lytton Strachey, Frances Penrose, and Dora Carrington. The author Vita Sackville-West appears in the photograph top right.

While he was studying to become a scientist, Roger Fry developed a great interest in art and took up painting. The experiences of his first Italian journey steered him toward the history of art. After lecturing on the history of art from the middle of the 1890s he soon embarked on a career as an art writer: he worked as an art critic, was one of the founders of the still highly regarded Burlington Magazine, and published his first longer studies of art history. At the same time he also took an interest in contemporary art, not least because he himself was having increasing success with his painting. When he first saw the works of Paul Cézanne in 1906, he recognized the painting he had always sought: the colors of Impressionism combined with the composition of the Old Masters. In several articles in the Burlington Magazine he wrote about such new artists as Gauguin, Van Gogh, and Matisse. In 1910 he organized an exhibition of their works under the title "Manet and the Post-Impressionists," which caused a veritable scandal. The shocked visitors either flew into a rage or burst out laughing when they saw the abstract, expressively colored paintings. While Fry was being vehemently attacked both in the press and by his former art history colleagues, he was already working on a second exhibition. He was now no longer a learned expert on Old Masters, but became instead a champion of the modern, which cost him some of his old friends, but also brought him new ones, like the "Bloomsbury Group." This loosely bound group of young artists and authors, which included Vita Sackville-West and the sisters Vanessa Bell and Virginia Woolf as well as Duncan Grant, E.M. Forster, and Lytton Strachey, received the new painting and Roger Fry with great enthusiasm. It is possible that Fry also expected some relief for his melancholic wife from the liberal attitudes, liberty, and openness of the young people. He frequently invited the "Bloomsberries," as they were sometimes contemptuously called in the press, to Durbins.

Unfortunately his efforts were in vain: In 1919 his wife Helen was admitted to a sanatorium and Fry decided to sell Durbins. Later owners tried for a number of decades to make Durbins into a less open, less avant-garde house by repainting and remodeling. A German family bought the property at the end of the 1970s. By careful rebuilding and reconstructing they are trying to bring back the spirit of Roger Fry and Bloomsbury, taking care not to turn the house into a museum. For Durbins is what it should be: an English house.

Left: Durbins in Surrey, designed by the artist and art historian Roger Fry in 1909, is the perfect example of a "reformed" English house. Windows almost as high as the walls provide light and openness and seem to integrate the garden into the two-story living room.

Opposite: Roger Fry's murals in the stair well at Durbins reveal the influence of the work of Henri Matisse.

South Kensington is one of the quietest, most exclusive areas of London.

CITY LIFE

THE CAPITAL

In Great Britain city life is summed up above all by life in London, Europe's largest city. It may mean something different to each of its eight million inhabitants, but some main groups can be distinguished among them.

Firstly, there are the Londoners who were born and bred there. They cannot imagine living anywhere else, and in this respect they are no different from the inhabitants of other great cities, such as New York or Paris. Just like the real New Yorkers and Parisians, they are well aware that their home is one of the most important cities in the world.

Then there is the large group of Londoners by choice who have moved to this city of their own free will. They may be fascinated by the British capital for some reason, or the city may offer them particular opportunities. For example, young fashion designers are often keen to move to London in order to train and seek inspiration there. Londoners by choice also include the German waitress who works in the restaurant at Fortnum & Mason's and can climb the career ladder much faster than she could back home, the artist from Barcelona who believes he can feel the pulse of time in London, and the barman from South Africa who works temporarily in a London hotel.

There is another group of temporary Londoners: those who also enjoy the buzz of London, but only come for a short while. Indeed, the tourists are just as much a part of London as Big Ben or Buckingham Palace. After all, 25 million people visit the city every year, and in some areas they dominate the scene more than the Londoners themselves.

Apart from the people who are in London because they were born or have gone there by choice, there are also large numbers of people who are forced to live there by circumstance. They are often immigrants from poor regions of the world who have found work in the capital of the Commonwealth and now earn a living far from their

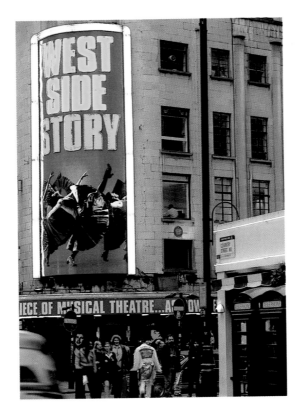

In the evening many visitors and residents love to go to a spectacular musical in London's "theaterland." This even has an impact on the restaurant guides, which often indicate a "pre-theater menu" that allows diners to eat early before they go to a show.

homes. There are over 300,000 immigrants from the Caribbean living in London, more than 250,000 from India, and thousands of Africans and Chinese. They have no real interest in the city as such, and most have never been to the Tower of London, Madame Tussaud's waxworks museum, or Harrods in Knightsbridge. They have more than enough to do to keep themselves and their families fed and clothed to be concerned about seeing the tourist sites of a city that was once the center of a global empire.

The situation is rather similar for temporary Londoners who may not have been forced to the city directly by economic necessity, but are drawn there for primarily economic reasons. These are people who would actually far rather be living in the country and only come to London because they have to earn money there. It helps to have an address in the capital if you want to pursue a career in many of the most prestigious areas of business, such as the stock market, banking, public relations, publishing, or international commerce. As the rents in London are very high indeed, ambitious young people often share a flat in the nicest area of the city they can afford, such as South Kensington. Of course, they drive out into the country again at the weekend, preferably at the invitation of well-heeled friends or relatives. In this way many people spend the decisive decade between 20 and 30 commuting between urban and rural life. This can be seen from the clothes these Londoners choose: Some small detail such as wearing a waxed jacket could betray that the wearer leaves the capital every Friday night. Their choice of car is also indicative – a station wagon or a Land Rover could suggest that someone owns a house in the country. If this is not the case, it is probably intended to create the impression that their city flat is just a second home where they stay from Monday to Friday.

These Londoners dream of living permanently in the country, or at least that is what they claim. Then they could spend every day with their horses and dogs instead of struggling through the London traffic and putting up with all the dirt, noise, and poor air of the city. It is probably better not to go into the question of whether life in the country would be quite as agreeable as they like to think. Certainly, these lovers of country life make the most of the London night life until they get into their thirties.

The happiest people are those whose jobs allow them to work from home. They can combine business with pleasure, living in the country but still earning money. Despite their dislike of the place, these convinced country boys and girls still travel to London regularly. In the end, there is nowhere better to obtain the good things in life than the city's traditional specialist shops, whether you are interested in a magnificent clock that is going to be sold in one of the auction houses and would look lovely on the mantelpiece, half a dozen shirts from Hilditch & Key, stocks of marmalade and tea from Fortnum & Mason, wine from Berry Brothers & Rudd, a bottle of *eau de toilette* from Penhaligon, or a cricket pullover from Lillywhite for your godson.

In summer every spare minute is used for sunbathing. At lunchtime the city's parks are suddenly transformed into crowded green beaches.

Beauty and pomp, ugliness and poverty – London is a city of contrasts. Most visitors are familiar with the area around St James's whereas many are not acquainted with the other areas of London, such as the East End. The old division between the East End and the West End has never been truly overcome. One event though which brings all ranks together is the "Proms". Short for Promenade Concerts, the "Proms" are an annual series of concerts which take place in the famous Albert Hall.

The locals make the least use of the full range of opportunities offered by London's museums, theaters, galleries, sights, and shops. Only for a lucky few does life in the capital consist of a dizzy whirl of exhibition launch parties, first nights, and auctions. For most people, London is simply "their" part of the city, where they go round the corner to the supermarket or the pub, a place they hardly ever leave, except on weekend excursions. They see Piccadilly Circus as infrequently as a visitor

With its distinctive design, there is no mistaking a London taxi, though there never seem to be any in the streets on rainy days. In dry weather, however, it is always possible to flag down one of these spacious and maneuverable vehicles. A taxi is often the quickest way to make short journeys.

from the Continent who flies in once a year. They have often never visited the National Portrait Gallery, the Tower of London, Madame Tussaud's, and the other famous tourist attractions. And they are more than happy to leave the crowds in Oxford Street and the trek round the famous department stores, such as Harrods, Selfridges, and Fortnum & Mason, to their foreign guests. For Londoners life in the capital of the United Kingdom is normality – but, by comparison with other places in the world, it is a normality that always holds open the possibility of some extraordinary event.

The *coffee shops* in the City of London always have plenty of business at lunchtime, when hungry brokers and bankers stream out of their offices in search of nourishment.

Midday is sandwich time. The break is not long enough for much else. The great exception is the business lunch, which is enjoyed in some style.

In summer the lunch break becomes a little picnic with tea and sandwiches in the nearest park.

Princess Anne is the Queen's only daughter. She is just two years younger than Prince Charles and bears the honorary title Princess Royal. Her London residence is St James's Palace (left).

St James's Palace is used as a residence by many members of the Royal family, among them Charles, the Prince of Wales, the Queen's eldest son. His apartments and the offices of his staff are located there.

Princess Alexandra is highly popular, though she is only 21st in line to the throne. When she is not staying at St James's Palace, her home is Thatched House Lodge in Richmond Park.

Prince William lives in student lodgings for most of the year. When he is in London he has an apartment at his disposal in Kensington Palace (right).

Prince Harry, William's younger brother, lives in Kensington Palace when he is not enjoying the holidays at his father's country residence.

Princess Diana lived for many years in Kensington Palace. Since she died in a car accident in Paris many people have made the pilgrimage to her former home.

Princess Margaret is the Queen's younger sister. When she is in London she lives in an apartment in Kensington Palace.

Buckingham Palace (above) is the Queen's London residence. The flag that is raised above the palace when she arrives there signifies the presence of the monarch.

The Queen's second son is Prince Andrew, who was given the title Duke of York on his marriage. He too has rooms in Buckingham palace available as his city residence.

Prince Charles's youngest brother is Prince Edward, the Earl of Wessex. He has the use of an apartment in Buckingham Palace whenever he is staying in the city.

Clarence House is situated behind St James's Palace. It was built in 1825 by John Nash and has been the residence of Queen Elizabeth the Queen Mother since 1952. The Queen Mother enjoys great popularity with British and foreign devotees of the royal family. Her annual birthday appearance in front of Clarence House is always an international media event.

The early Georgian town house (like the ones found in this street in London's Spitalfields) was usually a terraced house. This highly economical way of using space met the rapidly increasing demand for housing, as well as accommodating the exploding land prices in the capital.

THE TOWN HOUSE

Until the 19th century living in London meant living in a house of one's own. On account of the high property prices it may have been extremely small, but at least no one had to share their house with anyone else. Great Britain has remained a land of home owners to the present day.

The preference for town houses led to terraced houses becoming very popular in Great Britain as early as the 17th century. The extensive estates of terraced houses that were often planned as investment projects sprang up on what were then the outskirts of London. The terraced house came to be the typical dwelling of the capital's residents in the 18th century, as well as being found in many other cities. Since the 17th century people had followed the principle of building as large a house as possible on the land they had. The appearance of the London town house was determined both by the unwritten rules of contemporary taste and by very restrictive building regulations, which were introduced following the Great Fire of 1666, a catastrophe that destroyed a large part of the City of London. As a result, for example, wooden houses were banned and fire walls made compulsory. This had far-reaching consequences both for individual houses and for the entire urban landscape. The regulation according to which the frames of the sash windows could no longer be built flush with the walls, but had to be set back ten centimeters also changed the character of the facades significantly. It was hoped that this measure would prevent flames from spreading between the different stories of the same building. These regulations only applied in London, but were also followed by architects in other British towns and cities – after all, no family wanted its house to look provincial just because it did not meet the requirements imposed in the capital.

The great popularity of these small terraced houses, as they are known, says a great deal about the British character. For one thing, terraced houses meet the need the British feel to be masters in their own

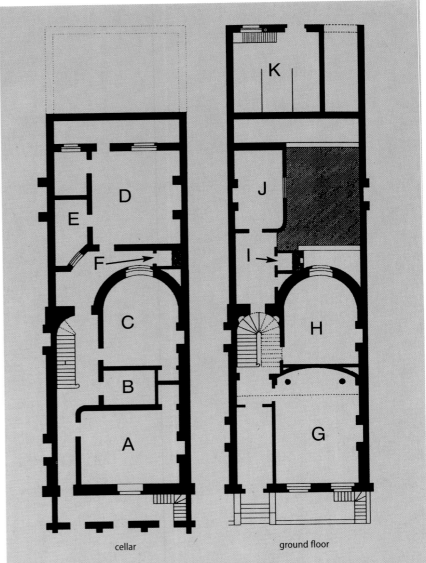

cellar   ground floor

The typical town house was a terraced house with four to six stories, each with different functions. One was used for eating and daily life, one for sleeping, the cellar was used for cooking, and the attic was originally intended for the servants. This plan shows the cellar and ground floor of a large town house. The cellar accommodates the front and back kitchens (A and C), the wine cellar (B), the servants' dayroom (D), the pantry (E), and a water closet (F). The ground floor consists of the dining room (G), the library (H), with its elegantly curved back wall, the toilet (I), the bathroom (J), and the stable block (K), though this could only be reached from the back of the property.

Opposite page: Terraced houses remained a typical form of urban residence for the British during the 19th century. The close succession of doorways here shows that these family houses are built on tiny, narrow plots of land. During the 19th century whole rows of streets were built in this particular style, in Notting Hill, for example.

homes. At the same time, the uniformity of the facades gives a sense of belonging and satisfies a desire for understatement and discretion. However, the monotony of the terraced houses in the cities should not be taken for a lack of individuality. Someone who has to live behind a rather unoriginal facade in the city – no matter how elegantly – will not want to go without architectural extravagance in the countryside. There are a good many people who own a Georgian town house who also possess one or more country residences of a size and magnificence that take the visitor's breath away.

Anyone who wants to gain an impression of how people lived in London in earlier times should visit one of the town houses owned by the National Trust, which has several of these terraced houses in its care.

Above: In the decades leading up to 1900 many of the older terraced houses in the London borough of Chelsea were demolished and replaced with apartment houses in the style of the Arts and Crafts Movement. The interlocking elements of these buildings were intended to be reminiscent of medieval and rural architecture.

Right: In 1812 the Prince of Wales, at the time Regent for his father George III, who had gone mad, commissioned the architect John Nash with the design of Regent's Park. By 1828 he had not only converted this area of heathland into an elegant park, but had also built a series of exclusive terraced houses and detached villas along its edges. In this way he made his mark on the grand Regency style.

The small-paned transom windows, brick facades, and curved gables of the Queen Anne houses built around 1700 are reminiscent of Dutch architecture. These features appear once again at the end of the 19th century.

In the years between 1810 and 1830 buildings were erected in the elegant Regency style in all the larger towns of Great Britain. This sizeable house in Hastings, Sussex has a white stucco facade and sports an iron balcony that was probably added at a later date. Nevertheless, it is less exuberant than buildings of the same period in London.

No. 24 Cheyne Row stands in the borough of Chelsea. This Queen Anne house was built in the early 18th century and was the home of Thomas Carlyle, the historian and writer who lived here with his wife from 1834 until his death in 1881. Not only does the house bring the Carlyles to life, it also gives a vivid impression of how people who did not have great riches, but were still not absolutely starving, used to furnish and decorate their homes in mid-19th-century London. Although the house looks very small from the outside, it still offers plenty of space. The kitchen and the housemaid's private rooms are in the cellar, at ground level we find the library and the dining room, people slept or withdrew during the day in the two stories above, and Thomas Carlyle used the sound-proofed attic as his personal study.

The house is laid out on the same floor plan as many urban terraced houses, with two rooms opening off the landing on each story, except in the cellar and the attic. It is still possible to live very comfortably in a house divided up in this way – visitors are received in the cellar, the father and mother sleep on the ground floor, guests are accommodated on the first floor, and the children have their rooms under the roof. For many Londoners it would be a dream come true to be able to call a Queen Anne house like this in Chelsea their own. But properties of this type bring exorbitant prices.

A different development of the English town house can be viewed in the London district of Belgravia. The white houses that are lined up here around green squares were built approximately 100 years after the Queen Anne houses in Chelsea. Stylistically they fall in the late Regency period and historically they date from the reign of George IV (1820–1830).

The monarch gave the initial impulse for the development of Belgravia with his decision to have Buckingham House converted into a palace. Certainly, we may assume that it was mainly the proximity of the new royal residence that suddenly made this previously rather uninteresting part of London highly desirable. There is practically no other way to explain the huge sums of money invested there by the developer Thomas Cubitt from 1821 on. He leased the land he needed from its owner, Lord Grosvenor, drained the marshy areas, and made it possible to build there by consolidating them with massive quantities of earth transported from the excavation work for the construction of St Catherine's Dock near the Tower of London. The earth was carried up the Thames on freight barges and stored temporarily at Millbank. Cubitt's investment paid off, because Belgravia soon became a popular address, and the freshly crowned Queen Victoria took up residence at Buckingham Palace in 1837, just ten years after the completion of the new houses around Belgrave Square.

Above: With its radiant white terraced houses and apartment blocks, Belgrave Square has been the epitome of a high-class residential area since the first houses were completed in 1825. Today many of these impressive Regency buildings are used as embassies.

Far left: In King's Bench Walk there are still a few houses preserved that were built in the style of English Baroque shortly after the catastrophic fire in 1666. This London street is therefore a popular location for filmmakers shooting historical dramas. This porch dating from 1677 now decorates an early-Georgian town house.

Left: No. 37 Dover Street in London was built in 1772 by Sir Robert Taylor in the style of the Italian Renaissance architect Andrea Palladio and was intended as a town house for the Bishop of Ely.

THE DEVELOPMENT OF THE TOWN HOUSE

Unlike urban areas on the Continent, the expansion of the British towns and cities, London above all, was the work of a relatively small number of private developers, who were almost all successful bricklayers, carpenters, or stone masons. These individuals were able to execute large projects because they had the necessary experience of construction work, access to materials, and useful contacts in the trade. They would lease a large area from a landowner, who was usually a member of the nobility, build as many houses as they could on it, then sell them at a profit. The remarkable thing about the whole process is that the houses were built speculatively with no actual buyers in mind – for the market, one might say – and that this was being done on such a large scale at such an early date. Of course, it was cheaper for the builders if a house shared one or more of its walls, so they concentrated mainly on the construction of terraced houses. These were built on precisely staked out plots that had to be leveled first into terraces – hence the terms "terrace" and "terraced" house. For the most part, the individual houses were grouped together in square or semicircular complexes – squares, crescents, and circuses – around a central open space. A single facade would unite all the houses in these developments, good examples of which can be seen in London's Grosvenor Square, Bedford Square, and Regent's Street. Interestingly, these places are not named after the architects and builders who created them, or their prominent residents, but the aristocrats who originally owned the land.

The appearance of the streets of London changed fundamentally after the Great Fire of 1666. Due to the fire regulations, structures with projecting wooden beams were no longer allowed, so the structural elements of the buildings were now built of brick, and natural stone or light artificial stone was used for the decorative features. From the middle of the 18th century builders also worked with fine exterior rendering or "stucco," as it is known. On the one hand, this made it possible to create a stone facade – if only an illusory one – at a low price. On the other, the stucco would cover up untidy or damaged brickwork. Artificial-stone decorative elements could also be produced and put in place much more quickly than carved natural stone. Where the brickwork was to remain visible, decorative artificial stones could be added at key points to provide cheap, impressive architectural ornamentation. For example, the entrances to the prestigious houses on London's Bedford Square, built between 1775 and 1780, are decorated with imitations of roughly hewn ashlar and ornamental key stones made of what is known as "Coade Stone". In 1769 Eleonora Coade took over the management of the Coade family firm, whose artificial-stone products were exquisitely modeled and amazingly durable. Mrs Coade marketed the company's relief panels, decorative moldings, capitals, decorative vases, etc. with great success, issuing catalogs that were used by the best architects of the day. As the composition of Coade Stone was a jealously guarded secret, it was lost when the business went bankrupt at the beginning of the 19th century.

The facades of 18th-century houses are usually flat and rather inconspicuous. In fact, the dull exterior walls often conceal magnificently decorated rooms. You can only gain some idea of the glory of the interiors if you go walking in the evening and your gaze falls on the illuminated stuccoed and painted ceilings of the upper stories. These houses were the product of a new professional class that replaced the earlier entrepreneur bricklayers and stone masons: the professional artist-architects. Their most famous representatives included Robert, James, and John Adam, and John Nash. While Nash built Regent's Park and Regent's Street in London under contract from the Prince Regent, who subsequently reigned as King George IV, during the first decades of the 19th century, the Adam brothers had begun to work as private building contractors

some 50 years earlier. In 1768 they leased land by the side of the River Thames in London and spent a fortune embanking it. By 1772 they had built a large block of eleven terraced houses looking out over the Thames and two more streets at right angles to them: the development known as the Adelphi. With their simple, flat pilasters and courses modeled in stucco, the facades were based on the delicate interior decoration for which the brothers were renowned. For some time this classical, elegant, and affordable style of exterior ornament became an essential feature of fashionable new terraced houses.

From 1800 on the facades of the town houses became rather more lively. The entrances were now often preceded by a columned porch, while the windows began to project from the walls again with their more prominent surrounds. In the course of 19th century facades tended to become even more informal, with emphasized or projecting entrances and bay windows. Apart from this, the Victorian terraced houses are characterized by a less classical formal language and a tendency to mix architectural features based on medieval models. However, streets of Victorian terraced houses often make an unpleasantly monotonous impression on account of the mass construction of the houses, and the lack of squares and other public spaces.

The district to the west of Kensington Palace was developed and built up mainly during the 19th century. Many Victorian terraced houses were built here.

Parks – the Lungs of the City

Many city-dwellers dream of having their own garden. The traditional terraced houses that have room for a couple of flower beds and a small lawn at the back are highly prized very much for this reason. For example, someone who owns a Queen Anne house is able to savor the special pleasure of seeking refuge from the hurly-burly of city life in the tranquility of a walled garden. Anyone who lives in a block of flats or some other kind of urban dwelling without a garden has to satisfy his or her need for grass, trees, and flowers either during a weekend visit to the country or in public parks and gardens. Fortunately, there are a great many of them in London. Most of the Royal Parks are found in the heart of the city – St James's Park, Green Park, Hyde Park, Kensington Gardens, and Holland Park, which belongs to Holland House. Further out there are the other Royal Parks, such as Regent's Park, Greenwich Park, Richmond Park, and Bushy Park, as well as parks that are not owned by the Royal Family, such as Chiswick House Gardens, Fulham Palace Gardens, Bloomsbury Square, Victoria Embankment Gardens, Victoria Tower Gardens, Battersea Park, and the Chelsea Physic Garden. On the outskirts of London we find Osterley Park, Kew Gardens, Syon Park, Marble Hill Park, Ham House Gardens, Ham Court Palace Park, and Crystal Palace Park. There are also a number of areas of former common land that have been traditionally accessible to all, such as Hackney Marshes, Hampstead Heath, Wormwood Scrubs, Wimbledon Common, Putney Heath, Clapham Common, Wandsworth Common, Streatham Common, Plumstead Common, Woolwich Common, and Blackheath Common. As well as those we must not forget Kenwood Park, Ruskin Park, Lesnes Abbey Woods, Alexandra Park, and the Jubilee Gardens.

There are even green spaces in the City of London – such as the Bowling Green in Finsbury Circus and Bunhill Fields. The City can also boast a great many patches of greenery in churchyards and ruined churches, which provide shelter for over 2,000 trees. The total number of trees in London is about five million, though this does not include trees in private gardens. It is not necessarily considerate town planners whom the Londoners should thank for

Anyone who gets worn out in the midst of London with its population of eight million can recharge his or her batteries in one of the city's many parks. Walking, reading, lying on the grass and dreaming, or even rowing in Regent's Park are among the most popular leisure pursuits of the city's residents – in summer, at least.

their parks. Many of the Royal Parks are former hunting grounds where Kings and their retinue used to enjoy the pleasures of the chase. However, some of them were already open to the public by the early 17th century, such as Hyde Park, which was originally used by the Royal Household, but to which the populace was given access by Charles I in 1637. After the king had been beheaded, Oliver Cromwell divided the park into three parts and sold them off. The new owners suddenly began charging Londoners entrance fees, but, following the restoration of the monarchy, these charges were abolished in Hyde Park under Charles II, much to the pleasure of his subjects. St James's Park was also a popular destination for excursions in the 17th century. However, in the early 18th century Queen Anne wanted to control visitors to St James's Park in order to raise the tone a little. She therefore forbade people from wearing clogs, walking on the grass, drying their laundry, or trading in the park. Indeed, among other things, it was common for people to sell milk – direct from the cow grazing on the grass behind them. In the 18th century George II's queen wanted to go even further and drive the common people out of the park altogether. According to legend, she is supposed to

London's parks and gardens are well organized recreational facilities. There are neatly laid paths with clear signs almost everywhere, so no one has any need to take a wrong turning or lose their bearings completely. In some parks, such as St James's Park, it is necessary for those who desire the luxury of a deckchair to buy a ticket from a park keeper for a small fee. Feeding the pigeons, however, is free of charge.

have asked the Prime Minister Robert Walpole how much this measure would cost. His answer was ambiguous: "Just three crowns," by which he meant not only the coins of the same name, but also power over the three kingdoms of England, Ireland, and Scotland.

During the Victorian period many parks were built as places of relaxation and recreation for the urban population. For example, Battersea Park, which was created in an area prone to flooding by the Thames. The reputation of this location, Battersea Fields, was by no means promising, because, apart from the fact that asparagus was cultivated there, nothing good had ever come of the place. Not only was a wide variety of popular entertainments held there, it was also the scene of many violent crimes and duels. This all ended with the creation of the park, which was extremely expensive, as the wet marshland had to be drained before it was laid out. After its opening in 1858, Battersea Park soon became a much loved and fashionable place for day trips. Many large events are still held there, such as the annual Easter Parade.

However, organized entertainment is generally unusual for London's "green lungs" – if it is possible to talk of anything being typical in view of the great variety of parks and gardens there. These green islands in the sea of London's houses invite hurried city-dwellers to relax, take a gentle stroll, quietly study the plants on display, bask in the sun, take a sandwich and a cup of tea during the lunch hour (a more common pastime), meet for romantic trysts, or engage in energetic sporting activities. The grassed areas are not just admired, but really used. Indeed, in most parks the grass looks as though it suffers pretty rough treatment, but what is the point of the most beautiful piece of turf if you cannot sit on it.

Few Londoners have a garden, but there is such a rich choice of parks and green spaces that no one need suffer for lack of grass, trees, flowers, lakes and ponds, swans, ducks, squirrels, and rabbits. London is a green city, and this makes it both bearable and loveable for its residents. The tourists and business travelers who descend on the British capital in their millions every year also love to take a break on the grass.

Cricklewood

Hampstead Heath

Parliament Hill

Highbury

Islington

Clissold Park

Hackney Downs

Gladstone Park

Fortune Green

Haverstock Hill

Kentish Town

Highbury Fields

Dalston

Willesden

High Rd

Finchley Rd

Holloway Rd

Caledonian Rd

Paradise Park

Stoke Newington Rd

London Fields

Brondesbury

Willesden

Adelaide Rd

Chalk Farm Rd

Camden Town

York Way

Caledonian Park

Camden

Barnard Park

Hoxton

Shoreditch Park

Haggerston Park

Mare St

Roundwood Park

Willesden Sports Gardens

Brondesbury Park

Willesden Lane Cemetery

Belsize Rd

Primrose Hill

Kentish Town Rd

King's Cross Station

City Rd

Kingsland Rd

Bethnal Green

Harlesden

Queen's Park

Kilburn

Maida Vale

St Johns Wood

Regent's Park

Euston Station

Euston Rd

Bloomsbury

Coram's Fields

Finsbury

Bunhill Fields

Liverpool St Station

Harrow Rd

Kensal Green

Paddington Recreation Ground

Paddington

MARYLEBONE STATION

Marylebone

Baker St

Marylebone

Russel Square

Holborn

City

Finsbury Circus

Whitechapel Rd

College Park

Wormwood Scrubs

Westway Motorway

Portobello Rd

PADDINGTON STATION

Oxford St

Soho

Lincoln's Inn

Fleet St

Temple Gardens

FENCHURCH ST STATION

Shepherd's Bush

A 40 (M)

A 41 (M) West Cross Route

Nottinghill

Bayswater

Bayswater Rd

Marble Arch

West End

Piccadilly Circus

Strand

CHARING CROSS STATION

Waterloo Bridge

CANNON ST STATION

The

Hammersmith Park

Holland Park Av.

Kensington

Kensington Gardens

Hyde Park

Park Lane

Mayfair

Piccadilly

St. James's

Trafalgar Sq.

Whitehall

Southwark

LONDON BRIDGE STATION

W. Curtis Park

Tower Bridge

Coldhawk Rd

Holland Park

Kensington Palace

Buckingham Palace

St. James's Park

Jubilee Gardens

WATERLOO INTERNATIONAL STATION

Tower Bridge Rd

Bermondsey

Ravenscourt Park

King St

Cromwell Rd

Westminster Abbey

Houses of Parliament

Archbishop's Park

Geraldine Mary Harmsworth Park

Fulham Palace Rd

Westminster

VICTORIA STATION

The Victoria Tower Gardens

Lambeth

Kennington Rd

Walworth

Old Kent Rd

Castelnau

Rec. Ground Fulham Cemetery

Brompton Cemetery

Fulham Rd

Chelsea

Burton's Court

Ranelagh Gardens

Grosvenor Rd

Kennington

Kennington Park

Camberwell New Rd

Camberwell

Burgess Park

Fulham

King's Rd

Battersea Park

Battersea Park Rd

Larkhall Park

Clapham Rd

Brixton Rd

Barnes

Barnes Common

Bishop's Park

South Park

Hurlingham Park

Eal Brook Common

York Rd

Battersea

Brixton

Ruskin Park

Peckham

River Thames

Upper Richmond Rd

Wandsworth Park

Clapham

Herne Hill

Peckham Rye Park

Putney

Wandsworth

Side Spencer Park

Clapham Common

The Avenue

Clapham Park

Brockwell Park

Brixton Hill

Dulwich Village

Roehampton Golf Course

West Hill

King Georg's Park

Wandsworth Common

Balham

Christchurch Rd

Dulwich Park

Southfields

Wandsworth Cemetery

The Central London Golf Course

Balham High Rd

Streatham Hill

Dulwich Common

Dulwich & Sydenham Hill Golf Course

Kingston Rd

Wimbledon Common

Wimbledon Park

Garratt Park

Steatham Cemetery

Tooting Common

West Norwood Cemetery

Streatham

Wimbledon

Heathrow

Windsor

Kew

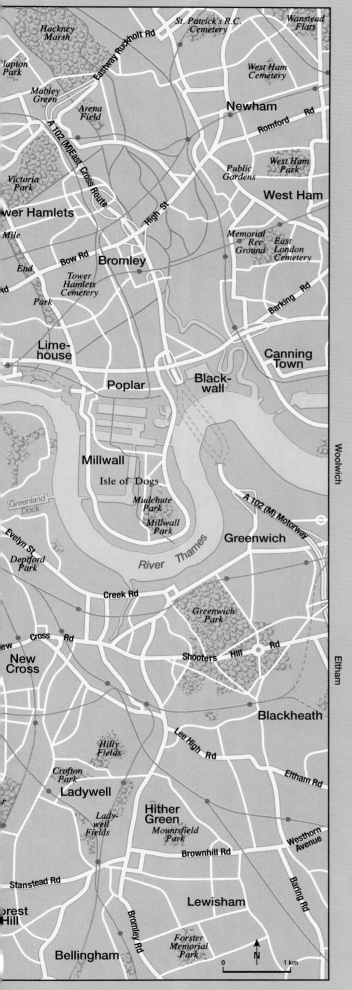

Parks and Gardens in London

Archbishop's Park
Arena Field
Barnard Park
Barnes Common
Battersea Park
Bethnal Green
Bishop's Park
Brockwell Park
Brompton Cemetery
Brondesbury Park
Bunhill Fields
Burgess Park
Burton's Court
Caledonian Park
Clapham Common
Clapton Park
Clissold Park
College Park
Conram's Fields
Crofton Park
Deptford Park
Dulwich and Sydenham Hill Golf Course
Dulwich Park
East London Cemetery
Eel Brook Common
Finsbury Circus
Forster Memorial Park
Fortune Green
Garratt Park
Geraldine Mary Harmsworth Park
Gladstone Park
Greenwich Park
Hackney Downs
Hackney Marsh
Haggerston Park
Hammersmith Park
Hampstead Heath
Highbury Fields
Hiley Fields
Holland Park
Honor Oak Park
Hurlingham Park
Hyde Park
Jubilee Gardens
Kennington Park
Kensington Gardens
King George's Park
Ladywell Fields

Larkhall Park
Lincoln´s Inn
London Fields
Mabley Green
Memorial Recreation Ground
Mile End Park
Millwall Park
Mountsfield Park
Mudchute Park
Nunnhead Cemetery
Paddington Recreation Ground
Paradise Park
Parliament Hill
Peckham Rye Park
Primrose Hill
Queen's Park
Ranelagh Gardens
Ravenscourt Park
Regent´s Park
Roehampton Golf Course
Roundwood Park
Ruskin Park
Russell Square
Shoreditch Park
Side Spencer Park
South Park
Southwark Park
St James´s Park
St Patrick´s R. C. Cemetery
Streatham Cemetery
Temple Gardens
The Central London Golf Course
The Victoria Tower Gardens
Tooting Common
Tower Hamlets Cemetery
Victoria Park
W. Curtis Park
Wandsworth Cemetery
Wandsworth Common
Wanstead Flats
West Ham Cemetery
West Ham Park
West Norwood Cemetery
Willesden Lane Cemetry
Willesden Sports Garden
Wimbledon Common
Wimbledon Park
Wormwood Scrubs

From top left to bottom right:

St James's Park is the oldest of the Royal Parks in the British capital. Henry VIII bought the land in 1532 and used it for hunting. In the 17th century an attempt was made to transform the layout of St James's Park in a different style. Charles II wanted to turn it into something approaching a mini-Versailles, the famous royal park outside Paris, so tree-lined avenues were planted and a straight canal constructed. The architect John Nash disposed of these features in the 19th century and gave the park its modern appearance. On account of its proximity to the Houses of Parliament, St James's Park is popular with politicians and civil servants, who enjoy stretching their legs here.

Green Park lies in a triangle between Hyde Park Corner, Buckingham Palace, and the Ritz. Some of the luxurious rooms in this famous hotel, which was built in 1906, look out onto the green expanses of the park. Henry VIII purchased this land together with the area that was later to become St James's Park, and used it for hunting and grazing livestock. A garden was first created here in the 17th century, when it was known as Upper St James's Park. Green Park may sometimes be very overcrowded, but it is the ideal place for a brief, relaxing break.

Like Green Park and St James's Park, the land now taken up by Hyde Park was used originally by Henry VIII for hunting, but the area had been made accessible to the public by 1637. After 1689 2.6 hectares of the park were hived off to build Kensington Palace. To compensate for this, the landscape architects built a lake in 1730–1731, the Serpentine, which certainly made up for the area that had been lost. The first World Exhibition was held in Hyde Park in 1851, attracting more than six million visitors. Today the park, which is 142 hectares in area, is a place of solace for Londoners and tourists who yearn for a piece of inspiring natural scenery in the center of Europe's biggest city.

Kensington Gardens were originally the grounds of the country residence that William III had built in 1689 in South Kensington as a place where he could relax and take the country air. The royal road to St James's Palace was known as the *Route du Roi*, which the Londoners corrupted over the years into Rotten Row. George III opened the gardens to the people in the 18th century, but there were servants at the entrances to the park who made sure that visitors were respectably dressed. Today you can wear whatever you want, and stroll past Kensington Palace in shorts and a T-shirt. The residents of the palace probably sometimes wish that they themselves could wander so informally in their gardens. The sights of the park include the Albert Memorial.

We have the ambitious plans of the architect John Nash to thank for Regent's Park. When this land reverted to the Crown in 1811 at the end of a long lease, Nash wanted to turn it into an exclusive residential complex surrounded by gardens. This undertaking was never completed in full, but the patron after whom the project was named, the Prince Regent, was absolutely delighted by the concept that Nash presented to him. The fact that the park was to bear his own name certainly gave his enthusiasm greater warmth. William IV, the Prince Regent's successor, was already on the throne when the park was thrown open to the public in 1835. London Zoo was opened in Regent's Park in 1828; at that time its only keeper wore a top hat.

Greenwich Park was laid out on a piece of land 88 hectares in area that the Duke of Gloucester had enclosed in 1433 in order to build the Bella Court palace there. The complex was later expanded with the construction of Queen's House, but demolished after being sacked by Cromwell's soldiers. There was a plan to build a new palace, but this foundered on a lack of money. So a naval hospital, now the Royal Naval College, was built on the site of Bella Court. The park has been altered many times during its history, most recently in the 17th century under Charles II, who called on the services of André Le Nôtre, the designer of the gardens at Versailles. Anyone who makes an excursion to Greenwich should therefore definitely include a visit to the park.

Background: With an area of 1,000 hectares, Richmond Park is the largest of London's Royal Parks. It also has some of the richest game reserves. About 400 fallow deer and 250 red deer live there. Richmond has been a royal residence since the 12th century. The palace had a stormy history behind it and had already been rebuilt three times when Charles I fled there in 1625 to escape the plague in London. In 1637 the ruler had a hunting ground near the residence enclosed with a wall. However, in order not to offend the local population, he allowed them continued access to the park. Charles was only able to enjoy hunting at Richmond for another twelve years, because on January 30, 1649 he was executed in Whitehall. Today Richmond is one of the most beautiful parks in London, and the visitor who climbs up Henry VIII's Mound on a clear day will enjoy a unique panorama that extends from Windsor Castle all the way to the dome of St Paul's Cathedral.

A Sandwich in the Park

The British enjoy making the best of good weather. People who work in the center of London like to recline on the lawns of the nearest park during their lunch-break. They can be seen there in their office clothes or shop uniforms, eating the light lunches that they have bought from one of the mobile stands. It is not always English tea sloshing around in the plastic cups, because *cappuccino*, *caffe latte*, and *espresso* are becoming ever more popular, and Italian sandwich-shop owners sell authentic, strong coffee. Once they have purchased their meal, they sit down on the grass, or what the sun and innumerable feet have left of it. The longer the summer goes on, the more battered the lawns in the parks become. Nevertheless, no one would ever think of stopping people from walking on the grass. After all, the grass in a park is there for you to sit on. Just as the British are remarkably resistant to the cold, they do not appear to be in the least bit bothered by the prospect of sitting on grass wet with rain. An old newspaper or a plastic bag is quite sufficient as provisional seating. After eating they stretch out briefly on the cool turf before going back to work. Then the park is taken over again by tourists, pensioners, and school trips, at least until the next lunch break.

Left: In the summer, as soon as it is time for their lunch-break, the office workers stream out of London's banks, publishing houses, insurance companies, and government buildings, and hurry to the nearest park to relax, eat a sandwich, have a drink, and spend a quarter of an hour dreaming about their weekend in the country.

Below: The sandwich shop is the main place of refuge for hungry workers of all types. There is often a long queue of customers during the lunch-break. In many of these establishments you can have your sandwich tailor-made to suit your own taste. The selection ranges from lettuce, tomato, and cucumber to roast beef, smoked salmon, egg, bacon, Parma ham, and various types of cheese.

Bottom left: Although tea is still the British national drink, a great deal of coffee is also consumed at midday. Italian food is very much in fashion in Great Britain, so it is no wonder that *cappuccino* is increasingly replacing tea in the country's plastic cups.

Bottom center: At midday the sandwich is the favorite food of shop and office workers. It is available from small sandwich shops and fast food chains that have specialized in sandwiches and sell them in vast quantities. Most sandwich fans have their preferred sources, which they swear by and may even prefer to keep secret.

Bottom right: The sandwich shops also offer a wide selection of cakes and sweets. Various types of chocolate cake are highly popular and are to be found on sale wherever you go. Depending on the recipe – and the imagination of the shop owner – you may be offered fudge cake, chocolate brownies, millionaire's shortbread, or fudge fingers. What these delicacies all have in common is their unsuitability for anyone who is at all worried about their waistline.

It was the elevator that first made the multi-story mansion blocks a really attractive alternative to the town house of the older style. After its invention, these blocks of flats mainly attracted prosperous bachelors. The best of their spacious apartments looked out on wonderful views.

Opposite page: Apartment houses of the late-Victorian and Edwardian period often have neo-baroque elements. Brick facades decorated with white stucco or sandstone courses and curved gables are typical of what was known as the "Hampton Court Style."

THE TOWN FLAT

Until the late 19th century people in British cities preferred to live in their own houses. The elegant squares with their regular facades dominated the street landscape of many urban areas and, by comparison with the large cities of Continental Europe, apartment life was discovered at a rather late date. In Berlin, Paris, and Madrid it had long been common to live in a single story of a town house, in England the mansion blocks, as they are known, only came into fashion during the Edwardian period.

Normally the Edwardian era is defined as the time between the death of Queen Victoria and the outbreak of the First World War in 1914. However, as with all such definitions, this name for the stylistic period is an abstraction that was coined at a later date. Victorian style did not suddenly fall out of fashion on the death of the Queen. Nor, strictly speaking, does the term Edwardian apply to the entire period up to 1914, because Edward VII, Queen Victoria's eldest son, only reigned from 1901 to 1910. His son, who reigned as George V, was on the throne during the last years before the Great War began. Nevertheless, his early reign is still generally subordinated under the stylistic label of his father, and George V did not give his name to a style or social mood even after the signing of the Versailles Treaty.

When, after many years of waiting, Edward VII finally became king in 1901, Great Britain was experiencing an era of great prosperity and carefree confidence that seemed as though it would never end. What in hindsight has been transfigured into the swan song of a dying era was viewed by contemporaries as an unprecedented economic boom accompanied by ever greater technological triumphs. When the Prince of Wales, who was known familiarly to his family as "Bertie," ascended to the throne, Great Britain was the richest country in the world. In 1901 the country's gross national product grew by a dizzying and, in modern terms, unbelievable 50 percent.

The modern, luxurious apartment was just what people wanted in this period, because, with central heating, running hot water, a connection to the sewers, electric lighting, and an electric elevator, it offered a completely new dimension of comfort. One might even say that it was only the comforts of modernity that made the mansion blocks attractive.

The people who moved into these mansion blocks must have felt that their new residences provided an ideal lifestyle. Most of the people who had the means to buy or let an apartment of this kind also owned a country residence that afforded the spacious accommodation of a proper house. This meant that they were also familiar with the disadvantages of life in a large building. When they stayed in the city, they could now live comfortably in their apartment with a comparatively small domestic staff. And because the mansion blocks were fitted with central heating, there was no need to light innumerable fire places or heat water for baths – both extremely time-consuming tasks for the servants.

The modern bachelor flats therefore enjoyed great popularity, particularly among unmarried gentlemen, as the name suggests. Apart from modern comfort, these apartments often offered additional facilities that

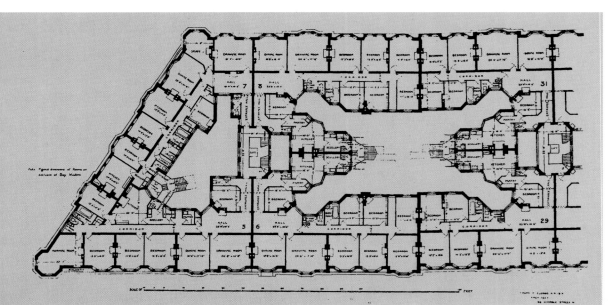

The Edwardian apartment block North Gate on the northern edge of Regent's Park was built in the first decade of the 20th century to the design of Frank Elgood. The facade of red brick with ornamental stone courses is neo-Baroque. From the outside, this mansion block looks like a town hall or government building, on account of the powerful formal language that it shares with these kinds of structure. Inside, the architects sought to provide for its residents' need to impress by creating spacious apartments and exuberantly decorated entrance halls.

The apartments were reached via central square stairwells with elevators, each with four flats opening off it on every story. Steps led from the inner courtyards to the servants' quarters, the kitchen, scullery, and storerooms. The flats at the front with the angular, projecting tower had a total of five bedrooms, a living room, and a dining room, while the room in the tower was used as a library or study. The tiny bathroom was hardly any larger than the bathtub itself.

designed in a grand style based on what people were thought to be familiar with from their country houses and villas in the city. The great interior decorators of the period profited greatly from the new enthusiasm for elegant apartments, because a modish bachelor pad had to be decorated stylishly as befitted the resident's status – and shops like Hampton, Maple, Waring & Gillow, Trollope & Sons, and Liberty had more than enough work on their hands.

The style of the new mansion blocks could be described as eclectic. Interesting variations on the baroque, with characteristic facades of red brick and contrasting white stone, were particularly popular. The dominant influence on these neo-baroque buildings was either English (Queen Anne Style) or Dutch. Dutch Style houses can be identified by their curved gables. Examples of this kind of mansion block can be seen in London's Cadogan Square. One of the most popular architects of this baroque revival was Richard Norman Shaw, whose most famous buildings include Lowther Lodge in South Kensington. The Royal Geographical Society now occupies this building not far from the Victoria and Albert Museum.

The architectural richness of London allows the interested observer instructive comparisons between the original baroque buildings dating from the reign of Queen Anne and what was made of the style during the Victorian revival. There are still many original English baroque buildings in London, on Queen Anne's Gate in Westminster, for example. By comparison with the delicate three-story houses built in the early 18th century, the mansion blocks of the Edwardian era can look overbearing and bombastic.

Nevertheless, no one would now contest the historical and architectural importance of these early urban apartments, dating as they do from a period that held to a deep faith in progress as it careered toward its decline. The mansion blocks continue to remain as popular as ever among their modern residents, not just on account of their spaciousness and their excellent locations, but also because they are reminders of a time that is viewed as a period of greatness unequalled by any other in Great Britain's history.

were very much tailored to the needs of the unmarried gentleman and his servants. As in a hotel, there were comfortable lounges and dining rooms that were available to the residents of the mansion block for social activities, while there was a porter on duty at the entrance whose job it was to make sure that shopping was done or messages were delivered.

Not for nothing are these buildings of apartments known as mansion blocks. The word "mansion" included in the term denotes a large or stately house owned by a rich landowner, and that was exactly the kind of image that appealed to their residents. The interiors were therefore

Top: Many apartment blocks were built at the beginning of the 20th century using architectural elements common during the Renaissance or the 17th century, but there were also buildings that used a completely modern formal language, such as this London apartment house from the 1920s.

Far left: While the windows with their small panes, the high gable, and the prominent use of red brick are drawn from the Queen Anne Style, which was influenced by Dutch architecture, the height of this building and its asymmetrical facade indicate that this mansion block must have been built toward the end of the 19th century. It is one of an ensemble of four houses that were built in 1887 by Richard Norman Shaw in London's Cadogan Square.

Left: If only on account of their size, the Albert Hall Mansions in Kensington look like the fashionable apartment blocks of Paris, Rome, or Berlin. They were built between 1879 and 1886 by Richard Norman Shaw.

Opposite page: The projecting key stones over the windows of this mansion block in the London borough of Battersea are characteristic of the Edwardian period.

A Nation of Collectors

The British are known as a nation with a great love of eccentrics. However, it is questionable whether British collectors are really viewed as eccentric by their compatriots. Most British people find the inability to part from apparently useless objects utterly normal. Collectors only come to be seen as eccentrics if they are interested in particularly strange objects. It is said that the Prince of Wales, for example, collects toilet seats from all around the world. Unfortunately, no one will ever see his collection: for the very good reason that it does not exist. No matter how intriguing the idea that Prince Charles decorates his guest bathrooms with toilet seats may be, the story is simply not true, according to his press office, at any rate, and they should know. They are also very happy to explain the origins of this often repeated and enthusiastically elaborated story. The Prince of Wales was once presented with a toilet seat by his fellow sailors in the Royal Navy. Over the years this has become a whole collection and the royal equivalent of an urban myth. Nevertheless, there seems to be a genetic predisposition to collecting in the Royal Family. For example, King George V collected stamps. His collection fills 325 albums and is one of the most valuable in the world. Apart from this, he and Queen Mary collected snuff boxes. Queen Mary was also reputed to have

Portobello is a magic word to many lovers of the kitsch, the artistic, and bric-a-brac. Every Saturday hundreds of junk dealers set up their stands on and around Portobello Road to sell all sorts of beautiful, silly, old, or amusing things. The real collector will not be irritated by the overwhelming variety, but will always carefully check the goods on sale that fall within his or her area of interest.

a love of small *objets d'art* and all kinds of ornaments. Supposedly, this passion went so far that her hosts would ensure that any particularly precious or interesting pieces they owned were hidden away as a precautionary measure before Her Majesty came to visit. Augustus, the Duke of Sussex and son of King George III, was a book collector. He owned over 50,000 works, along with 5,000 editions of the Bible. The Duke of Windsor and his wife, Wallis, collected porcelain pugs, and Prince Philip, the Duke of Edinburgh, collects caricatures and cartoons of himself, which are rumored to hang on the walls of the toilets at Sandringham. King George IV had a passion for paintings and furniture. Although his interest was exceedingly expensive at the time, it has proved to be a good investment. His collection is now extremely valuable and is regarded as one of the most important in the world. The more unusual objects collected by the family include the portraits of dead friends, relatives, and even servants assembled by Queen Victoria. Although Prince Charles does not possess a collection of toilet seats, he does have a weakness for garden gnomes. He liked to put them on the mantelpiece until his wife, Princess Diana, put a stop to this habit.

The fervent passion for collecting is also widespread among ordinary Britons. It is not just pieces of art that are hoarded, but even quite unassuming consumer goods. For example, Simon Khachadourian collects cocktail shakers. He owns about 400 samples of the most varied kinds and price classes. Egg cups are a favorite item for collectors. Isobel Whatrup owns over 2,000, including real masterpieces from Meissen and Spode. Some people are interested in paperweights, such as Vera Marshall, who is regarded as an expert in this field. Others hoard old clothes, costumes, hats, handbags, umbrellas, snuff boxes, clocks, cigarette lighters, or jewelry. The list could go on for ever, because, in the end, there is nothing that cannot be collected. One of the most peculiar collections is that of Julian Litten, who has an obsession with funeral equipment. He collects the catalogs issued by funeral directors, coffin makers' price lists, and death notices. Of course, there are also many collectors who are interested in the Royal Family. Margeret Tyler owns over 5,000 pieces of royal memorabilia, including 16 concrete corgis and a Prince Charles garden gnome. With which we find that we have come full circle. Is it not the case that the Prince of Wales also collects garden gnomes? As one collector to another, he could surely ask Margeret Tyler for "his" gnome, and she would probably give it to him in exchange for an autographed photograph.

The probability of finding valuable antiques at bargain prices in London's Portobello Road is rather low. Nevertheless, collectors of everyday objects and small knick-knacks will always hope to find something or other here, particularly if they have specialized in a rare or arcane area of interest. For this reason real junk lovers will dive into the crowds of thronging tourists and spend hours examining the weird and wonderful selection of items on display.

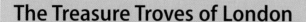

Whether you go to Alfie's Antique Market in Church Street (top left) or the small dealers in Portobello Road (top center), there is nothing quite like a British antique shop, whether it is full of fine collector's items or piled high with tat (top right).

The Treasure Troves of London

Auction Houses

Christie's
Christie's at No. 8 King's Street is the oldest auction house specializing in art and antiques. It was founded in 1766 by James Christie and is today regarded by many as the most distinguished auction house in London.

Sotheby's
Sotheby's was founded in 1744 as a bookshop and has made a reputation for itself with its spectacular auctions. Artworks, jewelry, books, wines, and memorabilia are among the objects in which it deals.

Phillips
This auction house was founded in 1796 by Harry Phillips and once counted Napoleon among its customers. The sales departments range from Old Master paintings to furniture, sporting memorabilia, and ceramics.

Bonham's
Bonham's in Montpellier Street is the smallest of the London auction houses. Founded in 1793, it deals in furniture, books, non-European tribal art, pop memorabilia, and much more.

Flea Markets

Bermondsey Market (Fridays)
Flea markets like the one around Bermondsey Square are really something for people who know what they are looking for. Otherwise there is always the danger that you will buy a cheap copy instead of an original.

Camden Market (Wednesdays, Thursdays, Saturdays)
You can find all sorts of things in Islington High Street and Upper Street. Apart from this, there is a number of interesting antique shops in the area.

Portobello Road Market (daily)
The stands in the narrow passages of Portobello Road are a rich hunting ground for collectors of artworks and curiosities.

Antique Markets

Alfie's Antique Market
There are over 140 dealers crammed together in the cramped accommodation at these premises in Church Street, including some specialists who are very much to be recommended.

Antiquarius
This antique market has been an institution on King's Road for over 20 years. Some of the dealers are quite famous, such as the suitcase specialist Martin Lee.

Chenil Galleries
This market is also in King's Road at No. 181–183. It is easy to find your way around and you can purchase large objects, as the dealers have plenty of space.

Gray's Antique Market
This market is very close to Sotheby's in Bond Street, but collectors do not have to bid for the pieces that take their eye here. The range on offer is very extensive and the quality is high.

Dukes Yard Antiques Market
This palace of delights for collectors and browsers is a bit further out from the center in Richmond's Duke Street. 60 shops offer almost everything between useless junk and precious antiques.

Kensington Church Street Antique Centre
Some noteworthy dealers have established their permanent bases at this market in Kensington Church Street. Collectors of jewelry, art, and English furniture will almost always find something to their taste here.

Even someone who is not bidding will find an auction at the old and respected art auction house Christie's an interesting experience. The dates and themes of the auctions are published on Mondays in *The Daily Telegraph* and Tuesdays in *The Times*.

A Prince with Principles

When Prince Charles delivered a speech before the Royal Institute of British Architects (RIBA) in 1984, he remarked that the proposed extension for the National Gallery in London looked like a "monstrous carbuncle on the face of a much loved and elegant friend." This was the first time he had spoken in public as a critic of architecture. After this he wrote and presented a television documentary about postwar architecture, which, in his opinion, has been inhuman and overly obsessed with technology. The program, *A Vision of Britain*, was first shown in October 1988, and was followed by a long, heated debate about aesthetics and the basic principles of modern architecture. Many British people took part in the discussion, passionately defending their views in the pub on the corner of the street, in letters penned to their local newspaper, or in the forewords of academic architectural journals.

A year later the Prince published a book of the same title setting out his views in detail. In it he emphasized the necessity of maintaining the typical character of British cities, towns, and villages, and of creating a form of architecture attuned to the needs of "ordinary" people. What is more, Prince Charles was not to be satisfied with mere theorizing, he also provided concrete proposals as to how his ideas could be implemented.

"A Vision of Britain"

In the book of his documentary *A Vision of Britain*, which the Prince of Wales made in 1988 with the BBC, he set out his own architectural ideas as "Ten principles we can build upon," hoping they would become generally accepted as a "code" that architects would follow, just as we all follow the rules of grammar and good manners.

- The Place: An understanding of the landscape and the creation of architecture that blends in with it
- Hierarchy: The size of buildings in relation to each other and the relative significance of their various elements
- Scale: The relation of buildings to human proportions and respect for the scale of the other structures around them
- Harmony: The adaptation of the building to its architectural and natural surroundings
- Enclosure: The limitation of the size of a development, and its division by means of open spaces and courtyards
- Materials: The use of local traditional building materials and avoidance of standardized products
- Decoration: Skilled craft work that decorates every part of a building appropriately
- Art: Art is a part of the environment, and can introduce symbolism and give meaning to a development
- Signs & Lights: Well designed road signs, advertising in its proper place, and carefully controlled lighting
- Community: Pride in one's surroundings and the feeling that everyone has contributed to their planning and organization

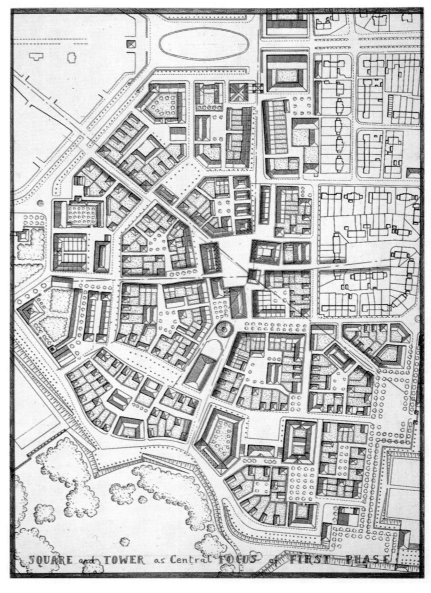

Plan of Middle Farm, the first phase of the Poundbury Project. The focal point of the village is a trapezoidal square dominated by a rectangular tower that can be seen for miles around. From this central meeting place, main streets radiate out toward the new areas planned to the north west, the already existing suburbs to the east, and the public park situated to the south. The most important communal buildings are arranged along a line leading from the park through the covered market, the round library, and the town hall to the central tower. The organization of the residential buildings around small planted open spaces is clearly shown. The development is bordered by landscaped promenades planted with trees.

SQUARE and TOWER as Central FOCUS of FIRST PHASE

The Poundbury Experiment

In recent years the Prince of Wales has often expressed his views as a critic of architecture. His opinions have met with approval from some, but also drawn accusations of dilettantism from many architects and town planners. It is true that the successor to the crown has no formal qualifications in architecture, but a professional training is hardly a precondition for the ability to express an opinion on this subject. This is particularly so in view of the fact that the Prince may be assumed to have a certain appreciation of aesthetic matters, if only on account of the circumstances of his life, living as he does in some of the most beautiful houses in Great Britain. So it is probably fairest to the Prince to describe him as an amateur. *Amateur* means "lover," and a person who spends time and energy on an issue as an amateur therefore does so out of love. Early on the Prince sought out challenges in practise, and in 1987 he found the ideal site for experimentation in the county of Dorset. The ancient town of Dorchester was to be expanded to the west in order to create new residential areas. The town council inquired about the purchase of the land required from the Duchy of Cornwall, which owned the parts of the district designated for development. The request made by the city fathers was presented to Prince Charles in his capacity as the Duke of Cornwall, and it was this that gave Charles the opportunity he had been looking for. Instead of simply selling the land and washing his hands of the matter, he wanted to exert an influence on the process and make his own vision of Britain a reality. The town council of Dorchester could hardly say no when they were informed of the Prince's wishes. However, they probably also recognized that the future king's commitment to the project would bring great advantages with it. Certainly it gave the new development widespread publicity, no doubt improving the chances of attracting employers to the area.

The Prince wanted to call his model town Poundbury. Under this working title and in close cooperation with his royal patron, the American Leon Krier drew up a plan that provided for the construction of 3,000 homes over a period of 25 years. In his work he followed closely the principles that the Prince had articulated in the book *A Vision of Britain*. This meant designing the development to fit in with the landscape, using traditional regional building techniques, and sourcing construction materials locally. The aim was to build on a human scale, creating a development that would look as if it had grown organically: a place that would blend harmoniously into its surroundings. On no account should it just attract pensioners or commuters. Rather the inten-

The Prince of Wales has been interested in alternative architecture for many years. His ideas, which were brought together in 1989 in his book *A Vision of Britain*, were realized for the first time in the model town of Poundbury, where he has worked with respected architects and town planners, and cooperated closely with the local authorities.

Dorset has rich natural resources. This has made it possible to deploy the whole range of *vernacular architecture* in Poundbury, using local construction materials, such as Purbeck Marble, Portland Stone, reeds, straw, brick, tiles, and limestone.

tion was to create an organic community where people would "live, shop, work, and play."

The basic features of this ambitious project were presented to the public in the presence of the Prince of Wales in 1989 and comments invited. Poundbury was not supposed to be one of those developments that are created without any consideration of their future inhabitants. So the team were glad to accept the delays brought about by the consultation process and the revision of the designs to take account of suggested changes and improvements. In 1993 the plans were finalized and the building work could begin. By December 1997, 137 houses had been built and sold. It proved to be an advantage that the project was realized more slowly than had originally been planned. This meant that it was possible to benefit from the practical experience gained in the parts of the development that had already been completed. For example, the planted areas in the squares proved to be too large and were reduced in favor of the gardens. In February 1998 about 300 people were living in the new community, where a number of business had already located. This was very much due to an innovative start-up program that supported new businesses with advice and assistance. Even though Poundbury looks like a traditional village at first sight, the infrastructure has been built to the highest standards of modern technology, and offers the residents all the advantages and opportunities of the information society. Every house has its own Internet connection.

Of course, it is difficult to give a conclusive judgement on a project like Poundbury after just ten years, but the balance so far is very positive. People now live, shop, work, and play there – just as Prince Charles wanted. The residents appreciate the architecture, which shows that the Prince's theories are not simply muddled or old-fashioned nonsense. Rather, Poundbury combines a sense of tradition and a concern for organic growth with respect for human beings and nature. Sound British business sense adds a very practical dimension to the whole project, giving the development a healthy economic vibrancy and preventing it from degenerating into a lifeless museum piece. If Poundbury is anything like a model of the kingdom that Prince Charles would one day like to reign over, his subjects really will be able to think themselves luckier than the citizens of many other countries.

The Suburbs

The suburbs are a transitional zone: not quite city, but not quite village. The suburbs are for people who cannot afford life in the middle of the city but do not want to be too far away from it, an ideal place from which to drive into the city every morning to work or just pop into the center for a quick shopping trip at the weekend. For others the suburbs symbolize the luxury of life with a hint of rural idyll. These "conscious" suburbanites probably once lived on one of the main trunk roads through the Moloch of the great city and are now overjoyed to have escaped from the roar of traffic. They like the fact that the milkman stops in the morning to have a quick chat, that there are no fights over the last parking space outside the local corner shop, and that a typically drowsy suburban atmosphere descends in the evenings.

Many of the suburbs around London date from the Victorian era. The building boom that began in the second half of the 19th century was a result of the desire felt by the rising middle classes to live close to their workplaces, while still keeping one foot in the countryside. At the same time, however, it was a response to the rapidly increasing demand for housing that could no longer be met in the heart of the city.

Rows of suburban houses were built one after the other, particularly in the area of North London. The southern suburbs were developed slightly later, and mainly date from the late Victorian period or the 1930s, 40s, and 50s. The rule of thumb is that the further you go from the center of London, the more recent the suburbs are. However, the development is continuing – places that were still quiet villages a few years ago are now being incorporated into the city and will soon have been overtaken by its urban sprawl.

Anyone who cares to take a stroll through the suburbs of South London – more recently developed areas like Morden, Rosehill, Stoneleigh, Cheam, Raynes Park, and Colliers Wood, and earlier, typically Victorian districts like Wandsworth, Tooting, Streatham, West Norwood, Catford, Eltham, and Charlton – will notice that the petit-bourgeois dream – feared by some, loved by others – is still very much alive. The typical middle-class family of legend and cliché, with its 2.3 children, is the dominant force in places such as these. The British have traditionally lived in terraced or semi-detached houses, and the fact that the whole suburb is dominated by a single architectural style and that the individual houses are the same in every detail does not seem to bother anyone. The semi-detached, or terraced, house is a good way to live – and why should anyone change something that has proved its worth for generations? The same is true of the interiors of these homes. You are as unlikely to find existential black here as postmodern style or avant-garde designer furniture.

These islands of middle-class prosperity and respectability still set the standards for the suburban way of life. The air here is much better than in the center of London, the pavements are clean, the gardens are a picture of carefully tended glory, the unemployment rates are much lower than in the areas of the city-center, there is less street crime – aside from the inevitable burglaries – and in some suburbs, such as Cheam, there are not even parked cars to spoil the view because nearly every house has its own garage.

Today people who move to a suburb often do so very consciously. They are choosing a peaceful, manageable community for themselves and their families in preference to the hectic anonymity of the capital. They accept that there will not be as many cinemas and theaters, and possibly not as many different kinds of restaurant as in London or the other large cities of the British Isles, but in exchange, they can happily invite over friends and relatives for a barbecue, and at last find time and leisure for the national hobby of gardening. People who have children (or dogs, or both) are particularly likely to view a terraced house in the suburbs as a preferable alternative to life among heavily used roads and overcrowded parks, even if they are forced to travel much further to work as a result.

Opposite page: Long, straight streets dominated by rows of terraced houses. This is Crewe, Cheshire, in the north of England, but it is a picture that could have been taken anywhere in the British Isles. There are not many facilities in these areas, which are often purely residential, but there are always plenty of places to park.

Right: The tranquility of life in the suburbs has its price. People who work in the city have to endure long journeys to work as commuters.

Below: Another modern suburb. Fanciful Tudor elements have been used in an attempt to raise this row of houses in a suburban area of London above the usual monotony.

Close Encounters of the Third Kind

Anyone who has a tendency to depression when faced with fog, drizzle, cold, and constant gray skies should avoid the United Kingdom – at least during the months from October to April, but it is not just the climate that disturbs the locals and their visitors on dark winter nights. Rather, it is supernatural forces that have often prevented travelers from finding the rest and relaxation they were seeking, and spooky experiences that have made a few keen to get away from the country at the end of their stay.

Great Britain is a tolerant, cosmopolitan land. Not only does it offer a new home to immigrants from the Commonwealth, it also shelters many residents who have actually been dead for some time, but have still not found rest. It is quite natural for the ghosts found in haunted houses and castles, poltergeists, fairies, gnomes, and apparitions of all kinds to be treated with a certain friendly respect. North American ghost hunts like those depicted in the film *Ghostbusters* are unthinkable here.

The old lordly mansions and dusty castles offer just the right environment for the undead. The further to the north they are, the colder the masonry, and Scotland is particularly well-suited to ancient bones, though Wales can also offer attractive places to haunt. The impenetrable magic woods are preferred places of resort for fairies and wood spirits that sometimes just want to have fun, but can sometimes be dangerous.

However, Her Majesty's ghostly subjects also feel at home in the heart of the capital and the small suburbs around London. Here they lead a more or less peaceful existence in beautiful old buildings or seek out parks and neglected cemeteries. Wimbledon alone has five principal haunted sites. The Tudor Palace of Hampton Court is home to the ghosts of Henry VIII's many wives, and Greenwich is claimed by nine different ghosts, while Pluckly, which is just an hour from London by car in the delightful landscape of Kent, is even able to boast of being "England's most haunted village." There have been ghosts on every corner of the village for many years. In the early 1970s a group of occult researchers managed to persuade the vicar to give them access to St Nicholas's Church for a night so that they could investigate mysterious lights that had appeared there on several occasions. The next morning the researchers complained that they had not seen or heard a single ghost, just the vicar's little dog, which had pottered in to spend some time there with them. The trustworthy vicar then had to explain to them that he did not own a dog and that there were no pets living in the neighborhood. Anyone who visits the church and then wants to shake off the unusual atmosphere with a bite to eat and a pint of beer would be well advised to avoid the nearby Black Horse Inn, because it is haunted as well. The ghost there particularly enjoys slamming doors and locking out the landlady, Laura Gambling, and he finds it just as amusing to move glasses on the bar with an invisible hand or worry the pub's dog.

Lindisfarne Castle, Northumberland mantled in fog on an autumn morning – who could seriously doubt the existence of ghosts and spirits when looking at this view?

London – the Haunted Capital

Anyone who has ever taken the time to meditate on the unique characteristics of the supernatural will tend to assume that ghosts and other specters are most likely to be found in rural areas. This is not necessarily the case. There may be a great many ghosts active in the British countryside, but London is also haunted by countless apparitions. Not for nothing is the city regarded as a center of the occult. The shades of the departed have taken up residence in dusty attics cluttered with old trunks and spider webs, damp cellars full of moldy wine racks, private town houses, theaters, pubs, Royal palaces, and disused underground stations. So a certain amount of caution is required by anyone going about their business in London.

Thirsty sightseers who wish to recover from their tour through Belgravia with a beer at the Grenadier in Wilton Row need nerves of steel, because the pub is visited by the ghost of an officer who allegedly deceived his comrades so outrageously during a game of cards that they flogged him and stabbed him to death. A short while later the pub was invaded by a ghostly presence. To the present day objects are moved by invisible hands, chairs and tables shifted, steps echo from empty rooms, and sometimes gentle groaning can be heard from the cellar.

A couple of streets further on, the renowned Cadogan Hotel is a place of comparative safety. The hotel may be haunted by the ghost of Lillie Langtrie, the legendary mistress of the Prince of Wales and later King Edward VII, but the apparition appears to be of a generally reserved nature and traditionally only appears on very quiet days. It may be that Lillie simply does not have the time to haunt the hotel properly, because some people believe that she also visits the ladies' toilet of Rules restaurant on Maiden Lane in Covent Garden. While she was alive she went here so often with her royal companion that the management built a rear entrance specially for the secret couple. However, her ghostly activities are not at all dangerous, and there is no need for the ladies to be afraid. The worst that ever happens is a door being locked or the faucet turned on – by a gentle, ghostly hand, of course. Even if female ghosts are sometimes more reserved, they should still be treated with respect. Particular care is also required in front of the entrance to the prestigious department store Fortnum & Mason. The journalist Nancy Spain once had a strange encounter there. She was in a great hurry to get to an important appointment, but was unable to flag down a taxi. When a vehicle eventually stopped for her, an elegant, red-haired elderly lady alighted, but was unable to find her money. In order to speed matters up, the desperate journalist said she would pay for the old lady's journey. Once she was firmly ensconced in the back of the cab, the driver laughed and explained that the old lady had been the amazingly rich Lady C. A few days later Nancy learned that Lady C. had already been dead for three days by this time – she had died in a terrible fire.

On the Tracks of Jack the Ripper

Jack the Ripper is one of the most infamous serial killers that the world has ever seen. The name immediately conjures up associations with Victorian London, gaslight, dark alleyways shrouded in autumnal mist, and bestial horrors, quite apart from the mysterious fact that the series of murders he committed ended without the murderer ever being found.

It all happened during the late summer and autumn of 1888. In the early hours of August 31 the driver Charles Cross found the body of a woman. The Police were called quickly to the scene and discovered that the woman's throat had been cut through to the spine. A thorough examination the next day established that the body of the victim, a prostitute called Mary Ann Nicholls, had been slit open and all of her intestines removed. The scene of the crime, Buck's Row, came to be known as Murder Row, and its name was eventually changed to Durward Street at the request of the residents.

On September 8 the Ripper struck again. This time his victim was another lady of ill repute. Annie Chapman was found in the gray light of dawn, just before six o'clock, in the back garden of No. 29 Hanbury Street. The body had been brutally mutilated in a similarly gruesome way to that found in Buck's Row. The Police worked intensively on the case, but the evidence still remained strangely vague.

At half past eight in the evening of September 29 the custodians of the law picked up a drunken prostitute called Catherine Eddowes close to St Botolph's and took her to the police station in Bishopsgate. By midnight the woman had sobered up. She was released again, only to run straight into the arms of the Ripper in Mitre Square. Catherine's body had been brutally mutilated when it was found the next day.

Another murder took place on September 30. However, it remained uncertain whether this case should also be ascribed to the elusive murderer, because the body of Elizabeth Stride had not been mutilated – though this could also have indicated that the murderer was disturbed and was not able to complete his horrible work.

The last murder in the series was perpetrated on November 9. This time the victim was the 25-year-old Irishwoman Mary Kelly. At around four o'clock in the morning her neighbors in Miller's Court heard a woman's voice crying, "Help, murder," but none of them took any notice of her pleading. When the landlord's agent arrived to collect Mary's rent the next morning, he found a vision of horror. The young woman's body had been so horribly mutilated that initially it was thought it would be impossible to identify her.

As has already been noted, the culprit was never found, but the rumors spread like wildfire. The various individuals who were suspected of these awful deeds included Queen Victoria's nephew (the Duke of Clarence), an American doctor, a poor Polish Jew called Kosminski who lived nearby, and many others.

It is still possible to see the London of Jack the Ripper and his unhappy victims by joining guided walks through Spitalfields and Whitechapel. In 1999 Richard Jones published a book that should be given to anyone who is interested in unexplained phenomena. *Walking Haunted London* describes 25 routes through the city, leading the dauntless visitor to the darkest places in its history – and into its most haunted pubs. After all, even ghost hunters need refreshment from time to time. This little book can be used to find the most famous haunted streets and squares in the City of London, as well of places of historical and supernatural interest beyond its boundaries. The tour through Hampton Court Palace is also much to be recommended, since this Tudor palace is regularly visited by the ghosts of the six wives of Henry VIII, particularly Anne Boleyn, Catherine Howard, and Jane Seymour.

Durward Street in London's Whitechapel still has a rather unnerving atmosphere. In 1888 it was called Buck's Row, and was the scene of the murder of Mary Ann Nicholls, the first victim of the serial killer Jack the Ripper.

It was common to use the entrance hall as a dining room during the 16th century. However, no one would have dreamed of doing this by the 18th century, when the entrance hall was seen as a place where guests were received, while the life of the house went on elsewhere. Sometimes a rather smaller vestibule might be placed in front of a magnificent hall with an ornate staircase.

THE ENTRANCE HALL

THE VISITING CARD OF A BRITISH HOUSE

The entrance hall of Elton Hall in Cambridgeshire has the authentic character of a medieval *great hall*. The bare beams in the ceiling, the large fireplace, the wood-paneled walls, and the long table are typical of a 15th-century country mansion.

Anyone who is invited into a British house will go in through the entrance hall, which gives the visitor a first impression of his or her hosts' status in life. Until the 14th century the great hall still made up practically the entire inside of the house. It was not just a room through which people passed and in which they were received, but could be described as a two-story residential landscape, where people cooked, ate, and slept, just like the large spaces of a modern loft. Over the centuries various chambers were split off from this large hall, and the familiar plan of the modern house, with its separate rooms, developed. Up until the first half of the 16th century the hall gradually lost more and more of its functions. It was often used as a dining room, but in winter it was terribly cold in spite of its huge fireplaces. As a result, in the second half of the 16th century people began building smaller halls with larger windows or putting in lower ceilings.

By the mid-17th century the staircase leading to the upper stories had developed into a main feature of the hall. In the early 18th century the hall took on its modern form and function, and came to be used increasingly as a reception room. Halls may have still been equipped with hearths at this time, but they were no longer used as living rooms. By the end of the 18th century entrance halls had become even smaller, and in farm houses they had already been reduced to the modest space they constitute today. Only in sizeable manor houses were halls still constructed on a large scale. The hall was rediscovered with the rise of neo-Gothic architecture in the early 19th century. Thanks to the influence of A. W. Pugin, great halls became common after 1830, since they were believed to be places of old English hospitality. Like the original great halls, the hall was now used again as a multi-purpose space, either as a living room or a ballroom, depending on the size of the house. As in the baronial halls of the middle ages, balls were organized for the nobility and local farmers, while the lord of the manor might hold an annual dance for his tenants or the servants of the house. The furniture and decorations were kept dark, as was the fashion. However, this changed in the early 1930s, when halls began to be decorated in a brighter, more inviting style.

In modern times there are no strict limitations on what can be done with this space. Depending on its size, and the way it is divided up, it can either be used just for receiving guests and hanging up coats, or furnished as a reading room with an inviting couch and an occasional table. If there is sufficient space, afternoon tea can be taken there or small parties entertained.

But, however large or small a hall may be, and whatever its other functions, it is always used to control access to the rest of the house. It is no longer the outer world, but usually not quite an interior room. People who enter it have not really arrived yet. Visitors can take off their coats here, check their ties or dresses, take a last deep breath, and finally go through into the reception room. Unwelcome guests leave their visiting card and can be shown out by the domestic staff or a secretary, if there is any doubt as to their credentials. Suppliers and couriers drop off their deliveries and wait for the receipt to be signed. For new visitors the hall is like a strip of no-man's land where they have to wait before they can enter foreign territory.

The entrance hall is also the first room that guests see. True to the principle that you never get a second chance to make a first impression, much value is therefore placed on the decoration of the hall in the British Isles. In country houses it presents a still life of Wellington boots, waxed rain jackets, riding coats, tweed caps, and walking sticks, but this should not be misinterpreted as disorder. Although these garments appear to have been carelessly tossed aside, this has been done very consciously to create a particular impression: that one is entering a traditional British country house.

Color has great significance in this respect. It can be inviting or off-putting, and can also make a room appear larger or smaller than it really is. However, in Great Britain the color of a room would not be chosen according to the principles of some psychological theory of color, but for decorative reasons or on account of historical accuracy. For example,

The original form of the medieval entrance hall continued to be common in 16th-century houses. Before the division of the house into various rooms intended for different activities, the hall was used as a combined living, eating, and sleeping space. In consequence, very old country houses sometimes have entrance halls that lead directly into the kitchen.

Right: The entrance halls of country houses are supposed to be comfortable and uncomplicated rather than formal and imposing. After all, they have to survive invasion by hordes of wet dogs and visitors in dirty Wellies undamaged.

Far right: In 18th-century houses the entrance hall is often dominated by a staircase, because at this time reception rooms were located on the first floor, the *piano nobile*, as it was known – a fashion imported from Italy. From the 19th century on reception rooms were relocated to the ground floor, which meant that impressive staircases became more of a rarity.

green would be the correct choice for a house dating from the 18th century, because this color was very popular then. However, it is also important to realize that the range of colors available was much smaller in the past than it is today. If particular colors were used a great deal in a certain era, this is usually a result of the technical limitations of the time.

If you place particular emphasis on authentically decorated walls, you should avoid bright colors. This is particularly the case with interiors that date from the Victorian period or even earlier. If it is not possible to find an authentic shade, you can at least work with modern matte paints. If you prefer wallpaper, it can also be used to change the viewer's perception of a room's size and shape. Vertical stripes make a low room look higher than it is, particularly in combination with a light ceiling.

So a wide range of design methods is available when decorating, and it is typically British that they are used with such care in this apparently insignificant room. However – and this is also very British – the careful planning of the entrance hall should on no account be visibly evident. On the contrary, a hall is only really perfect if it does not obtrude on visitors at all, but simply spreads an atmosphere of welcome.

The halls of 19th-century country houses are often divided into two parts. Visitors first enter a relatively small vestibule, and are then asked into the more imposing hallway, from where they can be led directly into the ground-floor reception room, as here at Melbourn Bury in Hertfordshire.

The British climate has certainly influenced the layout of the entrance hall. A small vestibule would be placed in front of the large hall with the imposing staircase leading up to the reception rooms. This served to retain the heat laboriously generated in the house.

Above: A British entrance hall is not just a place where you leave your hat and umbrella. Rather, it is the visiting card of an English house and introduces visitors to the ambience in which their hosts live.

Far left: Hooks and racks for hanging up coats and hats are to be found in almost every entrance hall. The form of the coat rack will differ, depending on whether you are in the country or the city. In the country it may be simply be a construction improvised with a pair of magnificent antlers.

Left: The umbrella stand is still an important piece of furniture in Great Britain, not just because umbrellas are essential in this rainy country, but also because an umbrella stand holding a variety of umbrellas and walking-sticks looks highly decorative. Many people like to keep their umbrella or walking-stick in a large vase.

A mirror in the entrance hall can make the room look larger and gives you the opportunity to check your clothes and make-up one last time before going out.

Armchairs are popular pieces of furniture in British halls. Depending on the size of the room, they may simply invite you to while away the time or even be grouped together, making the perfect place to take afternoon tea.

Many entrance halls have grandfather clocks. Not only do they tell the time, they can also help to make low rooms look higher than they really are.

Interesting pictures will transform a hall into a little gallery. They are a good way of telling your visitors about yourself before you have even met each other.

The hall does not always have to be decorated with refined flower arrangements. A simple bouquet can be a refreshing contrast in a formal context.

Dried flowers can look very charming, and there are so many different ways of prettifying a hall in this way. You can put them in a vase like fresh flowers or lay them in a basket.

A pot plant is an eye-catching feature in any room. The type and size of plant will depend on the scale of the hall and the amount of light it gets during the day.

A woven wreath of flowers or straw is a favorite decorative feature, particularly in the halls of country houses. If there is glass in the main door, a wreath like this will prevent people looking in.

Old sporting equipment, such as battered tennis rackets, golf-clubs, cricket bats, and croquet sticks that have been passed on from generation to generation add character to any hall.

Doors – a Brief Style Guide

From the 15th century to the 17th the function of house doors was primarily protective, as their appearance showed. They were simply constructed from vertical planks or slabs of wood held together by cross or diagonal bars. The heads of the nails that fastened the wood to the metal bars were often visible on the outside, and this was usually their only decoration. The handle would be a heavy metal ring.

Only from the mid-17th century did the door slowly become an important decorative component of the facade. It was often the immediate surroundings of the door, the lintel and the door-frame, that were heavily decorated. One particularly popular style had steps leading up to the entrance, and columns to the right and left of the door supported a classical pediment. Glass also began to come into use at about this time, but usually only if protective outer doors were placed in front of the actual house door.

In the Georgian period – from the mid-18th century to the early 19th century – the door developed into the central architectural element of the front side of the house. The door itself was kept very simple, but its surroundings were designed like the facade of a temple. The columns on either side of the door-frame were often reduced to plain pilasters, while their capitals supported a portico, which often rests on consoles.

In the Regency period – the first three decades of the 19th century – simpler entrances gradually began to become common. Above their doors you find undecorated brick or stucco arches. Lights – usually semi-

This baroque doorway is intended to impress the owner's status upon the visitor, even from some distance away. It would be unthinkable on a town house, but it has the space to unfold its full effect in the facade of a country house or palace.

An aedicule, or "little house," frames the classical door of a small country house dating from the early 18th century. The proportions of the columns, entablature, and pediment are derived from ancient temples.

The door of this Georgian country house is framed by a projecting portico with double columns. A narrow, molded stone band is the only decoration round the door itself.

After about 1750 semicircular fanlights were added more frequently above doorways. They are usually glazed with bars of glass radiating from a central point so that they look like opened fans.

Georgian houses usually have a light over the door to illuminate the entrance hall. There is also a semicircular recess at ground level in the wall by this door. It contains an iron cross bar for use as a boot scraper.

These two doorways lead into different terraced houses, which not only share a wall, but also the central part of the wooden doorframe. The door to the right is decorated with a fine Regency fanlight.

circular – also began to be added above doors more frequently. In the Victorian period they became larger and more various in form, while the pediment over the door tended to become a canopy. Glass panes in a range of colors and forms are typical of the period. Wooden doors were usually painted green.

The Arts and Crafts Movement, dating back to the last three decades of the 19th century, sought inspiration in the past and combined elements from very different periods. For instance, you might find doors in the style of the 15th century, doors reminiscent of the Georgian period, and doors decorated with stained glass or carved wood. In the Edwardian era, between the beginning of the 20th century and the First World War, the variety of colors available increased and designs became more flexible as doors came to be produced on an industrial scale. The doorways built

with lavishly elaborated canopies on terraced houses are typical of this period. Depending on the style of house, the light over a door might be glazed with stained glass or decorated with lavish ironwork.

The end of the Edwardian period marked the dividing line between classic British furniture and modern interior design. Traditional British doors also went out of fashion with the outbreak of the First World War. In the 1920s and 30s we find entrance doors made of metal as well as wood – sometimes in combination with glass. Instead of lights over doors, windows on either side were now popular, as were small windows in the door itself. Modernism had an impact in the form of very simple, minimalist solutions and graphic decorative features. In the early 1980s, with the rise of postmodernism, there was a revival of Georgian stylistic elements that has continued into the new millennium.

The frame around the door of this town house from the Regency period consists of a wide, molded strip with a decorative keystone that has lost its structural function.

This Regency door is flanked by two playful half-columns, creating an effect that is anything but Classical. The capitals do not support an entablature, but two consoles, which, in turn, hold up a tiny canopy.

This simple, early 19th-century door has no side columns, but is decorated with a fanlight and a typical urn-shaped brass door knocker. There is a decorative band around the light inspired by the profile of the Classical entablature.

This large light with its French-style ornamentation suggests that there is an extended entrance hall behind this door. At the end of the 19th century British architects often used French models for urban buildings. There was a particular interest in Parisian architecture.

The ceiling of the entrance hall in this 1920s house is rather low, so, instead of a light over the door, two windows have been placed on either side of it. A sense of unity is imposed on these three elements by the long cornice over the doorway.

This simple, functional entrance door on a detached country house dating from the first half of the 20th century could almost be taken for a back door.

Ways with Doors and Windows

Doors and windows in the entrance hall are not just decorated in line with aesthetic criteria, but also according to practical considerations. After all, this room is a transitional area between the house proper and the outer world, and is therefore exposed to considerable wear and tear. Residents and visitors carry in dirt, and dogs also leave paw prints and hair behind them, particularly in country houses. For this reason the curtains covering the doors and windows are usually made of some robust material – if curtains are put up at all. Anyone who cannot do without curtains should calculate their length so that the hem does not reach the floor. Long, low drapes may look very effective, but the bottom edge will soon look tatty. The material should also be a strong weave with a bold color for the same reason. A wisp of white muslin may create a lovely atmosphere, but it will not last long if there are cats or children rampaging round the house.

Whether a curtain is required at all depends on three factors: firstly, whether it is necessary to keep out drafts; secondly, whether you want to stop people looking in; and thirdly, whether you have sensitive furniture, artworks, or carpets that need to be protected from the light. If none of these considerations applies in your hall, the windows might just as well remain undecorated.

Nevertheless, some people decide on a curtain for purely aesthetic reasons. They may, for example, wish to hide the shape of a window, soften the light in a room, or create a background for furniture or ornaments. Not only that, curtains are very good reflectors and in some circumstances can be an effective way of brightening up a room. At the same time, the contrasts between textiles and flooring materials can be very interesting: for example, smooth, shiny tiles look very good in combination with a coarse woolen cloth.

Doors usually only need curtains if they have panes of glass in them. In this case, a net curtain will stop people looking in. Visitors should not be able to see from the outside what awaits them in the entrance hall and what is happening in the private rooms of the house.

If the door is very old and lets in cold air, it is a good idea to put up a heavy woolen curtain to keep out the drafts. Such curtains are not necessarily masterpieces of interior décor, but do a good job and are therefore quite acceptable, particularly in the country. The important thing is never to forget that the hall is the visiting card of a British house, so it has to be arranged with as much care and attention as possible in order to make a good first impression.

Doormats – The Medium is the Message

In Great Britain a doormat is more than just something you place in front of your door on which to scrape the dirt off your feet. It is often a medium through which a message is communicated to visitors before they even enter the house. This is done with pictures or text, or a combination of the two. For example, doormats with amusing mottoes enjoy great popularity. "Oh no, not you again" is a real classic in this category. These mats are remarkably cheap and can be purchased at agricultural shows or similar events that attract the kind of British people who appreciate the sense of humor expressed by these mottoes. Anyone who fails to see what is so funny about this kind of joke, but would still like a personalized doormat, can have one made with the name of their house on it. The Kingsbridge-based company Cloakrooms provides an excellent mat-making service. They will supply one-off doormats in any size and with anything printed on them. The production method is very simple, allowing almost any subject that can be depicted in a few colors and drawn as a silhouette to be printed on a mat. Apart from images of all sorts, they will also make mats decorated with brand logos, club badges, or regimental coats of arms. The imagination knows no boundaries. So why not give someone a really different present? Instead of a T-shirt printed with a photograph of the birthday child, or a tea cup with his or her name on, how about a doormat that says "Best

Wishes"? The same technique is also used to make the standard range of Happy Mats, a company that advertises in the classified section of almost every British house-and-garden magazine. The company produces mats with striking, evocative names, such as *English Garden*, *Scottish Hedgerow*, *Rose*, or *Green Lattice*.

You can argue about taste, and there are many Britons who would not wish to lay this kind of flowery, more or less amusing doormat in front of their door, but people who put one on their doorstep seem to be saying that the world inside their house is still in order as far as they are concerned.

If you have mud and stones stuck in the treads of your boots or shoes after a walk over muddy ground, often the only thing that will help is an iron boot scraper. They are set into the wall by the entrance steps of many country houses – a wise precaution!

The folding boot jack is exactly the right thing for particularly tight-fitting riding boots. After use it can be folded up and placed to one side. If even this device fails to do the trick, you will have to find a strong friend to pull off your boots.

A boot jack is extremely helpful when pulling off Wellington boots. The nice thing about this implement is that you do not have to handle the dirty heels of your boots while you are taking them off.

A *wader boot rack* is a clear indication that there is an angler living in the house. It is used to hang up the long waders that are needed for fly fishing. Features of this kind will only be found in a hall where country pursuits enjoy top priority.

Where to Keep Your Wellies

The hall of a country house is not complete without a doormat, a boot jack, and a special rack for green Wellington boots, or "Wellies." If you have just come back from a rainy walk through the garden or a hunting trip, the treads of your boots are bound to be full of mud and stones. The practical British have invented a whole selection of instruments that can be used to scrape off this dirt. They are available in the most varied forms. Some of them look like hedgehogs with spines on which you brush your shoes to remove the mud. Others look like normal coarse doormats with taller bristles on either side that can be used to clean the edges of your shoes. Alternatively, dried mud can be scraped off with a metal bar, while you hold onto a long stick to stop yourself from falling over. Once you have pulled off your boots with the aid of a boot jack, they can be hung up on a special rack to dry off. Adverts for the devices pictured appear regularly in the small-ads sections of the magazines specializing in old houses, lifestyle, and classic décor – the best proof that muddy boots are as much a part of British country life as the country house itself.

The various patented bootracks used to store Wellington boots can be found in cloakrooms as well as entrance halls. These rooms usually hold huge collections of coats, hats, and caps, though their owners have often disappeared long since or are quite unknown to the master of the house.

Flowers in the Hall

Every British house needs flowers. Frequently, guests are greeted in the entrance hall with a welcoming display. Depending on whether the house is in the country or the city, this will be a relaxed mixture of wild flowers or a perfect bouquet of hothouse blooms. The art of arranging flowers can be learned to a certain extent, but, as with all aesthetic disciplines, talent is the most important prerequisite. There are no fixed rules for the creation of a beautiful flower arrangement, but anyone who trains their senses a little will soon be able to combine colors and shapes to assemble very pleasing compositions. First of all, you should learn about the plants themselves. Someone who has difficulty telling tulips, roses, and daffodils apart will tend to have a rather limited repertoire.

People whose houses are full of individual creations usually have a flower garden of their own. A carefully tended garden will ensure you always have fresh supplies, which will only occasionally have to be supplemented with bought flowers. Cultivating your own flower garden also encourages your knowledge of the sorts and varieties of flowers, and so extends your understanding of what can be done with them. The possibilities really are as numerous as the flowers and plants that nature has to offer.

Above: What could be a nicer way to greet a visitor than with a flower arrangement reflected in the well-polished mahogany of a Georgian table.

Left: A well stocked florist will have everything you need for elegant flower arrangements. If you are very lucky, you will be able to pick the raw materials in your own garden.

Center: The English summer greets you at the door with a simple bunch of wild flowers picked on a peaceful walk through the garden.

Right: The great attraction of working creatively with flowers is the fact that you can make something new every time with a limited number of components.

Anyone who has worked enough with flowers and has developed a good eye for colors and forms can start to think about accessories. The selection of natural materials that can be used is quite inexhaustible. Interesting effects can be created with dried twigs, pine cones, autumn leaves, or pieces of bark. Intensive observation of nature will sharpen your feel for its hidden beauties. The longer the amateur flower arranger spends in gardens, parks, or woodland areas, the more ideas he or she will pick up for interesting combinations of flowers and accessories. A stroll through the vegetable market can also throw up innumerable ideas, and even the kitchen, with its spice jars, can be a great source of inspiration. Finally, you may also wish to consider materials such as textiles, wire, and paper, but self-limitation to the simplest resources has often proved to be the best way of liberating a flower arranger's creative powers. Achieving impressive effects with a few simple materials should be the first aim of anyone starting to learn about flower arranging.

Flowers are welcoming to visitors and put them in the right mood for the house, its special atmosphere, and its residents. For this reason, the arrangement should be tailored quite specifically to fit in with the architecture and interior décor. Should guests be welcomed heartily or feel respect on entering? Should they sense cheerfulness or austerity, respectability or relaxed gaiety, grandeur or simple elegance? Certainly, there will be no mistaking the unflappable British attitude that comes from the consciousness that there is no need to aim for exaggerated standards of perfection.

The Chelsea Flower Show

The Chelsea Flower Show is more than just an exhibition of flowers and innovations in garden design. It is the unofficial opening of the social season, as well as one of its high points. It is held at the end of May and lasts for five days. This prestigious horticultural event takes place on a site between the Thames and the Chelsea Royal Hospital and mainly draws enthusiastic gardeners. In addition to this, however, there are always people who just like to be seen in the limelight of a truly exclusive event.

On the first day the gates of the Chelsea Flower Show are opened exclusively for the honorary guests of the Royal Horticultural Society, which organizes the event. They always include members of the Royal Family. The second and third days are reserved for the members of the Royal Horticultural Society, which was founded in 1804. Only on the last two days are normal mortals allowed to have a look at the displays.

It is not just flowers and plants that are on display at the Chelsea Flower Show, there are also complete gardens that have been designed and laid out specially for this occasion, as well as all the equipment that a gardener's heart might desire. Understandably, there are never any problems attracting enough visitors to the show. On the contrary, it is always very well attended. In order to make the tour round the beds, borders, hedges, flowers, garden accessories, and lawns as pleasant as possible for the paying public, the numbers admitted are always limited.

Several precursors of the current event were held by the Royal Horticultural Society at various locations in London. The concept that is still used today first took shape in 1913. The location and name of the show have remained unchanged ever since, so, like Ascot and Henley, the Chelsea Flower Show has been a part of English society life since Edwardian times. The British are united by a deep love of gardening, which even transcends the significant social barriers that still exist. Although the Chelsea Flower Show is very much a gathering of the upper and middle classes, it also belongs to the ordinary British people. British television broadcasts detailed reports on the show in order to keep everyone who has not been able to obtain an entrance ticket up to date with the latest developments. These unfortunates also miss out on the opportunities that are presented by the last day of the show, when the magnificent displays that have been laid out and brought together over the previous four weeks are sold off for next to nothing. Anyone who wants flowers for their garden or a palm tree for their entrance hall can purchase magnificent specimens for a couple of pounds or less. Many houses give pride of place to some plant or feature purchased as a souvenir of the most famous gardening show in the country.

For many visitors the gardens that are laid out specially for the occasion are the main attraction of the Chelsea Flower Show. Gardeners and designers from all round the world come here to compete for the plaudits of the knowledgeable public.

In 1745 William Hogarth painted this self-portrait with his pug Trump, one of several dogs of this breed that he owned.

Opposite page: Eight different breeds of hunting spaniels are found in Great Britain, all descended from gundog breeds. Many spaniels like swimming and are therefore very useful when shooting ducks or other water birds.

MAN'S BEST FRIEND

In the rural areas of the British Isles the dog is regarded practically as an equal member of the family. Not only because it accompanies its master or mistress on strolls round the estate, but also because it makes itself very useful when hunting by tracking down game or retrieving animals and birds once they have been shot – without eating them, of course. On large estates where livestock is farmed, a dog is also indispensable as a guard over the herds or flocks. Even if the family sometimes yearn for a comfortable flat in the city and the rich variety of cultural life in London, they stay in the country because "doggy just wouldn't stand it in the city." It cannot be denied that the countryside really is much nicer, even if it is more difficult to get to the cinema, theater or the opera from time to time. How thoughtful of the dog to hold his owners back from the madness of giving up the fresh air and peace and quiet of the country for the noise and bustle of the city on a mere whim. Things are a little different as far as the many commuters who live in the country are concerned. They may live outside the city limits, but the daily journey to work takes the bread-winner into the metropolis every day from Monday to Friday. Of course, in the majority of cases, this does not mean that their four-legged friend also has to go with them. It is the dog's master who suffers from the consequences of this arrangement, as he is the one who is deprived of the company of his faithful companion for most of the day. Unless he has had the good sense to choose a breed or mongrel that is suitable as a constant companion: after all, it is quite possible to have a dog with you all the time if you work in some professions.

Nevertheless, despite all the dogs that are taken for walks in the parks of the cities, in the consciousness of most British people the dog is associated with country life. A deep-seated feeling for what is right and natural leads most of the people in the United Kingdom to be of the opinion that the city simply is not the right place for a real dog. And a real dog is not some pampered Chihuahua that shivers with cold at the first gust of wind, but a robust sheepdog or hunting dog, such as a Labrador retriever. Labradors come very high on the popularity scale – in all sectors of society – and this breed, whether black or yellow, could well be described as the British national dog. Labradors are regarded with affection by the man in the street and the Chairman of the Board, and in the pub this shared enthusiasm will immediately get you into a lively conversation, particularly if you happen to have your particular specimen with you on a lead.

Celebrities and their Four-Legged Companions

The Queen is by far the most famous dog owner in Great Britain. She keeps Pembrokeshire Corgis, a dog breed from south-west Wales that has only been recognized relatively recently. The Welsh Corgi is not a lapdog, as its size might lead one to believe, but a sheepdog. The monarch's passion for her short-legged darlings goes back to 1933, when the seven-year-old princess fell in love with a Corgi. Her parents then allowed themselves be talked into purchasing an animal just like it. At the age of 18 the future Queen was given the first Corgi that was exclusively her own. There is now a whole dynasty of much loved companions descended from this dog, which went by the name Susan, and there is very little that will stop the Queen from feeding them in person.

People who choose a pug as a pet are saying a great deal about themselves, particularly that they do not care one jot about the judgements of their fellow human beings, who often enough ask why they have not selected a "cute" dog. The Duke and Duchess of Windsor owned a whole succession of dogs, and in later years they were almost all pugs. Their love of this breed is also demonstrated by their large collection of Meissen porcelain pugs. The first dog they owned together, when they were still unmarried lovers, was a small Cairn Terrier called Slipper, whom Edward presented to his future wife for Christmas in 1934, while he was still the Prince of Wales. This much loved animal, who was nicknamed Mr Loo, later died in France after being bitten by a snake.

The Jack Russell Terrier is particularly popular with people who like riding, and wherever they gather you will find large numbers of these energetic dogs. In the 1990s Jack Russells also became popular and fashionable outside riding circles.
One of Prince Charles's favorite dogs answers to (or ignores, as the case may be) the name Trigger. The Prince's four-legged friend peers into the camera with a quizzical, alert look in many photographs of the successor to the throne and accompanies the future king on long walks.
The next generation of British Royals has also taken this spirited little canine close to their hearts. Trigger particularly likes playing with the Princes William and Harry.

The Pekinese was introduced to England from China during the 19th century and is still very popular as a lapdog. The breed has been granted literary immortality by the stories of the English country vet James Herriot, who wrote most amusingly of Tricky Woo, the spoiled Pekinese owned by the eccentric widow Mrs Pumphrey. Barbara Cartland, the uncrowned queen of the British romantic novel, was not just famous for her love of pink, but also on account of her weakness for little white Pekinese. Just about every photograph of the diva shows her in the company of one of her little snub-nosed dogs. It is said that they were always in the room whenever the lady dictated a new chapter to her secretary, because Barbara Cartland could not bear to spend her later years without dogs or writing.

The Collie is a sheepdog breed from the Scottish Highlands. It is found in various colors, such as black and white, or yellow and white. The Sheltie is related to the Collie, though this breed of sheepdogs from the Shetland Isles is more of a rarity. Shelties are also found in the same colors as Collies.

The Labrador is a retriever – so called because it retrieves shot game for hunters. Both black and yellow Labradors are extremely popular on the British Isles, not just as hunting dogs, but also as family pets.

The Border Terrier comes from the Borders where Scotland and England meet. Terriers were used for hunting underground, flushing out small animals that had gone to ground in their burrows. The Border Terrier was bred by crossing the Scotch Terrier with the old Fox Terrier and was specialized in hunting for otters.

The West Highland White Terrier became very popular during the 1990s. This relatively recent breed is very brave for its size and is certainly an extremely entertaining animal with which to share a house. Like all Terriers, which are really hunting dogs, the Westie needs plenty of exercise.

The Beagle is related to the Foxhound, of which it is a rather smaller version. It is usually kept as a pet, though it makes a very good hunting dog that is used to track down smaller animals, such as rabbits and hares.

The ancestors of the English Bloodhound arrived with the Normans from the Ardennes. Since then they have been bred into the form in which they are common today on the British Islands. The Hound of the Baskervilles that featured in the Sherlock Holmes story of the same title should be imagined like the dogs shown here.

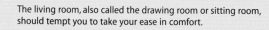
The living room, also called the drawing room or sitting room, should tempt you to take your ease in comfort.

THE LIVING ROOM

A Room to Live in

At the beginning of the 1970s, it was considered chic and modish to have an open-plan living area serving many different purposes, instead of the separate living room and dining room of the past. However, although this was thought avant-garde at the time, it really just harked back to the past. As far back as the 14th century, the great hall – today's entrance hall – was the large inner area of the house, where people ate, chatted, and slept. Rooms with specific functions did not develop until several centuries later. It is therefore not surprising that the modern trend toward a single room was quickly consigned to the trashcan, because it takes more than a mere fashionable trend to brush away something that has become established and has proved itself over time. Thus in the United Kingdom today, many people once again assume that the living room and dining room will be separate. The architecture of most old houses makes this obvious anyhow. A medium-sized house from the Edwardian era, i.e. between 1901 and 1914, still had a dedicated living room and a dining room, then came the billiard room and conservatory, followed by the gentlemen's room, which combined the functions of library, study, and smoking room.

In medieval times, people withdrew from the medieval great hall to smaller rooms, the forerunners of the living room. The current common English term, "drawing room," recalls this fact, because it is an abbreviated form of the term "withdrawing room." This was originally an antechamber of the bedchamber. "Withdrawing rooms" per se, with no connection to the bedroom did not come into existence until the 17th century. The less intimate the room became, the more suitable for receiving guests. It became bigger and was more impressively furnished. In the 18th century the drawing room was one of many reception rooms in the house. It was to this room that the ladies withdrew after dinner, whereas the men remained in the dining room to smoke and talk without restraint, joining the ladies later. Over time, the drawing room became more of a general reception room for guests of both sexes. They were provided with every conceivable comfort to make them feel relaxed and at ease. This gave rise to that mixture of grandiose formality and relaxed coziness that is a particular charm of the British living room.

Nowadays, the drawing room (also called the sitting room or living room) is a reception room as well as a family room. The furnishings alone make this obvious. There are family photographs and works of art, cozy seating arrangements and valuable period furniture, holiday souvenirs and mementos of social events, weddings, trophies, and knick-knacks. In short, the living room is the place for anything that could possibly be of interest to family, friends, and visitors. It shows who the host wants to be and, perhaps, who he really is. All these more or less decorative – and more or less valuable – items are arranged in separate groups around a focal point, usually the fireplace. As in the past, the fireplace is still of almost mythical significance in domestic life. If the house or apartment has no genuine, functioning fireplace, then an electric or gas imitation does the job. If this is not to people's liking, they create a visual fireplace replacement, such as a side-

The room layout in 19th-century British terrace houses is always very similar. The living room was usually in a room facing onto the street in the basement. Many people in Britain continue to use this architectural device, because this is also where the best fireplace is usually to be found.

board, the top of which replaces the mantelpiece and is decorated with framed pictures, vases, urns, a clock, or porcelain figurines. The seats are arranged in the room so as to form three sides of a rectangle around the fireplace or its substitute. Right back in Georgian times, this arrangement would have been extremely unusual, for during that period it was customary to line the furniture up along the walls, moving the seats out into the room only as required. Before retiring for the night, obedient servants spirited all the furniture back against the wall.

Things went to the opposite extreme in Victorian times, when living rooms were filled with so much furniture that there was barely room to move. Today in Britain, people prefer a look somewhere between homey coziness and spacious roominess. The living room, with its seating, coffee table, occasional tables, sideboard, corner cupboards, and book shelves, has to include a whole range of things, but the room should also look as though it could be rearranged easily and at any time. Most importantly, the furniture should not restrict the visitor's freedom of movement. Ultimately, the main purpose of the living room is for socializing. It is vital that the room is arranged so that, even after a couple of gin and tonics, a visitor can find his or her way out again without endangering him- or herself or the furnishings.

The living room provides a good example of a typically British characteristic: it should look as though it has been furnished and decorated effortlessly. It would just not be British to go to such expense on the living room that the host was always on edge in case his visitors should disturb or upset the tasteful arrangement, thereby making a relaxed conversation impossible. Everyone should feel at home in the living room. The host is not seeking an adulatory mention in an interior design magazine or to impress the guests with valuable antiques and furniture. This is perhaps why there are often clashes among the carefully selected and tastefully arranged ornaments on display in a British living room, which prevent giving the impression of everything being too perfect. And indeed that may be their intention, to remind visitors and hosts that the owners of such an otherwise perfectly arranged house are actually quite normal members of society.

Other countries apart from Britain also have country houses, such as Hilton Park in county Monaghan, Republic of Ireland, that, in line with the British model, have several living rooms to receive visitors. There were also practical reasons for this, as it made it possible for the occupants of the house to be in a sunlit room at any time of day. In the 18th century, following the Italian example, living rooms were situated on the first floor, known as the *piano nobile*. In Regency times, they were once again planned on the ground floor, so that the occupants of the house could walk out over terraces into the garden.

Right: Sofas and armchairs are arranged so that everyone can see the fire and can stretch out cold feet toward its warmth if necessary.

Far right: For many British, sitting in a softly upholstered leather arm-chair at the fireside in a cozy library is the best place on earth.

Opposite: The fireplace is the architectural focal point of any living room. Furniture and décor further emphasize its central position.

Below: The fact that an open fire might be insufficient to heat a room was of little concern to architects right into the early 20th century.

Classical Seating Arrangements

British living rooms, even those of major individualists, are governed by an unbreakable rule of interior design: the room must have a focal point, and this focal point is the fireplace or the item of furniture that replaces the fireplace. Under no circumstances can there be any deviation from this design dogma. It therefore comes as no surprise that a British living-room is always arranged around the fireplace. The three-sided rectangle can comprise sofas, armchairs, upholstered footstools, and occasional tables. The important thing is that the fireplace should be the focal point. A further concern regarding this established seating arrangement is that it should provide its occupants with every convenience. For this reason behind the sofa there is often a small table for glasses. This table is often home to the gin bottle, the ice bucket, and the essential tonic water.

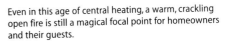
Even in this age of central heating, a warm, crackling open fire is still a magical focal point for homeowners and their guests.

sight throughout the whole of England. As the smoke was now conducted straight outside, it finally became worth decorating ceilings. This subsequently totally changed the way houses were decorated.

There is no rational explanation for the fact that the open fire continues to be so popular in the United Kingdom. It must have something to do with the appearance and the smell of burning logs and glowing coals, because with modern central heating there is no need for a fireplace. Until the late 19th century, people in large houses continued to sit and shiver in front of the fire. The situation in such houses did not improve until the introduction of various methods of central heating offered some respite.

By the end of the 19th century, nearly all houses, including those in the country, had some heating system. But this did not mean that open fireplaces became superfluous. Although they may not heat the rooms sufficiently, they certainly warm the cockles of British hearts. The British still like nothing more than spending an evening at the fireside, which is why every room is clearly arranged around its fireplace: the furniture is arranged around it, and it is the undisputed center of attention. Until the First World War, even in new houses, it was customary to have a fireplace in bedrooms and reception rooms, even when the dwelling had a modern heating system. After all, you cannot beat a fireplace for coziness, and the central heating can always break down.

Nor, at the beginning of the 20th century, was it a problem getting hold of the necessary staff to manage the numerous open fires. In a large house with multiple fireplaces, keeping up a supply of fuel was an elaborate logistical exercise, and a precise plan was required to keep all the coals and logs glowing. This system relied on a troop of domestic servants, available from early morning to late evening. When they gradually relinquished their positions to take up jobs that gave them a proper day off work and more social recognition, many owners of medium-sized and smaller houses were of necessity forced to look after the open fire themselves. But that deterred very few of them from continuing to use the open fire. In 1937, W.H. Auden wrote in his "Letter to Lord Byron:" "Preserve me above all from central heating/It may be D.H. Lawrence hocus-pocus/But I prefer a room that's got a focus." Britons share his oppinion even today, and manufactureres of authenticly reproduced fireplaces are as busy as ever.

The Magic of the Fireplace

The British appreciate open fires more than almost any other nation. This is no mere cliché, but a preference that has been passed down from generation to generation. Whereas in 17th-century continental Europe, open fires were being replaced by freestanding tiled stoves, and the Dutch, Scandinavians, Germans, and Russians were making themselves comfortable on the bench by the stove, in the British Isles people continued to gather round the open fire. They were not, however, oblivious to the fact that, although an open fire was good for warming the front, it left the back cold. But instead of abandoning the fireplace as something that had had its day, they preferred to invent the wing chair.

From the late 11th century, the fireplace moved to the wall of country houses, and from the end of the Middle Ages until the beginning of the 19th century, this position was the norm. An open fire in the middle of the room required a chimney in the ceiling, making it difficult to use the story above. A fireplace in the wall, on the other hand, meant that a single chimney could go through several stories up to the roof. The fireplace thus became an integral part of the construction. If it was incorporated into a central wall of the house, it could form a double fireplace that could even be used by two rooms. The rooftop chimney became a typical

THE MANTELPIECE AND ITS ORNAMENTS

The mantelpiece acts like a magnet for all sorts of knick-knacks. Large and small works of art stand peaceably alongside holiday souvenirs, personal mementos, or a variety of collectors' pieces. The mantelpiece can of course be arranged with extreme care, so that it reflects the room and its decorative style. Some might prefer to leave it totally bare or adorned with just one or two favorite things. This, however, would not be in keeping with the fundamental principles of British interior design. Perhaps it is the height of the mantelpiece that makes it an irresistible repository for all sorts of junk. Anything left there is instantly obvious, and that is why people often put things there that they do not want to forget, such as car keys, mobile phone, or the invitation to the next ball.

The basic principle is that the more ambitious the man or lady of the house in terms of interior decoration, the more sophisticated the miniature exhibition above the fireplace. If the house has several living rooms, the mantelpiece in the most prestigious reception rooms will often be laid

China dogs, known as Staffordshire Dogs, are so typical of mantelpiece decoration that they have almost become a cliché. Family photographs are obligatory on the mantelpiece, and silver and gold picture frames also count as decorative objects.

out as though in a museum, but in a family living room you will invariably find an intimate hodge-podge of objects.

To readers of detective novels, the mantelpiece will also be a place to keep an oriental slipper, such as the one in which Sherlock Holmes, the Victorian detective, kept his opium. Today, we prefer to smoke less harmful substances, and it is more likely that you will find cigarettes and pipe tobacco on the mantelpiece in the smoking-room, although there are bound to be a few houses where substances of more narcotic effect are to be found. In contrast, the porcelain animal figures that are without doubt one of the timeless classics of mantelpiece decoration are morally beyond reproach. China dogs have long been particularly popular. There are, of course, much more original ornaments than these ever-popular four-legged friends, but anyone wanting to be typically British can always fall back on them. It is, however, becoming increasingly difficult to find an authentic, in other words genuinely antique, pair of Staffordshire Dogs.

Vases, porcelain jars, and urns are right at the top of the list of popular mantelpiece ornaments. They are especially sought after in pairs to achieve symmetry. A single vase can be placed to good effect in the center of the mantelpiece, flanked by two candelabra or lamps.

As its name suggests, a precious fireplace clock is the perfect choice to adorn the fireplace. Placed exactly in the middle, it shows the time – or perhaps not, for many an old specimen has long since stopped ticking. But that is no reason to part company with the treasured heirloom.

The Reproduction Fireplace – Pros and Cons

In his multi-volume work, *Das englische Haus* (The English House), published in 1903, the German architect and historian, Herman Muthesius, commented that it was indeed true that here and there you could find gas-operated imitation open fires, especially in houses belonging to philistines. Refined British people would rightly reject such fakes. Although this claim may have been valid in Muthesius' time (1861–1927), it would no longer be applicable today. The real-flame gas or electric fire has now gained general acceptance and adorns private living rooms, restaurants, and up-market stores alike.

Even just after the First World War, there was a whole range of electric fires that worked like heating radiators. The 1920s saw the arrival of coal-effect fires, and in the 1950s you could even get artificial glowing coals with gas flames that made them look so real they led to a revival of the traditional fireplace. People who had formerly ripped out their fireplace because it did not seem to be in keeping with the modern postwar apartment now reconverted the bare space back to its former glory with a replica fire acquired at great expense. There is now a wide range of electric and gas real-flame effect fires. A cheerful flame now appears at the touch of a button – even in apartments that never had a fireplace in the first place. Thus even people who are not lucky enough to live in a lovely old house can enjoy a real fire. Is a real fire from the socket or gas mains really so reprehensible? After all, we no longer roast our meat over an open fire – and if the electric cooker is a good enough substitute for the old stove to create coziness, why shouldn't the symbol of an open fireplace do the same?

The most important thing is to have a real flame – so say devotees of gas-operated real-flame effect fires. Whatever you may think, there's no denying one great advantage: there's no need to cart about logs or coal, or to think about sweeping out the dusty fireplace.

Fireplaces – a Brief Lesson in Style

A simple fireplace dating from the 16th century, with its distinctive stone lintel and brick hearth.

Ornate corbels and broad uprights enjoyed great popularity throughout the Regency period of the early 19th century.

Even in the Baroque period, fireplaces in ordinary houses were kept simple. People who could afford it preferred the expensive model with its highly decorative mantel.

Classical-style fireplaces were extremely popular in Georgian times. Town houses increasingly burned coal.

The 19th-century Victorian fireplace had cast iron grates for better air intake and slightly more economical fuel consumption.

The fireplace designers of the Edwardian period wanted to reduce fuel consumption by means of slanted sidewalls, direct air intake, and smaller grates.

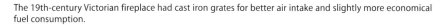

Companion Sets

Companion sets are essential to keep the fire going. Tongs are used to place the log in the best position in the embers. The poker breaks up the embers, and the shovel is used to add coal. The bellows are particularly useful if flames are not forthcoming.

It used to be the job of the domestic servants to keep the various fires of a large property burning, and this was no easy task. When a large country house was full of guests at the weekend, it took practically an army of servants to tend properly to each fire in each room. No considerate host wanted to run the risk of their guests complaining of cold feet or frozen wash basins. However, after the First World War, when the number of housekeepers, butlers, maids, servants, and other helping hands decreased noticeably, many homeowners suddenly found themselves forced to grab hold of the coal shovel and ash bucket. Companion sets, which until this time had been only of primarily aesthetic interest, were scrutinized carefully for more practical detail now that the masters of the house had to use them themselves.

You need a range of instruments to tend a fire and fireplace. Before lighting the fire, the fireplace should be thoroughly swept. The fire brush, which is used in conjunction with a suitable shovel, is appropriate for this task. If the fireplace has an integral grate, this will also need to be thoroughly cleared of dust, ashes, and deposits from time to time. This is best done with a long-handled brush. It is best to keep a couple of days' worth of logs or coal in a log basket or coal scuttle right by the fire. It goes without saying that neither the scuttle nor the basket should look so unattractive that they spoil the drawing room.

Just because the logs and coals have been laid and lit does not mean that you can leave the fire to its own devices. To set a fire correctly demands not only experience but also the right equipment. A poker and a small coal shovel are good when it comes to making the best use of logs or rearranging coals.

Managing an open fire sounds like a lot of hard work if you are used to the comfort of central heating and the electric radiator, but there is hardly a homeowner or guest who does not enjoy gazing dreamily into the flames. Looking after the burning coals can be very soothing. Even friends of a nervous disposition calm down when entrusted with the task of supervising the fire.

The materials storeroom at the Antique Fireplace Warehouse contains all types of raw materials needed to refurbish, repair, or construct new fireplaces, fireplace panels, and fittings. In addition to the various types of wood, it houses all sorts of parts and ornaments made of stone and marble until they are needed. There is a strong probability that you will find a solution here to almost any fireplace problem.

PARADISE FOR REAL FIRE DEVOTEES

Even in Britain there were some philistines who simply ripped out their old fireplaces, leaving the chimneys idle. Subsequent tenants or owners have not always bothered to restore the fireplace. But nowadays there are more options to help in such cases. For one thing, a look round an architectural salvage yard or a trip to the antique shop can sometimes prove worthwhile. Specialist fireplace stores are another possibility.

One such is the Antique Fireplace Warehouse in London run by brothers Paul and Nick Chesney. It was founded in 1982 and is now one of the leading suppliers of fireplaces and fire surrounds in all sorts of styles. If you want to see this paradise for fireplace devotees, just tell the cab driver to go to Battersea Park Road No. 194–202, where you will find the show-room displaying the firm's extensive range.

In the Antique Fireplace Warehouse, there is a solution to practically any fireplace problem. For one thing, it stocks over 120 English and French originals from the 18th and 19th centuries. New acquisitions constantly supplement this store of antique objects. The range really is staggering, from simple Victorian bedroom fireplaces to the most exquisite marble chimney pieces dating from the 18th century. If you don't hit lucky with the old originals, you can turn to an extensive range of true-to-style reproductions from the company's own workshops. These are exact copies of the most beautiful antique examples and are manufactured with the utmost care by hand.

If you have enough money, you can also have a fireplace specially made. In this case, mantelpieces or even whole fireplaces are designed exclusively for the client and then constructed using stone or marble by experienced craftsmen. This can be interesting when an existing fireplace in the house needs to be copied for another room. The custom-made fireplace service is also good if you want to bring individual and original ideas to life.

The Antique Fireplace Warehouse also offers a wide range of cast-iron grates and fire baskets for both coal- and wood-burning fires. Whatever you buy in Battersea, it can be delivered and installed throughout the United Kingdom, so it is certainly worth a visit for anyone interested in fireplaces.

To restore a marble fireplace, a craftsman needs sensitivity and flair. The natural material is extremely fragile and excessive force on the chisel will cause it to split immediately. The company stonemasons also finish stone fireplaces and supply individual commissions. This is where their work overlaps with that of curators of monuments and restorers, who often turn to the specialists in Battersea when the fireplaces in a historic building are involved.

Old fireplaces and reproductions wait for a buyer in the sales rooms. If, despite the huge range, you can't find what you're looking for there, don't give up. The Antique Fireplace Warehouse also supplies fireplaces made to order.

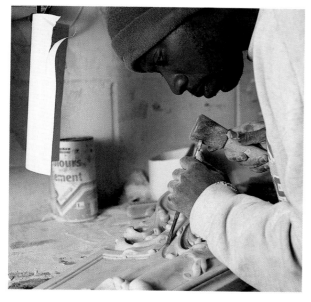

Typical Living Room Furniture

What good would an armchair be without an occasional table? It's essential, of course, to have somewhere to put your drink!

Although British living rooms may sometimes seem to be a mish-mash just casually thrown together, their owners usually apply an obvious principle of room furnishing. The pieces are often arranged around the fireplace symmetrically, so you immediately feel at home in any house furnished in a traditional style.

Whereas in other countries of the world the boundaries between dining room, living room, library, and even kitchen have been deliberately blurred to create multi-functional living spaces, many people in Britain still divide the rooms up strictly according to use. As a result, the furniture and fittings of the living room usually serve the main functions of that room: conversation, relaxation, television, card or board games, or just drinking tea. The seating is of primary importance. Armchairs and sofas come in all sorts of shapes and sizes, inviting in their soft upholstery. But alongside the main group of seats, there are also single armchairs for

anyone who does not want to join in the conversation, perhaps because they want to read a magazine or book. Tables and benches of various heights and sizes, depending on their function, are an essential complement to these sofas and armchairs.

The idea that living room furniture should have a fixed position dates from the 19th century. In the 18th century, however, the custom was to move the furniture as and when needed. Only when the room was vacated, before retiring to bed for example, would the occupants, or more probably the servants, return the chairs and tables to their place along the wall. The middle of the room was left clear. The flexible arrangement of the furnishings was, of course, also necessary because of the sources of heat and light used at that time. During the day, the occupants of the house stayed by the windows because of the sunlight, moving in the evening to the warmth of the open fire.

The sofa just has to be the most important piece of furniture in a British living room. It comes in a wide variety of shapes and in innumerable covers. The main requirements of a sofa are comfort and a cover that can be removed for cleaning or of the kind that won't show the dirt.

The wing chair is a real classic. This type of chair came into fashion as early as the late 17th century. It was designed to provide protection against dangerous drafts from behind.

Even though the British are thought of as a nation of tea-drinkers, they actually also drink a lot of coffee. The quality of the dark brew has improved considerably in the last few years. Whereas tourists used to be able to claim with justification that people in Britain drink tea only because the coffee is so bad, this is no longer the case. To be in keeping with British style, coffee should be served on a low coffee table from the Regency period.

The ottoman is an absolutely typical accessory of the British living room. It is used for storage and as an extra seat. It often has castors instead of legs, so it can be pushed wherever it is required.

Nowadays, the Canterbury is mostly bought and used as a newspaper rack. Originally, however, it was used to store sheet music and music notebooks. The Canterbury is a popular item not only in the living room but also in libraries and smoking-rooms.

The pier table is a narrow table placed along the wall between two windows. It nearly always has a mirror above it. This traditional arrangement acts as a focal point in a room, especially if there is no fireplace, and emphasizes the symmetry of the windows.

The mirror is an absolutely typical feature of the British living room. It usually hangs above the mantelpiece, but can sometimes be found above the pier table. Mirrors help to enlarge and brighten a room. A mirror can reflect and almost double the light of a lamp or the sunlight streaming in through the window.

The drum table is just as likely to be found in the living room as in the entrance hall or library. It usually dominates the middle of the room and is used for reading, writing, or as a table for books or magazines. Writing paper and equipment are kept in its drawers.

The butler's tray is a tray on a foldaway frame or with extendible legs. This way, the tray could be laid with tea, biscuits, and cutlery, carried, and then set up wherever people wished to take their refreshments. This makes it still extremely useful.

Like the sofa, the armchair is an essential part of the living room. It has the advantage that you have it to yourself. Although not furniture, paintings and drawings are still essential. They really give the living room its sense of tradition and family history.

A desk is no stranger to the living room. It is often placed behind a sofa so that it is incorporated into the overall arrangement of the room.

A British living room would be inconceivable without at least one table lamp. However, they look even better in pairs. The preferred position for lamps is to the right and left of a piece of furniture, since this reinforces the idea of symmetry.

A Sofa for the Living Room

Nothing makes a living room more inviting than a large, softly upholstered sofa. That is why every British drawing room has at least one of them, for here comfort has a capital C. This is particularly true of the living room that is actually used by the family. In formal reception rooms, on the other hand, such as are found in large houses, people would feel less inclined to relax and put their feet up on the sofa.

The traditional sofa differs from the modern designer models chiefly in its sumptuous upholstery and dizzying pattern. There are good reasons for both of these. The upholstery ensures comfort, and the pattern makes this well-used piece of furniture impervious to stains. Specks of dirt are less obvious on luxuriant flowers or brightly-colored checks. As nearly all dogs are allowed to sit on the sofa at the side of their masters, loose covers and throws that are easy to remove and clean are extremely useful.

Most people in Britain believe a sofa should be upholstered in such a way that only a few minutes after sitting down you will feel an overpowering need to sleep. In actual fact, nearly all sofas of British origin have this property. The size of the sofa depends on the dimensions of the room. If there is enough space, choose at least one large three-seater sofa, or preferably two if at all possible, facing each other in front of the fire.

Then there are the various armchairs, principally for guests, for three people hardly ever sit together on a sofa – unless they are family or very close friends. Since upholstered seats were originally a great luxury that only the seriously rich could afford, sofa designers did not have to take small living rooms into consideration in their work. Such upholstered furniture was not adapted to the dimensions of smaller living rooms until industrialization brought sofas and armchairs within the reach of everyone's pocket. In the 1920s, the average suite comprised a two-seater sofa and two armchairs. Owners of large properties, on the other hand, are blissfully unaware of the problem of lack of space. The problem they face is that in their spacious drawing rooms even the largest sofa looks rather lost.

The basic shape of the sofas commonly found today developed from the divans of Classical times and the settles of the Middle Ages. Thus the sofas of the 18th century were constructed like a bench with upholstered seat, back, and arms, but with the remaining timber framework visible. Although some seats may look to us like two-seater sofas, they were in actual fact intended for only one person. The seat was actually made wide because of the fashion of that time, since it enabled the ladies to sit down despite their voluminous skirts and stiff crinolines.

Above: A sofa is no good unless you can stretch out comfortably on it to watch the evening news (or the children's programs). That is the unanimous view of many inhabitants of the British Isles. Beautifully shaped designer furniture, with its uninviting seats, is therefore unpopular.

The chaise longue – also called a daybed, reclining couch, or *récamière* – is not really a sofa, but actually an armchair with an extremely elongated seat. These pieces of furniture, often firmly and generously upholstered, were particularly common in the Regency period.

Knole sofa with collapsible arms. Extremely comfortable for an afternoon snooze or as an emergency bed after a dinner party.

The time between the Victorian and the modern era produced excellent reproductions, as for example this two-seater sofa in neo-Regency style.

Modern two-seater sofa in 1920s style. Such sumptuous upholstery was not possible until the invention of spiral springs at the end of the 19th century.

The seat was often relatively shallow compared with the high back of the chair. This was to prevent slouching. To be accurate, people actually lay down only on 19th-century chaises longues. It was not until the Victorian era, from 1837 until 1901, that sofas grew to the size that we now consider so typically British. Cushions were influenced by oriental divans and became huge and plumped up. They were an expression of a furnishing style that almost overloaded the rooms with furniture and decorative items. In the Edwardian period, from 1901, interiors became slightly more relaxed once again, and in the 1930s a furnishing style developed that can still be seen today. It involves a mix of styles that combines the elegance of the 18th century with the dark leather, deep buttoned Victorian club atmosphere, but permeated by the 20th-century feeling of cheerful formlessness. In contrast to the originals from this time, nowadays timber parts are usually no longer visible, the basic carcass being totally covered with upholstery and covers. Only the wooden feet are still sometimes left exposed. Only designer furniture that toys with Classical ingredients still reveals the wood. This mixture of old and new that is so typical of British rooms leads to other differences in

the seats. Whereas people like to invest in old armchairs, easy chairs, and ordinary chairs, it is totally acceptable to buy a new sofa. Old upholstered furniture seldom pops up in the antiques trade, and the fastenings on the covers and upholstery are rarely the originals or are badly worn. Another advantage of a new sofa is that it can be custom-made for a specific living room. If you are prepared to spend the necessary cash, you can even today get very high-quality craftsmanship. Thus the floral chintz sofa that would send shivers up the spine of any admirer of functional, minimalist furniture can easily cost several times as much as an elegant piece made of leather and chrome. And as well as comfort, it has the invaluable added advantage that it will be contemporary for much longer, precisely because of the fact that it was never fashionable in the first place.

Georgian-style three-seater sofa. Original 18th-century furniture was not fully upholstered.

Edwardian three-seater sofa, highly decorative, yet still comfortable. It differs from the Chesterfield sofa in the more slender shape of the armrests and back.

Chesterfield. With its leather upholstery, it is mainly to be found in rooms that receive many guests, such as clubs or hotel lounges for example.

How an Armchair is Made

Even the coziest armchair was originally made of hard wood. It takes the skill of the upholsterer to make it comfy. Depending on the shape of the armchair, the back is filled with upholstery material, buttoned, or sprung. A timber frame forms the base of the back. Elastic or spiral springs can be used to add extra cushioning to the back padding. Felt and molded strips are used to shape the front ends of the armrests and the edge of the back. The armrest is formed from layers of webbing, sacking, stuffing felt, high-density foam, and fibers. A fire-resistant lining is stretched over the base of the chair. The cushion and padding fillings are also fire-resistant.

Foam rubber or real feathers or down can be used for the seat cushion. It is really just a matter of personal taste. In the case of a good armchair, the covers will be cut and made up by hand, so that the nap of the material runs smoothly between the various parts of the chair. Sacking and synthetic fibers are used to line the cover fabric to protect against wear and tear. The front edge of the seating area is finished with a molded section, fitted over several layers of foam rubber, felt, and fibers, to produce a durable yet flexible base. Struts are then fitted to the corners of the timber frame, sometimes together with casters. All in all, a lot of work, most of which can be done only by hand. But such an armchair will last a good bit longer.

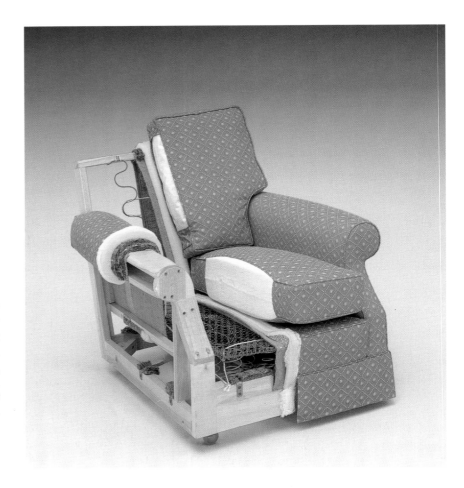

Above: Sectional view of an armchair made by the famous manufacturer Duresta of Nottinghamshire, showing the various components of the armchair.

Top, far left: The frame of a high-quality upholstered chair is made from solid hard wood, carefully doweled, bonded, or screwed together by hand. The sections for the frame are also cut by hand.

Top, left: Firms such as Duresta still upholster armchairs, sofas, and benches by hand. Such furniture may of course be a little more expensive, but it will last much longer than many cheaper examples.

Below, far left: It is a long way from the length of material as it comes from the mill to the finished armchair. First the material must be cut to keep the continuity of the pattern, then sewn together, and finally the individual buttons are put in place.

Below, left: At Duresta, many details are handsewn onto the fabric cover, such as piping, which can add interest to the edge of a chair. It takes a great many hours to complete a piece of furniture.

The Sofa Cushion

A sofa needs at least two cushions. The sofa shown above has so many that there is hardly any space between them. To British minds, upholstered furniture is not correctly and sufficiently adorned until you have difficulty finding room to sit.

All you need to do to fully appreciate the importance of the sofa cushion for the character of a room is to imagine the interior without this movable padding. The furniture suddenly looks empty and dull; the room lacks a certain something. Barely any other decorative ploy says so much about the arrangement of a room as the careful positioning of attractive sofa cushions. Of course, it is reliant on it being the right cushion arranged in the correct way on the sofa. Both of these aspects are totally different from the neat, serried ranks of cushions on parade in continental living rooms, which are not considered really beautiful until the housewife has applied the finishing touch with a well-directed slap with the side of her hand. Under no circumstances should you dare to disturb or push aside such cushion sculptures, or even use them for their original purpose. They are as sacrosanct a part of the decoration as the collection of cups in the carefully locked china cabinet and the unread magazines in the newspaper rack.

The British sofa cushion has nothing in common with its untouched, dust-harboring relatives in mainland Europe. Its sole purpose is to enhance the comfort of the sofa user. British cushions can take a lot of punishment. They don't mind supporting tired backs, being squashed up under your head for an afternoon snooze, or making a cozy nest for the cat. British cushions are also hard-wearing and provide a contrast with the usual mix of styles. As a general rule, the cushions should not match too closely in color and decoration, because they should look as though they had been scattered on the sofa by chance. Analysts could spend a long time contemplating a typically British sofa with its collection of cushions in an attempt to discover the underlying hidden logic of its composition. The fact of the matter is that there isn't any logic behind it. Patterns, colors, and materials are chosen for each individual cushion intuitively and affectionately. Roughly

speaking, the motto is: "I love Paisley, I love Tattersall check, and I love tartans, so let's have them all on the sofa." Fans of matching décor are constantly surprised how well this hodge-podge looks in the room. It would also be terribly boring if a pale blue sofa always had only three identical cushions with dark blue, pale blue, or even pink stripes. It is also quite important to avoid too close a match between the cushions and the curtain material, as this gives the room the air of sterile perfection found in a humorous catalog photograph.

In Britain, you can buy cushion covers anywhere that sells furniture, fabrics, curtains, and accessories. If you cannot find ready-made cushion covers to suit, you can always have them sewn up, or alternatively reach for the scissors, thread, and sewing machine yourself. You can often buy cheap remnants of wonderful fabrics that make excellent cushions. Experienced cushion sewers also like making use of old textiles. It does not matter if they are slightly damaged and can therefore no longer be used for a chair cover or curtain. With a bit of ingenuity, you can stumble across real gems in the fabric departments of major stores that, when made up into a cushion, give the sofa a really personal note.

How the House was Lit

The further back you go in history, the darker the houses were. Medieval houses must have been almost terrifyingly dark. Hardly any sun could get through the tiny windows, so that meager tallow lamps or candles were lit even during the day. In the kitchen, the hearth with its open fire provided a little brightness. In the 16th century, people built larger windows, but glass was still the preserve of the rich. They were also able to afford luxurious torchères, or suspend candles from the ceiling. But even these did not light the rooms at all brightly.

Although the trend toward ever larger windows did at least provide for somewhat brighter rooms during the day, people still had to resort to candles with the onset of darkness even in the 17th century. The candles were now placed in reflective wall brackets. As with the chandeliers that were beginning to come into fashion, their purpose was to reflect the light by way of glass crystal and gilt decoration. Until the second half of the 18th century, the number of candleholders increased constantly and people experimented with large mirrors, but despite this, there was no significant improvement in the lighting situation. People were always having to move the important furniture to follow the light. Apart from the pieces of furniture that were part of the primary arrangement of the room, occasional tables or groups of chairs, tables, and chairs were now so light that it was easy to move them to the brightest window.

There was no sign of any end to the dark ages until the middle of the 19th century. In addition to candles and oil lamps, the first gaslights now burned in ceiling and wall lamps. There had already been initial attempts with this new technology in the 18th century, when, for example, George Dixon, a miner from Durham, lit his house using gas in 1789. He achieved this by heating coal in a kettle, conducting the gas produced through a system of pipes made from tobacco pipe stems stuck together with glue, and then lighting the gas at the exit points that he had drilled into the pipes at regular intervals. The engineer William Murdoch subsequently managed to develop a similar system to a practical level.

The tallow lamp used to be a cheap but time-consuming alternative to the candle. The fat-soaked wick from the peeled stem of the rush was fitted into a special holder and then lit. It had to be pushed upward again every 15–20 minutes to prevent the flame from going out. Despite this, tallow lamps continued to be used into the 20th century.

Gaslight marked significant progress over candlelight, especially the invention of the incandescent mantel by Baron von Welsbach in the 1890s. This technical discovery not only emitted a brighter light, but also helped to save gas. English houses were not lit by electricity until 1881. However, it was another 40 years before electricity could reach every corner of the United Kingdom.

Together with his partner, Samuel Clegg, he developed the first gas lamps for industrial concerns. These produced so much heat that they had to be erected outside, in front of the workshop windows. By the mid-19th century, gas lamps were increasingly popular in private houses, bringing about significant progress over earlier times.

The invention of the light bulb by the American Thomas Edison and the Englishman Joseph Swan in 1878 marked the beginning of a new era. However, at first only a few households could benefit from electric light. Lord Kelvin in Glasgow and Lord William Armstrong in Cragside were among the first people to be able to switch their lights on and off to their hearts' content as early as 1881. But it was a good 40 years before everyone could enjoy the revolutionary lighting system.

One reason for this was that the government granted the gasworks lobby a long transition period. As with all technical innovations, warning bells were sounded with the introduction of electric light. It was, for example, thought that the excessive brightness of electric light would put too much strain on the optic nerve. There were also fears that human and animal life spans could be shortened if the nightly rest period was suddenly brightly lit and the day no longer came to a natural end. At the beginning, there were of course technical difficulties and accidents. And many people simply refused to exchange their gaslights for electric ones, although not always for ideological reasons or even plain fear. In his capacity as Director of the Clevedon Gas Company, Sir Ambrose Elton protested against the new competition by continuing to use gaslights in his house until his death in 1951. Even so, the triumphal procession of electric light was unstoppable. It marked the dawn of a new era, in which you could banish the darkness of the night from your house at the flick of a switch.

A ceiling light is necessary, especially in larger living rooms. In this case, small table and standard lamps often provide insufficient light. A ceiling light can provide constant basic lighting or deliberately highlight the center of a room.

CONSTRUCTING A LAMP

Christopher Wray Lighting in London's King's Road is one of the most interesting places for homeowners looking for lighting. It is almost impossible not to find what you are looking for among the 6,000-plus fittings and accessories on sale there. You can choose from original and reproduction antique lamps.

At the beginning of the 1960s, there was nothing to suggest that Christopher Wray would make his fortune illuminating houses and apartments, for at that time acting was the profession of the future lighting expert. But the dream part never came, and so in the Swinging Sixties Wray specialized in selling old oil and gas lamps, which were coming onto the antique market in the mid-1960s as many country houses went over to electricity.

Wray did such a roaring trade in the old originals that he started to manufacture reproductions. In order for their construction to be as close as possible to the originals, the resourceful ex-actor acquired two tradi-

tional firms that guaranteed the supply of authentic lamps. Landon & Co. in Birmingham, established in 1898, supplied brass and copper parts, and Grantley of Yorkshire, which had been founded in the 1940s as Translucent Glass in Wakefield, supplied the glass components. Christopher Wray considered the major expenditure incurred in manufacturing the lamps to be absolutely justified: "It may take longer to make our lamps, but they last a lifetime."

The expert in Victorian and Edwardian light fittings also knows that design did not come to a halt with the outbreak of the First World War, which is why one of his numerous branches is devoted solely to selling modern light fittings. For a good many years now, Christopher Wray has even been designing his own models. "No matter how much I love old lights, I just cannot ignore good, contemporary design. On the one hand, I buy lights from specialized European designers, on the other I produce modern lamps and increasingly my own designs. It is an extremely exciting new development for us."

Weights are dropped to shape the copper or brass lamp bases. This process is known as drop stamping.

Molten lead is poured into a stamping die for drop stamping. The metal that is going to be worked with this positive die must first be heated to make it soft to prevent the workpiece from cracking.

Before varnishing, the individual components of the lamp are polished. Even if machines are used, each of the tiny parts still needs the craftsman's attentive eye to detail.

Many of the lamps manufactured in Christopher Wray's Birmingham factory are made up of numerous, labor-intensive component parts soldered together by hand.

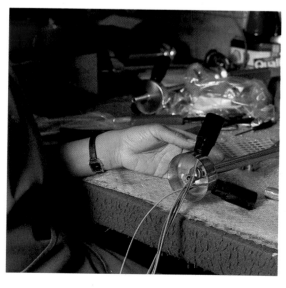

The component parts of the lamps are then screwed together and the cable drawn through. This is also done by hand, of course. But it takes a great many working hours for the lamp to get to this stage.

When the lamp is finished, it is put through a thorough test, not only to check that it works perfectly, but also that it complies with European safety standards.

Restoring a Crystal Chandelier

Top left: The first step is to dismantle the chandelier totally. This alone requires a considerable degree of skill if there is to be no damage. It is also important that nothing gets lost or comes apart, as you should have just as many parts at the end as you did at the beginning, and it must be possible to put everything back in its place again.

Top center: It is important to use the correct cleaning solution for the basic frame of the crystal chandelier. All parts are then cleaned and later polished again by hand. A very expensive job, but worth it, however, in the view of many Britons. Specialist firms cannot complain of a lack of orders for restoring antique chandeliers.

Top right: Over many decades, the steam rising from the food and the smoke from the cigars have left their mark on the crystal elements of an antique chandelier. It therefore comes as no surprise that the chandelier has lost its luster. A thorough polish frees the hand cut crystals from the deposits of such pleasures and returns them to their original brilliance.

Far left: The difference between a crystal chandelier and a used car is not as great as you might first think. Both can increase considerably in value after a thorough clean. Nowadays the antique dealers keep the restorers in business.

Left: No "before and after" comparison could be more striking than that of a crystal chandelier before and after cleaning. Like a mirror that, when it's been dusted thoroughly, seems to open a window on the wall facing it, a crystal chandelier looks as good as new after its treatment.

The crystal chandelier may seem very English in all its splendor, but in actual fact it did not find its way into British living rooms until very late on. Crystal chandeliers were not manufactured in the British Isles until about 1780, when they also began to be used more in house interiors. The older examples were imported from Venice, their real place of origin. The crystal chandelier cannot really be considered as being an essential part of British home décor until Regency times. Lavish costume dramas used to suggest a different, considerably brighter picture of the light situation, but film directors have recently changed over to lighting evening scenes as they really used to be. And they looked very dark indeed. This was due in part to the price of high quality candles. Sir Thomas Robinson reported in 1728 that, at a dinner held to mark the visit of the Duke of Lorraine, the hall of Houghton Hall in Norfolk was lit by 130 candles and the drawing room by 50 wax lights, entered in the books at £15 a night.

Despite all its disadvantages from an objective viewpoint, the crystal chandelier lit by genuine wax candles has not yet totally disappeared. People still like cozy, flattering candlelight. This is why antique chandeliers continue to be brought for repair to specialist firms such as Christopher Wray Lighting, so that it is possible for them to sparkle with their original luster once more.

CLEANING AND CARE

Owning a house and making it beautiful is one thing – looking after it and keeping it clean is quite another. That involves the daily battle against dust and dirt, not only for purely aesthetic reasons but often also for reasons of hygiene too – especially in areas where food is handled. A glance in the carefully tiled dairies where milk was made into butter, cheese, and other perishables, or the larders where food was stored in historic country houses gives an idea of the high standards of earlier culinary practice.

But other areas of the house were also kept fastidiously clean. The army of chambermaids and other servants was commanded by the housekeeper and was equipped with a wide variety of implements for the laborious and sometimes strenuous work. The floors of much-frequented halls and corridors required particular care. Dust was best swept away using a broad broom (top right), whereas stubborn or ingrained dirt was removed using a coarse scrubbing brush. Then, depending on the type of floor covering, the floor would be scrubbed, polished, or treated with special preparations for parquet flooring. The fact that some of the wonderful floors have been preserved is due to the meticulous care lavished on them in the past.

Floor coverings were not the only things to be maintained and preserved. Many properties owned by the nobility and upper middle classes housed extensive collections of valuable furniture, lamps, silver, and other treasures. Protecting them all from harm was one of the housekeeper's main tasks. If some rooms were not in use, they were thoroughly cleaned, and the furniture covered with large sheets to protect them from dust and, of course, sunlight, which would otherwise rob the fine upholstered covers of their brilliant color.

Rooms that were in constant use had to be heated daily or the fires had to be lit daily – at least in the winter. The fireplaces made for extra dust and sometimes even rust. As each cleaning job had an intrinsic risk of damage or even breakage, there was a whole range of special brooms, brushes, and feather dusters. The fireplace itself was cleaned using an ash pan set. Then the floor in front of the fireplace had to be swept with a dustpan and brush (center). Fragile ornamental items such as vases, clocks, statues, and sculptures were dusted with a feather or fine goat hair duster, while a smaller kind of dusting brush was used for smaller ornaments. But it was not just dust and rust that kept the domestic servants on the go. There were also insects and vermin to contend with. These intruders were removed from cupboards using a special cupboard brush (second from the left), and the spider brush (second from the right) was used to remove spiders and their disfiguring webs.

Cleaning Silver

The large silver collections in many houses in the British Isles often date back to times when servants were charged with the responsibility of cleaning the precious metal that is so quick to tarnish. Nowadays, many a castle-owner has to reach for the cleaning cloth himself – and probably now appreciates that the laborious task of cleaning silver is one of the more thankless household chores.

Silver quickly oxidizes and becomes tarnished. Regular cleaning is the only solution. As well as creams and liquids that are applied and then polished off, there are also cleaning solutions and gloves impregnated with a cleaning agent.

Gleaming silver would be easier to enjoy if it stayed that way for longer. However, unfortunately it is never long before it becomes tarnished and you have to reach for the cleaning cloth again.

AFTERNOON TEA

The idea of afternoon tea is perhaps the most persistent cliché applied to England. It may well be the case that there are people in England who have never thought of meeting up for an afternoon tea of sandwiches, scones, and clotted cream, because they reject this ritual as being only for tourists. Perhaps many British people would now even prefer a cappuccino or a coke. Nevertheless, afternoon tea does still exist, and most British people partake of it either at home or in a hotel – whether or not the tourists do too.

A visit to the Regent Room in the renowned Claridge's Hotel, or the tearoom in the Ritz, or Fortnum & Mason's restaurant proves that this time-honored tradition is still held in high esteem, and not just by the blue-rinse brigade. Quite simply, high tea is just a popular meal that restores you after a shopping spree. It is also a good occasion to discuss business matters.

The ritual is always the same. In the event of an invitation to tea at someone's house, the host or hostess behaves in exactly the same way as the waiter in a hotel. First, tea is served when the guest has expressed their wishes with regard to the type of tea. Large hotels often offer their own blends, which are then brought to the table freshly brewed in a large teapot. There is also another pot containing hot water to dilute the tea if it becomes too strong during the course of the meal. The tealeaves are usually left in the teapot, where they can carry on infusing. A small silver strainer prevents them from being poured into the cup. The food starts off basically wholesome, and then progresses to the sweet things, in just the same way as at lunch or dinner.

English afternoon tea or high tea, whether taken at home or in a hotel, is always a full-blown nutritious meal.

Although they can be double-deckers, the sandwiches are small enough to be eaten with the fingers. Typical fillings are roast beef, cream cheese with cress, cucumber or smoked salmon. For the sweet part of afternoon tea, the cook's imagination knows no bounds. As well as scones (tea cake) with clotted cream and jam, English muffins, apple pie, meringues, or sponge cake, there are also petits fours or proper desserts such as sticky toffee pudding.

At a private afternoon tea with friends, guests can be served totally different delicacies, as the lady of the house sees fit. Whatever is served, however, afternoon tea is usually a main meal where you are best advised to try just a little of everything on the menu, so that you don't have to capitulate too soon.

Tea is served in all the large hotels during the afternoon, but usually from as early as two or three o'clock. It is advisable to book at the famous addresses, such as Claridge's or the Ritz. If you turn up as a tourist in shorts and T-shirt, you run the risk of being turned away, especially if you have not reserved a table. If you have not had time to telephone beforehand, wearing a respectable suit should increase your chances of getting a table. Though, a tie no longer seems to be compulsory, not even in Claridge's.

Outside of London, there are also a great many hotels, restaurants, and tearooms serving excellent afternoon teas. There are plenty of beautiful places to chose from when you set off on a trip to the country side such as one of the many renowned National Trust sites. In any event, it is worth a look.

Claridge's, the traditional London hotel, still remains one of the best places to experience a stylish British tea ceremony.

It is advisable to book if you want to take afternoon tea in the Savoy. It is also best to look presentable, perhaps a smart skirt and jacket for her, and jacket and tie for him.

No proper afternoon tea is complete without scones (tea cake). They must be moist yet crumbly in texture. Experienced scone eaters can see as soon as they cut into the little cake, or more precisely from the way it crumbles, whether this has been successfully achieved.

Clotted cream is served in a bowl with the scones. It looks like a mixture between whipped cream and butter and is the classic accompaniment for this crumbly pastry. Spread thickly or thinly on the scone, it forms the base for the jam.

Jam is then spread on the buttered scone and clotted cream. After sampling this delicacy, you may begin to feel the first hints of having eaten your fill. Marmelade, as continental visitors know it, is called jam. The British marmelade is made of citrus fruits – usually oranges – with thin or thick cut slices of the peel, and to the foreign tongue tastes rather bitter.

Far left: Tea was totally unheard of in Britain until 1657. This situation was changed by a gentleman called Thomas Garway, who ran a coffeehouse in the city of London. It was in that year that he offered his customers the curious, exotic beverage for the first time. However, it was not until the middle of the 18th century that tea gained general acceptance.

Center: A real sandwich must be very soft. Even the crusts are removed in sophisticated circles. Typical sandwich fillings are cream cheese, cress, cucumber, or smoked salmon.

Left: After the scones (tea cake), you should have no compunction about going on to enjoy more sweet delicacies. A petit four is still permissible, and many a hardened afternoon tea connoisseur would even have room for a portion of sticky toffee pudding or chocolate cake.

Below: Boiling water is added to a specific amount of tea, which is then left to infuse. This ensures that the professional tea taster can reliably check that the quality of the tea remains constant. The tealeaves are left on the inside of the lid to await expert scrutiny.

Most British houses regularly have guests to stay for the weekend. Visitors are never bored, because they can always take time out to leaf through the coffee table books laid out ready for them.

Coffee Table Books

The book on the coffee table is an integral part of the British living room, just like the fireplace and the chintz sofa. Coffee table books are mainly large-format picture books – serious novels or copies of the classics are usually banished to the library. The books displayed in living rooms, on the other hand, should not present any excessive mental demands, but should merely invite the reader to leaf through them casually. This predilection for large-format, glossy books may have something to do with the British dislike of open displays of intellectual ideas. It demands just as much attention to look at a photograph album as it does to read the *Tatler* or the magazine *Country Life*. The British living room is in any case no place for learned discussions or demanding reading. It is somewhere to chat, to have a bit of a laugh, but not

Many a book enthusiast may turn up their nose and say that books in British houses are really only there for decoration rather than to be read. But it is precisely these large-format, lavishly-illustrated coffee table books that give every living room its cozy, interesting, cheery feel.

to put your education under the spotlight. A book of color photographs is a picture book for grown-ups, and is usually used as such – for entertainment.

Sometimes these books are actually just pure decoration. Magazines are provided for anyone who finds a thick art book too heavy-going in every sense of the word. The magazines may even be read attentively if they concern horses, homes and gardens, or are humorous. A typical British selection of magazines might contain the society magazine *Tatler*, together with *Horse and Hound*, the staple of all horse lovers, *Private Eye*, a humorous and satirical magazine, together with the *National Trust Magazine*. Other magazine classics are *Homes & Gardens*, *Country Living*, and *Period Living & Traditional Homes*. Catalogs are just as popular as magazines; for example those issued by Sotheby's or Christie's auction houses, or by interior design companies such as Laura Ashley, Mulberry, Habitat, and department stores such as Harrods or Liberty. Of course, everyone has different interests, and depending on the host's ambitions in matters relating to style and taste, a magazine that is perhaps too focused on the country house style will be replaced by the *Architectural Digest*. The choice of reading matter generally reflects the appropriate taste in interior design, and the one could lead you to make a reasonably accurate guess about the other. Anyone buying the hunting magazine *Field* from the station kiosk is probably on their way to a traditional home with chintz, mahogany, and brass. *Elle Decoration* and *Architectural Digest*, on the other hand, would suggest a modern, trendy interior. Naturally, the homeowner's particular hobby is reflected in the titles made available, whether they are car magazines, a specialist magazine for ornithologists, or a publication for arms buffs.

OTTOMANS AND FOOTSTOOLS

A typical feature of British furnishing style is the upholstered table, bench, and footstool, which go by various names in English depending on size and style: stool, footstool, ottoman, or box ottoman. They are usually placed at the center of a group of seats arranged around the fireplace and take the place of the sofa table popular in continental Europe. Depending on the firmness of the upholstery, they are used more as a seat or table, although they often fulfill both these functions. In Great Britain the sofa table is placed behind, not in front of the sofa, so the tea tray is placed on the ottoman or footstool, where it is within easy reach of everyone. The table behind the sofa, on the other hand, is often used as a small bar or for vases, plants, and other decorative objects.

Some ottomans can be opened like a chest to reveal practical storage space, often used for board games, old newspapers, and magazines or toys. These are called box ottomans. If the chest-shaped cavity is not accessible, they are simply ottomans. If they are too small and low to sit on, they serve as footstools. If they can be used as a seat or as a low table, they are usually called a stool or ottoman. Appropriately, the footstool is placed in front of an armchair, whereas the undefined stool, on the other hand, is placed in the middle of a group of seats or even in front of the fire. In the case of sofas and armchairs that are placed far apart, there can be both a stool and a couple of extra tables to fill up the space between the upholstered furniture with places to put drinks, etc. In most cases, however, the stool is so heavily laden with books or magazines that it can be used neither as somewhere to sit nor as somewhere to put the tea tray.

In most British homes, however, whether grandiose houses or small flats, no objection would be raised to a courageous attempt to clear a stool or ottoman, because a museum-like, "Please do not touch" atmosphere is definitely taboo. So many books on interior design and décor advise the reader to arrange the furniture so that a new grouping can always be created if required. Above all else, in the rooms lived in by the family, comfort and informality have top priority. No other piece of furniture expresses this idea better than an ottoman that can be used to support a heavily-laden tray, as a table for a game of Monopoly, as the cat's favorite spot, or as an improvised TV chair. That is why the ottoman in all its guises is practically an essential part of the British way of life.

There is often an ottoman instead of a coffee table. It has the advantage that it can also be used as an extra seat.

A somewhat lower ottoman can also be used as a somewhere for a tea tray or as a footstool.

An upholstered footrest may be a wiser choice in a smaller room, where an ottoman would be overpowering.

The circular ottoman looks inviting from all angles.

The fabric cover of an ottoman or footstool can add a colorful note to a room.

Country House Pastimes

When the weather is so bad that even the hardy British won't set foot outside their door, this is the time for country house pastimes. Rainy Sundays and long winter evenings may have lost some of their horror through television and radio, but traditional diversions are still popular. Unlike passively watching entertainment programs, handicrafts, making music, sewing, reading, and letter writing give the satisfying feeling of having done something worthwhile. From the 16th century to the beginning of the 20th, particularly in the countryside, there were not many diversions. As a result, people stayed at home, often by extremely poor light and with fingers numb with cold, creating lavish embroideries, repairing items of clothing, arranging shells collected on the coast into intricate pictures, building models, devouring novels and travelogs, filling albums with cut-out pictures, postcards, and drawings, and the pages of diaries with exhaustive reports. The fact that even today many Britons spend time in a creative way cannot just be a question of nostalgia, but must also be seen as a way of ensuring traditions do not die out.

Television is an essential part of modern life, in Britain just as much as anywhere else in the world. But the TV set is often thought out of place in the drawing room. People therefore prefer to keep it in private rooms, such as the bedroom, dressing room, library, or study.

When people talk of handicraft as a way of passing the time in the British country house, they do not mean the maid darning socks, or the washerwoman repairing a sheet. What they really mean is the lady of the house making long winter evenings or endless rainy days pass more quickly by doing her tapestry. Cushion covers decorated with pictures, names, or proverbs are particularly popular.

Music has always played a major role in British country life. House concerts had a firm place in family life in times before any interest in music was restricted mainly to listening to tape-recorders. Before they became generally available, you either had to play an instrument yourself or else employ musicians.

Many British country houses have libraries that would fill any keen reader with enthusiasm. Even today, spending a happy hour reading on the sofa or armchair is still one of the favorite pastimes in Britain – not just in the country, but also in the town.

Jigsaw puzzles are said to be one of the Queen's favorite pastimes. She shares her passion for this test of patience with thousands of her subjects, who while away many a long winter's evening creating pictures out of an apparently infinite number of individual pieces.

There is nowhere better to write letters than in an English country house, sitting at an antique desk and writing an amusing report of last weekend's huntball – naturally on personal headed notepaper from the aristocratic stationery store of Smythson's in Sloane Street.

The game of billiards became popular throughout British country houses from the 17th century. In the late 18th century, the green table was even part of the standard furniture of such an estate. Initially, it was placed in the entrance hall. In Victorian times, the separate billiards room came into fashion, often connected to the smoking room. It was usually on the ground floor of the house, as the table with its slab of slate was too heavy for the upper floor. Women even joined in the game. Thus in Wilkie Collins' novel *The Woman in White*, the protagonist, Marian Halcombe, promises the new arrival, Mr Hartright, an evening's entertainment that includes a game of billiards: "I don't know one note of music from the other; but I can match you at chess, backgammon, écarté, and (with the inevitable female drawbacks) even at billiards as well."

Card and board games have been very popular in the United Kingdom for centuries, as evidenced even by the furniture. Practically every historic house has at least one card or games table. People particularly liked playing cards, often for money. The king of card games is bridge. The dedicated group of enthusiasts does not merely play bridge, but practically celebrates the game.

THE ARTS AND CRAFTS MOVEMENT

The English Arts and Crafts Movement began in the mid-19th century as part of the Gothic Revival. Its main exponents were the architect Augustus Welby Pugin (1812–1852) and the artist and art historian John Ruskin (1819–1900). Faced with the onset of industrial mass production, which was often of poor technical quality, these artists harked back to the craft traditions of the Middle Ages and the formal austerity associated with them. The Pre-Raphaelites Edward C. Burne-Jones and William Morris, who had met at Oxford as early as 1853 and had painted the Union Society Building together, were influenced by Ruskin and Pugin. Soon after, Morris gave up painting and devoted his energies to designing furniture, but also primarily fabrics and wallpapers. His work already displayed the basic ideas behind the nascent Arts and Crafts Movement: structural unity of the building, which should be integrated into the landscape and the structural surroundings, practical design, sensitive room arrangements, use of local materials, and above all a deep respect for traditional construction methods and craftsmen's skills. The studio he shared with other Pre-Raphaelites finally developed into a firm that took as its model the Art Manufactures founded in 1845 by Felix Summerly. Although Morris withdrew from company management as early as 1865, he still continued to have a considerable influence on the firm, which gradually became popular with the upper middle classes

The artist craftsman and socio-political thinker William Morris (1834–1896) was the mainstay of the Arts and Crafts Movement.

when an exhibition hall was opened in London in 1877. Morris & Co. excelled as decorative artists – decorations that are still popular even today on wallpapers, upholstery fabrics, and carpets, and which incorporate medieval as well as oriental influences. Moreover, from 1880 Morris represented positions that were both antagonistic and far-reaching. Thus on the one hand he founded a company to maintain old buildings, while on the other hand he joined the Democratic Federation and outlined in an essay and a novel a utopian socialist commonwealth entitled *News from Nowhere*. In this utopian commonwealth, according to Marxist prophecy, the State had disappeared and the distinction between town and country had ceased to exist, and it was a society where people worked freely and without compulsion in the guild or associations. This may have been contrary to the ideas held by Morris' clientele from the English upper classes, but the idea of a garden city in particular had enormous consequences. William Morris' students transformed the movement into an institutional form. Thus his company partner, Walter Crane, represented the same ideas, as did the architects Arthur Mackmurdo and William Lethaby, and finally the more modern artists, Ashby, Voysey, and Newton. In 1882, Mackmurdo founded the *Century Guild in the Arts and Crafts* in London, a forerunner of Art Nouveau. The architect and artist Voysey also became important. He rejected the mixture of patterns advocated by Morris' circle and cultivated a more austere form of decoration: either the wall hangings, or the furniture, or the wallpaper could be patterned, but not all of them. This new formal discipline was especially important for the centers of the

Today William Morris is famous not only for his furniture but especially for his floral designs. This *Lea* wallpaper pattern originates from 1885.

The *Rose* design is one of many fabrics and wallpapers designed by William Morris.

Above: William Morris designed this interior with furniture, wallpaper, and carpets, in the 1860s. The reconstructed original can now be seen in the Victoria & Albert Museum in London.

The bedroom in the attic of William Morris' house, Kelmscott Manor in Oxfordshire, was created in 1861. Ford Madox Brown designed the green-stained furniture. With its puritanical austerity and art nouveau shapes, the room follows the principles of the Arts and Crafts Movement.

more austere and geometric Art Nouveau: Vienna and Glasgow. In Glasgow, a group developed called the *Glasgow Four*, Charles Rennie Mackintosh, Herbert Mac Nair, and Frances and Margaret MacDonald. The work produced by this group of architects and designers is distinctive due to its simplicity of form and color and the lack of any historical references. The *Arts and Crafts Exhibitions Society* was finally formed in 1887 under the direction of Walter Crane, but its most influential artist was William Lethaby. In 1892, Lethaby published his essay *Architecture, Mysticism, and Myth*, which declared that older architecture was always marked by cosmic and religious influences, and therefore imposed the demand for magical construction. In the years leading up to the First World War, however, Lethaby distanced himself from this symbolic concept and became one of the advocates of functionalist architecture in England. Thus in 1915, with his help, the *Design and Industries Association* came into being. Here he recommended that the German Works Association be taken as an example, which in its turn had been influenced by the Arts and Crafts Movement.

FIONA CAMPBELL – INTERIOR DESIGNER

Anyone buying a house or elegant city apartment in Britain – and anyone who has the necessary cash – will probably not be furnishing and decorating it themselves to the standards befitting their social status, but will commission an interior designer to do this work. A stroll through the Pimlico district of London gives an idea of just how popular it is to treat yourself to you own interior designer. Here there is one specialist store after another for this luxury essential, all able to offer assistance to the most discerning of customers. Whether you are looking for a particular curtain material that is perfectly in keeping with Victorian surroundings, or suitable soap dishes for an Edwardian bathroom, or even if you want a complete design for a Queen Anne-style bedroom, London's interior designers have the answer to everything.

However, Pimlico Road and the adjoining streets right by Sloane Square are not the only places for these oases of British taste. Quite a bit further west in the ever-chic Chelsea, the windows of stores specializing in furniture and furnishings lure people inside. This is the case at 259 New King's Road, for example. The eponymous proprietor of the shop is Fiona Campbell, a charming lady to whom you would be happy to entrust your home. The ground floor of the store houses numerous pattern books and fabric swatches ready for customers to peruse. There are also examples of accessories, wallpapers, paints, curtain tiebacks, curtain rails, carpets, and much more. Using the patterns and the examples of work captured in photographs and sketches from stylish houses and apartments, you can immediately order furnishings for a whole palace.

Fiona Campbell started her career in 1967 with her first small commissions. In the same year, the magazine *House Beautiful* published photographs of her apartment, after which she was asked to provide designs for a couple of apartments on Lowndes Square. The customer insisted that the curtains came from her own workshop, so Fiona Campbell had to sew them herself, which she did with the accuracy and precision that she now demands from her eight employees.

Following personal recommendations from satisfied customers, the firm grew rapidly, and in 1970 Fiona Campbell was able to buy the premises in New King's Road for £7,000– a price that seems remarkable for this location today. Do not be deceived by the small commercial premises. From this headquarters, Fiona Campbell and her team manage an army of specialists and outworkers, who follow a perfect plan. Everything must follow a definite course that makes sense only if adhered to absolutely. This is essential if design commissions, which are sometimes very large, are to be accomplished successfully. In the basement of the store, Fiona Campbell has her workrooms, where up to six machinists can be working. Here they sew up made-to-measure curtains,

The store of the internationally renowned interior designer Fiona Campbell can be found at no. 259 in the more up-market end of London's King's Road. The ground floor of the shop has recently been refurbished.

individual cushion covers, bedspreads, or special table linen. Having her own workshop means that Fiona Campbell can supervise the execution of her design ideas right down to the last detail. Many of her colleagues would not treat themselves to the luxury of their own workroom. They prefer to have their ideas carried out by subcontractors, which does, however, present problems for quality control.

Looking into the workshop is like peeping through the entrance to a secret and hidden world. It is well worth doing, because here even the layman can appreciate the great care that goes into bringing the designs to life. This has the added advantage that the cost and labor required to make up the commissions by hand are immediately obvious to any client. If required, Fiona's firm can also take care of worn-out sofas and dilapidated armchairs. Working closely with carefully selected workshops, she can arrange for new upholstery, a brand new cover, or even for the complete renovation of antique wooden frames.

Fiona Campbell's work differs from the many other interior designers primarily because of the attention that she personally devotes to the tiniest detail. As a result, her range spreads from very clear, simple, almost sober designs right up to extremely lavish items, most of which are made by hand. Very few decorating firms are in a position to offer their clients this type of service, perfectly planned and executed right up to the last detail.

Respect for detail is a defining feature of Fiona Campbell's work. As a result, she sees more than her client can ever fully appreciate. She therefore often uses photographs and sketches to illustrate what she means by successfully working with the nap of a material. Using the example of a bedspread, upholstered armchair, or a curtain, she explains to the astonished client how important it is that a design runs perfectly across each seam and edge. Every object must ultimately look as though the fabric had been created for that particular shape. The layman can appreciate the fact that a great deal of effort goes into producing this effect only when the working method is explained. Fiona Campbell is forever saying that a pattern must flow, it must continue to flow on almost organically, whether it is on a carpet border, a curtain, or on the canopy of a fourposter bed.

Most clients come to their interior designer with no clear idea of what they want. Experienced designers such as Fiona Campbell can translate even the vaguest ideas into an achievable design.

If you cannot find a suitable article in the many samples displayed in the pattern books, Fiona Campbell will arrange for that very special border, that perfectly matching lining, that particular cord, or whatever else it may be, to be made up for her customer. There are no compromises.

Attention to detail should not, however, distract from the fact that Fiona Campbell always has an eye for the overall effect. It is an example of the experienced designer's modesty that she often explains her flair to the layman by comparing it with mastering the craftsman's art. However, alongside the precise technique, the root of her success lies in her great aesthetic intuition. Because it goes without saying that it takes more than

a mastery of all the necessary skills to give a room an unmistakable atmosphere or feeling. And that is precisely what Fiona Campbell manages to do time and time again.

In closets, chests, and filing cabinets, Fiona Campbell keeps a huge selection of fabric swatches and samples of materials. If, against all odds, you cannot find the right one, she commissions special orders.

Floor Coverings for Living Rooms

Anyone visiting British houses is soon struck by certain similarities in the way the floor is treated. In homes with timber flooring, carpets are always of such a size that they do not quite reach the walls. In other words, the timber flooring can still be seen at the edges. Perhaps this is because the owners want to show that the carpet is not a floor covering. And if there is floor covering in the house, then it is often in a color known as greige (a word combining gray and beige) or somewhat more dramatically as dead mouse. This neutral gray-beige color provides an excellent background for oriental carpets. As the English have far fewer reservations about combining strong patterns than most people in mainland Europe, brightly colored knotwork can sometimes be found even on highly patterned flooring. Small patterns are popular, often surrounded by a border.

Owners of country houses usually prefer floor coverings made of vegetable fibers to a woolen floor covering. Sisal, coconut, or sea grass creates an interesting contrast to the delicate masterpieces from the Orient. They are laid wall to wall like carpets or just loose as runners. Generally, the oriental carpet is still the most popular floor covering. Like furniture, carpets count as genuine antiques when they have reached a certain age. The unavoidable traces of wear and tear are therefore not considered a cause for anxiety. Many carpets would probably be in better condition, however,

The floor covering is not exempt from the predilection for mixing patterns. Two competing carpets can often be found meeting – or more precisely clashing – at the threshold between two rooms.

if people went barefoot or in stocking feet over them, as is done in their countries of origin.

Whereas today furniture, wallpapers, and carpets usually come from different places, in the 18th century it was the norm to have an architect design not only the suitable furniture for a room, but also the appropriate floor covering. An example of this is in Osterley Park, a house that was renovated and altered by Robert Adam between 1765 and 1780. Gems such as a carpet woven using the design of the famous architect have now become extremely rare.

In many country houses, the visitor can see that carpets are laid sparsely, to highlight the beauty of a timber or stone floor. You could almost go so far as to say that the more rustic the house, the emptier the floor. This is particularly true in old houses – because carpets would have been far too good for people of the 16th and 17th centuries to lay them on the floors – instead they were hung on walls. At that time, floors were covered with reeds, which were not swept out when they got dirty, but simply covered with a new layer. Sometime in the 16th century, people had the idea of weaving the reeds into mats instead of scattering them loose over the floor. To this extent, this floor covering, which is thought so typical of the British country house, really is the authentic choice.

Carpets in British houses are basically laid so that the floor underneath can still be seen at the edges. Floor coverings made of jute, sea grass, woven reeds, coconut, or sisal can create an attractive contrast to an oriental carpet.

Runners made from vegetable fibers are an authentic choice for the country house, since reed matting was already common in the 16th century.

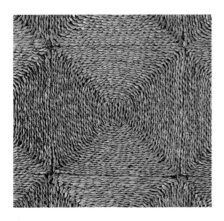

Far left: Carpets were being woven in Kidderminster, Worcestershire, as long ago as the beginning of the 17th century. Production did not begin on a large scale until the middle of the 18th century. The firm of Brinton's moved there in 1819.

Left: Strict quality control together with good raw materials and careful processing ensure the high quality of Brinton's floor coverings.

Below: Carpets are not a modern invention. They were widespread in England as long ago as the middle of the 18th century. At that time, however, looms were not wide enough to carpet large rooms in one piece. Narrower strips of carpet were sewn together instead.

THE CLASSIC ENGLISH CARPET

Anyone treading British floors will sooner or later come across a product made by the firm of Brinton's, because Brinton's is Britain's largest carpet manufacturer. As half of its production is exported, the visitor's feet may well have enjoyed Brinton's long before their arrival in the British Isles. At Chek-Lap-Kok airport in Hong Kong, for example, with its 176,000 square yards (135,000 square meters) of carpet. The design was created exclusively for this major commission. Gigantic orders such as the one from Hong Kong are a specialty of the company, which also supplies carpets for palaces, government buildings, company headquarters, golf and sailing clubs, hotels, and casinos.

Orders for huge quantities from China or even the USA (for example for the 5,000-room building of the MGM Grand Hotel and Casino in Las Vegas) are produced in their entirety by Brinton's using their four factories in the United Kingdom, one in Portugal, subcontractors in Australia and the USA, and a spinning mill in New Zealand. These will soon be joined by a factory in India. This ensures the high quality standards that have made Brinton carpets famous.

It may come as a surprise that this carpet empire with an annual turnover of over £100 million still belongs to the Brinton family and is even still actively run by them. In actual fact, Brinton's is one of the last businesses of its size still to be under the total control of its founding family. Michael Brinton is the sixth-generation company boss. Family members of the seventh generation are already working in the business who are his son and niece.

The company history began in 1783, when William Brinton set up a yarn-weaving mill in Hill Pool near Chaddesley Corbett. In 1819, his son moved with the concern to Kidderminster. This town offered the ideal conditions for setting up numerous carpet weaving mills – wool for the pile, cotton for the backing, and water for washing and dyeing the wool and for driving the looms. Kidderminster also had enough inhabitants to provide a workforce for the flourishing carpet industry, and some of their descendants are still employed there today. For these reasons, during the 18th and 19th centuries, this town in the county of Worcestershire became the center of the carpet manufacturing industry in Great Britain and the whole world.

One hundred years later, Brinton's was an important employer in the region. Only an international disaster such as the Second World War could put a temporary stop to the company's success. At first, they managed to continue some carpet production, but from 1942, only armaments left the factory. Carpets were not woven here again until 1946. In the 1980s, the British carpet industry collapsed, the number of employees falling from 45,000 to 10,000. Brinton's survived the crisis relatively unscathed, although there were redundancies even in this giant of the industry.

Today, Brinton's is not only the largest private firm in Britain, but has also become the largest manufacturer of woven carpets in the world by acquiring Axminster, Inc. in Greenville, Mississippi (USA). The company's strength lies on the one hand in the experience it has gained from its long history and on the other in its highly technical means of production. At Brinton's, for example, one of their own departments designs the looms. It goes without saying that the most up-to-date CAD technology is used in the design studio.

The company's success should be sufficient proof of the fact that traditional British firms are still thoroughly competitive today. They manage this in part due to extremely high quality requirements, which are ensured by family tradition alone, and also due to that eccentricity that seems so typically British to some. At any rate, it cannot have been a mere financial calculation that moved Brinton's in 1993 to take Vivienne Westwood of all people on board as a carpet designer. The avant-garde fashion designer created the carpets on the advertising pictures awarded the *Flooring Industry Award for Advertising*. More advertising campaigns are planned to follow, which should establish Brinton's in the public consciousness for what it has been since the 18th century: a typically British family firm, with a strong sense of tradition, top quality, and above all success.

SASH WINDOWS

This is a situation familiar to any visitor to the British Isles: you have arrived at your hotel or bed and breakfast and want to open the window to let some fresh air into the room. You have pushed the heavy curtains aside, but instead of a window handle, there is only a crossbeam, and this is just the first surprise you encounter in your attempt to open the window. Depending on the age and condition of the sash window, you have to exert more or less force to slide the frame and the glass upward. If you manage it and if you are lucky, the window will stay open. If you are unlucky, it will slide down again, trapping your finger, or even worse, your neck.

This typically British window design is called a sash window and first appeared in the 1670s. Chatsworth in Derbyshire is reputed to have been the first building to have such windows, although there were examples of simpler versions a good 30 years earlier in France. Basically, a sash window comprises two glazed timber frames that can be moved by means of a system of weights, pulleys, and cords in the window jambs. This system made the classic window-cross superfluous and made it possible to move even large and therefore heavy panes of glass with relative ease. From then on, windows hinged at the sides and known as casement windows were found only in smaller houses or in the door-sized French windows of the 19th century. In the 18th century the typical sash window comprised two moveable windows, each glazed with six panes of glass — hence the term *six-over-six*. Until 1709, the window frame was built flush with the wall, but after that a law stipulated that it had to be moved four inches (10 centimeters) inward. It was thought that this measure would help prevent the passage of flames from one story to another in the event of fire. In Victorian times, glass became cheaper, and as a result only one

pane of glass was used per sash, instead of several smaller ones. From the turn of the century until the First World War, sash windows were also made with six panes in the upper sliding window, while the lower one contained only one or two panes.

Since the 1980s, neo-Georgian buildings have come into fashion once more, and it goes without saying that, true to style, these have traditional sash windows. The aesthetic qualities of such windows may be beyond dispute, but the fact that they also present practical disadvantages does not seem to cause much concern among post-modern builders. One such disadvantage is that sash windows are rather prone to stick. Another is that the glass is hard to clean. They also rattle in strong winds. On the other hand, the fact that they are not very draft-proof is seen by many on the British Isles as being beneficial from a medical point of view, because the constant exchange of air improves the atmosphere in the room.

As sash windows continued to be built in most new houses right up until the early 20th century, and many of these houses are still standing today, it is highly likely that any visitor will have to get to grips with the design of this window. A tricky task for the inexperienced. Most homeowners prefer to repair these old windows for as long as possible instead of simply changing them for a more modern design. People believe that they are worth repairing, as even a half-broken old window is always better and more true-to-style than the most attractive, contemporary copy. That is why it is important to learn how to deal with sash windows if you are to have a successful stay in the British Isles.

First release any locking device. Otherwise you will be expending your energy in vain.

The window frame can now be moved, provided the mechanism is not too decrepit.

Push the window up with some force. Be careful when leaning out, as the window can slide down again.

Windows from the 15th century to the 17th still look rather like firing slits. The stone window jambs were fixed in the wall as it was built.

Such ornate baroque window cases are now rare in Britain. They were probably very unusual even in the 17th century.

The ground floor of Georgian town houses often has this type of very simple sash window.

Rectangular windows crowned with ornamental corbels or tympana are typically Palladian. This particular example dates from the 18th century. Above you can see the wooden shutters that are pulled out from the window jambs from the inside of the house.

In keeping with the doors, windows from the Regency period were also often semi-circular at the top.

If windows in Georgian times were usually flush, the typical Victorian façade again jutted out, such as the oriel or bay window, for example.

The bottom half of this Edwardian six-over-six sash window has been replaced with a single pane of glass. Usually this half is also divided into six small panes.

Fixed frame windows that push open outwards have never been very popular in Britain. This type of window, as in this modern example from the 1930s, is rarely found.

TYPICAL TYPES OF WINDOW

Historic British windows date from the 15th century up to the outbreak of the First World War. The earliest types still bring to mind firing slits. Glass was a rare and expensive commodity, and very few of these early windows could be opened.

During the baroque period from the mid-17th century until the first quarter of the 18th century, people began to design more architecturally ornate window jambs. The introduction of the sash window at the end of the 17th century meant windows could be made bigger, since the invention of the sliding mechanism made them relatively easy to move, despite their great weight. In the Georgian period from the early 18th century to the beginning of the 19th, the sash window continued to become established quite simply as the typical British window. The window shutters inside were also part of the standard fittings in most houses. Originally, windows were built flush with the facade, but the new regulation had a great effect on the appearance of the front of the building.

French windows – large windows that open to the outside – became fashionable in Regency times. The windows on the first floor became more elongated and elegant, whereas the window cases themselves remained comparatively plain.

In Victorian times, the oriel window, also known as the bay window, became more common. The repeal of the window tax in 1851 led to an increase in windowed areas. Exterior blinds shaded the facades and were primarily intended to protect the furniture and interior decoration against fade. With the Arts and Crafts Movement, smaller windows made a comeback. Stained glass made the colors also become very popular in those days.

In a high-ceilinged room, curtains can be draped to great effect.

Decorating the Window

In most houses, the living room is not only a private sitting room but also a reception room for visitors. The living room window can therefore be decorated in a rather more striking way. People often choose a heavy fabric for the curtains, and price does not matter here. The drapes should be lined with a neutral fabric if possible, since this prevents light penetrating, protects against the fading effects of the sun, and improves the fall and hang of the folds. Experienced interior designers always advise against skimping on curtain material, since window decor that is measured too exactly looks anything but elegant.

If the living room has a high ceiling, as in Georgian or Regency houses, undulating edgings are another option. Depending on the taste and style of the furnishings, these can be made from swags of white fabric or from a slightly stiffer material. Valances and pelmets are also very popular. However, they only look really good in very grand rooms. In smaller rooms, they can easily detract from the window and have a dominating effect.

The simplest and often the best solution is a pair of curtains with a gathered or pleated trim. Depending on how the curtain material itself is handled, a simple window decoration can look very elegant too. Of course, the choice of curtain rail is also very important to achieve the desired effect. It is true to say that the more visible the curtain rail, the more rustic the impression that is created. A bright fabric hanging from the rings of a plain brass or wooden curtain rail is one of the simplest solutions. Draping or pleating a length of fabric over the curtain rail or hiding it behind a fabric blind would create a more elegant effect. Another way to hang curtains directly beneath the ceiling is to use special tracks with moveable or fixed hooks.

Curtains are usually held back to the left and right by tiebacks. These are made either from the same material as the curtain itself, or match the blind material. Ready made tiebacks come in a wide variety of shapes and colors, so that you can choose just the right one for your living room. Brass holdbacks, fitted straight onto the wall, are another alternative.

Symmetry can be very effective with curtains too.

A pale-colored curtain is always the best option in a light interior.

A brass holdback provides an interesting contrast to the curtain material.

Tiebacks made from the same material as the curtain provide a very elegant solution.

A roller blind will protect against the sun if you want to keep the curtains open.

A rustic Venetian blind is often the best solution for an informal interior.

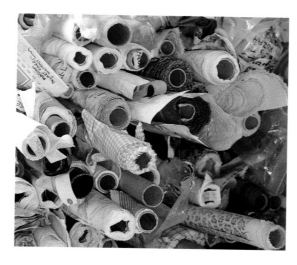

At Fiona Campbell's store, clients can choose from hundreds of different curtain materials, not just in a great variety of designs and colors, but also in different types of fabric.

Naturally, space is limited in the interior designer's storeroom. It would be impossible to keep such a big selection in stock. If you do not find what you are looking for on the rolls of fabric, you can look for your dream material in the cloth merchants' books of swatches.

Detail is of vital importance to the overall effect of the curtain. Borders and tassels can provide either a positive or negative finishing touch. A heavy velvet tassel would ruin a lightweight printed cotton curtain.

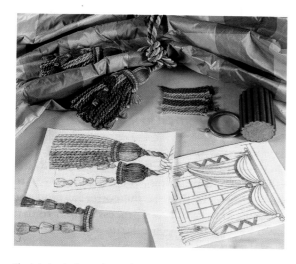

The interior designer always shows the customers sketches to provide a better idea of how the window will look with its new curtains. As soon as they have agreed on a common idea, an exact pattern can be made for the machinists and decorators.

Curtains are usually lined, primarily to add weight to lighter materials and to create a better feel, but also to make translucent fabrics less transparent. A lining also hides the unattractive wrong side of the material. Curtains are lined to protect light-sensitive materials from the sun's fading rays.

In the ground floor of Fiona Campbell's store there is a small workshop where very important pieces of work are carried out by the company's own specialists under the supervision of the designer. Not many interior designers can afford the luxury of their own studio. Fiona Campbell would not be without it.

When the new window decoration is finally ready for hanging, the excitement rises in Fiona Campbell and her colleagues. Because no matter how carefully everything is planned out, only now will they be able to see whether everything has been done correctly. But thanks to the designer's great experience, it always has.

It is especially important to use patterned fabrics correctly. When you look at the finished curtain with its perfectly positioned design, you would not know how much work it often takes to match up lines, checks, flowers, or images correctly.

All suppliers of quality custom-made work face the problem that they can rarely show actual samples of their work. Everything they design and convert into reality disappears into the houses of their customers, never to be seen again. A photograph in their briefcase is often all that remains, apart from the memory.

You can eat superbly in the dining rooms of British houses – and not just because of the grand surroundings. The delicacies and drinks are excellent too.

THE DINING ROOM

PERFECT SETTING FOR DINNER PARTIES

During the 18th century, the idea of a separate room for eating – the dining room – became the norm in middle- and upper-class homes. Until then, on grand occasions, people had eaten at long tables in the spacious halls of the large houses of the nobility, while on less important occasions, they ate in the living-room, putting smaller tables together to form a dining table. In this case, every diner had to find somewhere to put his legs among the confusion of table legs. At the end of the 18th century, tabletops rested on large, branched bases, very long tabletops requiring two or more bases. At this time, it was the custom to lay the table in the same way as we do today. Before that, people ate straight from the bowls and platters placed in the center of the table. The increasingly informal British society of the 18th century wanted a more private room for social gatherings, so

Choosing and positioning the furniture carefully in smaller rooms can create an atmosphere that is both genteel and cozy. Candlelight adds to this effect.

that the dining room developed as a room in its own right, often built as an adjunct to the drawing room and counterbalancing it in the house. When the dining room had become established, homeowners and designers began to put great thought into its design. Special furnishings were soon designed to serve the purposes of the new room: side tables for food, cutlery, and crockery, and urns with taps for hot and cold water, the former for washing the cutlery, the latter for drinking. Sophisticated wine coolers were also devised with an integral iced water dispenser, as were serving trays on a revolving base, on which all the dishes could be attractively arranged. This

device was called a dumb waiter, and made it possible for people to serve themselves without the need for a servant to be in constant attendance. The furnishings were completed with ingenious closets and dressers with integral devices for keeping the plates warm. All in all, the furnishing of the dining room is impressive evidence of the inventiveness of 18th-century cabinetmakers.

After the late-18th century, a new dining etiquette came into being: people now ate *à la Russe*. This meant that one waiter served three or four guests, placing the dishes before them one after the other. Previously it had been the custom to bring all the dishes to the table at once, which necessitated having one waiter for each guest. Later still, it even became fashionable to eat the evening meal at several small tables, no longer together at one large table.

A dining room is still essential for anyone managing a large house. Particularly in the United Kingdom, it is a popular form of evening entertainment to invite friends to dinner. Going to a restaurant with a group of friends, as they do in France, for example, has only recently become socially acceptable in Britain. In the country, the private invitation to a dinner party is still the most usual form of social intercourse, not least because of the lack of good restaurants in some remote regions of the island. Many homeowners find it a pity that they cannot use such a large room as the dining room every day, and that is why the dining room often fulfills several functions, such as being a library or study during the day.

People even like to use the kitchen as a dining room nowadays, if it is large enough, but it can be difficult to create a formal atmosphere in among all the pots and pans. Some guests find the odors and fat fumes from the pots and pans distracting. For a real black tie dinner, in other words a formal dinner party demanding formal dress, only a separate dining room will do. With close friends and relatives, on the other hand, you can sit just as well in the kitchen and enjoy a simple meal. People then chat into the early hours, while tucking into a huge stilton cheese.

When people decide to have a dining room, their choice of furniture can define the style of the surroundings in which people will subsequently eat. A long, rectangular, plain wooden table reflects the Middle Ages, an oval table belongs to the 18th century, and a circular table relates to the 19th century. Admittedly, this is just a rough guide, but it does make it easier to find the right shape of dining table for the age of the house. The same is true of the chairs, their covers, and the other furnishings.

The style of the room affects its atmosphere. Should it be formal or more rustic, stylish, or casual? In Britain, it is usually a mixture of them all. The British are dab hands at combining formality and informality, and move effortlessly from one to the other. As a result, the dining room basically offers a rather formal setting where everything can be extremely informal.

Even in a smaller house, heavy curtains and candlelight can give the dining room that certain grandeur that is celebrated in Great Britain with a mixture of deep earnestness and a wink. But do not be put off by the luxurious impression such a dining room initially creates. It is primarily a private invitation to have a good time – the fact that you are invited into a stylishly

Syon House is the London home of the Duke of Northumberland. Starting in 1762, the Scottish architect Robert Adam redesigned the property. The dining room is an outstanding example of his style.

furnished room has nothing to do with ostentation but reflects the high esteem in which the host holds his guests. So you are sure to have an excellent time even at a dinner in evening dress or dinner jacket. The only thing is – and this is the problem – you have to be sufficiently aware of the etiquette to know when formal dress is and is not expected. If in doubt, ask your hosts, and whatever you do, try not to be boring. If you play by the ground rules, and never talk about politics, money, or illness, you will have a good chance of being invited back.

Chatsworth in Derbyshire was built in the 16th century, although the exterior of the house is more reminiscent of the 18th and early-19th centuries due to the redesigning work carried out at that time. The dining room of the huge house is a good example of a stately dining hall of princely proportions.

If you think the fireplace in the dining room might hark back to the hearth, you would be only partly right. Although people cooked, roasted, and grilled on an open fire in the great hall of medieval times, the idea of a separate dining room did not become fashionable until the 18th century, when the dining room fireplace served only to heat the room.

Many large dining rooms are no longer in constant use. Even in houses that are not half-transformed into museums but are actually still home to a family, the large dining room is used only for special occasions.

THE CORRECT TABLE SETTING

The size and furnishing of the dining room are fundamental in defining the impression that the guest takes home after an invitation to lunch or dinner. But even the most beautiful antiques could not compensate for the bad marks consciously or subconsciously given to the host for a badly laid table. Even the best menu would not be remembered half as well if it were not properly served at the table. That is why British hosts usually make very sure that their dining room table is laid perfectly. After all, it will be on view to the guests all evening. The table linen and napkins must therefore be freshly washed and ironed, and new candles placed in the holders. The silver must be gleaming to compete with the sparkle from the glasses, which of course should have no fingerprints or lipstick marks.

But even before laying the table, experienced hosts pay great attention to the seating plan, to which the British still attach great importance. In many cases, it is still thought important that the seating plan should reflect social status. The host would therefore usually sit at the head of the table, with the most important female guest on his right. The hostess would sit at the foot of the table with the most important male guest on her right. The spouses or partners of the two most important guests sit on the left of the host and hostess respectively. This also complies with another basic rule that states that spouses and partners – including same-sex partners – should not sit together. Furthermore, the guest list should be planned in advance so that there is an equal number of men and women. This produces what is known as the alternate ranks, the arrangement where a man always sits next to a woman, and vice versa.

Long rectangular tables, called rectory tables, often come from vicarages or schools. They look good in a rustic dining room. It is becoming increasingly difficult to find genuine antique examples, as there is now a burgeoning trade in reproduction rectangular tables.

Circular dining tables, where all the guests can talk to each other without difficulty, became fashionable in the 19th century. One disadvantage with larger circular tables is that they take up a lot of space. Another is that conversation is very difficult for those guests sitting at opposite poles.

A Windsor chair would go well with a rectory table, but would look very out of place in a formal dining room. Rustic seats from the 18th century are now becoming popular even in more grand interiors.

Chairs popular in the early 19th century go well with a dining table. Ones with rectangular backs in the style of the cabinetmaker and designer Thomas Sheraton are a practical alternative.

A crystal chandelier is a splendid sight, but it is not always easy to adapt its light to suit the room. Sometimes it does not give enough light to illuminate the dining room sufficiently, while at other times it is almost dazzling. If in doubt, choose a model that provides too little light, and then place additional lamps in the room.

The dumb waiter is a tiered table and appeared in this form in the first half of the 18th century. It made it possible for the waiting staff to withdraw once they had placed the food and drinks on their wooden helpers. In this way, the conversation could continue at table without interruption.

The sideboard is an 18th-century invention. It was originally a narrow table on which food and drinks were placed before being served. The architect and designer Robert Adam made the sideboard a sort of outpost of the kitchen by adding urn-shaped water tanks containing hot and cold water.

China cabinets often look out of place in a formal dining room. However, wall shelving is very useful if there is no other place to put the china. Like bookshelves, they can be made to fit the room. Laden with plates, cups, pots, and bowls, such shelves have a charm of their own.

Once you have made the seating plan, you can proceed to lay the table. As a basis, you can use either a tablecloth or table mats. A tablecloth looks more elegant, whereas tablemats leave some of the table visible. This can be an advantage if the tabletop is especially worth seeing. If you use a tablecloth, it is advisable to have a woolen or cotton-felt underlay. This protects the tabletop from the heat of the dishes and absorbs the clatter of glasses and china on the table. The next step is to arrange the centerpiece in the middle of the table. It should not be so large as to obstruct a guest's view of the person sitting opposite them. Depending on the style of the furnishings in the dining room, a splendid silver service can look good, or just a simple porcelain or crystal bowl containing fruit, flowers, or candies. The degree of sophistication, whether you match the color of the table decorations to the furnishings of the room, for example, is a matter of personal taste and imagination. However that may be, it is worth going to the expense for British guests, because as seasoned dinner-goers, they have a good eye for the details of the arrangement. The next thing to do is to lay the cutlery, china, napkins, and glasses.

Many British hosts still think it worth bothering with different cutlery for each course. They consider using the same knives and forks for different courses to be a sign of meanness, and that is why the domestic dining room often displays an impressive arsenal of knives, forks, and spoons next to the plates. As in continental Europe, they are laid in the order in which they are used, starting from the outside with the first course of the meal. At a formal meal, the dessert spoons, forks, and knives for cheese and fruit are not placed above the plate, but to the sides. Traditionally, the plate for the main course is not laid at the start of the meal in Britain, although it is increasingly making an appearance now, sometimes flanked by a side plate for bread and butter. The napkin, always a proper fabric one, is placed either on the main plate or on the side plate. There is no need for any elaborate folding. The wineglasses are usually lined up above the tip of the largest knife in the order in which they are used, starting from the inside and working outward. The glass for water is placed slightly to the left. As for the shape of the wineglasses, this too reflects the British predilection for tradition.

A British Menu

A typical starter would be mulligatawny soup, a hot, curry-flavored soup containing vegetables, meat, apples, tomato paste, and rice. Fish comes next, trout for example, which, like other freshwater fish, is usually cooked in one of two ways: poached or sautéed in breadcrumbs. The meat course might be roast beef with Yorkshire pudding. The pinky-red sirloin of beef is served with seasonal vegetables. Yorkshire pudding is not actually a pudding or dessert, but a warm vol-au-vent made from flour, egg, salt, milk, and beef dripping. For dessert, or pudding as it is sometimes called, there might be an apple and blackberry crumble or a sherry trifle, a real explosion of calories made from sponge cake soaked in sherry (hence the name), seasonal fruits, raspberry jelly, custard, and cream. When cheese is served, it is usually the legendary stilton, which does not actually come from Stilton, but is produced mainly in Belvoir in the country of Lancashire. It comes in two varieties: as a strong, highly flavored blue-veined cheese (blue stilton), and as a mild white cheese (white stilton). In Britain, too, a good meal is rounded off with a strong cup of coffee. Recently, more and more restaurants and private hosts have taken to offering their guests an Italian espresso.

Mulligatawny soup

Fish course: Trout

Meat course: Roast beef and Yorkshire pudding

Pudding: Apple and blackberry crumble

Cheese: Port and stilton

To finish: Coffee

FROM LUNCH TO DINNER

The sightseeing tourist rarely experiences the pleasure of an invitation to lunch or dinner. However, if they go to Britain on business or have made friends with British people, you are sure to be asked, almost out of pity, to lunch, a business lunch, or an evening dinner party. The usual European table manners will be appropriate at any of these occasions, but there are a couple of idiosyncrasies that should be observed.

Plenty of time is always needed for business lunches. If lunch is planned to start at one o'clock, it will not finish before three o'clock. Sometimes it is even advisable to have no other commitments for the rest of the day, because a lunch can easily go on until four o'clock in the afternoon. The remaining hours of the working day are needed just to recover from lunch. Despite the American trend toward mineral water as a mealtime drink, a British lunch is usually still served with alcohol, a gin and tonic or Champagne aperitif, then wine, followed by a brandy or whisky digestive. Even if you do not actually drink alcohol, there is bound to be enough in the food to make work impossible.

At a dinner party, a dinner jacket is often *de rigueur* for men, a suit or little party dress for women. Business people who appear in office clothes, i.e. suit, dress, or skirt and jacket, are excused. The dinner party follows the usual tradition of starter, main course or courses, pudding, and cheese.

People usually have their aperitifs while standing around chatting and amusing themselves in informal groups.

Despite their sense of humor, the British expect certain rules to be observed at lunch and dinner. Foreign guests may be granted a certain license, but an awareness of the three simple principles can do no harm. Firstly with regard to table talk: you are basically expected to be equally attentive to each of your neighbors at the table. Regardless of how interesting the conversation with a British person, after a certain period of time he or she will, without warning, turn away and strike up a conversation with their neighbor on the other side. This is the high time for you to start to pay attention to another guest. Secondly, guests should be aware that soup is drunk from the side of the soupspoon. It is considered bad manners to sip it from the front. Thirdly, with regard to smoking: tobacco fans should wait for a formal announcement before lighting up cigarettes, cigars, or pipes.

Silver services give any table a formal yet romantic feel. A traditional table setting calls for a white damask tablecloth. Gaudy or flowery extravaganzas are the preserve of the breakfast table on a sunny terrace.

The Macclesfield Wine Cooler

The huge Macclesfield wine cooler that can be admired in London's Victoria & Albert Museum is one of a three-part wine service that magnificently reflects the customs and traditions of the dining rooms of the nobility during the 1720s. The service, made from Britannia standard silver, comprises a water tank, a water receptacle, and the wine cooler itself. It was used throughout the meal as a kind of washing machine and also as a refrigerator.

From the 17th century onward, it was thought improper to place wine bottles directly on the table. The guests did not even have wine glasses in front of them. If they wanted a sip of wine, they called the waiter, who then served them with a full glass on a small tray. The guests quickly drank the wine, replacing the empty glass on the tray. The waiter then washed the glass, running water from the water tank into the receptacle. Once dried, the glass was then ready for further use and could be refilled with wine from the cooler on request.

Such silver services were extremely expensive. The price for the three pieces must have been somewhere in the vicinity of £1,220. This does not sound too bad to present-day ears, but it must be remembered that in the early-18th century you could buy a carriage for £60, and your own portrait in oils for around £35.

So who was this man who adorned his dining room at Shirburn Castle with such an expensive wine service? He went by the name of Thomas Parker and was the son of a lawyer from Staffordshire. He followed in his father's professional footsteps and quickly made a name for himself in the Midlands. He then gained a seat in parliament and was subsequently knighted. Parker later became Lord Chancellor, receiving £14,000 on his appointment.

In 1721, Thomas Parker became first Earl of Macclesfield, but just four years later the gifted lawyer had to vacate his office because of an indictment containing 24 charges. Among other things, he was found guilty of accepting bribes and of having used his customers' possessions for his own benefit. In the same year, 1725, he had to give up all his posts. From then on, Parker sat in enforced early retirement in his castle and devoted himself to the sciences. He was also a generous patron of the mathematician William Jones, whom he allowed to live at Shirburn Castle for many years. It is highly likely that the learned guest was served chilled wine from the Macclesfield wine service, because Parker was allowed to keep this memento of past fame.

The Macclesfield wine cooler is part of a three-part wine service dating from 1719 or 1720. Over two and a half feet (80 centimeters) tall, and about four feet (120 centimeters) wide, it just has to be one of the largest wine coolers in the world.

A ROYAL STATE BANQUET

A state banquet in Buckingham Palace is always held in the Ballroom, which was built between 1853 and 1855 to plans by Sir James Pennethorne. The Ballroom is the largest of the palace's many state rooms – 123 feet (37.5 meters) long, 60 feet (18.3 meters) wide, and 45 feet (13.7 meters) high. It was officially opened in 1856 with a glittering ball to celebrate the end of the Crimean War.

Despite its name, the room is now used solely for state banquets and other formal occasions. The table, arranged in a U-shape, seats about 170 guests. The Queen sits in the middle of the closed side of the horseshoe, with the official visitors and other members of the royal family sitting on her right and left. The guests include the delegation of visitors, members of the aristocracy and the British government, other personalities from the world of politics, Commonwealth dignitaries, ambassadors, and business people who have a special relationship with the country for whose representatives the banquet is being given.

Preparations for a state banquet last three days, and that is just setting up the Ballroom. On the first day, the benches arranged against the walls of the room are removed. The remaining two days are spent laying the table. Measuring poles are used to position the individual place settings exactly, so that each plate is the same distance from the center of the table and the neighboring place setting. This is customary when laying any large table and is not just a peculiarity of British state banquets. Following international convention, the cutlery is arranged from the outside inward, so you begin at the outside and work your way inward with each course, ending with the dessert or pudding.

Each place setting has six crystal glasses for wine, champagne, and water. They are part of a Stourbridge service made in 1953 on the occasion of the coronation of Queen Elizabeth II. Each glass bears the Queen's initials, engraved by hand.

The china is also very select. For example, on the occasion of the visit by the Brazilian president on December 2, 1997, dessert was served on a 17th-century dinner service. This Sèvres masterpiece, decorated with painted flowers and fruits on a turquoise background, was originally an official gift from the French king Louis XVI to the wife of the fourth Duke of Manchester when the Peace Treaty was signed at the end of the American War of Independence in 1783. King George IV subsequently acquired the service in 1802.

More treasures from the Queen's collection are displayed on the sideboards, for example a Royal Rockingham dessert service that was first used at the festivities to celebrate the coronation of Queen Victoria in 1837, and subsequently at the coronation of Queen Elizabeth II. It would not take two days to lay the table if, in addition to each place setting, the center of the table and the tables against the walls of the room did not also have to be decorated. Here, numerous examples of precious gold plate are displayed, such as lamps, plates, and vases, and of course fresh flowers, some of which come from the gardens at Windsor Castle. For the Brazilian state visit we have already mentioned, the palace florist selected and arranged flowers in autumn colors ranging from cream to yellow to coral red and bronze.

Between 1992 and 1998, no state banquets could be held in Windsor Castle, since it had been badly damaged by fire in 1992. Today the Queen's favorite residence has been restored to its former glory.

The staff are dressed in different-colored uniforms according to rank. Footmen, for example, wear red liveries. The servants are responsible to the *master of the household*, the most important court official in matters relating to waiting on the guests. This position was created in 1539 as part of a reform of the royal household, and at that time there were four more masters. In the late-17th century, there was only one master, and the job was highly prized. In the 19th century, Prince Albert, consort to Queen Victoria, strengthened the position of the master when the royal household was again reorganized, giving him responsibility for organizing all domestic matters. Today, although the *master of the household* may in theory be responsible to the Lord Steward, in practice he bears sole responsibility for staff, care, and maintenance at all the royal palaces and during state visits abroad. As Buckingham Palace is now the only official residence to have a permanent, full complement of staff, the *master of the household* also transfers servants here and there between the official residences. At a state banquet in the Ballroom, the *master of the household* supervises every detail, from the guest list to the invitations right up to drawing up the menu. When the Emperor and Empress of Japan visited on May 26, 1998, the menu comprised *Consommé de Veaux aux Champignons Sauvages*, *Loup de Mer aux Fines Herbes*, *Selle d'Agneau Printanière avec Petits Pois Gourmande*, *Pommes Champignol*, salad, and for dessert *Soufflé Glacé aux Fraises*. The following wines were served: Puligny Montrachet, Les Perrières, 1989 Domaine Louis Carillon, 1981 St Julien, 1988 Moët et Chandon, and 1970 Warre.

Of course, all these tasks can be managed only with a large staff, and for this reason the department of the *master of the household* has 195 employees, who take care of domestic matters in the official residences. For special occasions such as a state banquet, additional staff are brought in from outside.

Guests at a state banquet must observe certain rules with regard to dress. Ladies choose a long evening dress or a national costume, together with their tiaras and medals. Gentlemen wear evening dress, knights of the Order of the Garter wear knee breeches, soldiers wear uniform, and a national costume is also permissible.

Speeches are usually given at the start of a banquet, but this is not a hard and fast rule. They are the only part of the whole event that is filmed. For the rest of the occasion, cameras are taboo. The Queen is the first to speak and closes her speech with a toast to the guest, who responds with his speech and a toast to the Queen. A band from the *Household Division*, the land forces, provides light musical entertainment during the meal. The program on the occasion of the visit of the Emperor and Empress of Japan included a Schubert March, the ballet music from Gounod's *Faust*, and a medley from the musical *Hair*, to mention just a few, all conducted by Major P.E. Hills. The repertoire is divided into 12 sections: march, overture, waltz, selection, ballet music, suite, waltz, selection, march, descriptive, selection, march. Scottish music is sometimes played at the end of the evening. When dessert has finally been eaten, the guests rise from the table and take coffee and liqueurs in any of the various state rooms.

Henry Poole & Co. – Royal Livery Maker

When you first find out that the state liveries, the uniforms of the servants of the English royal court, are made by a bespoke tailor, you might wonder about the expense incurred. But no one other than a tailor could make the liveries, since they cannot be bought off the peg. Even in England, there is no shop for court requisites.

Henry Poole & Co. were granted the honor of supplying the royal household under Queen Victoria, and the traditional concern has continued to do so to this very day. The company was founded in 1806, when the Shropshire notions dealer James Poole opened a store in London's Everett Street. Legend has it that he became a tailor quite by accident when, in 1815, he joined a volunteer corps that had been raised to fight against Napoleon. The amateur soldiers had to make their uniform themselves. With the help of his wife Mary, James Poole did this so well that he caught the attention of an officer with the uniform kilt he had made himself. When asked if he was the tailor, James Poole smartly answered yes, which got him his first commission.

Until the battle of Waterloo in 1815, there was such a flood of orders that the notions business expanded to become a uniform tailor's business. In 1822, Poole opened a store in the then new and highly fashionable Regent Street. A year later, he moved to 4 Old Burlington Street, which runs parallel to Savile Row. His second son, Henry, entered his father's firm when he was 15 years old. His elder brother Jim had found a job at a stockbroker's, and so it was up to Henry to learn the tailor's craft. The young man, however, found no pleasure in this difficult profession, and so his father decided that his son had better go hunting for customers. Equipped with exquisite custom-made clothing and a carriage, Henry set about gaining a place in society to reach customers of sub-

stance. This was no easy task for the son of a humble tailor, and his entry into the circles of rich bachelors was only gradual.

His first success was becoming acquainted with the Earl of Stamford, who had shocked High Society by marrying a circus girl. It was at his house that the almost apocryphal story unfolded that has gone down in the annals of the firm. Henry was playing an after-dinner game of billiards with a few gentlemen and witnessed how one of the men was lamenting the fit of his suit. Henry at once seized the chalk really meant for the billiard cues, and used it to mark the necessary changes on the ill-fitting garment. He then asked the guest to bring the suit with the markings to the store in Old Burlington Street, so that it could be altered.

Of course, young Henry's marketing activities were not restricted just to such clever moves, and he gradually managed to penetrate the circle of the prosperous huntsmen. His father was soon able to open his own sporting department to devote much of his time and energy to the very promising riding wear business.

However, it was not until after the death of the firm's founder in 1846 that Henry Poole really hit the big time – both in person and as a firm. Henry Poole's premises in Old Burlington Street backed on to Savile Row. Henry now made the back into the front and was thus one of the first "Savile Row Tailors" in the true sense of the term. Toward the end of the 1850s, the tailoring firm was able to develop and extend its premises, commissioning the well-known builder Thomas Cubitt with the work. His development of Belgravia was one of the projects that made him famous.

In the new business premises, illustrious clients gathered not only to look at fabrics or to have clothes fitted, but also to drink, chat, and smoke. As early as 1869, Poole's commercial premises had expanded to cover three houses each in Savile Row and Old Burlington Street. There was a branch on the corner between Savile Row and Clifford Street that was solely in charge of the livery business, which was injected with new life when appointed "livery tailor" by Queen Victoria.

Above: Henry Poole & Co.'s store in London's Savile Row.

Right: The liveries made by Henry Poole & Co. are used for years or even decades. They are so intricately made up that it is better to alter them than to order new ones for each generation of servants.

Far right: Only very few tailors are now expert livery makers. Such specialists are much in demand in Savile Row.

THE SMOKING ROOM AND ITS HISTORY

Ever since tobacco was introduced to England in the 16th century, the smokers' weed had guaranteed strong reactions: it was greeted with either passionate devotees or fierce opponents. One of the latter was King James I, who reigned from 1603 to 1625. He increased the tax on tobacco quite steeply, thereby ruining the pleasure for many smokers. In the 18th century, it even looked as though snuff would supplant the pipe. When cigars and cigarillos came into fashion, more and more non-smokers complained of the smell.

But it was not until Victorian times that it became customary to provide special smoking rooms. Previously, the ladies often withdrew to take tea in the drawing room, while the men remained in the dining room and talked business, politics, or less refined topics. There were also houses where the smoking gentlemen were banished to the garden, the terrace, or to the servants' quarters. Queen Victoria was herself a declared anti-smoker. She had No Smoking signs put up at central points in Windsor Castle, which are said to have had an intimidating effect even on royal visitors. The Saxon King Albert managed to refrain from smoking at least for two days, before he finally remembered his royal status and pointedly ran around with a long cigar.

Even Victoria's beloved consort, Albert, had to submit to the smoking ban, and therefore had his own designated smoking room at Osborne House on the Isle of Wight. The doors were adorned just with his initial, "A," in contrast with the other doors, which were marked with an intertwined "V & A."

Many smokers envy the inhabitants of British country houses for their cozily and comfortably furnished smoking rooms. Initially, these were not taken to voluntarily, however. It was more a question of the ladies' dislike of the tobacco smoke that made them advocate the establishment of smoking rooms. Exiled to the smoking room, the men could then sit in their own fumes, smoke, and drink brandy far from any sensitive noses. Only when smoking became more popular with the ladies could the smokers return from their places of exile to the drawing room. The English author Evelyn Waugh, however, often preferred not to make use of this remission. His diaries imply that he preferred to smoke his cigars only in male company.

Smoking Rooms then became increasingly fashionable. And as though a smoking room in itself was not a sufficient indication of the isolation for the lonely tobacco fan, people persisted in choosing places as far as possible from the living-rooms, next to the conservatory, for example, as in Mentmore, the house of the first Lord Rothschild. Frequently, smokers were exiled to cold garrets, such as at Breadsall Priory in Derbyshire or Cardiff Castle.

The trend toward having a small smoking room next to the billiard room, on the other hand, promised to be more comfortable. Over two thirds of the British country houses built between 1835 and 1870 had their own games room together with a smoking room annex. This is where the gentlemen withdrew after dinner to relax with tobacco and brandy. This reflects the increasing separation of the sexes, often thought to be so barbaric on continental Europe, and therefore associated with the fact that occasionally liberal, eyebrow-raising erotic works of art were to be found in the smoking and games rooms.

A jacket that you wear when smoking – that's all a smoking jacket is really. Smoking tobacco was a male preserve when it first became fashionable. The idea that the smell of smoldering tobacco leaves should not offend the delicate female nose took such a hold, that not only did the men withdraw to a separate room, but they even changed their jackets to prevent the smell of the smoke clinging to their clothes after they had finished smoking.

A glance at the velvet smoking jacket and smoking cap makes obvious the original purpose of the velvet slipper, now a popular inside shoe. The toe cap of this shoe, which usually has a quilted lining, is often embroidered with initials or a coat of arms, for example. Today this combination of smoking jacket and velvet slippers often also looks good on the host of a private dinner party.

As with tea, port, and sherry, the British have successfully adopted many imports. The Havana cigar has become an integral part of their way of life. A dinner party would be incomplete without a cigar.

At Davidoff's of 35 St James's Street, London, cigars are kept in a walk-in humidor. They also sell all the accessories a cigar lover could wish for.

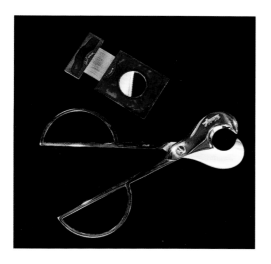

Biting off the tip of the cigar is neither particularly stylish nor does it do the cigar any good. It is better to use a special, sharp instrument. Such instruments come in many shapes, such as the form of scissors or as a small guillotine. The latter sits well in a waistcoat pocket.

The humidor is essential to prevent cigars from drying out over a longer period. This air-conditioned container comes in all sizes, from the size of a shoebox to a walk-in wardrobe.

A cigar smoker does not really care what is written in an ashtray. The main thing is that the cigar can be propped up in it without damaging the burning end. For this reason, there are indentations in the sides of the ashtray to hold the cigar.

The cigar case holds a day's supply of the precious rolled tobacco leaves and its firm sides provide optimum protection for this delicate commodity. Such cases are available not only in cigar stores, but also from exclusive haberdasher's stores or manufacturers of quality accessories.

THE BAR

The pre-prandial drink is an important part of British dining ritual. The choice of drinks on offer to relax the mind and stimulate the appetite is relatively limited. Gin, usually served with Indian tonic water, must be the classic British drink. The Dutch juniper-flavored spirit probably crossed the Channel to England in the 16th century and was an immediate success. The gin from those days would not appeal to the modern drinker, however, since it did not acquire the dry flavor we know today – "London Dry Gin" – until the end of the 19th century.

If you do not like the taste of gin, you can replace the juniper-flavored spirit in a gin and tonic with vodka. As well as the original Russian makes, brands made by Russian exiles are also popular in Britain, such as the American Smirnoff, for example. People also like Scandinavian vodkas, such as the Swedish Absolut vodka, or Finlandia.

As an alternative to white spirits, many British people have a whisky before the meal, usually with ice and soda water. After lunch or dinner, whisky is again served, but this time either neat or with ordinary water. Alongside gin, whisky is the most famous British spirit. Although it is really a Celtic drink, the British have long adopted it as one of their own national drinks. The way it is spelt hints at its country of origin, whisky being from Scotland, and whiskey from Ireland. American bourbon really has no place in an English decanter. Despite the high regard in which many single malts are held, every house bar nearly always has a few "solid blends" as well. These are much prized by connoisseurs, since they are of a consistent quality. Brands such as The Famous Grouse, Cutty Sark, or VAT 69 are especially popular. Some enthusiasts even drink their whisky during the meal

The house bar is often found in or within easy reach of the dining room, because, for most British people, the pre- and post-prandial drink is an integral part of the pleasure of eating, if not quite the most important aspect of the whole occasion.

instead of wine, a habit that Princess Margaret, the Queen's sister, is alleged to practice.

If you prefer less alcoholic drinks, you can always have sherry. The British predilection for this Spanish drink dates back to 1587, when the great English seafarer Sir Francis Drake seized 3,000 barrels of wine in Cádiz. The name "sherry" originates from the Britons' inability to properly pronounce the Spanish town this wine comes from: Jerez de la Frontera. The quantities in which British travelers buy up this Andalusian specialty in duty free shops proves the continued popularity of this classic drink.

After the meal, British hosts serve port. This is actually a Portuguese product adopted by the English in the late-17th century. In the 18th century, port was drunk in large quantities even during the meal, in the same way as we drink red or white wine today. Even in the 19th century, decanters mounted on rails circling the table served thirsty guests with a constant top up. Along with this mobile decanter, such heavy consumption of port is now a thing of the past, but the ruddy complexion of some of Her Majesty's subjects could still be a result of the Portuguese wine even today.

The after-dinner drink is a great British ritual. The heavy crystal decanters in which the precious liquids are kept are an essential part of this ritual. Whisky or cognac really does taste just that little bit better when served in sparkling crystal glasses. There are also special decanters for red wine. In the past, they really were essential, because the wine had often been stored for a long time and had to be exposed to the air before being drunk. For this reason it was poured into a bulbous decanter.

London is the perfect place to buy genuine British decanters for your house bar. You can buy old and new, expensive and inexpensive decanters in numerous antique stores or flea markets. Old decanters are more expensive when bought as a pair rather than singly. Engraving increases the value, as does silver decoration. An exact date is often difficult, since signatures and markings are not always found on the base. Usually only experts can assess whether the old object in question is of value, whereas a new decanter made by Asprey of New Bond Street, for example, is definitely valuable.

Red wine needs to be decanted only if it is old or very old. If you prefer to drink your red wine young, you will not usually have to contend with any sediment at the bottom of the bottle.

Antique Crystal Decanters
– Care and Cleaning

All a second-hand or antique crystal decanter usually needs before being ready for use again is a quick rinse. If the dirt and calcium deposits prove to be resistant to just a normal wash, you will have to resort to a brush or abrasives.

If ordinary washing in water and detergent is not enough, you should first try cleaning it with a bottle-brush. Its bristles will loosen stuck-on remains, without damaging the glass.

Decanters that are only moderately dirty need only be washed in water and detergent like normal china. This will get the inside clean enough so that it can be used for its original purpose once again.

Some deposits cannot be removed without resorting to abrasives. But be careful, as shaking the decanter too enthusiastically can damage it inside.

In the kitchen of an old house, historical accuracy and matching styles can be achieved only to a limited extent. So even in a Tudor house which has been authentically restored in every respect, you'll find hot running water, a fridge, and an electric cooker.

THE KITCHEN

THE CHEF'S DOMAIN

Medieval houses did not have kitchens as we understand them today, and cooking was done above a large open fire in the great hall, the forerunner of today's hall. Not until the 16th century were separate rooms used for food preparation. These early kitchens were far more than simply primitive versions of present-day ones; both architecturally and in terms of facilities they were surprisingly sophisticated. Just about any form of cooking could be done on the hearth, and the kitchen itself was as carefully planned as today's streamlined designer versions.

The main difference between modern kitchens and those of previous centuries is that the number of rooms used for the storage, preparation and cooking of food has greatly decreased. In the 16th century, for example, apart from the kitchen itself there were special rooms for storing food, making dairy products, curing and smoking meat and fish, and for any jobs involving the use of water. Today, all these processes are carried out in a single room. Produce is mostly kept in the kitchen itself unless the refrigerator, freezer, and other storage facilities are located elsewhere, for example in the cellar, to save space. Part of the reason why modern kitchens are a lot smaller is that we now have so many electrical appliances doing jobs that were once carried out by humans and required more room. Also, today we tend to buy produce such as bread, jelly, and dairy products rather than making it ourselves.

The second difference is the change in the social function of the kitchen. Once it developed as a separate room, it ceased to be a place in which the owners would spend time. It was not until the First World War brought about dramatic social changes that it became not only acceptable, but necessary, for the owner of the house to become actively involved in the work that went on in the kitchen. Before this, if you could afford to employ kitchen staff, you did so. However, the idea of dining informally with guests in the kitchen itself, or actually sharing the cooking with them, is a relatively modern phenomenon.

In the late 16th century, after the kitchen was displaced to the basement, the owners of the house would scarcely have been aware of it for most of the time. It became a purely functional room, and there was virtually no reason to enter it unless you were employed to work there. This does not mean that the myth of hearth and home does not exist in Britain. On the contrary, it is a firm part of the national consciousness, but it relates more to the open fire in the living room, and ideally in all the other rooms, than to that in the kitchen. In the past – particularly before the First World War – it was possible to create a homely atmosphere without ever venturing into the kitchen.

Today the wheel has turned full circle, and wealthy home owners either pay other people to do their cooking for them, or spend hours practising it as a hobby. Making sauces and knowing which kind of knife to use is regarded as a sign of a sophisticated lifestyle, guests sit in the kitchen and chat with the host as he or she does the cooking, and kitchens are often open-plan so that they form an integral part of the living area. Their design, and whether they are fitted or unfitted, will depend on how they are to be used and whether they are intended for living, working, or both.

A traditional fitted kitchen is very much a status symbol in the western world, and Britain is no exception, but here the way people use their kitchens is partly to do with how they perceive themselves and their position in society. Many Britons look down on the kitchen, seeing it as the territory of the servants or au pair, and try to maintain the pretence that they never set foot anywhere near it themselves. In practice, this often means using fittings which are not too obviously expensive, and perhaps doing without a fitted kitchen, to give visitors the impression that the kitchen is not nearly as important as the reception rooms. It may be crammed with state-of-the-art electrical appliances, but a tatty-looking cupboard or sink can be used to spoil the effect, and the kitchen can be deliberately arranged to create a sense of chaos using piles of unwashed dishes.

While some modern kitchens have a carefully cultivated patina of age, with dried flowers cookery books, and bric-a-brac, many have genuinely changed little since before the First World War. But as every gourmet knows, the quality of your food has nothing to do with the age of your kitchen. People cooked no less well in the past than they do now; quite the contrary. And if the Aga is doing a perfectly good job, why exchange it for an electric cooker?

Far left: The kitchens of stately homes were very spacious because large households had huge numbers of visitors. They were often located well away from the dining room to ensure that guests could not glimpse behind the scenes.

Left: The kitchen of Lanhydrock in Bodmin, Cornwall, gives a good idea of the state of the art in 1881. It was built as part of the reconstruction following a devastating fire.

Opposite page: It is perfectly possible to have a modern kitchen in an old house, as this one in an 18th-century country house in Dorset shows.

Many British homeowners take great pride in their old cast-iron stoves, which act as a magnet for the inhabitants and their guests in winter.

Every kitchen needs a table unless it has fitted worktops. In a country-house kitchen, a beautiful old table is both a work surface and a place to eat, and can even be used for purely aesthetic reasons if people rarely eat in the kitchen.

Pots and pans of all shapes and sizes line the simple shelves in the kitchen at Chatsworth. The slightly improvised-looking style of storage is extremely practical, although it may not entirely comply with the everyone's idea idea of a perfectly designed kitchen.

The choice of kitchen chairs largely depends on the style of the rest of the furniture. The Windsor chair is particularly suited to the country-house kitchen, and was first made toward the end of the 17th century, reputedly in Buckinghamshire.

Many British country-house kitchens have large enameled Belfast sinks, which are deep enough to wash even big piles of plates. If you are not fortunate enough to have one in your house already, you can always get one made to order.

This large free-standing kitchen dresser serves a similar function to the cupboard units of a fitted kitchen. Items like this can be bought either as originals or modern copies, made to measure if necessary. The shelf units above the lower cupboard section can be used to display plates.

Kitchen tools can be stored above the worktop for easy access and to save space. This very British solution is given a modern note with sunken downlights.

Also typically British are these cast-iron corner shelves for pots and pans. Open storage is recommended only if the utensils are used frequently. Otherwise, particularly in rural areas, they quickly get dusty.

THE FITTED KITCHEN

Each year, many Britons realize a dream by buying a beautiful old house in the countryside, far from the noise and pollution of big cities. But a new home can often prove to be a nightmare, with many years of renovation and rebuilding required before it is completely habitable. And in many cases, the kitchen is the biggest problem. If you invest in a Georgian, Victorian, or even medieval house, you don't want to ruin its charm by replacing historic features, but at the same time it is impossible to manage without modern conveniences such as a refrigerator, freezer, microwave, dishwasher, and extractor hood. The problem lies in reconciling the two contrasting needs by having a kitchen which uses modern technology but matches it to the style and period of the house; the solution may be to bring in kitchen designers.

For many Britons, a country-house-style designer kitchen combines the cozy, idealized world of the past with the comfort and convenience of modern technology.

One example is the company established by Howard Robinson and George Cornish, which for the past 15 years has been supplying fitted kitchens, baths, and specialist living room furniture. During this period, it has become the most sought-after business in the industry.

Howard Robinson began his career as a cabinet-maker. Later, he attended Leicester Art School and went on to study graphic design at Coventry Art College. He gained further experience of furniture manufacture by working for a cabinetmaker who had studied with Edward Barnsley, whose workshop in Petersfield counts the royal family among its clients. The more knowledgeable Howard Robinson became, the more interested he was in antique furniture.

George Cornish has a background in hotel management, which gave him an insight into the world of catering and kitchens. He also loves antiques and furniture restoration.

Since the mid-1980s, Howard and George have been planning and building kitchens under the label Robinson and Cornish. The company's most obvious trademark is that it has no trademark; there is no such thing as a "Robinson and Cornish kitchen" which is immediately recognizable from specific details. Rather, their philosophy is to produce a wholly individual design for each project, and it goes without saying that the materials and appliances they use meet the highest standards of quality.

In 1987, Robinson and Cornish breathed new life into an item of kitchen furniture known as the Belfast sink. They did this for one of their customers, Mrs Montgomery, the granddaughter of the famous Field-Marshal Montgomery. She had owned a Belfast sink herself, but it had long since been banished to the basement laundry, so she asked Robinson and Cornish to build one in her kitchen. The idea caught on elsewhere, and these sinks are now much more widespread than they used to be. They are very deep, providing plenty of room for mountains of saucepans, crockery, and cutlery.

Over the years, Robinson and Cornish have transformed numerous kitchens in Britain. They now also design bathrooms, living rooms, and specialist tailormade furniture, and customers have come to appreciate the highly personal service they provide.

Once you decide to commission them to plan and build a kitchen or other project, all it takes is a phone call. George Cornish or Howard

Right: Even an old London townhouse can be fitted with a modern kitchen, as this example in Fulham shows. The designers have succeeded in incorporating the owner's requirements, right down to the smallest detail.

Far right: Until the 18th century, the kitchens of country houses were mostly dark, stuffy rooms which nobody went into unless they had to. Today, they could not be more different: they have become bright, modern living spaces.

The Aga often takes the place of the old hearth as the centerpiece of the kitchen. Like many kitchens by Robinson and Cornish, this example is fitted with a traditional Belfast sink.

Robinson will pay you a visit as soon as possible. They believe it is particularly important to meet customers face to face, find out what they want, and decide whether this is aesthetically and practically feasible. And they also believe it is very important to consult the customer at every stage of the process; after all, the customer knows best what they need, and in many cases already has specific ideas which can be realized only by an expert.

After this meeting, Howard Robinson produces a set of sketches and costings, and if these are acceptable to the client, work can begin. Howard and George are available to answer questions throughout the process, advising on such subjects as electrical appliances, flooring, and wall tiles.

Robinson and Cornish's designs are always traditional ones, because they believe that traditional design will suit any room. Perhaps the best way of describing their style would be "understated," and the biggest compliment a customer can give them is to say "It looks as though it's always been here." This says two things: firstly that the design fits its surroundings and is seamlessly integrated with the house in every respect, and secondly that the new kitchen is nearly as good as an old one; after all, people are convinced that just about everything was better in the past.

The Stove

No traditional British kitchen would be complete without a traditional cast-iron range, combining a stove, oven, and boiler. The first patent for such a device, which has never really caught on outside the British Isles, was awarded to Thomas Robinson. He had found a way of using the fire in a stove to heat the oven at the same time. His fellow Briton Joseph Langmead perfected the invention by adding a hot water boiler to the stove and oven, a combination which became widespread in large parts of the country during the decades that followed, particularly in coal mining areas. Elsewhere, it took slightly longer before people stopped using traditional open fires in their kitchens, but in 1813 it was noted that in Derbyshire there were hardly any houses that did not have cast-iron ranges.

Later, the system was further enhanced so that the hot air from the stove or oven could be diverted. Users could therefore choose whether to use it to heat the boiler or oven, or close a flap to keep it in the stove. A range which trapped and reused the hot air was known as a closed one. In Victorian times, the closed range was the most popular and common combination of a stove, oven, and boiler, and the first patent for such an item was awarded to George Brodley of Exeter in 1802. One of the most successful manufacturers of this improved system was William Flavel, of Leamington.

Following the British preference for open fires in the hearth, closed ranges were nearly always placed against the kitchen wall, and freestanding ones which could be accessed from either side never became really popular. As the closed system meant that little heat could escape, it was sometimes quite dangerous to use such a device for cooking and heating. It actually required a certain amount of skill to limit the huge amount of heat and make optimum use of it.

In the 1920s, gas-fired stoves and ovens began to replace coal-burning ones and a Swede, Gustav Dahlen, invented the most famous of all British ranges. This was the legendary Aga, a development of the closed range which became the embodiment of the cozy British kitchen. It consisted of

Opposite page: To many Britons, a large Aga or Raeburn range is as essential a part of a kitchen as an open fire in the living room. For this reason, it is not uncommon for people to use non-functional ranges purely for decoration, and to cook on an ordinary electric cooker when no one is looking.

two extremely well insulated ovens and two hotplates. One oven was very hot, the other slightly cool. The hot oven was heated by the radiant heat from the coke fire inside, while the cooler oven and hotplate were heated by the dissipated heat from the hot oven.

Even though the Aga was soon replaced by gas or electric stoves, many people kept them in their country houses. Today, used Agas are restored by specialist companies and sold as antiques, and a number of manufacturers, such as Stanley Cookers in Wrexham, make Aga-style cast-iron and enameled ovens. These modern versions can be operated using gas, electricity, wood, or coal, and the boiler often provides the whole house with heating and hot water. This sophisticated development of the traditional system is very much in the tradition of the first cast-iron ranges of the 18th century,

and many Britons still feel more comfortable with one than with a continental cooker. These ranges are still often found in traditional houses.

Right: The forerunner of the closed range was the early 19th-century open range, itself a development of the open fire. This example is in Saltram House in Devon.

Far right: The National Trust property of Dunham Massey in Cheshire has a huge Aga in the kitchen, dating from 1938. Agas of a similar age are still in use in many homes.

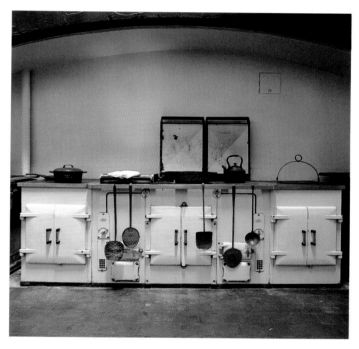

Right: This kitchen at Lanhydrock, Cornwall, represented the state of the art in the late 19th century. The closed range is a forerunner of the legendary Aga.

Far right: Free-standing stoves and ovens in the middle of the kitchen never really caught on in Britain. This example from the 19th century therefore has rarity value.

Colorful Printed Tea Towels

No kitchen in the British Isles is complete without a tea towel. Up and down the country, they are to be found hanging up to dry on cooker handles, and as long as people continue to do their washing up by hand or use old crockery which is not wholly dishwasher-proof, this will go on being the case.

As from many details of interior decoration (such as the hand towels in the bathroom and the number plate on the front door), you can tell a lot about the owner of the house from their tea towels. Some use simple white ones with blue or red checks; this design was common throughout Europe in earlier times, and goes very well with an Aga or a country house kitchen. Others use Arts and Crafts tea towels based on designs by William Morris. Little old ladies in cozy country cottages may favor the typical flower patterns which are available at the London store Liberty's, while those seeking to display their love of Britain's architectural and rural heritage may buy theirs from National Trust shops.

Alternatively, if you want to demonstrate your sense of humor, there are plenty of tea towels bearing witty motifs and slogans to hang in your kitchen.

But don't be deceived: a tacky or badly designed tea towel does not necessarily reflect on its owner's tastes, and some people deliberately choose the worst ones they can find. So it is sensible not to judge the rest of the house by one item since there may be a collection of valuable 17th-century antiques in the next room.

The best place for tea towels is on a rack by the cooker, where they are within easy reach and can dry out when not in use.

KITCHEN CLASSICS

If you're a frequent visitor to British homes, you'll be familiar with some typically British items of kitchen equipment. Take the electric kettle, for instance, which is not the cheap plastic water boiler of the kind sold in electrical and department stores all over the world, but a proper, solid steel kettle with a built-in heating element. One particularly beautiful example of an electric kettle is made by Russell and Hobbs, and is a direct descendant of the legendary K1 Automatic Kettle designed by Bill Russell and Peter Hobbs in 1955. Alternatively, if an electric kettle is too modern for you, you can simply place a normal one on the stove. Real traditionalists use copper ones, not just on aesthetic grounds (they look extremely warm and welcoming), but also to reduce the waiting time for a cup of tea, since the metal is highly conductive.

Another unusual sight for many foreigners is the nutcracker, which unlike elsewhere in central and northern Europe is not just used at Christmas. The British love to eat nuts all year round, and you'll find this handy utensil in just about every kitchen.

One popular patent nutcracker looks like a cross between a C-clamp and a vise, and works on the same principle. The nut is placed between the jaws of the device and cracked using a screw mechanism. It is made of heavy cast iron, which might seem a bit like using a sledgehammer to crack a nut, but

Every cook knows this problem: you want to follow a recipe from a cookbook, but it won't stay open. This bookstand makes life much easier, with its heavy cast-iron page holders.

you can't beat the satisfaction of shattering the hard shell of a Brazil nut into a thousand tiny fragments.

A full British breakfast will always include eggs in one form or another, perhaps scrambled or fried. But there are also two less well known but very British ways of cooking eggs which involve utensils made specifically for the purpose. One is an egg coddler, a porcelain container roughly the shape and size of a very large egg cup with a screw-on metal lid. To make this delicacy, you break an egg in a cup, whisk it, season it with salt, pepper and Worcester sauce to taste, and pour it into the egg coddler. Next, put the lid on and place the container in boiling water to cook the egg.

The second typically British method of boosting your cholesterol levels at breakfast time involves the use of a simple metal ring with a handle, which is placed in the frying pan (see illustration). A broken or beaten egg is then poured into the so-called egg poacher, which prevents it from spreading out to the edges of the pan, so that bacon or other ingredients can be cooked at the same time.

This handy metal ring keeps the egg in shape and stops it from spreading across the pan.

A Quick Cuppa

Just as the Germans, Dutch, and Finns love their filter coffee, so the British are addicted to tea, though espresso and cappuccino are becoming increasingly fashionable. Drinking tea is not some elaborate ceremony that takes place on the dot of 5 o'clock, with the steaming brew being delicately poured into Wedgwood or Spode porcelain cups; no, your everyday tea is made by placing a teabag in a mug and pouring hot water onto it. Go into any office in Britain and you'll see empty mugs strewn all over the desks, waiting to be filled with fresh tea.

Some connoisseurs claim that British teabags make the world's best cup of tea, and Tetley's and other brands still make popular souvenirs for visitors to Britain. Other countries have never quite managed to create a teabag that gives an authentically British aroma, though as the Marks & Spencer store chain continues to expand onto the continent, there is hope for Anglophile tea drinkers abroad.

Teabag tea is not tea unless drunk from a mug. These come in a huge range of colors, designs, sizes, shapes, qualities, and prices. Any London souvenir shop worth its salt will sell them, probably decorated with Union Jack motifs and portraits of the Queen. You can also buy mugs bearing the logos of famous department stores, companies, and institutions. And if you don't want to sully your lips by allowing them to come into contact with a common-or-garden earthenware mug, you can always buy one made from the finest porcelain.

Many mugs bear messages, such as the owner's name, a witticism, or aphorism. Environment-conscious households will inevitably have mugs bearing invocations to save the whales or the rainforests, and most people's crockery cupboards are home to a chaotic jumble of colors and advertising slogans. Often, the cheapest mugs survive the longest, not infrequently lasting longer than the company they are promoting.

The tea mug is as much a part of everyday life in Britain as tea itself. Together, they provide an opportunity to switch off, put your feet up, and contemplate the meaning of life. Nothing symbolizes a refreshing break as well as an earthenware mug.

Right: The dairy was an important part of houses in earlier centuries. It was used to store milk and make cream, cheese, and butter, so hygiene was a major priority.

Far right: Before the electric refrigerator was invented, food and drink had to be kept at low temperatures using ice. This was stored in ice houses, chests, or cellars. During the winter, people could make their own ice; at other times of year they had to buy it in.

FOOD STORAGE

Another essential feature of any genuine country house is a well equipped pantry. Here, you'll find home-made dairy products, preserves, pickles, and relishes; fruit and vegetables from the garden, and homemade ham, bacon, and sausages. The pantry has a long tradition in Britain, and every country estate from the Middle Ages onward had its own home farm, making it virtually self-sufficient. From the mid-16th century, this was often located well away from the house where its smell would not offend the inhabitants.

Elsewhere it remained an integral part of the house itself; examples include Uppark, built toward the end of the 17th century, and the 18th-century.

The home farm provided not only meat from cattle, sheep, pigs, and poultry, but also milk and eggs. Members of the landed gentry had a very varied diet; they owned pigeon lofts, hare and rabbit hutches, fishponds and game enclosures, and also grew their own cereals. Agricultural produce could be processed in the house itself; butter, cream, and cheese were made in the dairy, which was also used to store eggs, and there was often a bakehouse and a brewhouse. Baking and brewing were usually carried out by the same person, since they used many of the same ingredients such as malt and hops. In many cases the bakehouse and brewhouse were situated next door to each other.

Produce not intended for immediate consumption was preserved by salting, smoking, drying, or freezing. Fruit and vegetables could be boiled, or stored on shelves in the cellar. Game had to be hung and processed separately from the rest of the meat because of its strong aroma, and some estates, such as Uppark, had separate buildings for this purpose.

Storage techniques such as chilling and freezing were common long before the invention of the electric refrigerator. But as the United Kingdom has never been a particularly warm country, full-scale ice houses were not built until the 17th century, perhaps after travelers saw them being used in Italy. A well constructed ice house could be used to store ice for two years. If you couldn't make your own ice, you bought it; there was a flourishing trade in the early 18th century, and in the 19th century it was actually imported via a scheduled shipping route between England and Norway. This meant that ice could be obtained at any time, and the huge ice house in London's Haymarket was used to store up to 1,500 tons at a time.

Later on, houses stored ice in separate cellars or cabinets, and mobile ice chests appeared around the middle of the 19th century. These simply slowed down the melting process, and refrigerators as we know them today were first mass-produced in the United States. The first domestic electric refrigerators appeared in the shops in 1913, and made their appearance in larger British kitchens during the 1930s.

The salting room at Tatton Park in Cheshire was used to preserve meat. Once it had been salted, it was wrapped in clean cloths and hung on hooks from the ceiling.

Robert Adam built Kedleston Hall, in Derbyshire between 1770 and 1772. This monumental estate also includes a lake and a small fishing house. This had two boathouses and an unheated swimming pool on the lower floor, and a fishing room on the upper story where people could keep dry and comfortable while casting their lines. Among the fish that can be caught here are (left to right) trout, river perch, tench, carp, perch, and eels.

Only a few of the many different preservation methods are still used today. The most common is probably the storage of potatoes and the boiling of fruit and vegetables to make jams, jellies, and pickles. Despite the overwhelming variety available in the supermarkets, this type of home cooking is still practised by many Britons, partly out of nostalgia and partly due to the need for independence which results from living on an island. The British also like to offer their guests home-made jellies, pickles, relishes, and wine, and in most cases they rightly display a great deal of pride in these.

Left: Jam is among the classic home-made preserves. Others include pickles and relishes, which give added flavor to cold meat and sandwiches. They are made using tomatoes, gherkins, carrots, apples, cabbage, and onions, which are finely chopped and cooked in vinegar.

Far left: Today, the large drawers of a modern fitted kitchen replace the pantry of yesteryear. Many Britons in the country still stock their larders with home-grown fruit and vegetables, partly out of nostalgia and partly because it tastes better and is rewarding to cultivate.

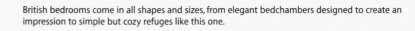
British bedrooms come in all shapes and sizes, from elegant bedchambers designed to create an impression to simple but cozy refuges like this one.

THE BEDROOM

The History of the Bedroom

The huge fourposter bed in one of the 175 rooms of Chatsworth in Derbyshire is more like a throne than a place of sleep.

Until the late Middle Ages, very few middle- and working-class homes had separate bedrooms. Most people slept in the great hall, which was also used for cooking and eating. Peasant families would often use the dining table as a bed by turning the tabletop over and placing a straw sack on it. Separate bedrooms first appeared in the 15th century, and were used not only for sleeping but as a place to which the women of the house could retire while the men caroused in the hall.

The bedchamber was initially a private place, though toward the end of the 16th century it also began being used as an elegant living room. During the following century, visitors were even invited into the bedchamber while the host was getting up or dressing; this reflected the influence of the French court and the daily rituals of the king, which were adopted by the English upper classes during the Baroque period. Aristocratic bedrooms were richly decorated, with magnificent, throne-like beds draped in huge quantities of fabric, frequently being the most valuable piece of furniture in the house.

In the 18th century people stopped receiving guests in their bedrooms, and these grew smaller. They were often replaced by dressing rooms which also served as living rooms, studies, and even bathrooms, with portable baths and three-legged washstands. In the mid-18th century it became common to take ice-cold baths on health grounds, and country homes had their own bathhouses built specifically for this purpose.

The most important item of bedroom furniture in wealthy households was the fourposter bed. The curtain material was chosen to suit the temperature and situation; while medieval beds used thick layers of fabric to protect against draughts, lightweight silk ones often sufficed in later periods. Instead of a canopy mounted on four pillars, some people preferred to have just two at the head of the bed. Using less fabric in the bedroom also had the advantage that pests such as moths, lice, fleas, and bedbugs were less likely to be a problem. Until the 18th century people slept sitting up, so beds were much shorter than they are today.

Modern British bedrooms differ little from their 18th- and 19th-century predecessors. Then, as now, they contained a large bed (with or without a canopy), a chest of drawers, a dressing table and of course seating, so that they could also be used as a dressing room and living room. But what aspects of this are typically British? Well, one example is the traditional fourposter bed with its quilt, and another is the bedside lamp with a fabric shade. Other traditionally British items include the chest of drawers and mirrored dressing table. And one distinctive feature you would not necessarily find in a French, German, or Italian bedroom is an item of furniture at the foot of the bed, such as a table, cabinet, or sofa. Britons seem to have a unique predilection for placing matching items of furniture together, for example a narrow table along the back of a sofa.

Having seating in the bedroom is a practice which goes back to the time when it also served as a reception room. This was the case elsewhere in Europe until the situation changed in the 19th century and the bedroom increasingly became a very intimate room purely for sleeping. In the Netherlands or Spain, no one would have dreamed of receiving guests in the bedroom; it would simply have caused embarrassment on both sides. The only outsider allowed into the bedroom was the doctor visiting sick patients.

You might expect a similar thing to have happened in Britain, but here the bedroom furnishings suggest otherwise. In their collective unconscious, the British still seem to have a vague memory of the time when bedrooms were also living rooms. As recently as the Victorian era, they were used for all kinds of purposes other than sleep. People breakfasted in the bedroom, not necessarily in bed but often on a small table near the fireplace. After this, they would use it as a dressing room to prepare for the morning's events. Later, they would return to change for lunch, and after this they would have a post-prandial nap on the bed or sofa. In the early evening, they would go to the bedroom to read books or write letters before changing again for dinner.

The fact that bedrooms were used intensively throughout the day was reflected in their furniture: not just a bed, bedside cabinet and chest of drawers, but also living room furniture which could be used for such purposes as breakfasting, reading, and writing.

For these reasons, British bedrooms are quite distinctive in character. They are cozy, rustic, and in some cases designed to create an impression. And they are also the ideal place in which to curl up with a good book and a cup of tea while a gale rages outside the window.

Opposite page: A night in Syon House is a journey back into history. Although the bedrooms have every modern convenience, if you took away the electrical installations you could be in the 19th century. This is Princess Victoria's bedroom.

Bedroom Furnishings

In a modern house or apartment, the bedroom is one of the most private rooms. If someone takes you on a guided tour of their home, they will show you the living room, dining room and, if they have a particularly luxurious house, the billiard room and wine cellar. But the door of the bedroom will usually remain firmly closed. Ask why, and they will tell you there's nothing worth seeing, or that it's in a bit of a mess. But this was not always the case. In earlier times, the bedroom functioned as a multipurpose living area and its furnishings were designed appropriately. An elegant bed occupied the central position to impress visitors, and there would be a suite of upholstered chairs and various tables, ideally placed near the fireplace so that the occupant could keep warm in winter. There might also be a writing desk at the window to ensure the maximum amount of light, and by the time wardrobes and dressing tables were included it could be quite cramped. But this lack of space, combined with the typical mixture of colors, shapes, fabrics, and styles, has always been a major factor in the distinctively cozy character of the British bedroom.

This bright, cheerful bedroom at Llangoed Hall in Wales has a traditional layout: a highly ornamental fourposter bed takes center stage, while a chair stands in the corner and a sofa at the foot of the bed provides a secondary focal point.

The British bedroom not only provides a relaxing night's sleep, but also serves as a study during the day to which you can retire to read or write. This inviting example is in Elton Hall, Cambridgeshire.

Chatsworth House, the seat of the Duke and Duchess of Devonshire, is idyllically located in Derbyshire. Its numerous bedrooms have a whole series of valuable fourposter beds. This one has been placed close to the window to give a view of the garden.

Opposite page: This elaborate, highly upholstered fourposter bed has been fitted neatly under the sloping roof.

Above left: The Mauve Room in Castle Leslie, Ireland, is a fine example of a spacious bedroom which is also suited to daytime use. The Royal Suite, with its ensuite dressing room and bathroom, has accommodated royals and rock stars such as Mick Jagger and Marianne Faithfull.

Above: While the voluminous curtains and canopies of a fourposter bed can look somewhat imposing, this ensemble is much more light and airy. The ornamental frame of the bed is echoed by the delicate structure of the chair.

Above: The fourposter is a classic among beds. It was originally designed to protect the occupants against drafts, cold, and prying eyes. As the canopy and curtains required large quantities of fabric, the bed was often the most expensive item of furniture in the household.

Far left: No British bedroom would be complete without the typical bedside lamp. These come in a great variety of styles, from the grandeur of gleaming brass to romantic flower patterns.

Left: You are unlikely to find modern art in a traditional bedroom in Britain. Instead, the walls will be decorated with watercolors, oils, old engravings, framed caricatures, and even paintings by the owners of the house.

Either one or two bedside tables are an essential feature of any bedroom. These are used to contain everything the occupants might need during the night, and may be round, square, or rectangular.

The washstand is a relic of times when houses did not have running water, and hot water for one's morning shave was provided in a jug by the servants. Today, washstands are a very popular form of decoration in country homes.

Above: The chest of drawers is another traditional item of bedroom furniture. Clothes requiring vertical storage are usually stored in a wardrobe in the dressing room, while the chest of drawers is used to store bedlinen, underwear, shirts, and sweaters.

Right: A small desk or bureau allows you to dash off a quick letter before bed, while a comfortable armchair can be used to read yourself to sleep.

Beds

To some people, a bed is simply a place to lay their head, while to others, it is their favorite place in the whole of the world. It is even possible to run an entire country from underneath a pile of blankets; the great wartime leader Winston Churchill followed the example of many kings by spending the morning in bed dealing with state affairs, making phone calls and dictating letters to his secretary while clad in his dressing gown, with his beloved cats for company.

In earlier times the bed was considered a prestigous object, and was designed and decorated accordingly. The late medieval box bed or cupboard bed was enclosed on three sides, with a curtain for privacy on the fourth side and a mattress which was supported by ropes. Every now and then these ropes had to be tightened; this what the expression "sleep tight" refers to.

The design of this early 19th-century Regency day bed is full of classical allusions.

Only the rich and famous could afford beds like these. During the 16th and 17th centuries, huge fourposter beds were common in wealthy circles; the heavy masses of fabric protected against draughts, but also provided an ideal breeding ground for pests of all kinds. The half-tester bed of the 18th century, with its half-canopy resting on two pillars at the head of the bed, did not significantly improve the situation. But at about the same time, people also began sleeping on couch beds which had no posts or canopies; as the curtain fabric was the most expensive thing about the whole bed, these offered a cheaper alternative. A further improvement in ventilation and hygiene occurred with the introduction of metal-frame beds during the Regency period.

Fourposter beds were way beyond the reach of most ordinary people. The heavy wooden frame cost a small fortune, the curtains were made from meters of expensive fabrics, and the canopy often bore gilt ornamentation in the form of the family crest or other motifs.

Narrow, couch-like beds like this one were introduced during the Regency period, and represented something of an innovation in British bedrooms. In the past, the bed had always projected out into the room, but this type could be placed up against the wall.

The half-tester bed appeared during the 1740s. Two posts at the head supported a relatively simple canopy and curtains, and there were no posts at the foot of the bed.

The traditional twin bedroom has wooden beds which can be placed either together or apart, and can be used as a bedroom for guests or older children.

Once it was realized that beds containing large quantities of wood and fabric were breeding grounds for bedbugs and fleas, the metal bed became more popular. This provided better ventilation and had the added advantage of being relatively inexpensive.

The shimmering gold finish of the brass bed gave it a smarter appearance than the iron version, and meant it could be used in the smartest and most formal of surroundings. During the Victorian period, brass fourposter or half-tester beds were very popular in country houses.

Bedroom Curtains

Choosing bedroom curtains might not seem like the most demanding of tasks. Strangely enough, though, many homeowners are dissatisfied with theirs, secretly annoyed at having paid through the nose for tailormade curtains which simply are not up to the job.

One of the most common causes of buying unsuitable curtains has to do with the time of year when you buy them. If you choose them during the summer, you are likely to end up with a bright, cheerful, and relatively lightweight fabric, which may prove to be a costly mistake as the fall approaches and you find there is a permanent draft and the room is never completely warm. Buy new curtains in winter, and the chances are they will be woolen ones, so that in the summer you will be woken by the sunlight streaming onto your pillow at six in the morning. In the dark days of December, you don't think of the possibility of using roller blinds to keep the July sun out.

Window coverings for the bedroom should always take account of changing light and weather conditions. They should also be easy to open and close, and it should not be necessary to shift piles of furniture out of the way to open the window in the morning.

As windows in British houses rarely close properly, most people tend to choose heavy curtains. But in fact, heaviness is not necessarily essential. Even fine silk can do the job if you sew a warm interlining of felt or cotton waste between the outer material and the lining. In a more rustically styled room, you could also use stitched quilting. A valance of the same or a different pattern as the curtains can be placed along the top of the window, and a tieback attached to the wall by a hook can be used to keep the curtains open during the day.

Right: Net curtains provide privacy, and filter out bright sunlight. Apart from these benefits, they also provide a visual link between the brightness of the window and the opaque curtain fabric.

Far right: Bedroom curtains should be chosen not only on esthetic grounds, but also on practical ones. If the room receives bright sun in the morning, particularly in summer, they need to be thick enough to stop you being woken up too early. They should also be easy to open and close.

Right: The strong upright lines of curtains held open by tiebacks provide an attractive contrast to the horizontal lines of the sash window.

Far right: This room breaks one of the fundamental rules of British interior design, which is to use a mixture of patterns. Here, the curtains used for the window and the fourposter bed are both made from the same patterned fabric.

HYPNOS – THE WORLD'S MOST COMFORTABLE BEDS

When night falls over Buckingham Palace and the Queen's servants prepare her bedchamber for the night, the mattress on the bed will almost certainly have been made by Hypnos.

Not far away, in Clarence House, Queen Elizabeth the Queen Mother provides daily evidence of the fact that nothing is more relaxing and orthopedically beneficial than sleeping on a Hypnos bed. Which is why this highly traditional manufacturer of beds, mattresses, and upholstery has been nominated as supplier to both courts, and is therefore entitled to print two royal warrants on its products and brochures.

The business is the result of a merger between two family companies, both around 100 years old and both located near High Wycombe in Buckinghamshire. George Henry & S. Keen Chairmakers was a highly respected manufacturer of items that were mostly made from native beech. They were regarded as almost indestructible, and were therefore popular with hoteliers and restaurant owners throughout Britain.

The other company was William S. Toms Bedmakers, which manufactured beds and other bedroom and dining room furniture and marketed it under the Hypnos brand name. Hypnos was the ancient Greek god of sleep, and the son of the night-goddess Nyx, and his blessing therefore guarantees a pleasant night's repose.

The two companies merged in 1986, but continued to use the highly appropriate and now very well known Hypnos label, together with the words "Makers of the most comfortable beds in the world." They are now seeking to prove this ambitious claim from their headquarters in Princes Risborough, not far from High Wycombe.

Reflecting changing conditions in the chair market, Hypnos now builds fewer of its hard, stable models for offices, and concentrates on more comfortable luxury seating for upmarket restaurants and other customers. While it no longer makes bedroom and dining room furniture, it is expanding its bed workshops. Hypnos supplies mattresses and beds for home use, and also to hotels, old people's homes and other institutions where a good night's sleep is particularly important. In addition, it can make individual products to order if they need to be of a non-standard size.

The secret of the Hypnos mattress' legendary comfort lies in its sophisticated multilayer construction and high-quality spring core.

Hypnos' upholstery and mattresses have a high-quality finish (many of the production stages are carried out by hand), and are known for their durability and orthopedic properties. They also comply with statutory fire resistance requirements; mattresses for home use must not catch light even if a newly lit cigarette is placed on them and allowed to burn down to a stub, nor if a lighted match is dropped onto them. Even stricter criteria apply to products used in institutions and smaller hotels. Here, a wooden tower is built on top of the mattress and set alight; this is known in the fire protection regulations as a "Crib 5." To ensure safety in old people's homes, mattresses must be sufficiently fire-resistant to survive the burning of a larger "Crib 7."

In common with all other manufacturers, Hypnos is required to test each new product thoroughly. Once the product becomes part of its permanent range, it must be fire-tested again at intervals of six months. Products made individually to order must also undergo testing.

For maximum comfort, the bands of pocket springs are placed as close together as possible so that the individual springs form a honeycomb pattern. The bands are then tied together by hand. By this stage, the final shape of the mattress is clearly apparent.

The spring core itself is obviously not at all comfortable, and is therefore covered in layers of the finest upholstery materials; soft white cotton felt, horsehair, polyester fibers, and silk are particularly suitable. Finally, the outer material is laid on top of the filling.

Once the pocket springs have been individually packed into their fabric pockets, they are sewn together to create a band. Each mattress contains several hundred springs to ensure that the sleeper's body is fully supported, no matter how much they toss and turn.

The sides of the mattress are finished by a master upholsterer using a long needle and strong yarn to ensure that they remain in place. This makes it impossible for the outer springs of the core to slip, and the mattress stays in shape.

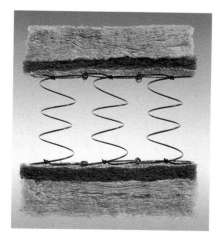

The core of a pocket spring mattress consists of individual springs which are packed into individual fabric pockets and then sewn together in a honeycomb pattern. This means that each spring can move independently and the body of the sleeping person is properly supported. The metal core is covered in several layers of upholstery material before the outer skin is added. Finally, the mattress is carefully stitched so that all the parts stay in place, creating the attractive deep-buttoned surface.

In an open-spring or open-coil mattress, the springs are not packed individually, but are connected with spaces between them. This structure means that the body weight is evenly distributed over the whole surface of the bed. Although it contains fewer springs than pocket-spring versions, it is just as comfortable. The spring core is covered in generous layers of upholstery fabric and the mattress is stitched together.

The Orthos range of beds caters for those who prefer a harder mattress. If space is short, some of the models contain built-in storage drawers in a variety of configurations.

The Queen carries out an extremely busy program of engagements for a woman of her age; perhaps the high quality of the mattresses she uses provides her with a good night's sleep, which helps her to fulfil all her royal duties. Both she and the Queen Mother have awarded royal warrants to Hypnos, providing a useful and highly effective form of advertising for the company.

Right: The Duchess deluxe model is a top-quality classic from the Hypnos range.

Far right: In common with all other models, the President Deluxe is available in normal or slightly harder versions.

Right: The Orthos range of mattresses is designed for those with more contemporary tastes.

Far right: The Sherwood Spacesaver can be expanded into a double bed. The second mattress is pulled out and raised to the same level as the first using legs that fold out.

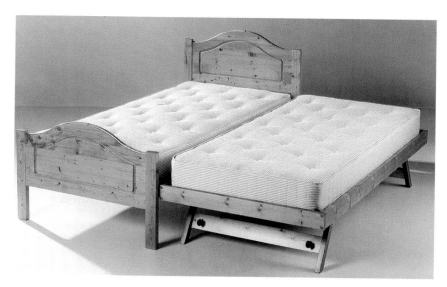

Hot-Water Bottles, Electric Blankets, and Other Survival Strategies

Generally speaking, it is never particularly warm in British houses, and in old ones it can be positively arctic. In summer, you may even find guests going outdoors to warm up. How can this happen in what is otherwise such a cultivated and advanced country? After all, central heating was invented a long time ago, and you'd think that everyone would have it by now. But in fact, many country homes are heated solely by open fires, and in rooms where there is no fire burning, the temperature can be absolutely freezing.

Many householders are put off installing central heating by the cost and disruption involved, but part of it is down to fear of change; people would rather don an extra sweater or wrap themselves in a blanket.

But not every old British house is like an icebox. Many have been centrally heated since the 19th century and had a couple of new systems fitted since then, but even these are never really warm. And in many modern houses which ought to be comfortable, you won't find the kind of temperatures that are taken for granted in other European countries. In fact, scarcely a single house in Britain is truly warm and comfortable from basement to attic – either in the city or in the countryside. Even when the temperature in the living room, kitchen, and bathroom is reasonably acceptable, you may still find it hard to suppress a shiver as you walk down the hall or up the staircase.

So the message for anyone receiving an invitation to such a house is: Take plenty of warm sweaters, and a heavy tweed three-piece suit and a comfortable wool-and-cotton shirt and warm underwear won't go amiss either. The low temperatures in British homes are part of the reason why in many cases, fashion is still stuck in the 1960s.

There is also a separate dress code for going to bed: lightweight cotton or thicker flannel pajamas, depending on the season. Warm bedwear is essential in winter if you don't want to be kept awake by the sound of your own teeth chattering; some houses are heated only by open fires, and when these die down in the small hours of the morning, the cold inevitably starts creeping in.

Don't worry if you forget to pack nightwear when you visit a British country house. Usually, the wardrobes will contain pajamas and nightdresses for guests to use.

A woolen nightshirt will keep you warm in the most arctic of stately homes. If you're not too worried about the way you look, a traditional nightcap makes the perfect finishing touch.

One solution to this problem is an electric blanket. Elsewhere in Europe, this is regarded as an outmoded device used by elderly people, but in Britain it can be a lifesaver on a bitterly cold night. Some visitors, knowing that their bedroom is going to be freezing and there is no electric blanket, will take their own with them. And when all else fails, there's always the good old hot-water bottle.

Sheepskin-lined slippers might not win any prizes for stylishness, but they make a very effective form of insulation.

This is the view that is likely to greet you in the morning if you visit a stately home in winter – it doesn't really entice you to leave the bed and seek out a freezing bathroom.

A rubber hot-water bottle is the ideal companion as the mercury plunges. Filling and distributing these to guests is a nightly ritual.

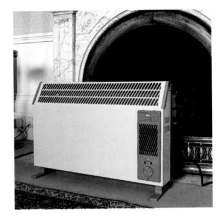

Convector heaters can be used to provide rapid relief in rooms which are particularly chilly, though their electrical safety sometimes leaves a great deal to be desired and they might cause power failure in very old country houses.

Left: A thick, heavy wool dressing-gown is essential if the bathroom is a long way down the hall.

Above: Even if you normally prefer to sleep nude, you may change your mind when you discover how cold British country houses are.

The Nightcap

Of course, the concept of the nightcap is not specific to Britain. All over the world, people like to partake of a final draught of Scotch malt whisky or fine cognac before settling down to their slumbers. It has a pleasure all of its own, with none of the social connotations usually associated with alcohol. In the words of the 18th-century British writer J.T.J. Hewlett, "The only glass that a man ought to take 'solus' is the night-cap tumbler."

But this institution has a particular resonance in the unheated bedrooms of Britain's country houses. It was in Britain that the word "nightcap" was first used to describe a drink rather than an item of clothing. You wore a nightcap to keep you warm at night, and you drank a nightcap for similar purposes.

The other ostensible reason for having a late-night drink is to help you sleep. As is so often the case, science has debunked this long-held preconception. Researchers have found that although alcohol does make you fall asleep more quickly, the sedative effect lasts only three or four hours. After that, the alternation of deep sleep and active REM sleep is disrupted, and you're far less likely to have a refreshing night's repose. Also, the sleep-inducing effect of alcohol diminishes as your body develops greater tolerance to it, so you need more alcohol to achieve the same outcome. And as if that weren't enough, you're more likely to snore after a nightcap.

THE BRITISH AND THEIR BEARS

Teddy bears seem to exert a particular fascination in Britain. They were not actually invented in the United Kingdom; the two most likely countries are Germany and the United States, though as with many great inventions it seems that a number of people on different continents had the same idea at roughly the same time.

In Germany, it was a company called Steiff that introduced the first prototype teddy bear. In the United States a Russian immigrant couple, Morris and Rose Michtom, came up with the idea and sold the first bears in their toy and stationery store in Brooklyn. They may have been inspired by a caricature published in the *Washington Post* on November 16, 1902 depicting President Theodore Roosevelt, who had gained a great deal of public sympathy by refusing to shoot a bear when he was out hunting.

But the Michtoms' bears did not achieve true success until 1903, when a wholesaler began distributing them nationwide. In the same year, Steiff launched its first bears at the Leipzig toy fair, and by a stroke of great good fortune, the American importer George Borgfeldt ordered no fewer than 3,000 of them. This paved the way for the teddy bear to become a truly international brand, and in fact the German company very soon became the

Roger Moore and his wife, the singer Dorothy Squires, returning from a vacation in the company of a large toy panda.

world's leading manufacturer. By the year 1907, Steiff was churning out nearly one million teddy bears every year.

In Britain, the first teddy bears were made by a company called J. K. Farnell in 1908. There was a cool response from the British public, and so most of its output was exported at first. At the same time, two other German companies began seriously competing with Steiff: one was Schreyer & Co. with its brand Schuco, and the other was Gebrüder Hermann KG. But the success of German bears was abruptly halted by the outbreak of the First World War, as German imports were banned in Britain. Many British manufacturers seized this opportunity; they included J. K. Farnell, Atlas, Bassett Lowke, Chad Valley, Deans Rag, Harwin, Rees, and Terry. Today, it is not always easy to identify which company made which bears, as only a few of them were clearly labeled.

The postwar period was a difficult one for many cuddly toy manufacturers both in Great Britain and elsewhere; people had more pressing needs than teddy bears. However, many very attractive and successful makes of bear came onto the market, such as the legendary Chiltern "Hugmee" which was manufactured for over 50 years, beginning in 1923.

Arguably, the real star of the novel and movie Brideshead Revisited is the teddy bear Aloysius.

The Bucknell sisters and their teddy-bear mascot taking part in a car race in Barnet, near London, in 1930.

These two Royal Air Force bomber pilots have been given a lucky teddy by their ground crew.

The Second World War left many companies ruined, but the market for traditional bears was revived in the 1950s and 60s. High-quality manufacturers – Steiff and Schuco in Germany and Chiltern and Chad Valley in Britain – were the most successful, thanks to an increasing amount of television advertising and cheaply produced mass-market toys.

But the golden era of the teddy bear was the Edwardian period. Significantly, probably Britain's most famous literary bear dates from this period: not Winnie the Pooh, the hero of those beautifully illustrated children's stories, or Paddington Bear, but a distinctly marginal figure in world literature: Aloysius, from Evelyn Waugh's 1945 novel *Brideshead Revisited*. The narrator, Charles Ryder, describes an encounter with his later friend, Sebastian Flyte. He is very taken not only with Flyte's extraordinary good looks, but also with his large teddy bear. The eccentric aristocrat has just

bought a hairbrush, not to brush its fur but to hit the unfortunate creature if it misbehaves.

It is not clear why so many British people still cling to their teddy bears when they are adults, though literary examples like this one may be a part of the reason. And in a nation of eccentrics, a love of small cuddly toys is a long way down the scale of odd behavior. Therefore it is not surprising that the best-known bear of modern children's literature, Paddington Bear, is clad in a typical country house outfit, with Wellington Boots, a raincap, and a big duffle coat.

Edward Heath, Conservative prime minister from 1970 to 1974, is accompanied on the piano by Kermit the Frog and Paddington Bear.

The most popular cuddly toy of all time reputedly takes its name from a caricature of US president Theodore "Teddy" Roosevelt published in 1902.

1960s British pop legend Marianne Faithfull clearly had a weakness for bears.

THE DRESSING ROOM

A separate dressing room is generally regarded as the epitome of luxury. Mention that you have one, and you are implying that you live in a really big house; few smaller homes would have space for such a room.

It was not until the 16th century that homes began to have small, separate apartments which might contain a bedroom, a small reading and breakfast room, and a personal dressing room. By 1590, for example, Elizabeth Talbot, Countess of Shrewsbury (better known as Bess of Hardwick) had a whole series of private bedchambers at her seat, Hardwick Hall. There was also a small room with an elegantly decorated "close stool," which contained an early type of toilet.

Towards the end of the 18th century the concept of the private apartment declined slightly in popularity, but many bedrooms still had adjoining dressing rooms, often furnished in a similar way to small living rooms.

These were used by only one person, and it was unusual for husbands and wives to spend long periods together. Each had their own rooms which the other could enter, but only as a passing visitor. The lady of the house usually had her own bedroom and boudoir in which she received her female guests during the day. The husband slept either in his bedroom or in the dressing room, which usually adjoined the study where he received friends, and had a separate bathroom.

During the Victorian era, space became short as the population grew dramatically. Large-scale housing programs were implemented, and furniture began to be mass-produced. Few members of the new middle classes had space for more than one bedroom, let alone a separate dressing room, and it was during this time that couples began sleeping in double beds and also using their bedrooms for storage. The dressing room remained a distant dream for many people as they squeezed past huge wardrobes and chests of drawers each evening on their way to bed. The only way to fulfill this dream was by moving to a large old house, and once they had done this they wondered how they had ever managed without a dressing room. Soon, it became one of the most popular rooms in the house.

Right: Early dressing tables were simple affairs with two or three drawers. Later on, in the Georgian period, they made clever use of shelves and compartments to maximize the amount of storage space.

Far right: An electric trouser press is another useful dressing room accessory.

This clothes stand, a stylized approximation of the human form, allows jackets, pants, and ties to be hung flat.

No dressing room is complete without a mirror. A new one is fine, but one that has been handed down through the generations is even better. If it is old, spotted, and not very effective, a new mirror can always be placed on the inside of the wardrobe door.

Elegantly designed hatboxes provide excellent protection against dust and sunlight, and are a must for all hat owners.

Luggage stands are usually associated with hotels and guesthouses, but they are sometimes found in dressing rooms.

In the past, the British distrusted dry cleaning and preferred to clean their own suits and other items where possible. A well equipped household would have different brushes for fine cashmere, coarse tweed, and medium-fine wool.

The chest of drawers is a traditional British item of furniture. The present-day form with five drawers first appeared in the 17th century. Even then, designs varied a great deal to suit users' differing needs.

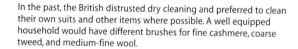

A WEEKEND IN THE COUNTRY

The country weekend is a world-famous British institution that has changed little since the beginning of the 20th century. The host invites friends, acquaintances, or business colleagues to spend Friday evening, Saturday, and Sunday in his or her country house. The invitation is issued orally or by letter; the bigger the house, the more formal the invitation.

Depending on the size of the household and the social status of the host, you may be received personally by the owner of the house, or by the butler or footman. If more than one set of guests is expected, there may be a list displayed on the wall showing who has been allocated which room, and how to find it. On the evening of your arrival, there will usually be an informal dinner preceded by drinks, providing an opportunity to get to know the other guests. After dinner, people may sit around talking, but there is unlikely to be a big program of events.

The weekend proper begins on Saturday morning with a cup of tea or coffee in bed, probably followed by a traditional cooked breakfast. The morning is spent engaged in a variety of activities, and sitting around doing nothing is definitely not on the cards. The agenda may include a spot of shooting, or a walk or drive in the local area; you will need to get as much exercise as possible in order to work up an appetite for another big meal at lunchtime. The same applies after lunch, since you now have to somehow find room for a sumptuous afternoon tea, perhaps consisting of sandwiches and scones with clotted cream.

Another long walk will prepare you for dinner, which is always the social high spot of the weekend, when you will be expected to dress up to the nines. After a menu consisting of a variety of courses – hors d'oeuvres, soup, a fish dish, a meat dish, and dessert are obligatory in most houses – the hosts may well provide entertainment, perhaps in the form of billiards for the men, charades and other ice-breakers, and possibly some amateur theatricals.

Only the biggest homes have more than one guest room, but they are an investment; the more guests you invite, the more return invitations you can expect to receive.

What to Pack

Dinner suit – This is essential if you are spending a weekend in the country, since the main dinner on Saturday night is likely to be a very formal affair.

Evening gown – If the men are wearing dinner suits, the women should wear evening gowns. If you are unsure of the exact dress code, it is quite acceptable to ask the host.

Tweed suit – This is a classic and very practical choice of clothing for both men and women. Steer clear of continental imitations, which are often too lightweight.

Tattersall check shirt – These are available in a wide variety of colors and check sizes, in lightweight cotton for the summer or wool mixes for winter.

Stout shoes – It is possible that the host will want to show his guests around and take them for a long walk to see the remotest corners of the surrounding landscape, so proper shoes are indispensable.

Warm sweater – A necessity both for long walks and poorly heated houses.

Barbour jacket – The Barbour is the ideal way of coping with the vagaries of the British climate. One owner reportedly lost his jacket and found it months later, buried in the mud, while building a new front drive. He hung it up to dry in the airing cupboard for a few days and gave it a new coat of wax, and it was as good as new.

Dinner suit

Evening gown

Tweed suit

Tattersall check shirt

Warm sweater

Barbour jacket

Stout shoes

On Sunday morning, you may be expected to go to church; for atheists, this is an opportunity to catch up on the Sunday papers. After lunch and afternoon tea, guests will gradually start to drift off home; if your host should invite you to stay for dinner, they will not normally expect you to accept the offer.

Make sure you leave a tip in your room for the staff if you want to be invited again. If you have a large enough circle of friends and acquaintances and are a reasonably likeable sort of person, you can expect to spend just about every weekend in this manner, and of course if you're lucky enough to have this kind of lifestyle yourself, you'll be expected to host such occasions. Some students enjoy a steady succession of weekends in the country with various friends, finding it an ideal way of stretching a limited budget and probably aware that at some time in the future, they will have to do the same for the next generation of young people. Because for all the changes that are taking place in British society, one thing is for certain: as long as there are country houses, there will be weekends in the country.

THE FULL ENGLISH BREAKFAST

One essential part of any weekend in the country is a cooked English breakfast. However, it is hardly an enticing prospect for vegetarians, because the few non-meat ingredients may well have been fried in animal fat.

As staying in a country house normally involves physical activity, you will need to stoke up on the calories at breakfast time. Bear in mind that a few hours after demolishing a pile of sausages, eggs, bacon, baked beans, porridge, and toast and marmalade, you face the prospect of tackling a lunch of roast beef and Yorkshire pudding. It is for this reason that walking, shooting, riding, and sightseeing are such an essential part of a country weekend; without them, you would not be able to do justice to the huge amount of food that gets heaped onto your plate. Sit indoors and do nothing and it is certain that you won't make it past afternoon tea, which would be a real pity. So forget everything you've ever been told about a healthy balanced diet, and throw caution to the winds.

The bread used to make toast should be white, thinly sliced, and of a typically soft, spongy consistency. The toaster magically transforms this into something edible, and it is then spread with butter and marmalade or jam (jelly).

The essential components of an English breakfast include freshly cooked items such as scrambled eggs, and cornflakes or other cereals.

Grilled or fried bacon is another vital ingredient, and needs to be cooked to just the right degree of crispness.

You will often be offered a choice between fried and scrambled eggs; other people prefer theirs soft-boiled.

Black pudding is a fresh blood sausage which is fried and served hot.

Grilled tomatoes are one of the few healthy ingredients of an English breakfast, and make an excellent complement to scrambled eggs and bacon.

Porridge is an acquired taste. Some swear by this hot oat cereal, served with cream and sugar or syrup; others detest it.

Fried or grilled sausages are an ideal way of stoking up on the calories before a strenuous weekend in the country. The best varieties reputedly come from Newmarket.

Kippers are salted and smoked herrings. Bloaters, which are less commonly found nowadays, are herring or mackerel which have been partially dried and smoked.

Baked beans in tomato sauce, perhaps the quintessential British dish, are now starting to catch on in other European countries.

Mushrooms fried in butter or oil make the perfect finishing touch to a British breakfast.

THE PERFECT GUEST BEDROOM

A good host is generous not only with the food and drink offered, but also with those little details that can make all the difference to your stay. One is a jug of water in the bedroom to satisfy late-night thirsts. Another is a new, sealed pack of paper tissues, because there's nothing worse than having an attack of the snuffles while in someone else's house and having nothing to wipe your nose on.

A pen and paper are ideal for jotting down those brilliant ideas that come to people in the middle of the night: poems, mathematical formulae, and the plot of your latest movie or crime novel, all of which may be the fruits of a weekend in the country.

And what are weekends for if they're not for reading? There's nothing worse than being caught short of books, and a thoughtful host will leave the guest bedroom stocked with a selection of titles by the likes of Agatha Christie, James Herriot, P.G. Wodehouse, and John Le Carré.

Another nice little touch is a selection of classic fragrances for guests to try; perhaps a bottle of Trumper's Extract of Limes, Penhaligon's Blenheim Bouquet, or Calèche by Hermes. A new bottle of shampoo and an unused bar of soap may be appreciated by guests who have stopped by at short notice. The emphasis is on the word "new;" guests cannot be expected to put up with messy, half-empty shampoo bottles and bars of soap with hairs stuck to them.

The finishing touch in this well equipped guest bedroom is a vase of fresh flowers that fill the room with their scent – provided, of course, that you do not suffer from hay fever.

Ideas of hot and cold vary a great deal from one individual to another. One person may be sitting there shivering while another complains about how hot it is, which makes it difficult for the host to know whether there will be enough blankets. To err on the safe side, it's always advisable to provide an extra one.

Visitors who wake up with a sore throat or a headache after the previous day's exertions will welcome a selection of remedies in the bedside drawer.

It is also a basic courtesy to provide one or two clean towels, particularly if your guest was not expecting to stay. And a freshly laundered dressing-gown will not go amiss either, particularly when the bathroom is outside in the hall and shared with other people.

It can be quite annoying when the guest discovers whilst unpacking that there are no coathangers in the wardrobe of the guest room. A good host knows this and will therefore ensure that there are enough coathangers for suits and dresses.

Top left to bottom right: Fresh water for late-night thirsts, paper tissues for attacks of the snuffles. Stationery for writing letters and jotting down ideas. Eau de toilette for guests who have left their own at home. Fresh flowers provide a friendly welcome. An extra blanket for those freezing nights, and remedies for the effects of overindulgence. Towels are a must, and so are coathangers.

THE BUTLER

The popular British television series *Upstairs Downstairs* chronicled the lives of masters and servants in a large house. Its worldwide success was the result of the nostalgia which Edwardian Britain arouses in so many hearts. The different strata of society were clearly defined, and everyone knew their place – whether they were satisfied with it or not.

After the First World War, the prospect of life as a housemaid or valet became increasingly unattractive. The servants lived under one roof with their employer, and in most cases were much more comfortable than at home, but in return they had to be available around the clock. The male servants reported not to the lord or lady of the house, but to the butler, while the housekeeper oversaw the female staff.

The word butler derives from the French *bouteiller*, the member of staff who in medieval France was responsible for managing the drinks. In Britain, however, the butler had to carry out a much wider range of tasks from the outset, which included ensuring that there was a plentiful supply of beer, milk, butter, cheese, and candles. In the first half of the 17th century, he also became responsible for bread, salt, cutlery, crockery, and wine. From about 1650 onwards, the butler supervised all the male employees and was assisted, and deputed for in his absence, by an under-butler.

By the beginning of the 18th century, the butler was in charge of just about everything that went on in the household, including serving meals, managing wine stocks, and storing and cleaning silver and glass. Only in very large, formal households did he report to a superior, the steward. As a rule, however, at least in the eyes of the other servants, the butler had more authority than anyone else in the household apart from the owner. He was like a company sergeant in the army, often having a clearer idea of what was going on than the owners themselves. By the 19th century, a butler was like a king with his own little domain, and a hundred years later he had his own rooms which served as an office, private apartment, and dining room.

There are very few households left in Britain where such formality prevails, or which employ more than one servant. In most cases, the butler has to do most things himself, and the view of this traditional role as portrayed in film and television is often a caricature of the reality. The butler would not have opened the door to guests; nor would he have carried their luggage

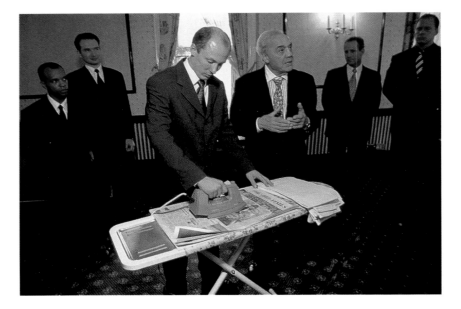

The purpose of the famous ritual of ironing the newspaper is not to smooth out the pages, but to prevent the ink coming off on your fingers.

up to their rooms. Rather, he would have delegated both tasks to the footman and maintained a discreet background role in ensuring that the job was done properly.

Some butlers achieved fame in their own right, but as in every profession only a very few reached the top. Training usually followed the principle of learning by doing, and a great deal of specialist tasks had to be mastered. A man rising to the rank of butler at the end of his career might have started out as a hall boy, and then been appointed as a steward's room footman, followed perhaps by a period as a storeroom or traveling footman. The next stage might have been promotion to valet, and after 20 years in the job, he might have taken the final step and become a butler. This was how the career of Charles Smith progressed. He took his first job at the age of 15, and for much of his life worked for Lord Mountbatten, whose butler had appointed him as a traveling footman. These days, it is rare for a servant to spend his or her entire career with one employer, and a butler is essentially a manager. As such he is no longer a minion, but a valued assistant to the master or mistress of the house.

Kazuo Ishiguro's novel The Remains of the Day provides a factually and psychologically authentic insight into the life of a butler obsessed with his work. The 1993 movie stars Anthony Hopkins.

Learning the Butler's Trade

In the days when every house had servants, there was no real need for a school for butlers. Nor was it possible to become a butler straight away; it was usually the culmination of many years in different posts. Few attained this elevated status, partly because, as with all management posts, there were not enough to go round, and partly because only a few applicants were suitable. But butlers sometimes managed huge houses and had levels of responsibility which would have left many a modern hotel manager seriously overworked. So there was only one route to the top: go into service as early as possible, and then gradually work your way up.

Ivor Spencer with Margaret Thatcher

At the beginning of the 21st century, this is no longer the case and the number of households with servants is constantly declining. Few people today would take on a 14-year-old boy as a full-time servant, not least because this would be classified as child labor. If you want to become a butler today, there is another, more direct route: applying to one of the numerous butlers' schools in Britain or abroad.

As the career of a butler is still inseparably associated with Great Britain, most choose a school located here in the home of this legendary profession. One of the best-known institutions of this kind is the Ivor Spencer International School for Butler Administrators, Personal Assistants, and Estate Managers.

Under the slogan "Our courses are an education. Our teaching is an experience," would-be butlers from all over the world are trained to carry out this demanding job. In the past it took a lifetime of practical experience to learn; today, it takes less than two months. But the variety of skills required is just as great. According to the school's brochure, they include buying food, wine, cigars, and clothes, and the administrative talents required to manage the house in a cost-effective manner and to high standards. A butler must also be well versed in every aspect of lifestyle and etiquette, and if necessary he should be able to teach these to a nouveau-riche employer. And it goes without saying, of course, that he should also be able to book flights over the internet or charter a yacht if necessary.

This six-week, carefully planned mixture of theory and practice provides a very effective substitute for learning by doing. Butlers from Ivor Spencer's institution go on to take up important posts with private households, hotels, and companies, and enjoy an extremely good reputation. One former student, now a successful butler, writes: "Mr Spencer successfully condenses into six weeks the skills which took the traditional butler 20 years to learn. Fantastic." Ivor Spencer still believes in transmitting his knowledge to his pupils in person, and with all the suavity you'd expect of a butler.

Ivor Spencer is famous not only for training butlers, but also as a toastmaster and after-dinner speechmaker.

Even bowing is an art that requires training. The deepest bow is reserved for one's own employer.

Ivor Spencer teaches butlers to serve champagne with a steady gaze and measured tread.

There is also a right way to pour champagne, and Ivor Spencer has taught hundreds of trainee butlers how to do it.

The school teaches theory as well as practice, and pupils learn to talk intelligently about champagne and other wines.

British-trained butlers are greatly in demand in the United States, not least because they can advise their employers on matters of style and etiquette.

THE SHOOTING PARTY

An invitation to a country house often involves shooting. When the British refer to hunting, they are usually talking about the pursuit of foxes; hunting in the continental sense is referred to as shooting. Both hunting and shooting are controversial sports in the United Kingdom. The skills involved were formerly passed down from one generation of a family to the next, or taught by a gamekeeper. Today, most people gain their first experience of using a gun at a shooting school. You should always have learned to use a weapon properly before accepting an invitation to a shoot.

In Britain, people have traditionally shot with side-by-side shotguns, which means that the barrels are side by side rather than one above the other as in the continental version. Those who can afford it have their own guns made to order by an old-established and renowned gunsmith such as Purdey or Holland & Holland. British shooters also wear very different clothing to their counterparts in continental Europe or the United States; the most important item is a three-piece tweed shooting suit with knee-length trousers, which might sound rather ridiculous, but has the advantage that your trouser legs do not get as dirty as they otherwise might. The outfit also includes a check shirt and of course a tie, and dressing up in this colorful, sometimes almost carnival-like garb appeals to the British sense of humor. However, very large checks or patchworks of different patterns remain the preserve of eccentrics.

The etiquette of shooting is similar in Britain to that which applies everywhere else in the civilized world. Always shoot at the sky; in other words make sure there is open sky visible behind the bird so that you do not hit anyone else by mistake. Always break and unload the gun when walking along, climbing over a fence or handing it to someone else. Make sure you are familiar with the game seasons during which specific animals can be shot, and check whether any other special rules apply before starting. And it is bad form to aim at birds which are already being targeted by other people, though if they miss it is perfectly acceptable for you to have a shot at it as well.

Shooters and beaters always eat separately, and the bag is divided up at the end of the hunt; the shooter usually receives a brace, which means a pair of birds, unless you are shooting grouse, in which case it means two pairs. The rest is sold to defray part of the cost of the shoot. Sometimes, the beaters and loaders receive a tip; if you're not sure, ask the host's advice. You should also write a letter of thanks the following day, and if the hunting invitation includes an overnight stay, a gift may be appropriate. Once you've mastered the etiquette of hunting and proved yourself to be a good guest, you'll undoubtedly receive more invitations soon.

Above: The snipe is a member of the shorebird family, and frequents marshy areas. The pheasant was introduced to Europe around a thousand years ago.

Below, left to right: The capercaillie, the largest European game bird. Wild ducks and geese can also be hunted in Britain.

The Main Game Seasons – What Can You Shoot When?

Grouse, ptarmigan, and snipe can be hunted from August 12 until December.

The partridge season lasts from the beginning of September until the end of January.

Pheasant and capercaillie can be shot from early October to late January.

The open season on ducks and geese lasts from the first few days of September until February.

The open season for woodcock is between early October and late January.

A Short Glossary of Hunting

Bag: the game killed on one day
Beaters: people employed to rouse or beat up game; also known as drivers
Bouquet: a group of pheasants
Brace: a pair (one male and one female) of grouse, partridge, or pheasant
Butt: a hiding place for grouse shooters
Clean shot: one which kills immediately
Couple: the unit used to count ducks
Covert: a thicket containing game
Covey: a group of grouse or partridge
Drive: to chase game toward the shooters
Ghillie: in Scotland and Ireland, a guide or assistant used in stalking
Gun: refers not only to the weapon, but also to a particular member of a shooting party
Hill: in Scotland, an area of moorland
Hot spot: an area of land where large numbers of birds can be expected
Loader: the person responsible for loading a shooter's gun, particularly when they are using two alternately, which is known as shooting double
Piece: in Scotland, a packed lunch
Stands or pegs: the places where the individual shooters stand
Wisp: a flock of snipe

The side-by-side shotgun is a traditional British weapon, but James Purdey & Sons also makes over-and-under guns.

HAVING YOUR OWN GUN MADE

The rifle and shotgun maker James Purdey & Sons, in London's South Audley Street, has a long history and probably the most illustrious client list of any company in the business. In fact there is hardly a prominent figure in the United Kingdom who has not come into contact with a Purdey rifle or shotgun at some time, either as a client or a descendant of former clients. In this tradition-conscious country, inheriting a Purdey gun is even more prestigious than buying one, because it proves that yours is old money.

The company was founded in 1814. Its first recorded blue-blooded client was the Prince of Leinegen, who ordered a double-barreled shotgun in 1823. The first member of the British royal family was the Duke of Gloucester, brother of King George IV, who bought a gun from Purdey in 1825. He was followed by the Duke of Cumberland, the Crown Prince of Bavaria and the Prince of Orange. And so the list goes on; today, the company's client database numbers some 28,000 people. You can see pictures of some of them if you visit the store; in most cases all you need do is ask nicely, and they will show you the Long Room, which is the company's hall of fame. Here, in the former dining room of the Purdey family, are photographs and letters of thanks from enthusiastic customers, together with historic shotguns and rifles.

Of course it's more expensive to have your own gun made for you, but the higher price is justified by the fact that it should suit you better and has involved many hours of work by master craftsmen. It takes over three years to complete a Purdey, and the client sees little of the process whereby this beautiful ornamental piece is completed. Halfway through it, you will be asked to choose the wood for the stock, a ritual which involves a second visit to the Long Room a few months after your measurements are taken. This time, you will select a rough wooden mockup, and the stock will be handmade in a lengthy and elaborate procedure designed to ensure that it exactly fits your body.

The outbreak of the First World War in August 1914 was disastrous for the company, because the 90-strong workforce needed a steady flow of orders to stay in business. Many of its best clients went off to war, and many were killed. The flow of orders from the empire of the German Emperors and from Austria-Hungary dried up, and the Russians were cut off from Britain by the war, which made it almost impossible to deliver completed weapons. A gun for the Russian count Paul Shuralov had to be shipped via Bergen in Norway, and in 1917 contacts with Russia were completely severed. During the Second World War, Purdey survived mainly by manufacturing tools, but this left no time for making its famous guns, and orders received from 1941 onwards could not be completed until after the war.

Even after 1945, the situation of this traditional company showed little improvement. The Labour government of postwar Britain made life difficult for luxury goods manufacturers, not least because former customers were now having to pay high taxes. But the company weathered this crisis

too, partly thanks to its overseas clients. Even today, a large part of its turnover comes from sales to the United States, Australia, Canada, South Africa, Japan, and South America.

A Purdey double-barreled shotgun will cost you upwards of £32,750 and, as with a car, the price can be significantly boosted by optional extras. Rifles are even more expensive, starting at £52,500. If price is a concern, then you should probably go somewhere cheaper. It's not as if Purdeys are the only guns; they just make shooting that little bit more enjoyable.

A well stocked gun cabinet is as essential a feature of a country house as a refrigerator or pantry.

How a Purdey is Made

If you'd like to own a Purdey rifle or shotgun, you have two choices: either buy one secondhand, or have one specially made. Either way, you will need to visit the store in South Audley Street. Buying a used gun has two advantages: firstly it is much cheaper, and secondly you can take it away with you. But a second-hand Purdey is never such a perfect match for the body and personality of its owner as a tailor-made one.

Apart from all the other advantages, buying a new gun also offers the pleasure of having something made specifically for you; it takes a long time, but that just increases the feeling of anticipation. The first stage in the process involves taking detailed measurements of your body: from middle of back to shoulder, neck to shoulder, shoulder to elbow, elbow to trigger finger, chest size, eye to chest level with shoulders, and the distance from this point to the shoulder. This is based on the conviction that if the gun is perfectly matched to your body, you will automatically raise it to the right firing position, and then all you need to do is take a sighting and squeeze the trigger. Of course, it helps if you're also a good shot.

Once the measurements have been taken, director Nigel Beaumont or chairman Richard Purdey will discuss other details with you, such as what type of game you want to use your rifle or shotgun for; this will affect the length of the barrel and the number of triggers. As soon as all these important matters have been dealt with, the factory in London's Hammersmith will begin building the gun.

Here, the first stage is to calculate the weights of all the components, both to comply with legal requirements and also to ensure that the gun is perfectly balanced. Next, the barrels are cut to the desired length and, in the case of double-barreled guns, they are soldered together. The breech mechanism and the front section are handmade and machine finished, and all the other steps are carried out by hand.

Once the breechblock and barrel or barrels are complete, work begins on the stock. This is made using French walnut from the Dordogne, which has exactly the right color, grain, hardness, and density. The shape of the stock will obviously be tailored to your measurements, and you will also be asked what type of engraving you would like. If you have no particular preference, standard engraving is used, but almost anything is possible for a price.

Next, the weapon is assembled and tested by experts on Purdey's own shooting range to ensure it is perfect in every way. After another inspection by the factory manager and a last check by Nigel Beaumont, the new Purdey is finally delivered to you, the eagerly expectant client, some three years after it was ordered. Many people order another one soon afterwards; once you've gotten used to shooting with a Purdey, nothing else will do.

Right: It takes at least five years to learn one of the eight specialist skills involved in building a Purdey: barrel making, action making, lock and trigger making, ejector making, stock making, engraving, and finishing. Here we see two barrels being joined together in the first stage, barrel making.

Far right: The very high price of Purdey shotguns or rifles reflects the fact that they are entirely handmade. What some might see as an anachronistic way of working in the computer age, others regard as traditional craftsmanship worth preserving.

Right: Apart from a single improvement, the ejector of a Purdey double-barreled shotgun works in exactly the same way as the original one designed by Frederick Beesley in 1880.

Far right: The stock of a Purdey rifle or shotgun is made from the finest French walnut. The chequering, or fine serration of the wood, is done by hand and uses over twelve lines per centimeter.

This bath in a country-house guestroom offers a perfect view of the grounds.

The Bathroom

Soap and Water

When visitors from continental Europe or the United States visit the bathroom of a British house, they are often amazed at how antiquated it is. Instead of the gleaming chrome-plated fixtures and fitted baths and washbasins they are used to at home, they find old-fashioned faucets, claw-foot bathtubs, and toilets with pull chains.

Even leading houses containing masterpieces of British interior design commonly have bathrooms of a standard which many foreigners would describe as primeval. But an old-fashioned bathroom of this kind is not seen as detracting from the quality of the house; on the contrary, it has usually been left in its original condition on purpose. Even modern ones bear many stylistic features from the first decade of the twentieth century. This has much to do with the British love of tradition, and after all, grandma's free-standing bath does just as good a job as a modern fitted one.

One drawback of British bathrooms is the fact that they often do not have mixer faucets. In traditional washbasins, the hot and cold faucets are placed one on either side, so that the hot water scalds you and the cold water leaves your fingers numb. The idea of being able to place your hands in a stream of warm water can only be brought to life by a double-ended rubber hose to act as a mixer. Some hotels and other establishments have made concessions to foreign tastes by installing devices that resemble mixer faucets and produce a single stream of water, but unlikely though it may sound, one side of the stream is boiling hot and the other freezing cold.

It is not just the love of tradition which makes a visit to a British bathroom a journey back through history. Performing your ablutions in a room which is fifty years out of date appeals to the British love of making do, which borders on masochism; people would rather stick with what they have than go through all the inconvenience of updating it, and their attitude toward anything remotely old-fashioned borders on religious veneration.

Many pre-20th-century homes did not have rooms specifically intended for washing, and there is therefore a widespread perception that standards of hygiene were poor. It is certainly true that people washed less often than they

Washbasins with hot and cold running water did not appear in British houses until the late 19th century. Before that, bathtubs and basins had to be filled by servants using large jugs.

do today, and they did so in the places where they removed their clothes, namely the bedroom or dressing-room. Until the early 20th century, they used washstands filled from jugs of water which had been heated over the fire either in the room itself or in the kitchen. Although baths with their own piped water supply are known to have existed in Westminster as early as 1169, they did not become widespread in Britain until the 18th century.

Portable bathtubs could be used almost anywhere in the house. There were various designs, though the slipper bath was particularly popular; this was shaped like an ankle-length boot, came up to the person's shoulders, and sometimes had a built-in charcoal stove to heat the water and keep it hot. Mobile shower baths were also surprisingly simple but effective, with a tank of water above the bather's head being emptied using a variety of mechanisms.

Bathhouses first came into fashion during the 18th century. Some wealthy aristocrats and commoners fitted their country homes with small-scale versions of Turkish baths or ancient Roman-style plunge baths. These were used not only for everyday hygiene, but also for specific health purposes, and had considerable prestige value.

In the 19th century, people began installing fixed baths and washbasins in their dressing-rooms, complete with running water. Many preferred to continue taking their baths in front of the bedroom fire, particularly if they had servants to fill the bath for them, and therefore saw no advantage in having water on tap. As a result, some of these old-style portable baths have survived until the present day, and you may still be lucky enough to encounter one in the guest room of a country house, preserved either out of nostalgia or due to a lack of facilities.

But many other bathrooms today are still of a standard more appropriate to the period between the late 19th century and the 1940s, typical features of which include free-standing cast-iron baths and boilers. Baths were first boxed in during the 1930s, but this concept never really caught on in Britain. Although a wave of modernization in the 1960s and 70s led to many old baths being scrapped, Edwardian ones enjoyed a revival in the 1980s. Many people ripped out their new baths and replaced them either with expensively restored antique ones bought at auctions, or reproductions. It is therefore sometimes difficult to tell whether an old-fashioned-looking bath is real or not, but either way, if you're a visitor to Britain and get the chance to have a soak in one, it will give you a feeling for what life was like at the beginning of the 20th century.

Far left: Victorian copper baths are a much sought-after item of traditional furniture, especially if they also have matching faucets.

Left: Hip baths were very popular, not least because they required less water than full-sized baths. During the 19th century they were available in many different designs, and sometimes, as in this example, had their own water supply.

A typical feature of British bathrooms is the use of carpets and other floor coverings, such as here in Holliday Hall. Although not very practical, these help to mitigate the coldness of many old houses.

Carpets, chairs, pictures, and other forms of decoration are rarely found in continental European bathrooms, but are taken for granted in British ones.

Above: Many Britons still prefer a good long soak in a bath full almost to the brim, whereas Americans and most continental Europeans would rather shower.

Far left: Bathrooms might be expected to have clinical white easy-clean tiles, but this is not the case in many parts of the British Isles, where bright colors and cozy decoration are the order of the day.

Left: As the demand for old country houses outstrips supply, other buildings such as stables and barns are often converted into homes, and therefore require bathrooms to be added.

The bathrooms at Elton Hall in Cambridgeshire are a joy for connoisseurs of British style, having changed hardly at all for generations.

This luxurious bathroom at Castle Leslie in Ireland's County Monaghan has been turned into something of an art gallery.

Not all British bathrooms are temples of nostalgia. Some owners of centuries-old houses have fitted glazed shower cabinets, underfloor heating, and sophisticated lighting.

At the beginning of the 20th century, it was realized that wood, carpets, and curtains were a breeding ground for bacteria in the warm, humid climate of the bathroom. Tiles, metal, glass, and ceramics were therefore used instead.

Baths with ornamental legs are rarely found in continental Europe, where fitted baths became the norm during the 1960s and 70s. In Britain, homeowners will often pay large sums of money for baths like this one, and turn them into a centerpiece. However, most have their own faucets and drainage; portable bathtubs are rare, though the chair beside the bath provides a reminder of a time when people bathed in their bedrooms and dressing-rooms. It also has decorative value, and makes a good repository for clothes.

The washstand is the predecessor of the present-day washbasin. Originally consisting of a simple bowl, it became a delicate and highly decorative item of furniture during the 18th and 19th centuries. Some were like writing desks, with marble surfaces for bowls, jugs, toothmugs, and other utensils; others consisted of a tripod with a matching bowl and jug. They were made of porcelain and stoneware, and were usually elaborately decorated with different motifs for men, women, and children. This painted Edwardian washbasin may once have had matching accessories.

Washing bowls and jugs may have fallen from favor, but they still make attractive and stylish bathroom accessories, perhaps in conjunction with a washstand.

A large natural sponge may not be cheap, but it is money well spent. Unlike the plastic version, it prevents the spread of bacteria and is also very durable.

These high-quality wooden bathbrushes can definitely cope with soap and hot water. Once a bathbrush has reached the end of its useful life, it can be hung on the wall as decoration.

When you have a free-standing bath, it is not always obvious where to put the soap. A beautiful old porcelain or stoneware dish is one solution to the problem.

Bottles of eau de toilette are an attractive and practical form of bathroom decoration. These may bear such famous names as Trumper's, Taylor's, and Penhaligon.

Bottles, glasses, and bowls of bath salts and oils stand within easy reach of the bath. These essences can be used to stimulate or calm, depending on your mood.

Showers

Given the important role that the bath has traditionally played in British culture, you might be excused for thinking that showers were not particularly popular. But in fact they are, and the great British spirit of invention has produced some interesting variations on the shower. The simplest method was obviously to pour buckets of water over yourself, but a more sophisticated way of doing it was displayed at the Great Exhibition of 1851. This consisted of a circular basin with four struts supporting a water tank above. The tank was opened by pulling a chain, and the water was released through a shower rose. It was then pumped back up the inside of one of the struts and into the tank to be used again. In some models, the tank was filled by climbing a ladder and pouring buckets of water into it.

Here, a 19th-century shower has been integrated with a modern bath.

The water in the tank at the top of the structure is released by pulling the chain.

THE GREAT VICTORIAN HYGIENE CAMPAIGNS

In the past, providing a house with water and sewerage systems was one of the greatest challenges facing architects. Buildings located close to rivers, streams, or springs were relatively easy to deal with, and in London mains water was available as early as the 16th century. But in the countryside, people obtained their water from wells, later with the aid of cast-iron pumps, and collected rainwater in tanks.

Pipes and storage tanks were made either of wood, which often leaked and rotted quickly, or lead. Pipes made from the latter material were much more durable, but many wealthy families that fitted their homes with full-scale pipe systems paid for this luxury with chronic lead poisoning.

In the second half of the 18th century, water suppliers such as the New River Company and the Chelsea Water Company began installing iron pipes. But the system was anything but comprehensive, and a large proportion of the population still had to make do with rainwater they had collected. The sewerage system was no better, as there were very few outflow pipes and these could not cope with solids, so blockages were inevitable.

Another problem was water pressure. The wooden pipes which were still widely used to transport water could not withstand high pressure, so many households had only a ground-level supply. It was not until the system was expanded, and lead and iron pipes were introduced in the first half of the 19th century, that the pressure could be increased and water could be supplied to the upper stories of buildings.

In the mid-19th century, most villages and many parts of London were a sanitary nightmare. In rural areas, a single water supply was often shared by many families, and there were hardly any drains or sewage pipes. In the cities, the existing system was failing to keep pace with rapid population growth.

Washstands were gradually replaced by ceramic washbasins during the late 19th century, their demise being hastened by the advent of mains water. The marble-style rim and cast-iron wall brackets are typical Victorian features.

As soon as running water was available in houses, there was an increased interest in alternatives to the traditional bathtub. This combination of a shower and a bath dates from the early years of the 20th century.

But at least by now people knew the importance of hygiene in fighting disease, and during the reign of Queen Victoria the water mains and sewer systems were expanded and improved so that nearly every household had its own water supply. Washbasins and baths were connected to the mains, and the tiresome task of filling them became a thing of the past. The first hot water-operated central heating systems were installed, and more and more houses had their own water closets. The Public Health Act of 1884 required houses to have toilets, and although these were often located outdoors, the first steps towards modern standards of sanitation had been taken. Things continued to improve during the 20th century, and the word "lavatory," which had previously referred to a bowl and jug used for washing, acquired its present-day meaning.

The Inventor of the Modern Flush Toilet: Thomas Crapper

People in Britain like to believe that Thomas Crapper of Yorkshire invented the WC. Unfortunately, this is not true, but he did introduce a technological innovation which was to be found in all toilets until the introduction of the modern water-saving flush mechanism. He called it the "valveless water waste preventer."

Until the 1870s, the water supply from the mains to the toilet itself was controlled by a simple valve. This meant that a huge amount of water was consumed, not only because the whole contents of the cistern was emptied into the bowl, but also because some people left their toilets flushing the whole time to keep them clean. Also, the valves were prone to leakage, and in London there were serious concerns that reservoirs might dry out.

Crapper invented a cistern in which the water was raised into the flushing pipe by air displacement. The chain operated a lever which reduced the pressure and sucked the water out of a small chamber, and after the chain was released, the chamber refilled for the next user.

This reduced both water consumption and leakage, and Thomas Crapper's reputation as a brilliant plumber was assured; in the 1880s, as a result of his invention, he was appointed as toilet installer to the court of Edward VII.

The bathroom should be an integral part of any authentic house restoration, and it is still possible to buy historically accurate reproductions of sanitary ware.

The design of the faucets used in washbasins, baths, and showers changed little for over a hundred years until the 1920s, when the mixer faucet was introduced.

Far left: The throne-like toilet in one of the many guest rooms at Castle Leslie in Ireland's County Monaghan.

Left: Chains are still a common sight in British bathrooms, even though modern handle-type toilets appeared back in the 1930s.

Perforated toilet rolls made their debut around 1880, and toilet-roll holders soon afterwards. Indoor toilets were becoming increasingly common, as were bolts with "vacant/engaged" signs.

A Very Private Place

In the age of the water closet, we tend to assume that our forebears were much less good at hygiene and waste disposal than we are. Although both towns and villages would have smelled distinctly unpleasant to modern noses, as the inhabitants simply threw their waste out of the window or tipped it into the gutter outside the door, British stately homes had sanitary facilities worthy of the name from a very early stage.

The fact that many of these houses do not contain bathrooms does not mean they did not have a "smallest room." In many cases, this took the form of a shed located as far away as possible from the living quarters themselves, to reduce the smell. Even in the 18th century, these private retreats had floor mats, candles, paper holders, and bookshelves.

If you felt the call of nature during the night but could not face the prospect of a long walk to the bathroom, you could use a chamberpot. Those of higher social status might have a close-stool, which was a seat with a lid that could be raised, concealing a bowl or pot. Close-stools were often disguised as small cupboards or chests and elaborately decorated, and it was the maidservant's job to empty the contents in the morning.

Earth closets first made their appearance in the mid-19th century. These were very similar to modern WCs, but the bowl was cleaned using earth or ash rather than water, and the waste fell through an opening into a container underneath.

Water was used in very early times to keep toilets cleaned. Outside toilets often used water from nearby rivers and canals, but indoors it was difficult to pump water and sewage through the primitive systems of pipes that were used. It was not until the 1870s and 1880s that the mains system was improved so that water would flow into the WC if a certain amount of pressure was applied. Also, people installed more modern toilet bowls which were easier to flush.

The study or library in many cases tells us more about the owner than any other room in the house, particularly as it is often a private place which few visitors see.

THE STUDY AND LIBRARY

FROM BOOKCASE TO INTERNET

A study can be a place for relaxation as well as work.

In the Middle Ages, British stately homes were not necessarily places of great erudition. Relatively few people were able to read, and it was not until around 1650 that the European Enlightenment led to an increased demand for education among the more affluent classes and books became more widespread. As a result of the great changes that occurred during the Tudor period, nobles connected with the royal courts needed to be educated if they were to take on new administrative tasks and keep pace with the sophisticated conversation of courtly circles. But only in the mid-18th century did people begin dedicating specific rooms in their houses to books, in a manner similar to the present-day library. The books were displayed in varying degrees of order in large shelves on the walls, with the higher ones being reached via a gallery or ladder. Chairs and lecterns were also provided.

Many landowners became great connoisseurs of literature despite having received no formal education. As a result, some stately homes in Britain have book collections which would be the envy of a university or museum. Among the most famous examples are the libraries at Chatsworth and Longleat, while the one at Sledmere House, the seat of the Sykes family, contained such treasures as a two-volume Gutenberg Bible. Unfortunately, this rarity was sold together with over 2,500 other works in 1824 because Sir Tatton Sykes needed money to finance his foxhunting.

From the late 18th century onwards, the library was also a popular place for socializing, which included playing charades and other guessing games, engaging in cultivated conversation, and reading to one another. Knowledge was seen as a form of leisure pursuit, and the nature of the library changed radically during the 19th century. It started out as a formal room used for educational purposes, and evolved into a living room which just happened to have its walls lined with books. Most importantly, even if it contained a valuable collection of books, it was a place not so much for mental exertion as for family meetings and the entertaining of guests. Even today, the library is often used as a television room or office.

In earlier times, the family library and the study of the master of the house were essentially two different rooms. Until the mid-19th century, a study was an absolute necessity for a busy landowner, and was used for administrative tasks and for meetings with employees, suppliers, and clients. It was therefore often located near the servants' wing, and in many cases had a separate door or staircase so that visitors did not have to use the same entrance as the staff.

This situation changed completely with the dawn of the 20th century. Country houses built during this time were increasingly intended for leisure rather than work, so they no longer had a separate study, though in some cases a writing desk was placed in the library. In old houses which still had separate rooms, the library and study could be combined, thus freeing one room which could then be used as a guest room or for some other purpose. As the country house ceased to be the administrative center of a huge estate, the study in most cases became the room where the master of the house smoked, read, and even slept. It became more like a gentleman's living room, with the desk serving purely as decoration.

In the late 20th century, the function of the study changed again as more and more people began working from home using modern communications technology. In this respect, the British often treat their historic buildings differently to continental Europeans. While a French or German might retain the old exterior but have a modern interior, the British prefer both the inside and outside to be as traditional as possible, and to conceal any modern technology. They will also go to great lengths to keep their offices or studies simple and unpretentious, which means decorating them in the same style as the rest of the house. You may find antiques, but you will rarely encounter modern designer desks or lamps. Even today, the average British study looks more like that of a Victorian academic or Edwardian landowner, even though the person working in it may be an architect, public relations consultant, or media mogul. This may be something to do with the fact that gainful employment is seen more as a necessity than a vocation, and the real sign that you have made it in the world is when you use your study solely as a place from which to manage your huge portfolio of investments.

A study should never look too much like a place of work. The only work left for such a person is signing cheques, and this may just as well be done at a small desk in the drawing room or entrance hall. Some studies are more like playrooms where the man of the house sits and contemplates his trophies and stamp collection, plays billiards, listens to music, and does anything else which is not the preserve of the family living room or the official reception room. More than any other part of the house, the study reveals a great deal about the character of the owner, which is probably why the door is so often kept firmly shut when curious strangers are present.

Opposite page: The office of Johnny Madden's Irish country-house hotel, Hilton Park in County Monaghan, is a mixture of old and new: traditional furniture rubs shoulders with an internet-linked PC.

Page 236: The Duke of Devonshire's desk at Chatsworth turns even the most onerous of tasks, like writing checks, into a pleasure. There are desks in several of the 175 rooms.

The Irish dramatist George Bernard Shaw moved into his house in Ayout St Lawrence, Hertfordshire, in 1906, and lived there until his death in 1950. In the summer, he worked in a small garden shed mounted on a turntable so it could be rotated to face the sunlight.

The writer and explorer Dame Freya Madeline Stark made extended journeys across Europe, the Middle East, and Asia during her eventful life. This photograph was taken in 1957 in her house in Asola, Italy and shows her concentrating on her work at the typewriter, probably on another manuscript.

Margot, Countess of Oxford and Asquith, was an influential figure in British society. She was the second wife of the First Earl Herbert Henry Asquith, who as a politician fought for votes for women. When her controversial autobiography was published in the 1920s, it caused a major stir in polite society. This portrait of her at her desk was taken around 1924.

The novelist William Makepeace Thackeray was born in 1811, and was known for his satirical works such as Vanity Fair and The Snobs of England. This photograph from 1862 shows him in a study of the kind that the Victorian photographer thought suitable for a man of letters. We do not know what Thackeray's real study looked like.

THE PERFECT STUDY

A study should first and foremost be conducive to concentration, and in theory should be designed and furnished to cause the minimum of distraction. This means choosing subdued colors for the walls, and a thick, sound-absorbing carpet which will withstand the constant wear caused by moving the chair. The desk is the nerve center of the room, and should be placed so that daylight falls on it from the left if you're right-handed, and from the right if you're left-handed. The chair should be positioned so that it will not place unnecessary strain on your body, and the shelves should be slightly further away but still within reach from a seated position. And of course proper lighting is vitally important.

So much for the theory. In practice, very few studies actually look like this, because they would be too perfect. A little clutter and disorder can be surprisingly conducive to inspiration, and so people make do with what they have instead of buying purpose-built office furniture. A big, heavy rectory table may be pressed into service as a desk, even though it is actually much too high; alternatively, a fragile bureau may be used, with a flap that folds down, even though this was not built to support the weight it is required to take. Instead of a smart modern swivel chair, a valuable deep-buttoned Victorian or Regency armchair may be used.

The wall is decorated with a combination of family heirlooms and more recent items, 19th-century daguerreotypes jostling for space with postcards and vacation souvenirs. And the desk is piled high with framed pictures, tools such as letter openers that might come in useful one day, and empty

Lecterns are ideal for quick consultations of reference books, or for jotting down notes. Some famous authors have written entire books standing at lecterns. They are very popular items of furniture, and thus rare on the antique market.

teacups. In surroundings like these it is almost impossible to keep important documents in any kind of order. But the owner is likely to feel quite at home amid all the chaos, and well-meaning attempts by others to tidy it will be vigorously rebuffed. The study is a place of spiritual inspiration, and there is no room for tidiness here.

Before the 17th century, desks were found only in buildings where writing was common, such as vicarages and monasteries, and in stately homes where there was a great deal of paperwork to be dealt with. It was not until the 18th century that they became widespread in ordinary homes.

A desk lamp doesn't necessarily have to be in a modern office-style design. A small lamp that gives plenty of light serves just as well and looks much homelier, as proven by the Duchess of Northumberland's desk in Syon House.

Office furniture can actually look more attractive if it is slightly the worse for wear, as in the case of this filing cabinet and armchair. The filing cabinet, which owner Johnny Madden bought for a song, has now become a much-loved item.

Even such trivial details as waste-paper baskets need to be carefully matched to the style of the study. It is no good having a traditional wooden desk and a futuristic, chrome-plated bin. Old ones can be found in antiques shops and – with luck – fleamarkets.

Some people have a passion for paperweights and have amassed large collections of them. Just about any small object fits the bill, provided it is heavy enough.

DOWNING STREET

Downing Street is a low-key, unassuming thoroughfare. Tourists strolling down Whitehall past the various ministries toward the Houses of Parliament and Big Ben often walk straight past this little side street without even noticing it. After all, there are plenty of other attractions round here: Trafalgar Square, the home of the National Gallery and Nelson's Column; the Palace of Westminster (as the parliament building is officially called), all the impressive buildings along Whitehall, the famous Horse Guards, and the daily Changing of the Guard. But Downing Street is still worth a glance. It has been closed to the public for many years, and the days when any citizen could saunter in and present a petition are long since past. The doorman would have banged on the imposing doorknocker, and a hand would have emerged to accept the document, but if you tried to do that today you would probably spark off a major security crisis.

The buildings in Downing Street were constructed in the 1680s by the diplomat Sir George Downing. A contemporary description of the project refers to "four or five large and well built houses, fit for persons of honor and quality, each having a pleasant prospect of St James's Park." The street was then rebuilt during the 1720s, and at some time between 1731 and 1735 number 10 became the office and official residence of the British prime minister. The modest exterior and plain front door are deceptive, since behind them lies a huge complex of around 100 rooms which are used by the prime minister and cabinet.

The first inhabitant of number 10 was Sir Robert Walpole, who received it from King George II. However, the word "inhabitant" is used advisedly, since most prime ministers found the private apartments too small and preferred to live in their own large houses.

Above: Tony Blair replaced John Major in 1997, and became the first Labour occupant of 10 Downing Street for 18 years. His primary goal was to modernize British society.

Far left: Robert Walpole was First Lord of the Treasury from 1721 to 1742. In 1730, he became Britain's first premier, and 10 Downing Street became the official prime-ministerial residence, also used by all following premiers.

Center: Benjamin Disraeli was prime minister in 1868, and again from 1874 to 1880. During his term of office, Britain acquired a majority shareholding in the Suez Canal and Queen Victoria became empress of India.

Left: Edward Heath was the Conservative prime minister from 1970 to 1974. He was a strong advocate of the European ideal, and supported British membership of the European Economic Community, which became a reality in 1973.

Next door, number 11 is politically just as important. This is the office of the chancellor of the exchequer, or finance minister. The ministry itself is called the treasury, and although the prime minister is traditionally the first lord of the treasury, in practise the department is run by the chancellor of the exchequer and the chief secretary to the treasury, who controls all public spending. Number 12 Downing Street is the official address of the government chief whip, who has overall responsibility for parliamentary party business.

Below: Margaret Thatcher ruled the roost at 10 Downing Street from 1979 until her resignation on November 22, 1990.

Right: Tony Blair brought a breath of fresh air to Downing Street both politically and personally, turning it into a family home complete with cat.

Desks and Bureaus

In the Middle Ages, a single item of furniture could serve as a chest, bench, and table all in one. Later on, furniture became more specialized, and by the 18th century, often regarded as the golden age of British furniture, items were described according to the specific purpose for which they were built: gaming tables, dressing tables, side tables, sofa tables, library tables. Writing desks formed a category of their own.

In British country houses, desks were not confined to the study. The aristocracy had discovered writing, and particularly letter writing, and since they were likely to do this in almost any room of the house, they might have several desks. There were many different styles, but all of them had to be relatively lightweight so that they could easily be moved to a window for extra light or toward a fire for warmth. In technological terms, too, the 18th century marked a turning point in the history of domestic furniture. New types of wood and woodworking methods were used to make finer and more elegant and imaginative pieces

The bureau à cylindre (cylinder-bureau) was an 18th-century French invention. The British acquired both the patent and the name of this often richly ornamented and finely constructed item of furniture, and made it an integral part of the classical Georgian-style interior.

During the 19th century, a lower drawer section was added to the cylinder bureau's barrel vault-like top section, with its drawers, shelves, and writing desk.

than ever before. The furniture industry also benefited greatly from the shortage of walnut; Great Britain was forced to import high-quality mahogany which was hard, dense, but highly suitable for cutting.

The job of the cabinetmaker also changed; instead of making items purely to order, they began producing furniture to their own designs. There were plenty of potential purchasers, since both the upper classes and the upwardly mobile middle classes were very well off financially. The designs that were developed in the 18th and 19th centuries are still in use today, and still serve as a source of inspiration to contemporary designers.

Since the beginning of the 18th century, the bureau and the bureau bookcase have been among the most popular forms of desk; in Britain, the word "bureau" refers specifically to a writing desk, whereas in the United States it is a chest of drawers. The combination of drawers and a desktop that folded down was extremely practical, as it provided lockable storage and also took up less space than a free-standing desk. Depending on taste and the local wood, bureaus were made from oak, mahogany, walnut, or elm. Today, just about every traditional British house has one, even if it is only a reproduction.

One close relative of the bureau was the secretary, also known as a *secretaire* or *escritoire*. This had what looked like a top drawer which could be pulled out and the front lowered to create a writing desk. Inside, there was a series of compartments and miniature drawers. A secretary could be placed anywhere in the house where people might want to write something down quickly, for example in the dressing-room, where visitors were also received and business matters dealt with.

Another interesting variation was the cylinder bureau, which was similar to a secretary but had fewer drawers and tall legs. The small writing desk was closed by shutting the flap and pulling the rounded lid down. Later, flexible rolling lids were used, made from slats like a Venetian blind. Both bureaus and secretaries had the disadvantage that the user was never sure where to put their legs. Unless the folded-down flap was unusually low, it was only possible to sit in front of it diagonally. The kneehole desk was designed to deal with this problem. This was a bureau with a desktop and a hole for the legs, with the drawers located on either side. One unusual version of this desk was the kidney table, so called because of its outline. It is believed to have been invented by the designer and furniture maker

Thomas Sheraton, who often made kidney tables with flaps that folded down. This creation had nothing in common with the kidney table of the 1950s.

The *bonheur du jour* was a typical lady's writing desk of the late 18th century. It was ornamental, with drawers and a richly decorated top section. But the archetypal British desk is probably the heavy pedestal desk, also known as a library writing table or writing desk. This had a heavy base and a leather top, which was usually green. It is an essential part of any theater designer's props list, usually used in conjunction with brown or green leather armchairs to convey the atmosphere of a study or library in a British club or ministry. These designs are still very commonly found as reproductions today.

The choice of desk will depend on the age of the house and the lifestyle of its owner. Some Britons are in the enviable position of never having had to think about their interiors because they have inherited houses complete with furniture and works of art, and will rarely be placed in the embarrassing position of having to buy a desk. But they are also missing out on a highly enjoyable experience, particularly in Britain, which has an unparalleled selection of beautiful old furniture.

The 18th century was a period of well designed and elaborately finished desks whose beauty was often not fully appreciable until they were opened. Designs for such desks were therefore very common in pattern books.

During the 1980s, the light-colored wood and strong architectural forms of the Biedermeier furniture of the German-speaking countries enjoyed a belated success in Britain.

Writing desks became more ornamental between the late 18th and early 19th centuries. The simple decoration of a cylinder bureau from this period harmonizes well with the informal interior of a British country house.

Winston Churchill's Study

It is probably no coincidence that Winston Churchill's study was right next door to his bedroom. After the statesman and winner of the Nobel prize for literature acquired his country house, Chartwell, in 1922, he had it renovated. The grandson of the seventh Duke of Marlborough, and born in Blenheim Palace, Churchill was in the habit of sleeping until late in the morning and then working from bed, so the bedroom and study were very close together both physically and metaphorically. When he was not working in his bedroom, he was reading and writing in the study, the creative powerhouse where he wrote his books and developed his political career. His prolific memoirs recount his involvement

Winston Spencer Churchill, former army officer, journalist, writer, and gifted amateur painter, was prime minister from 1940 to 1945 and again from 1951 to 1955. He was succeeded by Anthony Eden.

in two world wars: the first as commander of the sixth battalion of the Royal Scots Fusiliers, and the second as First Lord of the Admiralty, prime minister and defense secretary.

Churchill's study is more like a cozy lounge than an office. Its mixture of elegance and simplicity shows that he had a strong sense of style, and his unconventional personality is visible in every detail of the room. For example, it contains the lectern where he used to work standing up; this was a gift from his children in 1949, and replaced the coarsely made original which he himself had crafted. Churchill's study has all the authenticity one would expect of such an outstanding personality. No interior designer ever set foot here; this is the creation of a man who knew what he wanted from his surroundings.

David Linley's furniture often follows the motto "Less is more," and is therefore very much at home in postmodern surroundings.

Linley's designs are handmade using traditional British cabinetmaking techniques.

The forms of Linley's furniture, in this case a kidney desk, are based on 18th-century classical designs.

DAVID LINLEY

David Linley, the son of Princess Margaret and Lord Snowdon, was born in 1961. Perhaps it was the influence of his father, a photographer, designer and inventor, that led him to become a furniture designer; either way, this is an unusual choice of vocation for a nephew of the queen. Linley's stated objective is "to produce high-quality, functional, esthetically appealing furniture." This might sound like a commonplace that applies to any furniture designer, but too many people in this line of business create furniture which is neither beautiful, practical, nor particularly well made. Linley's motto is a highly ambitious one, which very few manage to achieve.

Beauty and functionality are relative concepts; quality is not. Every piece by David Linley is a work of meticulous, traditional craftsmanship, and 80 percent are made to order. If you visit his shop and headquarters at 60 Pimlico Road in London, you will find yourself walking past a whole series of antique shops; this is almost symbolic of the route followed by many clients before they commission a piece of furniture from him. They have seen furniture from very many different eras, and probably own works of art and modern designer items themselves, so they have a finely developed sense of judgment. They take it for granted that Linley will want to discuss

their requirements in detail before he starts. David Linley sees many advantages in this *modus operandi*, not least because it means that clients know what they want. Of course, he is also happy to provide advice and even discreetly point them in the right direction, and every now and then he turns down a commission because it does not fit in with his company's philosophy. But these are the exception rather than the rule, because Linley is a good businessman who hates to lose a client. In most cases, people are happy to be led by the hand a little, because they trust his specialist knowledge just as he respects their wishes and tastes.

Linley aims to create contemporary classics: tables, beds, and cupboards that are perfectly tailored to the room they were designed for, and which are brought to life by being used. In the artificial atmosphere of the showroom, these postmodern creations often look rather sterile and mannered, but their beauty emerges in their relationship with other items of furniture from different periods. This is a typically British trait, for much of the unique charm of the British interior lies in its combination of hand-me-down items and new furniture.

Left: David Linley's premises at 60 Pimlico Road serve as a shop, showroom, and design studio for the special commissions.

An exclusive collection of linen fabrics is available for upholstered furniture.

David Linley also makes smaller and more affordable accessories such as chandeliers and picture frames.

Right: David Linley offers something which was taken for granted until the beginning of the industrial age: individually made furniture.

Below: Linley's furniture is often decorated with marquetry motifs.

Marquetry

Marquetry is a decorative technique, not to be confused with inlays or veneers. Inlays are made by inserting a mosaic of pieces of wood of different sizes, grains, and colors into a base, such as a solid tabletop, and the result can be rendered even more ornamental by inserting pieces of mother-of-pearl and gold, silver, and other metals.

Veneer, on the other hand, can be used to improve the appearance of cheap or unattractive wood by cladding it with finely cut or turned sheets of wood of a better quality. This is usually done without producing a specific pattern.

The art of marquetry combines the two approaches by producing a veneer, but also using the inlay's mosaic technique. In this way, sheets of very different woods are used to create a painting-like effect. If the result is an abstract geometric pattern, the technique is known as parquetry.

The technique originally comes from France, and was developed by the cabinetmaker André Charles Boulle, who produced ornate decorations and furniture for Louis XIV at Versailles. After this time, marquetry became popular in the Netherlands, and arrived in Britain during the 18th century. It is now one of David Linley's trademarks, being ideally suited to his furniture, which is primarily inspired by that of the 18th century. Among his company's early projects were the Venetian wall screens in the VIP lounge at Heathrow airport.

David Linley only began making upholstered furniture in 1998, and his real specialty is still fine cabinetmaking.

Linley is best known for his neo-classical creations, but his repertoire also includes such standards as the drum table.

The company also specializes in miniature buildings incorporated into furniture, and model houses used as money boxes or humidors.

THE MOST BRITISH OF ALL BOOKS: THE ENCYCLOPAEDIA BRITANNICA

The *Encyclopaedia Britannica* may not be the world's oldest reference work, but it is the only one to have been continuously updated and improved since it was first published in 1768. It is therefore regarded as the mother of all encyclopedias.

But if it makes you think of leather-bound books in dusty, wood-paneled libraries, think again. Another title, *Compton's Multimedia Encyclopaedia*, was first published on CD-ROM in 1989, making it the first digital reference work anywhere in the world, and the *Encyclopaedia Britannica* followed suit in 1994. A single disk contains 73,000 articles and 8,500 photos, animations, videos, and sound recordings, making the process of reading an encyclopedia a multi-sensory experience. The same year saw the launch of *Britannica Online*, the first internet encyclopedia. Since 1999, this legendary reference work has also been available on DVD, with over three hours of video and animation and two hours of audio. The 16th edition of the conventionally printed and bound version is scheduled for publication in 2001, replacing the revised 15th edition of 1985, which took 11 years and $24 million to produce.

The home of the *Encyclopaedia Britannica* was Edinburgh in Scotland, where it was published as a twice-monthly partwork of 100 issues from 1768 onwards. It contained not only reference information, but also practical advice on such elementary subjects as toothache. The encyclopedia was almost unprecedented in its precision and comprehensiveness, but it did not gain universal favor; for example the article on obstetrics, accompanied by detailed illustrations, fell foul of moral crusaders. Three years later, in 1771,

the encyclopedia was complete – and work began immediately on the second edition, which was published from 1777 onwards.

One particular strength of this, probably the world's most famous encyclopedia, is the quality of its contributors. These have included such illustrious names as Benjamin Franklin, John Locke, Sir Walter Scott, James Mill, Matthew Arnold, Robert Louis Stevenson, Alfred North Whitehead, Harry Houdini, Marie Curie, Leon Trotsky, George Bernard Shaw, Albert Einstein, and T.E. Lawrence. All had either distinguished academic qualifications, or practical knowledge of the subject. For example, the author of the article on anarchism published in the eighth edition wrote from first-hand experience: he was the Russian prince Pyotr Kropotkin, who was exiled and then imprisoned in France for insurrection and incitement to strike. It was from here that he wrote his contribution to the encyclopedia.

The ninth edition, published in 1888, also appeared in the United States for the first time. This proved a wise move, as a large proportion of sales were made in Britain's former colony. However, at the end of the 19th century, declining turnover gave cause for concern, and the publishers joined forces with the *Times* newspaper, which was also having serious financial problems. These were solved by having the newspaper provide advertising space for the encyclopedia, and receiving a commission on every edition sold.

Today, as ever, the *Encyclopaedia Britannica* is in the forefront of the world's reference books, and users around the world are eagerly awaiting the publication of the new paper edition. Educational though the animations and sounds are, the click of a mouse is no substitute for the satisfaction of leafing through a beautifully leather-bound edition of the encyclopedia. The next edition will comprise 40 volumes, eight more than its predecessor in 1985, and will be available in two versions, differing only in their format. Multimedia enthusiasts will probably go for the digital one, since it costs only a tenth of the printed version. But true bibliophiles, sprawled in front of the fire in the libraries of their country homes, will always prefer reading a book to staring at a computer monitor.

The British Library

The British Library is one of the biggest and most important libraries in the world. It is also one of the world's foremost academic institutions, a powerhouse of knowledge, and the very mention of its name stirs the souls of intellectuals around the world.

But the famous library is no longer housed in the hallowed precincts of the British Museum. Gone are the days when hardworking students hurried past the great columns at the museum entrance each morning. And gone are the days when you could clear your head and relieve your writer's block by going for a stroll round the circular reading room, with its 50-meter-high dome and walls of books, or by paying a quick visit to the museum's department of Egyptian antiquities.

The British Library has now relocated to an ultramodern redbrick building in St Pancras. This was formally opened by Queen Elizabeth II on June 25, 1998, and since then users' lives have been transformed. Each reading desk has a socket for a laptop, there is a powerful computerized catalog, and the time spent waiting for books has significantly decreased. But there are still many who yearn for the history-laden atmosphere of the old reading room.

The library dates back to 1757, when George II gave his royal library of over 10,000 volumes to the British Museum, which had been founded four years previously. In 1883 it acquired the 120,000-strong collection of George III. By now the library was almost bursting at the seams, and so the site in Bloomsbury was expanded. The redevelopment plans, and the idea of a large dome, were the work of Sir Anthony Panizzi, a revolutionary who had fled from Italy. He was the head librarian from 1856 to 1866, and was determined to make the new rooms available to everyone, from impoverished students to established writers and men of letters. The architect Sydney Smirke implemented Panizzi's radical ideas.

As well as being one of the world's biggest repositories of knowledge, the British Library is also one of the most valuable libraries in the world. Among the priceless treasures on permanent display there are two of the four surviving copies of the Magna Carta of 1215, the Lindisfarne Gospels of 698, the first folio of Shakespeare's works, dating from 1623, and a Gutenberg Bible from around 1453. These alone are well worth a visit next time you go to London, and the new library is open to everyone, free of charge – just as Sir Anthony Panizzi would have wanted it to be.

Library Furniture

The Duke of Devonshire is an enthusiastic book collector, and his library at Chatsworth contains a number of important treasures. But he prefers to call the Lower Library "the duke's sitting-room," and likes to retire there for an afternoon nap. He has given it this nickname because he spends more time relaxing there than studying. This is not surprising, because although it has plenty of bookshelves and reading desks, it also boasts an inviting sofa and comfortable armchairs.

The great age of the library began in the 18th century, when members of the nobility and landed gentry sought to expand their education by touring Italy, France, and Greece, and studying travel literature, atlases, and scientific treatises. As a result, they inevitably accumulated collections of books. These had to be displayed for easy access, and of course they also had to create a certain impression. So cabinetmakers and furniture designers such as Sheraton, Hepplewhite, and Chippendale increasingly devoted themselves to making bookshelves.

As libraries were often located in tall rooms with ceiling-height shelves and bookcases, ladders were important requisites. These often took up space and caused an obstruction, and toward the end of the 18th century Thomas Sheraton invented a "table ladder" which, when not in use, could be folded underneath a decorative tabletop. Small steps or footstools on legs or castors served a similar purpose, and some were highly ornamental.

Some very fine examples of lecterns and library chairs were made during the Regency period, in the first 30 years of the 19th century. They were relatively lightweight and usually had castors so that they could easily be moved toward a window or a lamp. The Regency love of movable, fairly delicate items of furniture was also reflected in various types of smaller bookshelves that appeared during this period.

However, libraries did not become truly comfortable until the Victorian era, when sofas and heavy armchairs were introduced and people began using these rooms for socializing.

Floor-to-ceiling bookshelves, later made with glass doors to keep out the dust, were originally the preserve of large libraries.

A library ladder is necessary if the books on the upper shelves are to be easily accessed and dusted.

Portable or wheeled library steps of the kind popular in the Regency period were a good compromise if a ladder took up too much space.

In the early 19th century, as people began owning more books, there was increased demand for lightweight book storage which could be placed in any part of a room, such as this highly decorative dwarf bookcase.

The 18th century saw the introduction of a whole series of folding library furniture. This library chair has a drawer in the seat and a lectern-like extension on the back.

Square or circular revolving bookstands are another item typical of the Regency period. The shelves taper toward the top and rotate around a central pillar.

Old Books: A British Passion

People collect books for many different reasons. Many do not regard their love of books as a hobby at all, while others are interested in a particular subject and want to own every single title available, thus accumulating an impressive collection over the years without really having intended to do so. Some love books for their own sake and acquire them without any preference for specific titles or themes, but simply for the pleasure of ownership. And others have little interest in reading apart from the odd magazine about fly fishing or horses, and yet are the custodians of collections of rare books which they have inherited. In a country house, books are often the first things to be sold off when the owner is strapped for cash, but at least then they are bought by dealers and hopefully end up being owned by true connoisseurs of the printed word.

It is difficult to say which type of collector is most common in Britain. Most people collect books because they have a passion for reading and a nostalgia for everything which is old, venerable, and traditional, and have turned this into a highly enjoyable leisure pursuit, spending every moment of their spare time in antiquarian bookshops, and at rummage sales, auctions, and charity bazaars.

The whole business has a distinctly British touch, because it requires the instincts of a hunter and a considerable amount of detective work. In fact, one of the most famous book collectors in English popular literature was himself a sleuth. Lord Peter Wimsey, the blond, aristocratic hero created by British author Dorothy L. Sayers, is just as much at home tracking down villains as he is rare books. He regards both as a pastime, because he does not have to concern himself with such trifles as earning a living. On the very first page of his first adventure *Whose Body?*, published in 1923, Wimsey is sitting in a taxi when he realizes he has forgotten his catalog for the fictitious Brocklebury, an antiquarian book auction.

Those seeking to follow in Lord Peter's footsteps will need to know a few simple rules, which are not unique to Britain. Firstly, books are described as antiquarian if they were printed before 1820. Secondly, it is not the case that the older the book, the more valuable it is; there are many other factors which play a part in a book's value.

Of course, the rarer the book, the more it's likely to be worth. This may be the case with 16th or 17th-century editions that were put on the index and where most copies were wilfully destroyed.

First editions, even of very recently published titles, can be especially collectable, particularly if the author only subsequently became famous. A 16th-century edition of Homer with handwritten comments by Thomas More would be worth a fortune. A dust jacket in good condition can greatly increase the value of a book; so can inscriptions by the author or owner, signatures and the ex-libris, a bookplate, stamp, or inscription indicating the owner, often elaborately decorated with symbolic emblems. For example, one six-volume first edition of Winston Churchill's *The World Crisis* has become a collector's item of major importance because each volume is dedicated by the author to Edward, Prince of Wales. When the estate of the Duke and Duchess of Windsor came under the hammer at Sotheby's in New York in 1998, these six books bore a reserve of $30,000.

There are also a number of basic rules when it comes to handling precious books. For example, a book should never be pulled off the shelf by the top of the spine; instead, those on either side should be pushed back slightly so that it can be removed by the sides. Never thumb through an old book in the way you would a telephone directory, as this can mark the paper. And if you must write your name in it (assuming you're not famous), use a pencil.

If you can't afford to buy expensive antiquarian books, invest in cheap ones instead. With a combination of astute judgment and good old-fashioned luck, today's assortment of little-known titles can be turned into tomorrow's valuable and sought-after collection. But it is debatable whether a true lover

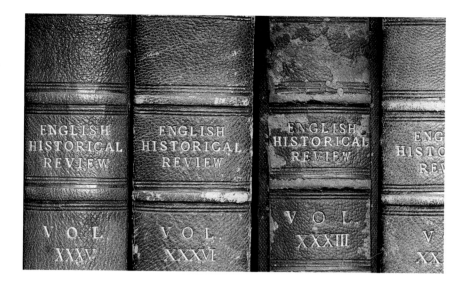

of books could ever sell these treasured possessions for a profit. To a bibliophile, a book is much more than an assemblage of paper, cardboard, linen, and glue. It is a valued and much-loved companion which the owner would not part with for all the money in the world.

A skilled bookbinder can restore a valuable leather-bound book to its former glory. Bookbinding is still largely done by individual craftsmen and women who may have long-term business relationships with many of their clients. A family coat of arms or other decoration can be added to a book cover; this bookbinder is using a spreading iron and individual stamps to blind-tool the outlines of the pattern, and then filling these in with a bone folder.

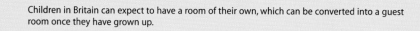

Children in Britain can expect to have a room of their own, which can be converted into a guest room once they have grown up.

THE NURSERY

THE CHILDREN'S PARLOR

The nursery at Chatsworth House provides visitors with a vivid impression of English Edwardian attitudes to children's rooms.

Developments in the nature of children's rooms mirror changes in parental attitudes towards their children. In other words, as the respect for, and appreciation of, children increased, so their living conditions improved while they also moved physically closer to their parents. Back in the 17th century, children were housed in modest attic rooms.

It was not customary for the upper classes to look after their own children. At least not in a way we would take for granted today. This was a task which was best handed to a nanny, who acted as the perfect mother-substitute. Parents were content to see their offspring just once a day. It was not uncommon for children not to see their mothers and fathers for weeks at a stretch whenever time was at a premium or parents had to be away from home. It is not surprising therefore, to discover that the nursery was not a haven of child-friendly furniture brimming with toys at that time. Such a room was more likely to have been a drab and dingy space, not much better than the servants' quarters. In such conditions children lived, took their meals, and slept.

Separate children's day and sleeping areas began to gain acceptance towards the end of the 18th century. The homes of wealthy families began to feature both a day nursery and a night nursery. The day room functioned as a combined sitting, dining, and study area for children and their attendants. While children were young, the night nursery was the bedroom for the children and their nanny. Older children were permitted to sleep unsupervised, but never alone, since they generally had to share their domain with several siblings. Not even children born into wealth were allowed the luxury of a bedroom to call their own.

This system for accommodating children was gradually perfected over centuries, and survived, almost unchanged, until well into the Victorian era. Infants and toddlers whiled away their time in the nursery and were cared for, day and night, by a nanny and her assistants. During the day, slightly older children occupied the schoolroom or day nursery, where they were instructed by a governess. Later on, boys were sent to boarding school, and girls educated at home until they were sixteen or seventeen years old. The only major planning consideration in the design of these sitting-, bed-, and schoolrooms during the 19th century was that children should not be a nuisance to their parents.

Consequently the nursery wing was generally located in a remote part of the family residence. Bringing food to the children's wing was a laborious and unpopular task fulfilled by the nursery maid, who was often still only a child herself. If she was lucky, the handyman, who answered to the other servants as well as to the masters of the house, would give her a hand.

Attitudes to children's education and accommodation gradually changed toward the end of the 19th century. Medical and pharmaceutical advances reduced infant and childhood death rates, and made it possible for children to lead a comparatively healthy life. Parents who would previously have expected no more than two or three out of ten children to reach adulthood, now had a much greater chance of seeing their babies actually reach maturity. The contribution made by architecture was, first, to design more suitable nursery spaces with better consideration of the little ones' needs, and secondly, to grant precedence to the nursery when allocating well-lit rooms within a building. Whereas the majority of mid-19th-century parents would have been loath to relinquish their bright bedrooms in favor of their children, Edwardian nurseries were increasingly located in the best part of the house with a view over the park rather than bare masonry.

Although no one today would subscribe to the Victorian attitudes and notions of raising children, some principles have survived. Many old-established families continue to refer to the children's room as the nursery and, as in the old days, their offspring continue to be looked after by nannies who often spend more time with the children than their own mothers do. Naturally, the pros and cons of this method of raising children are more openly discussed today than they were a hundred years ago. In fact, there is a lot in favor of entrusting the care of children to a kind and well-qualified person. First and foremost this approach enables women to continue pursuing their careers. Secondly, by employing a nanny mothers liberate themselves from the more tedious aspects of child-rearing, thereby giving themselves more opportunity for developing a more relaxed relationship between parent and child.

At first glance, late 20th century English nurseries appear almost identical to the domains of other smaller Europeans and Americans. Nevertheless, computer games, Tamagochis, and Barbie dolls do not disguise the fact that the British child's bedroom has retained a unique character. In typical

What child does not fantasize of having an entire attic to himself? In this room the dream has come true.

Winnie the Pooh and grandpa's child-friendly hunting trophy from India indicate that this room must be the dominion of a child.

British style, the contemporary nursery is generally furnished by combining the old with the new – bought antiques are placed next to heirlooms, and works of art co-exist with nicknacks. As anywhere in the prosperous west, furniture is complemented by a veritable mountain of toys. Modern parents who live in an old house with an old-fashioned, and hence unattractive, nursery wing, will occupy this area themselves so as not to saddle their off-spring with the dark rooms. This is also a suitable part of the house for spare bedrooms and study rooms, leaving the bedrooms which had once been the preserve of adults free for the children.

Outside of the British Isles, many people have to grow up in a style-vacuum of gaudy plastic furniture for children and easy-care, characterless floor coverings, but Her Majesty's younger subjects learn about British style from the cradle. The fact that their bedrooms contain more old pieces of furniture than anywhere else in the world, and that the substance of British buildings tends to be older, means that the taste of many children of the British Isles is molded in the early years by just the kind of style featured in this book. Furthermore, mothers never tire of reminding their offspring

that the cot in which they spent their first months was a hand-me-down from Aunt Sophie, and their cute little teddy-bear once belonged to Uncle William. Because of the importance of history and tradition, British adults have been known to feel distinctly uncomfortable unless a room includes at least one historic piece of furniture. Similarly, many of them never really learn to appreciate any food other than that they grew accustomed to in the nursery.

The Nanny

The nanny is a British institution which dates back to the 16th century. This particular type of nursemaid was entrusted with the care of boys until they were old enough for boarding school. With regard to girls, their education was handed over to a governess when the time came. On the whole, relationships between children and nursemaids were closer than with their natural mothers, since they spent more time in nanny's company than in that of any other adult. In any case, ladies of high society would not have known how to entertain their children, nor would they have had any of the practical skills required for looking after them.

The 19th-century nanny continued to exert a great deal of influence over her little charges. Her stories, poems, songs, and aphorisms often remained with the children throughout the course of their lives. The adult children of the gentry and the upper middle classes thought of their nannies in the same way as their mothers and grandmothers. The trend for parents to take a personal interest in their children did not emerge until the First World War was over. Yet this did not by any means entail taking care of children's daily needs. Children were merely awarded more space and importance in their parents' lives.

The key words nursery and nanny still have the power to awaken a string of associations in many contemporary British people. Nevertheless, it is no longer the norm for people, even those of the upper classes, to leave children entirely in the charge of nannies. Nowadays working mothers rely more on the au pair for help with the children. The au pair is normally a young person from abroad who wishes to combine a stay in another country with earning some money. Staying with a family is the ideal way of becoming integrated into the British way of life.

The myth of the nanny has merged with modern ideas of professional care. Hidden behind the nostalgic uniform lies a highly trained child-care and pre-school education specialist. She will have been trained at one of the specialized educational establishments such as the Norland Nursery Training College. This renowned institution was founded in 1892 by Emily Ward, an advocate

As a very young child, the Prince of Wales was taken for walks in his baby carriage around St James's Park by his nanny Helen Lightbody – quite unmolested by the media or gawkers.

of Friedrich Fröbel's methods. In 1816, the German educationalist opened his first boarding school in Thüringen, soon to be followed by further institutions in Switzerland. He also established further education for elementary school teachers and ran an orphanage in Burgdorf, where he came up with the idea of founding an institution for the promotion of the drive for creative activity and spontaneity in children and young people. In 1837 he realized this dream in Bad Blankenburg. Hence, he became the founder of the world's first kindergarten, although at the time it was known as a *"Pflege-, Spiel- und Beschäftigungsanstalt für Kinder"* (care, play, and occupational institution for children).

Emily Ward's education of her trainee nursery maids followed Fröbel's principles, and thus offset the treasure trove of experience gained by earlier generations of nannies with a modern theory of education. However, this did not mean that every one of the old guiding principles had lost its use. Warnings like, "You must wear clean underwear, you might get run over," are as relevant today as they were then.

A Georgian house in Denford Park in the county of Berkshire has been the Norland Nursery Training College's base since 1967. Trainee nannies undergo two year courses in which they learn about childcare and education as well as acquiring important accomplishments like cookery skills. They put into practice their theoretical knowledge in an in-house day nursery. Furthermore, all trainee nannies have to complete a period of work experience in schools and hospital baby wards.

After completing their training they have to undergo a trial period of nine months in a specially selected household. They are not given their diplomas until this practical test has been successfully completed. The superb training of British nursery nurses is admired worldwide, and explains why college graduates are inundated with offers of employment from abroad. The demand for this "export commodity" suits the British just fine, since it ensures the survival, for themselves and their children, of a typical profession which may otherwise be threatened by extinction.

Two nannies were in charge of the Queen's children, Helen Lightbody (pictured) and Mabel Anderson.

Classic baby carriages like that of the Duke of Devonshire, now on show in the nursery at Chatsworth, are currently back in vogue in Britain.

Classics of British cuisine (from left): pasta shapes with tomato sauce and milk, fish fingers with peas and creamed potatoes, and rice pudding with blackcurrant syrup.

Nursery Food

Great Britain ceased to be a culinary desert long ago and it is doubtful it ever was one. The quality of the United Kingdom's traditional fare is comparable to that of other northern, western, or central European countries, and uses more or less the same basic ingredients: meat, vegetables, pies, fish, and potatoes are equally popular in Germany, Denmark, Poland, and Switzerland.

For some years now, Mediterranean food has been the European continent's favored cuisine. Great Britain did not attract the attention of sophisticated gourmets until restaurants with a Mediterranean flavor began to be established in London.

Notwithstanding the trend for pasta and cappuccino, the bastions of traditional English eating culture have survived foreign culinary influences. By this is meant nursery food, the special dishes served to children and their maids since the 19th century. Many British people grew up with these nutritious and whimsically named delicacies, and hence they continue to prize them highly as adults. Mouths water when classics such as bread and butter pudding, spotted dick, jam roly-poly, rice pudding, toad-in-the-hole, or bangers and mash are listed in restaurant menus. This explains how these dishes come to feature among the oysters, venison, and lobster of some British restaurants.

The simple specialties of nursery food can indeed be very tasty. As with any other type of food, it is the quality of the ingredients and the skill of the cook which make all the difference. Fortnum & Mason's Fountain Restaurant, for example, is a reliable place to sample beautifully cooked nursery food. It is well worth the journey, as is testified by the many British people who join the tourists at lunch-time at the entrance of the restaurant on the corner of Jermyn Street and Duke Street.

However, for complete authenticity it is best to experience the nursery favorites in a British home. It may be a little bit easier to understand why so many British people swear by their nursery food after a gorgeous meal of bangers and mash and bread and butter pudding.

CHILDREN'S LIVING ARRANGEMENTS: CHANGING ATTITUDES

Designated spaces for children, freshly painted and decorated with bright, cheerful wallpaper, furnished with specially designed furniture which sometimes even grow with the child as the years pass, and shelves full of colorful toys as an encouragement to creativity and learning. This is a 20th-century ideal, which remains unfulfilled for many children even today.

Children's rooms were anything but child-friendly in the past, and their furnishings left much to be desired. For many centuries, childhood was regarded as a regrettable but unavoidable period of not-quite-adulthood. Children were seen as uncivilized creatures riddled with bad habits, which they had to be relieved of as expeditiously as possible. Children from wealthy families were rigorously trained in adult behavior from a tender age; as were poor children, whose families had to rely on their labor. From this point of view, the fact that adults did not waste much thought on child-friendly living spaces seems more understandable. This type of consideration is a 20th-century phenomenon which has its beginnings in the Victorian era.

The life of a child in England at the time of the Tudors and Stuarts began in a darkened, warm, and cozy room, in which stood a bed, covered in fresh, clean linen by the midwife in preparation of the mother's confinement. Diapers and vests were ready for the baby. A few hours after the birth, if successful, the new infant was laid into a cradle which, as recommended for example in the *Midwives Book* of 1672, also stood in a darkened space, to avoid either sunlight or moonlight shining onto the baby's face. Cradles were usually made of wood or basket-ware, and stood on rockers so that the mother or nursemaid could gently rock the baby to sleep. Apart from these little beds for newborn infants, there were very few items of furniture specifically designed for children.

Very little is known about the living spaces of older 16th- and 17th-century children, but it is unlikely that their rooms contained any furniture other than the type deemed suitable for adults, albeit without the adult level of comfort. Thinking back on her childhood, Lady Maud Baillie, a daughter of the Ninth Duke of Devonshire, described the nursery in Hardwick Hall, and could not but mention that the attic rooms were fitted with neither a gas nor electricity supply, and that the only lamp at the children's disposal emitted such a paltry amount of light that they were always frightened in the dark. It is notable that the year in question was 1908.

Things did not change all at once, but children's lives were transformed to a certain extent during the Victorian period. The monarchs' influence could be felt in this trend; unlike former generations of royal parents, Queen Victoria and her consort Prince Albert enjoyed the company of their children, and even looked after their welfare in person, thereby establishing something of a "family life". The children's rooms were moved closer to their parents' quarters, young and old now slept in adjacent rooms.

However, traditional ideas of childhood did not really change dramatically until the 20th century with its new medical and psychoanalytical insights. The adult world began to pay more attention to its offspring, and to protect it better from harmful influences (both physical and psychological). Light, air, child-friendly rooms, child-sized furniture, children's clothing, toys, good teachers: this was the emergence of the parental sense of responsibility.

When touring Britain's great castles, palaces, and country houses, visitors with a particular interest in the living quarters of children may be disappointed by most of the buildings preserved in their pre-19th century state. On the other hand, Victorian estates can prove very fruitful. Lanhydrock near Bodmin in Cornwall, for example, houses a typical Victorian nursery. The nursery at Nunnington Hall in North Yorkshire is also worth a visit. The atmosphere of a typical Victorian nursery can even be found at Castle Leslie in Ireland. There is a beautiful view from this cheerful room, with its antique toys and large-scale dolls' house containing state of the art sanitary equipment. Notwithstanding the influence of nannies and governesses, the Victorian (and subsequent) Leslie children were a mischievous bunch. The current Sir Jack Leslie tried to teach his toy chicken, known as "Hotwaterbottle," to fly by pushing it out of the nursery window. And the rascals enjoyed scaring the maids half to death by bringing bats and other small animals into the house.

The practical cribs commonly found in many toddlers' rooms today were not a feature of nurseries in the past. Once children had outgrown their cradles they were moved to austere iron or wooden beds.

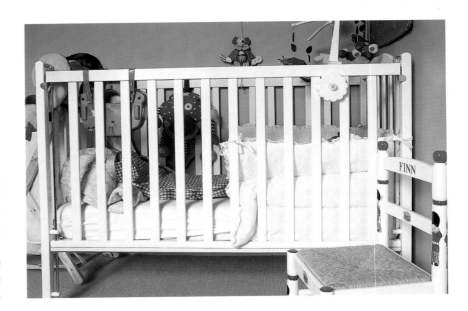

British children are exposed to their domestic national style from an early age. This explains why the ubiquitous wing chair in front of the fireplace is found even in the nursery.

The limited space available in a converted attic room with sloping ceilings is fully utilized by carefully selected and arranged furniture which takes the ceiling's slope into consideration.

A chest of drawers is perfect for storing baby's clothes. This piece of furniture can double as an educational tool. It helps to have somewhere to put things when trying to teach children about tidiness.

Curtains ensure that the children are not disturbed in their slumber by either the early morning sunshine or the light of the moon at night. If at all possible, the fabric should be selected to match the wallpaper or the furniture.

Beatrix Potter

Born in 1866, Beatrix Potter was one of the world's most successful children's authors as well as a superb illustrator. Her anthropomorphic animal tales have entranced children and adults alike since the publication in 1902 of the story of Peter Rabbit. This tells the tale of a little boy rabbit who will not do as he is told by his mother.

Since then the little book has become famous worldwide, but it was not originally intended for publication. Beatrix Potter wrote the story for the son of her last governess, sending him installments in letter form. It was not until some time later that she turned this into the book of *The Tale of Peter Rabbit*. A further 22 volumes followed this first work, introducing many more animal protagonists, each colored drawing of which was both life-like and immensely charming.

A study of Beatrix Potter's animal world is an absolute prerequisite for anyone who wishes to explore the universe of young British citizens. Despite the contemporary phenomena of Mr. Men, Thomas the Tank Engine, Mickey Mouse, and Pokémon, her familiar Edwardian characters are still at the top of the popularity scale. Peter Rabbit and friends even bridge the generations – grandmother adored them, and her grandchildren can still relate to their stories.

The nursery rhymes illustrated by Beatrix Potter are also highly regarded. Amusing memory training books like Appley Dapply's Nursery Rhymes were, and still are to some extent, an essential part of children's basic educational equipment. Many adults can still flawlessly recite the catchy verses from memory.

Beatrix Potter discovered her love of nature and animals as a child on vacation in Scotland and later in the Lake District. Her books' phenomenal success enabled her to make her dream of a life in the country come true. She acquired an old farmhouse in Cumbria, romantically named "Hilltop". The 17th-century house remained her home, where she lived in seclusion until her death in 1943. This is where she wrote and illustrated many of her stories. The successful and now famous author also occupied her time with breeding sheep, and she was a committed advocate of nature conservation and the protection of ancient monuments. This brought her into close collaboration with the National Trust, who now own her home near Sawrey in Ambleside, which is open to the public. However, it has become such a popular attraction that visitor numbers have had to be restricted to 800 per day. Visitors are keen to experience the domestic surroundings of the creator of favorite characters like Mrs Tiggy Winkle, Benjamin Bunny, Tom Kitten, Squirrel Nutkin, or Jemima Puddle-Duck. And it's all there: her home was not unlike those of her small protagonists; an almost magical, picture-book England.

Anyone harboring hopes that her little heroes may suddenly appear in one of the rooms will be disappointed. The rabbits, cats, and ducks love the countryside and seclusion as much as Beatrix Potter did, so they avoid the house and the crowds of meddlesome fans. The best way to get to know Peter Rabbit and his friends is by visiting the nearest book store.

Peter Rabbit features on a Wedgwood china design popular with parents and young children alike.

The best way of introducing British children to high tea is by serving it on Peter Rabbit or Mrs Tiggy Winkle china.

Many fans of Beatrix Potter's books collect tableware decorated with her characters.

We shall never know what Beatrix Potter would have thought of the intense marketing of her characters, but children will be delighted by the wide array of merchandise on offer. Naturally, the range now includes a cuddly toy rabbit.

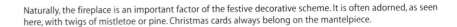

MERRY CHRISTMAS

Yuletide festivities in Great Britain are colorful, merry, and frequently noisy affairs. People wear silly paper hats and amuse themselves with Christmas party crackers. The primary objectives are, to spend some time with the family, relax, be merry, and distribute gifts among one's nearest and dearest. As anywhere else in the world, the lady of the house spends most of her time in the kitchen, because Christmas is a time for feasting. Most Christmas customs have been preserved, and British people would not deem it a proper holiday if there was no stuffed turkey on Christmas Day.

Preparations can begin weeks in advance. Homes are festooned with garlands and sprigs of holly, ivy, and mistletoe, and individual taste determines how the Christmas tree is to be decorated. Candles are lit, and Christmas cards are arranged on the mantelpiece or hung on a ribbon strung above the fireplace or over the door frames. Importantly, fake snow on window panes, or flashing electrical lights are not considered to be in good taste. In rural areas particularly, people like to come together to sing carols or perform nativity plays. In the past, it was customary for the local gentry or landowner to invite the entire village to a party at the great house.

In the United Kingdom, December 24, or Christmas Eve is mainly a day of preparation. An opportunity for last-minute shopping for food and gifts, and to work in the kitchen. A light, yet festive, dinner is served in the evening, after which some families like to attend Midnight Mass in church. Others go out drinking and singing in the pub and the streets are crowded. Children compose lists to ensure that Father Christmas loads the correct gifts onto his famous reindeer sleigh. Christmas stockings are hung from the bedpost or the bedroom door knob.

The festivities reach their high-point on Christmas Day, December 25. The day may begin with a visit to church. The gifts are exchanged during the course of the morning or after lunch. At last, the eagerly awaited roast turkey is served as part of a sumptuous Christmas lunch comprising two or three courses. In view of the colossal calorific content of the bird, which has been stuffed with chestnuts, minced pork, bread-crumbs, and sausage meat, starters are not strictly necessary. The turkey is served with roast potatoes, steamed vegetables, and cranberry sauce. This is followed by Christmas Pudding, also known as Plum Pudding. There is stilton and port for those who still have an appetite. In the afternoon, The Queen's Speech is broadcast on television, and the nation stops to listen. The next act of this culinary drama is served up in the early evening: Christmas Cake is a heavy fruit cake with a thick coating of icing. A broth and a little cheese are passed around before bedtime.

December 26 is known as Boxing Day, because this was the day in olden times when people would give their suppliers and members of staff a box which contained a small gift. Today it is a day of rest, when people recover from the after-effects of Christmas. Food is light, perhaps smoked salmon or cold, left-over turkey. Otherwise, people visit friends, go for long walks, or pursue a classic British country sport. Among the most noted families, some throw sumptuous hunting parties.

It is traditional for members of the royal family to spend Christmas at their Sandringham country estate near King's Lynn in Norfolk. Queen Victoria's eldest son, the future King Edward VII acquired the estate in 1862. His grandson David, later to become the Duke of Windsor, wrote in his memoirs entitled *A King's Story*, that the exchange of Christmas presents in his grandfather's house took place on Christmas Eve, in the German tradition. Queen Victoria and her German husband Prince Albert of Saxony-Coburg-Gotha are generally attributed with the introduction of Christmas trees to their royal residences, as well as to the living rooms of their loyal subjects. However, there is anecdotal evidence that it was Princess Charlotte of Mecklenburg-Strelitz who insisted on her annual Christmas tree after her marriage in 1761 to George III. It is said that she liked to adorn her trees with opulent decorations, including candles, small trinkets, and all manner of candy. Another matter for debate is how and when "Father Christmas"

Holly, Ivy, Mistletoe

A British Christmas would be incomplete without the classic evergreens *holly, ivy, and mistletoe*. The festive decoration scheme can be either traditional or modern, the tree may be forsaken for the sake of the environment, and the 'Christmas Cake' can be omitted for calorie-counting reasons, but the glossy foliage is an absolute must. And yet, this popular and decorative material was quite unconnected to the Christian festival originally. Indeed, folklorists and students of mythology think it most likely that these plants were highly prized by our very early forebears, who paid particular homage to them at around the time of the winter solstice on December 21, and even kept them in sacred places to be used as sacrificial offerings. The early Christian Church was aware of the solstice's popular significance, and guessed that it might be difficult to eradicate ancient cults completely. It therefore decided to adapt existing ritual customs by celebrating one of the new faith's most important holidays on December 24. This provided the framework for a gradual integration of the heathen festivals into the Christian liturgy, and for their reinterpretation in a Christian context. In this manner, a heathen celebration of the re-birth of light, growth, and fertility was transformed into the birthday of Christ, the son of God.

Holly, with its shiny, prickly, serrated, dark green leaves, and red berries, has had a large part to play in popular belief systems through the ages. Because it thrives, even bearing glorious fruit, in the depths of winter when all other trees and shrubs stand denuded in the cold, it symbolized fertility and the expectation of another spring. The accidental cutting down of a holly plant was seen as unlucky, whereas a sprig of holly placed in a barn had the power to ward off sickness and helped the livestock to thrive. Holly kept witches at bay and brought unfaithful husbands back into the arms of their wives. The church appropriated the controversial plant by claiming that the crown of thorns worn by Jesus was made of holly, the red berries of which signified nothing less than the Savior's droplets of blood.

Like many plants with symbolic properties, ivy was also endowed with many different meanings. On the one hand it brought bad luck, symbolized death, and was regularly used for burial ceremonies. On the other hand, how-

When it comes to Christmas decorations, British people are as particular about detail as they are about any other aspect of beautifying their homes. The basic materials are holly, mistletoe, and ivy. In more recent years, fir cones and twigs have been adopted from the Nordic repertoire.

ever, the delicate, winding leaves stood for the feminine principle. Wreaths made of smooth ivy and holly (which represented the masculine principle) had an overtly sexual message. Furthermore, ivy was regarded as the plant of Bacchus and Dionysus. In the Middle Ages, valiant revelers relied on ivy berries to relieve headaches after nights of heavy drinking. In Christian mythology, however, this attractive plant is associated with eternal love and marital fidelity.

Mistletoe is another plant which played an important part in ancient cults. Because it does not live in the earth like other plants but thrives in the lofty crowns of trees, the Celtic druids believed its origins to be divine. For this reason golden sickles had to be used to cut mistletoe, the plants had to be stored hanging up after harvesting, and care had to be taken that they were protected from contact with the earth. The druids considered the mistletoe which grew on oak trees to be the most valuable of all. These twigs and berries were efficacious against epileptic fits, healed ulcers and tumors, and were a reliable antidote to poison. It was also claimed that mistletoe could put out fires, open locks, and drive away evil spirits. Christian theologians took a serious view of the matter, and came up with the following story: once upon a time, the mistletoe was a big, strong tree – its timber was so strong in fact, that the bailiffs chose it for the Cross of Jesus' crucifixion. When the Lord perished upon the Cross, the trees felt shame and thus shriveled, and they have had to live as parasites ever since.

But what about the traditional kiss under the mistletoe? There are those who say that mistletoe over the door symbolizes a picture of a saint, and that the (brotherly?) kiss is therefore a confirmation of life lived in accordance with the tenets of the Faith. Others maintain that the custom is based on a link between mistletoe and fertility. After all, many Celtic women believed that wearing a garland of mistletoe around their hips would help them fall pregnant.

(Santa Claus) began to deliver presents around the British Isles. Whatever the origins, we know that the gentleman in the characteristic red suit uses a reindeer sleigh and enters through the chimney in England, whereas his continental equivalent carries a sack and proceeds on foot.

The Christmas tree did not come to the British Isles until the reign of Queen Victoria. The monarch, whose mother and husband were both German, thereby passed on a little bit of German tradition to her subjects.

TYPICAL CHILDREN'S TOYS

Paddington is a small bear who has a talent for causing havoc. His English adoptive family, the Browns, found him at Paddington Station in London, which is how he got his name. The author of these popular stories is Michael Bond.

It is no mere coincidence that this Peter Rabbit toy has a carrot in his paws. An illustration in Beatrix Potter's first volume of stories shows him holding the selfsame vegetable.

There is a wide range of building sets available, all of which stimulate the imagination. A simple set of wooden building blocks is as much fun to play with as a sophisticated construction set.

A. A. Milne published his children's books Winnie the Pooh and The House at Pooh Corner in 1926 and 1928 respectively. The books' main characters are a small bear called Winnie and his human friend Christopher Robin.

No child's room, whether on the British Isles or anywhere else in the world, would be complete without at least one stuffed teddy bear. Although we can generally be sure to find several, as in this picture.

Rocking horses are true nursery classics. They may seem old-fashioned, but their popularity among pre-school children is as great as ever. Some of these wooden quadrupeds even feature "real" manes, and are equipped with bridles and leather saddles.

Hamley's

The inhabitants of the British Isles are sometimes accused of exhibiting little interest in their offspring. This prejudice seems confirmed by the fact that they make their children eat supposedly stodgy and unhealthy nursery food, and pack them off to boarding school as quickly as possible, obviously in the belief that children thrive best the further away from home they are. Yet the people of Scotland, Wales, England, and Ireland adore their children, and love to spoil them with all kinds of toys.

One of the best places to buy toys is Hamley's at 188 Regent Street in London. Like many other typical English stores, this firm has a long company tradition to look back on. In 1760 John Hamley opened the Noah's Ark toy shop in High Holborn. The business flourished rapidly so that branches were subsequently opened in Regent Street and Oxford Street. Today's Hamley's store was built in 1906.

If it's not here, it probably doesn't exist. Six stories contain everything to make a child's heart (and those which maintain a little bit of childishness) beat faster. The range of time-honored teddy bears, historical dolls, and unbeatable model railway sets is as comprehensive as that of the latest computer games and Gameboys. Almost all the toys can be tried out on the spot, which helps avoid disappointment on the eagerly awaited birthday or Christmas. This also gives adults an opportunity to practise so that they can hold their own against their offspring when the time comes. Members of Hamley's team demonstrate how to play with the latest toys and games, which may not be entirely obvious at first sight. It is always advisable to find out the exact number of batteries required for the Space Invader and the exact location of the off-switch before paying for the toy.

Hamley's is worth a visit at any time of the year. It always attracts crowds, but Christmas shoppers need nerves of steel to work their way through the throng. It is advisable to leave young children at home. They should not see what 'Santa Claus' buys for them in any case.

Left: Can we conceive of a girl's life without dolls? Probably not. The ever popular Barbie doll is not the only possible option however. Doll's houses, especially those modeled on "historical" examples, have a particularly stimulating effect on children's imaginations.

A Royal Dolls' House

There are houses and there are palaces, there are dolls' houses and there is Queen Mary's Dolls' House on display at Windsor Castle. This is a masterpiece of miniaturization, and a major document of the period. A peep inside the gigantic miniature house, built on a scale of 1:2, is like taking a journey back in time to the beginning of the 20th century. This house demonstrates in detail the views held by the period's architects, craftsmen, interior decorators, and household management experts regarding the appropriate design and fitting-out of a monarch's household. Everything there is of the best quality and features the latest technology of the day. The ideal condition of the dolls' house as constructed by its builders has not been affected by either decay or modernization.

This is evidently not a child's toy. The furniture is much too delicate and dainty to withstand handling by children. Sir Edwin Lutyens was the creator of this, probably the most famous and, at 2.34 meters tall, presumably the largest dolls' house of all time. The architect and urban planner approached this work with zeal. Four years of hard work were needed to complete the design, construction, and finishes of the house, when it was at last ready to be handed over to the Queen in 1924. A multitude of artists and consultants were involved in the project. They considered it an honor to contribute to the diminutive palace. The list of suppliers reads like a "Who's Who" of trade, commerce, and culture.

Naturally, any supplier with a reputation to maintain in the big world wished also to deliver only the best *en miniature*. The wine bottles in the cellar, for instance, were supplied by the most renowned wine and spirits traders, and the library is full of works by G. K. Chesterton, Thomas Hardy, Rudyard Kipling, Joseph Conrad, Conan Doyle, John Galsworthy, or Hugh Walpole to name just the better-known authors. Many of these tiny books contain original works specially created for the dolls' house. The paintings,

No lesser an architect than Sir Edwin Lutyens designed the sumptuous dolls' house for Queen Mary in the 1920's.

sculptures, and caricatures were also supplied by famous artists.

Yet the design of the house is not merely a document of the architect's artistry, it also bears witness to his love of technology. An electric mechanism raises the external facade of the building to permit views of the interior. Every technical detail is in working order — from the door locks, via the gramophone, to the table in the dining room which extends from 14 centimeters to around half a meter. Even the combination lock on the safe in the treasure vault is fully functional, and the taps in the kitchen can drip either hot or cold water as required (a full stream of water is not possible because of the low pressure in the pipes). The architect's obsession with detail went beyond both technical and structural considerations. The household linen bears unbelievably small embroidered monograms, which took the incredible amount of 1500 working hours to complete.

This doll's house is now a particularly popular attraction. At the beginning of 21st century, it is almost impossible to find craftsmen and artists with the skills required to build and furnish a house like this at normal scale, at least not to the standards that would have been expected in 1900. The specialists needed to produce an accurate miniature would be even harder to find, if at all. In this respect the royal dolls' house is also a monument to a level of craftsmanship which has ceased to exist.

The floor covering of the entrance hall is made of, naturally real, blue and white marble.

The King's bedchamber offers every comfort, albeit on a small scale.

Above: A fourposter, mahogany Chippendale bed can be admired in the royal children's night nursery. In front of it, a tiny apple-wood cradle with silver and ivory embellishments.

Right: The King's library is one of the most impressive rooms in the doll's house: the shelves and bureaus hold tiny books and works of art, which can actually be read or viewed – with the help of a magnifying glass.

When the Victorian conservatory at Castle Leslie in County Monaghan was built, today's Republic of Ireland was still subject to the British Crown. Its charm, now slightly weathered, continues to enchant visitors.

THE CONSERVATORY

A Room Full of Winter Sunshine

Today's conservatories have developed from orangeries of the 18th century, where exotic plants, such as adorned the terraces and gardens of grand houses in the summer months, could be protected from Britain's chilly winter climate. The orangery was where delicate plants, preferably citrus trees, were kept, or conserved – which explains the origin of the English word conservatory to describe these plant houses. The name is said to have been coined by the landscape architect John Evelyn. In the summer, when orangeries stood empty, they were used as additional living spaces where concerts and sumptuous dinner parties took place. Very large glass houses began to be built when glass became more readily available toward the end of the 18th century.

The conservatory's popularity surged during the 19th century, inspiring architects and engineers to design and build ever bolder structures of glass and steel. The Victorians regarded the conservatory as a triumph of architecture over nature. The happy owners of these large and luxurious glass houses, some of which even had heating, could enjoy the illusion of an everlasting spring. However, this was not a cheap pleasure and, by the end of the First World War, not many people could afford to maintain them, even if rigid fuel rationing had permitted them to do so. Few of these magnificent sanctuaries for plants and people have stood the test of time; they either became structurally unsound or had to be demolished when maintenance costs became too high. The smaller structures stood a better chance of over-

Large houses such as Chatsworth used winter gardens and orangeries to grow rare plants as well as the tropical and exotic fruits which provided welcome additions to the kitchen's culinary offerings throughout the year.

coming this difficult period in their history, hence the conservatories of Syon Park (London) and Broughton Hall (North Yorkshire) survive to this day. Fortunately, the Palm House at Kew Gardens in London, which was completed in 1848, has also been preserved.

The large glass structures were no longer in favor after the First World War. The level of comfort to be found in country houses increased, so the trusty conservatory seemed a rather cold and damp place when compared to the coziness of the drawing room. In terms of comfort, the conservatories of smaller estates could not compete with the pompous constructions of grander and more important houses. Hence the conservatory, once so popular, fell into a long sleep from which it was not to reawaken until the 1970s. Advances in technology, thanks to which the means to construct them had previously been found, now brought about a revival, as modern heating and air conditioning systems could be installed in conservatories – just as in a modern home. This brought into being a whole new branch of the building industry, with specialist companies and architects-in-glass now supplying made-to-measure conservatories.

In the damp, cool climate of Great Britain, people take particular pleasure in their conservatories, surrounded by greenery, unaffected by the weather, and with all the advantages of a climate-controlled domestic space. Combining old and new, conservatory furnishings follow the usual rules typical of British style. Nevertheless, style purists may wish to ensure that pre-18th century pieces of furniture or decorative items are not included in their scheme – orangeries, conservatories or winter gardens did not appear in the British Isles until the 17th century. A conservatory's age and structure should also be carefully considered before selecting furniture. The earliest structures, built in the 17th and 18th centuries, cannot be said to have provided a suitable environment for any kind of furniture susceptible to either humidity or cold, unless, that is, the conservatories were at some time or other fitted with efficient heating and ventilation systems. If climatic conditions in the conservatory are harsh, the furniture chosen for it should share all the long-lasting properties of garden furniture. Even 19th- and 20th-century conservatories are not necessarily suitable for antique furniture and precious textiles.

A conservatory is the perfect place to eat breakfast or take afternoon tea. It also provides an atmospheric backdrop for dinner parties, and in candlelight it becomes a place of sheer romance.

The reason for the conservatory's incredible popularity in Great Britain can probably be found in the island inhabitants' general love of nature and outdoor pursuits. Thanks to the conservatory people can relish the luxury of withdrawing to a green space with a cup of coffee and a book without fear of either rain or snow marring their pleasure.

Left: The climate control systems of modern conservatories are much more efficient than those of 18th- or 19th-century glasshouses. Nowadays, conservatory furniture runs little risk of being ruined by high levels of humidity.

Right: English kitchen designer George Cornish has allowed the kitchen to spill over into the conservatory. To achieve this, the kitchen had to be relocated, because most 19th-century kitchens were in the basement.

Nevertheless, conservatories would not enjoy such a high level of popularity if they did not serve primarily to grow plants or protect them from frost damage. The British delight in pursuing their national hobby of gardening, and in winter they can do so in the conservatory. When everything outside is bare and dead, the plants inside the glass house provide a confident expectation of the spring to come, and there can be no better place to wait for spring than a conservatory.

The glazed verandah, like this one at Melbourn Bury, is the simplest form of conservatory. It creates a rain-proof refuge which can double as an airy, bright living-room from spring to the beginning of the fall.

The conservatory at Chatsworth House was a functional as well as an architectural feature of the gardens, since exotic plants, which in many cases had been imported specially from around the world, were kept in greenhouses through the winter.

Below left: It is worth visiting conservatories for more than just their wealth of plants. Many are architectural jewels, as demonstrated by the example of the orangery at Elton Hall in Cambridgeshire.

Below right: The Neo-Gothic orangery at Elton Hall is now principally used as a covered space in the landscape. There is no shortage of tropical fruit on the market, and people no longer have to tend orange and lemon trees, unless it's as a hobby.

Left: Wooden furniture was thought unsuitable for conservatories because of the prevailing humidity. Stone and iron were popular alternatives. Necessity brought about the emergence of a style of conservatory furniture which remains as popular today as it was then.

Right: Although not as durable as metal, rattan is also an ideal material for the conservatory. Wickerwork looks particularly attractive when combined with exotic plants, providing the modern conservatory with echoes of the colonial style.

CONSERVATORY FURNITURE

Conservatories are special. They can enhance the external appearance of a house and, on dull days, they are marvelous places for dispelling gloomy thoughts. The question, however, is how best to furnish this room? There is a tendency for filling conservatories with any old surplus furniture – on the premise that conservatories are damp and would ruin anything half-way decent. This approach can result in a charming and cozy hodgepodge. Yet there is also a great deal of satisfaction to be had in restoring an historical conservatory, and furnishing it with antiques which were made during the same period as its construction.

Late Baroque pieces of furniture and ornaments, or reproductions, would suit the oldest surviving orangeries and conservatories, built during the 18th century. However, one should not forget that conservatories were only used for particular purposes during that period – for concerts or grand

soirées (and then only in the summer). The conservatory had to wait until the second half of the 19th century before it could begin to cast off its purely horticultural function and become a living space for which specialized furniture was required. It is therefore somewhat easier to furnish a steel and glass work of art of the Victorian era in period style. Thanks to the birth of industrialization, a wide range of furniture and accessories began to be generally available. Cast iron tables, benches, and chairs were particularly popular, as was the colonial style of rattan furniture, often complemented by exotic accessories which may even have brought back from India, China, or Africa by the home owners themselves.

Cast-iron garden benches suit any conservatory. They are stylish and impervious to humidity, and colorful cushions provide comfort. Beautiful copies made of galvanized steel or aluminum are also available. Authentic Victorian pieces can still be found in antique shops and architectural salvage yards.

Like rattan, bamboo endows the winter garden with an exotic, colonial feel, whereby a natural finish is deemed more attractive than treated or even painted bamboo. Although lightweight, bamboo furniture is remarkably robust. With the addition of a couple of cushions this seat becomes a haven of comfort.

A bird-cage is the perfect conservatory accessory. Depending on the style of furnishings, the cage could be an antique, a flea-market find, or even a souvenir from North Africa. A bird is not compulsory, bird-cages are just as decorative when empty.

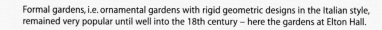
Formal gardens, i.e. ornamental gardens with rigid geometric designs in the Italian style, remained very popular until well into the 18th century – here the gardens at Elton Hall.

THE GARDEN

A Nation of Gardeners

The British and their gardens, in analogy to Samuel Adam's description of this island people as a nation of shopkeepers, the British could also be called a nation of garden keepers. But what makes a typical British garden? What immediately springs to mind are the landscape garden and the landscape park, justifiably regarded as the quintessential form of British garden design. While other garden types are rooted in ancient Rome, Renaissance Italy, or France at the time of the Sun King, England undeniably gave birth to the landscape garden. 18th- and 19th-century country houses are almost inconceivable without the generous park landscapes that surround them. The extraordinary appeal of these gardens lies in their natural appearance, despite the fact that they have been carefully designed and constructed by human hand. The landscape garden is typical of grand houses, but the cottage garden is particular to small country houses. The work of garden designer Gertrude Jekyll is widely acknowledged as having exerted most influence on modern interpretations of this form of small flower garden. Last but not least, there are the Italian-inspired Edwardian gardens, whose expanses of lawns positively invite you to a game of croquet.

A huge amount of time, energy, and money is spent in Great Britain on designing and maintaining gardens and parks, although another popular pastime is the study of English gardening history. Every child knows about the landscape gardener Lancelot "Capability" Brown, and even cosmopolitan Londoners have been known to fall into raptures at the sight of Kew Gardens' glasshouses. Nevertheless, research into gardening history has had limits imposed on it: with the passage of time, old gardens have been changed, and many have even grown wild. Preserving gardens over several centuries is very difficult to achieve. A building can withstand decay for a period even if

Entry to the Privy Garden at Hampton Court Palace was a privilege reserved to the king and his guests. The current layout follows King William III's design of 1702.

neglected, whereas a garden which has not been tended since the 16th century divulges nothing of its original layout. The task of the historians is slightly easier where gardens were built for particular houses or palaces, or were in some other way included in the architectural scheme. In these cases it is sometimes possible to make educated guesses about the original garden design based on the period of construction and the building's stylistic features. Nevertheless, very few English gardens are still in their original condition. Two of the most interesting examples are the gardens of Hampton Court and Kew Gardens.

After nature, the second enemy of historical gardens is man. Gardening fashions had a tendency to come and go in quick succession. As soon as a new trend emerged, everybody rushed to the task of transforming their own site. This process led to a ruthless disregard for the gardens which had been carefully laid out by preceding generations. New ideas were implemented unmindful of old trees, beautiful paths, or laboriously excavated lakes. This is exemplified by the fate of Blenheim Palace's gardens. Originally laid out in the French style by the architect Sir John Vanbrugh and the garden designer Henry Wise, in the 18th century much of the gardens was sacrificed to the ideas of the landscape architect Lancelot "Capability" Brown, and razed for the sake of a lawn. It was not until the 20th century, that Achille Duchêne took the gardens on and redesigned them to reinstate the French style. Nevertheless, other 17th- and 18th-century gardens are lost for ever, or exist only in pictures or plans.

Earlier generations seem not to have shared our desire to preserve, or even reconstruct, the testimonies of previous eras. Gardens were dug up, but valuable buildings were also demolished to make way on the old foundations for new buildings, which are now themselves regarded as historical architectural monuments. The passion for restoring gardens and houses to their original state is a 20th-century phenomenon, although the majority of British gardening enthusiasts do not have to worry about historical authenticity. Most own small gardens which they devotedly tend and maintain. Aside from some highly individual gardens, these gardens predominantly reflect a style which emerged after the Second World War. Regardless of size, every garden features a beautifully groomed lawn. This is only to be expected, as the lawn is the indispensable stage for every form of summer garden entertainment, from barbecues to Sunday afternoon games of croquet. Lawn maintenance permits no compromises, and when at last the grass has achieved the desired quality, the proud owner defends his lawn jealously against the encroachment of new trees, additional beds, or even the tiniest of weeds.

The design of private gardens is based on similar principles to those of domestic interiors. The foremost rule is that the garden should not appear too newly planted. This would disturb the artistically manufactured ambiance of old-established family tradition within the house. On the other hand the garden, like the living-room, has to exude generosity; in other words it should

Left: The gardens of Chatsworth, here the labyrinth, were last redesigned by the 6th Duke of Devonshire and his gardener Joseph Paxton. Paxton is best known for designing the Crystal Palace, built for the Great Exhibition of 1851.

Right: Since the 18th century, there has been little change in the gardens of Cawdor Castle in Scotland. The 17th Thane of Cawdor, who described the castle as an "ancient, honorable, and agreeable seat," could still find his way around today.

Fountains and pools were important garden design elements of the French style,
as here in the garden of Elton Hall.

Garden access via reception rooms was not a commonly established feature until the 19th century. Before that time, only large house of Palladian character provided such access via sumptuous flights of outdoor steps.

Most Tudor gardens were enclosed by walls. They contained plants with symbolic meanings that could provide counsel to people as they strolled through the garden. In contrast, the selection of plants in use today tends to be defined by aesthetic criteria, although this makes them no less appealing.

reflect the status of the house's mistress and master. Stone urns, ponds, and other ornamental features can help to introduce some of the grand park's magic to the gardens of terraced houses. Naturally, and without sacrificing order, the British garden must never look manicured. Like a sofa whose cushions invite one to take a seat, the garden and its lawn should be an enticement to linger at leisure.

There are many people with space and money who like to add swimming pools and tennis courts to their gardens. However, the swimming pools and tennis courts of even the grandest country estates can often surprise by their modesty. Since it is far safer to err on the side of maturity, which is by no means considered a defect, some of the country's wealthiest aristocrats splash about in antiquated pools, many of which were at the height of modernity 50 or 60 years ago. This is not deemed disagreeable because those people who are for-

tunate enough to own an old garden eschew the rashness of devaluing the natural patina of years by the installation of a vacation hotel-style pool.

In England, the French avenue became fashionable during the 17th century. These linear garden routes offered a new way of joining a house to the garden. Here, the avenue at Melbourn Bury.

There are a number of examples where a variety of design concepts co-exist within a single garden. Melbourn Bury, for instance, features aspects of both the formal style and the landscape gardening style of the 18th and 19th centuries.

Herb gardens, in which medicinal plants and aromatic kitchen herbs were cultivated, have a long-standing tradition in the British Isles.

The various forms of ornamental and pleasure gardens are supplemented by the kitchen garden. Its primary purpose is as a source of fruit and vegetables, although it also serves as a source of relaxation and the pure joy of gardening. Many British people make use of every square meter of garden to grow their own organic vegetables. This tends not to be for ideological reasons, but because they distrust modern fertilizers. Nevertheless, "green" ideas are gradually gaining acceptance in the British Isles, not least as a result of the Prince of Wales' commitment to environmental issues, once a subject for wry smiles, but now proven to be valid and worth emulating. Today even the most conservative gardeners can openly admit to having grown their pumpkins by organic methods, without having to fear derision at the village garden show. Yet the kitchen garden is not solely the preserve of fruit and vegetables, herbs too can offer an interesting, useful and sometimes even a medicinal outlet for the gardening enthusiast. Since the Middle Ages it has been an indispensable source of a variety of healing and aromatic herbs. Both monastic and secular houses were equally avid in their efforts to care for and raise these precious plants. A good example is the herb garden at Hardwick Hall in Derbyshire, which has been restored to its original Tudor style. However, the herb garden's place is not restricted to grand historic monuments. It requires only the smallest of sites, and keen cooks grow small selections of these useful ingredients, ranging from parsley through borage to mint, in small beds or even pots. Also, herbs keep away insects, lice and slugs and are therefore preferably placed near roses and other precious flowers.

Whether it is a grand park, a rural cottage garden, playing field, or vegetable plot, a garden always offers an opportunity for celebrating the country life so cherished by the British. This may be less important to the wealthy landowner whose estates are far removed from the cities than it is to the inner city dweller. After work and at weekends, Londoners are more likely to grab every opportunity to slip on their green Wellington boots and get to work in their gardens, regardless of their size. Because this is when they can feel like real country people and be in close proximity to nature — for a few hours, at least.

Above: Following the enthusiastic reception awarded to the architecture of Andrea Palladio and as a result of impressions gained on the Grand Tour, English gardens began to contain an element of Italian garden architecture. Here in Sezincote, the architect Thomas Daniell has used a dome structure to incorporate Indian influences. The garden was replanted in the 20th century by Humphry Repton.

Castle gardens were originally intended for growing vegetables and kitchen herbs. Ornamental plants were not introduced until the 16th century.

The Garden at Sissinghurst Castle

Sissinghurst's Tudor, tower-flanked gate house leads one to anticipate an opulent manor house beyond. However, this was demolished back in 1800. Nevertheless, the gate leads to one of England's most spectacular places: a garden created by the journalist Harold Nicolson and his wife, the novelist and poet Victoria "Vita" Sackville-West. When the incongruous couple acquired Sissinghurst in 1930, the gate house and garden were in a dire state of neglect. Harold produced the design and layout of the garden, and plant expert Vita set about its realization, including the fantastic color schemes of the flower beds. She had a preference for scented plants, roses in particular, which infuse the summer garden with the most beautiful fragrances, complementing the feast beheld by the eyes. Thanks to the large number of different roses in the garden, it is considered one of the most important old rose collections, many examples of which have completely disappeared from other places.

The garden is designed as a sequence of "outside rooms", each with its own color and formal scheme. Probably the best known of these is the "White Garden" which contains only flowers and plants with white and silver leaves or blooms, such as white roses, artemisias, and the silver-leafed pear. The garden also features a nuttery, a spring garden, a wildflower garden, and innumerable roses. The precision with which Sackville-West and Nicolson went about their gardening was almost scientific: every new planting was duly noted and dated. Each year they produced an inventory, which included the recorded measurement of every tree in the garden.

The stories that surround the couple are as fascinating as the garden itself. Harold and Vita were both homosexuals. Vita's love affairs with other women are particularly well known. In 1919, she ran away to Paris with her lover Violet, and the couple only returned to England thanks to their husbands' joint efforts of persuasion. Three years later, Sackville-West met the author Virginia Woolf. Woolf's 1928 novel *Orlando* was originally planned as a fictional biography of her novelist friend. The narrative tells an entertaining story which spans three hundred years in the life of an almost ageless aristocrat who experiences changes in gender. Vita wrote more than 50 books as well as newspaper columns and essays in addition to that. Sackville-West and Nicolson brought up two sons, one of whom later described this unusual union in the book *Portrait of a Marriage*.

Sissinghurst Castle Garden and the small biographical museum in the gate house now belong to the National Trust which has been entrusted with preserving the garden as it was left by Vita Sackville-West and Harold Nicholson. However, this has not always been possible, and some plants have had to be replaced as they outgrew their space and endangered adjacent plants.

Another problem has been the sheer number of people who come to visit this wonderful garden, thereby putting strain on the paving and flower beds. In order to limit the stream of visitors, the estate's administrators have introduced a ticketing system which permits visitors a strictly limited period in the gardens. This does mean however, that admission tickets to the garden can sometimes be sold out for months in advance throughout the summer months.

Discovering the Landscape

The "English landscape style" emerged in the early 18th century. This concept did not arise from one spontaneous idea, nor can it be attributed to a single person. Philosophers, politicians, and poets who adopted the ideas of John Locke (1632–1704) paved the way for the "natural style" of garden design. Thanks to Locke's argument that the law of nature gave rise to the freedom of man, nature became the focus of a number of people's reflections. The garden revolution, as the radical redesign of formal gardens into landscape gardens came to be known, was ushered in by literature. As early as 1685, Sir William Temple (1628–1699) criticized the architectural garden and called for the introduction of irregular design, but at the time his thoughts fell on deaf ears. A few years later, Ashley Cooper, the third Earl of Shaftesbury (1671–1713), Joseph Addison (1672–1719), Alexander Pope (1688–1744) and the essayist and garden designer Stephen Switzer (1682–1745) successfully took a position in opposition to the formal style of gardens, first through their writings alone and then by testing their ideals in real gardens.

Among the views formulated by Shaftesbury in his moral philosophy was the tenet that beauty and virtue were manifest in the divine order of untouched nature. "Nature in her primitive state" was interpreted as a symbol of freedom. This also meant that the Baroque garden, molded and quasi-subjugated by human hand, came to be considered as the quintessence of ugliness and constraint.

However, Shaftesbury's idea of nature was not clearly defined: on the one hand he speaks of untouched nature, yet on the other he seeks an ideal form which is only possible with the intervention of man. Joseph Addison, who invented the landscape garden before it existed de facto in the extensive design directions of his theoretical writings, also believed unspoiled nature to be superior to art. He called for the application of selective correction to achieve the "greatest perfection" of nature. "Improvement" was the slogan of garden design during the first half of the 18th century, a slogan enthusiastically adopted by the famous Lancelot "Capability" Brown (1716–1783).

Alexander Pope appealed for a return to the "friendly simplicity of untouched nature" and satirized the fashionable formal style with its clipped trees in his *Catalogue of Greens to be disposed of by an eminent Town*

William Kent was a somewhat untried designer before being commissioned by the Earl of Burlington to design the gardens of Chiswick House, and had only once previously assisted in designing a garden. Nevertheless, Kent succeeded in creating a garden far superior than a mere apprentice piece, and Chiswick House is now regarded as an early masterpiece of the English landscape style.

Gardener: "St George in box; his arm scarce long enough, but will be in a condition to stick the dragon by next April. A green dragon of the same, with a tail of ground-ivy for the present … A quickset hog shot up into a porcupine, by its being forgot a week in rainy weather …". In 1719, Pope retired to his country house in Twickenham where he transformed the garden by creating monuments and inscriptions with emotional and historic associations, and by taking the lyrical garden landscape of poetry and painting as his model. In so doing he allowed himself to be guided by the *genius loci*, the spirit of the place. Twickenham is considered the birthplace of the English landscape style, because it inspired an influential circle of acquaintances, the Kit-Cat Club, which included the third Earl of Burlington — patron of William Kent — to redesign their own gardens.

The landscape architect Charles Bridgeman (died 1738) was a key figure in this transformation, as were the famous garden designers William Kent (1685–1748), Lancelot "Capability" Brown (1716–1783), William Chambers

Tatton Park in the county of Cheshire is a day tripper's favorite. Humphry Repton designed the gardens of the 16th-century manor house, which was renovated in the 18th century to reflect changes in taste. These terraces were added by Joseph Paxton in around 1850.

(1723–1796), Humphry Repton (1752–1818), Joseph Paxton (1803–1865), and his pupil Edward Kemp (1817–1891). Some famous gardens were designed by amateurs like the banker Henry Hoare II (1705–1785) at Stourhead and John Aislabie at Studeley Royal.

William Kent, the "Father of Modern Gardening", was of humble origins. A painter of moderate talent, he was able to climb up the ladder of success thanks to his distinguished benefactors: Richard Boyle, third Earl of Burlington, introduced him to Pope's ideas, which inspired him to become a garden designer. As a follower of Pope, Kent designed gardens with the visual means of landscape painting in mind. A characteristic of the landscape garden was a rejection of rigid symmetrical garden plans and mirrored repetition of motifs. The growth of plants continued to be held in check, but it was no longer subject to the boundless excesses of the topiarists. Flowers and parterres went out of fashion at the same time as the living sculptures. Formal ponds and basins were replaced by irregular lakes. Surplus soil from the excavation of lakes was used to create gentle slopes. Regulated rows of trees were removed to make space for open lawns with occasional clumps of trees or specimen plants. Meandering paths led to a number of views and buildings. A variety of architectural styles, from Greek temples to Gothic ruins, were adopted to enrich the garden's design with variety as well as allegory. Addison believed that a garden should illustrate the ideal values of man (virtue and freedom). Garden walls were concealed, a measure which served to extend the view from the garden to the landscape beyond, its villages, woods, and countryside. This design feature was an invention of Switzer's, aimed at improving nature by artistic intervention to produce the ideal landscape.

The list of gardens and parks designed and constructed by Lancelot Brown during his 40-year career includes one of the most beautiful estates in England. He transformed the gardens of Syon House into a landscape of art for the Earl and Countess of Northumberland.

Kew Gardens. The Great Palm House was built by Decimus Burton and Richard Turner in 1844–1848. A storm during the 1990s destroyed many of the trees and buildings at Kew Gardens, and this is now one of the botanical gardens' few remaining original buildings.

Kent was successful in putting theory into practice at his benefactor's seat Chiswick House, and consequently was awarded further large-scale commissions. He designed the gardens for Carlton House, Badminton House (Avon), Claremont (Surrey), Euston Hall (Suffolk), Holkham Hall (Norfolk), Shotover, and the famous Rousham House (both in Oxfordshire) as well as Stowe (Buckinghamshire). In addition to planting expansive open lawns, he cleverly positioned buildings and sculptures to serve as eye catchers.

The "Temple of British Worthies" forms part of the "Elysian Fields" created by William Kent at Stowe. This monument is based on Roman tomb designs, and features the busts of 14 British paragons of virtue, including Queen Elizabeth I, King William III, Francis Bacon, and John Locke, William Shakespeare, Sir Francis Drake, and Isaac Newton.

Stowe is an outstanding example of the English landscape style and, as it is now, contains 32 preserved garden buildings that bear witness to many famous designers' work. The three distinct zones of the 17th century, terraced, formal garden were merged under the aegis of Bridgeman between 1715 and 1726. The small-scale buildings were designed by the architect Vanbrugh.

In around 1730, the garden's area was doubled, and a 4.5 hectare lake excavated. Kent's first task on taking over from Bridgeman was a redesign of the paths: they now wind their way through the landscape, incorporating views across the surrounding fields. The year 1735, or thereabouts, saw the creation of the "Elysian Fields", an allusion to the afterlife as conceived by the minds of antiquity. Lancelot Brown was employed as the estate's head gardener between 1741 and 1751, after which the owner Richard Grenville, Earl Temple (1711–1779) began to produce his own design for the garden's views and sightlines.

Lancelot "Capability" Brown came from a humble rural family, and dominated the landscape style for 35 years. Thanks to his time as an apprentice gardener, he was a master of his craft. Brown had the ability to translate his ideas into practical reality – he could visualize the "capabilities of a property's improvement", hence his nickname. Driven by the belief that nature was more beautiful than any work created by man, Brown radically metamorphosed his clients' sumptuous, formal gardens: In Blenheim Palace (Oxfordshire) he created two large lakes which flooded Vanbrugh's canal and cascade. The parterres and shrubbery beds made way for broad park areas. The fate of the gardens at Chatsworth (Derbyshire) was not dissimilar. He transformed more than 100 gardens into what he called "picturesque landscapes," including Warwick Castle (Warwickshire), Burghley House

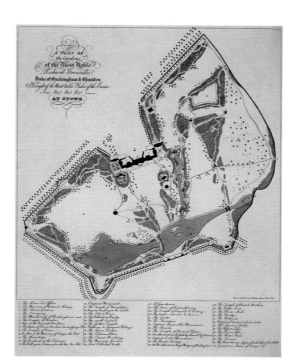

Plan of the gardens, ca. 1765.

(Lincolnshire), Harewood House (Yorkshire), and Hampton Court.

Brown's style was modified by his immediate successor Humphry Repton. We are indebted to the latter for reintroducing flowers, terraces, and stairs to the landscape garden. Despite only being an amateur rather than a trained architect or gardener, he earned many commissions for new gardens as well as modifications, including Holkham Hall and Tatton Hall (Cheshire). A protégé of the Duke of Portland, Repton did not come to garden design until after a short, unhappy, and unsuccessful career as a businessman. Highly educated, he wrote countless books on landscape gardening which became standard works in innumerable private libraries. Repton defined the Regency style. These gardens were flower sanctuaries surrounded by living hedges, full of the color of imported plants and new cultivars, and often divided into smaller garden rooms of varying styles within naturally styled gardens.

View of the triumphal arch. This composition features an eye catching triumphal arch on the horizon, and was created in 1765 when Earl Temple had already begun to involve himself in the design process.

Monopteros, Stowe. Clumps of trees have been planted next to Vanbrugh's Monopteros (pre-1730). Lancelot "Capability" Brown's hand is clearly discernible in the gently modeled terrain and the building's immediate environment.

Bounty of the Plant Hunters

The majority of people who wander through Great Britain's parks and gardens are unaware that many of the plants in them are not natives of the island. Many of the familiar trees, shrubs, and herbacious plants originated in faraway parts of the world. The discovery of America in the 15th century brought about an enrichment of the United Kingdom's vegetation. Tomatoes and sunflowers, to name but two examples, both originated in the New World.

Southern and eastern Europe were also popular hunting grounds for the garden designers and plant importers of the 16th, 17th, and 18th centuries. The conifer *Pinus pinea*, or "Umbrella pine" so characteristic of Spain and Italy, was brought to Great Britain from the Mediterranean in around 1550, and the poplar followed in around 1760. The spread of the Lombardy poplar, *Populus nigra* "Italica", a mutant form which emerged in Italy in around 1750, was particularly rapid throughout Europe. Planted along avenues or in groups, this tree can define a landscape's character. The tulip hailed from Turkey in around 1550. As early as the 12th century, Turkish gardeners considered this flower an indispensable adornment to their gardens. There have been commercial flower bulb nurseries in Holland since 1585. The tulip craze, which also affected England, reached its zenith in the period between 1634 and 1640. The hyacinth originates from the eastern Mediterranean region. The genus *Hyacinthus* contains only one species, that is the garden hyacinth *Hyacinthus orientalis* of which there are many attractive varieties now available.

The Yucca came to England from Central America during the early 17th century. This palm forms part of the Agavaceae family. "Geraniums", also known as hybrid pelargoniums, and not to be confused with the species of the genus *Geranium*, which belongs to the same family of Geraniaceae, came to England from South Africa in around 1710. Midway through the 17th century, the Dutch began to settle in South Africa, which became a British colony in 1806, and so began a brisk traffic of ships between England, Holland, and Cape Town. Of the original species which formed the basis for our modern varieties, *Pelargonium cuculatum* AIT was brought to England by Bentick in 1690. The Duchess of Beaufort introduced *Pelargonium peltatum* in 1701 and *Pelargonium zonale* in 1710. Bishop Compton was responsible for the introduction to Great Britain of *Pelargonium inquinans* in 1714, and *Pelargonium grandiflorum* was introduced by Masson.

From top left to bottom right:

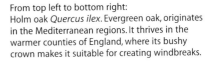
Holm oak *Quercus ilex*. Evergreen oak, originates in the Mediterranean regions. It thrives in the warmer counties of England, where its bushy crown makes it suitable for creating windbreaks.

Red Mulberry *Morus rubra*. There are around 10 species of the genus *Morus*. These shrubs and trees are popular in Great Britain and northern Europe, and probably originate in East Asia, Central Asia, and North America.

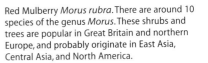
Conifer *Pinus pinea*. This characteristic conifer of Spain and Italy is not frost resistant in central Europe, although it is hardy in Great Britain.

London plane *Platanus x acerifolia*. A southern European hybrid of *P. orientalis* and *P. occidentalis* which was created in around 1650. *P. orientalis*, with its wide-spreading crown, is a native of Crete and the Balkan mountain regions.

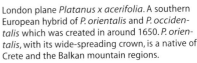
Horse-chestnut *Aesculus hippocastanum*. The chestnut is widely used as an ornamental tree and alongside avenues. It is a native of southern Europe, particularly northern Greece.

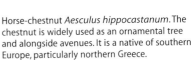
Swamp cypress of the genus *Taxodium*. With three species originally from North America and Mexico, this small genus of deciduous or semi-evergreen conifers is very popular. The name of this genus arises from the similarity of its leaves with those of the Yew (*Taxus*).

Cedar of Lebanon *Cedrus libani*. This attractive tree can grow to a height of 35 meters, and was introduced centuries ago to western Europe. Some selections have a conical or upright habit.

Poplar Populus. The Lombardy poplar emerged in northern Italy in around 1750 from where it rapidly spread through western Europe. They are grown alongside avenues or in groups to maximize their visual impact.

Araucaria, Monkey puzzle tree, Chile pine *Araucaria auracana*. A. Menzies brought this tree to Europe from a small region in the southern Andes. In its typical habit it is single trunked.

From top left to bottom right:
Cotoneaster *Cotoneaster* 'Cornubia'. This semi-evergreen shrub was bred in 1930 in Exbury in England, and may be a hybrid of *C. frigidus* and *C. salciflorus*.

Hyacinth *Hyacinthus*. This genus of bulbs originates in Asia Minor and central Asia, and produces flowers in the spring. The bulbs are planted in the fall.

Tulip *Tulipa*. Wild forms of this genus came to Europe from central and western Asia in 1544. There are over 100 species, and garden tulips are cultivars.

Yucca This genus originated in central America, and is principally found in natural gardens where it is successfully combined with succulents and grasses.

Nasturtium *Tropaeolum*. The brightly colored flowers of these annuals have made them particularly popular garden plants. The 87 species are natives of Chile and Mexico.

Red Hot Poker *Kniphofia*. These decorative herbaceous plants originate in tropical southern Africa. Crossbreeding has resulted in extremely attractive garden forms becoming available.

Geranium *Pelargonium*. All 250 species of this genus are popular pot plants, although they are equally happy in warm and sunny rockeries. They are relatives of the *Geranium* and *Erodium*. Many species originate in South America.

Hydrangea Most species are natives of the temperate climate zones of Asia, and of North and South America. The color of the flowers depends on the acid or alkaline content of the soil.

Plantain lily *Hosta*. The 40 species of this genus are grown for their decorative leaves. This native of Japan and China is frost hardy and easy to grow.

Probably the most famous plant collectors of the 16th and 17th centuries were John Tradescant the Elder and John Tradescant the Younger. They each have been dedicated a garden in the Museum of Garden History in London. John Tradescant the Elder was a gardener and nurseryman. He traveled to the European mainland on plant-finding expeditions, returning with numerous plants which have become widespread, including the oleander shrub and the fig. He has also been associated with the import of the European larch, which he is said to have discovered in Russia in 1618. His son made three journeys to America between 1637 and 1657, bringing back the swamp cypress among other interesting plants. This small genus, *Taxodium*, comprises three species which are native to North America and parts of Mexico.

A consequence of the discovery and importation of exotic plants to England was a need for conservatories and glasshouses to keep and propagate them. Orangeries provided winter shelter for sensitive plants which had originated in southern climates. By the 19th century this method of nursing plants provided thousands of flowers for new parks and gardens. Victorian innovations in construction made possible the erection of bold steel and glass structures which are still admired today. These glasshouses harbored pampered collections of exotic plants from around the world, many of which emerged from their glass nurseries onto Great Britain's green oases.

Great Britain was the greatest sea and colonial power of the period, and collecting exotic plants became both a pastime and a matter of prestige as her prosperity grew. This is what motivated English horticultural businesses, wealthy gardening enthusiasts, botanic gardens, and the Royal Horticultural Society (founded in 1804) to send botanists and plant hunters to the USA and the tropics in search of seeds, rootstocks, and bulbs.

A major nursery was the Royal Exotic Nursery, James Veitch & Sons (1808–1914), based in Exeter and London. 20 plant finders were employed by this company. In the early 18th century, as the English landscape garden began to replace the geometric style, collectors also traveled to Japan to acquire hardy shrubs and woody plants. The Loddiges Nursery began to publish the Botanical Cabinet in 1817. 20 volumes of this periodical were issued, containing 2,000 illustrations and descriptions of new plants. Veitch & Sons published a similar catalogue of conifers in 1888. Great Britain initially monopolized the introduction of new plants, and served as a model to businesses in Flemish Belgium, in the area around Ghent and Bruges, where major azalea, palm, and herbaceous plant suppliers became established.

ROSES

The rose is not only an extremely popular garden plant in Great Britain, it is also a major symbol of national identity. The red rose once stood for the House of Lancaster, and the white rose for the House of York. The wars fought between these two lines of the Plantagenet ruling family have gone down in history as the "Wars of the Roses". Henry Tudor put an end to the conflicts which lasted from 1455 to 1485 by marrying Elizabeth of York. This peace-brokering alliance was again symbolized by a rose, the Tudor Rose. A fusion of the red and white roses, it stands for the reign of the Tudors which lasted from 1485 to 1603.

The Lancaster and York Roses depicted by artists were modeled on Medieval shrub roses. *Rosa gallica Officinalis* was the model for the red rose of the Lancasters, and *Rosa alba Semiplana* for the white rose of the Yorks. Like wild roses, shrub roses are natives of the British Isles. Nowadays, they are described as "old roses" and include the Gallica, Damask, Alba, Centifolia, and Moss roses. They generally flower only once in the summer for a period of four to five weeks. Repeat-flowering Bourbon, Portland, and China roses are the exception to this rule. "Old roses" are still grown today, and many rose lovers have a particular fondness for the special appeal of the once-flowering types, a fascination they shared with the old masters who included them in many famous paintings.

The emergence of modern roses was relatively late. In 1867 the Frenchman Guillot crossed a remontant rose with a tea rose from China.

The resulting rose was baptized "La France" and entered the annals of rose-growing history as the first Hybrid Tea rose. Today, representatives of this group are among the most popular rose types in England, as elsewhere. They are distinguished by their large, fragrant flowers and long stems, which may bear the flowers singly or in clusters. Typical British Hybrid Teas are the red, very fragrant "Fragrant Cloud", thorny "Silver Jubilee" with its diverse shades of pink, scarlet "Alec's Red", yellow "Grandpa Dickinson", red and yellow "Piccadilly", faintly scented "Pink Favourite", snow-white "Polar", red "Precious Platinum", and, naturally, the award winning and ever popular "Peace" rose.

In 1875, Guillot created another ground breaking group, the Polyantha rose. These are characterized by abundant clusters of small flowers. In the 1920s, the Dane Sven Poulsen crossed a Polyantha rose with a Hybrid Tea, thereby creating the still popular Floribunda rose. It was introduced to England during the inter-war period as the "Hybrid Polyantha", but did not achieve the fame it deserved until after 1945. Since these roses are hybrids of rose types with relatively faint fragrances, some Floribundas give off no, or hardly any, perfume. This explains the belief that modern roses have no fragrance, but there are some highly scented types, like the yellow "Arthur Bell", "Champagne Cocktail" created in 1985, or "Fragrant Delight". Not only do Floribunda roses produce an abundance of flowers, they are also frost resistant. You will find a large number of Floribundas in British gardens. Popular varieties are the deep yellow "Amber Queen", Rose of the Year in 1984, scarlet "City of Belfast", orange and yellow "Dame of Sark", the less robust but equally beautiful "Elizabeth of Glamis" with salmon flowers, or the almost thornless "Pink Parfait" with pink and yellow flowers.

Hybrid Teas and Floribundas generally feature in beds and borders, providing the green of the lawn with splashes of color, or contrasting in front of shrubs and trees. When selecting a rose, the rose gardener takes onto consideration the color, number, and shape of its flowers, but also the height to which the plant will grow and the hue of the leaves. By so doing, roses can be harmoniously integrated into a garden's overall scheme. If a garden is unsuitable for Hybrid Teas or Floribundas, there are other roses to fall back on. Miniature bush and patio roses are a lovely alternative in a very small garden as they can be grown in containers. Miniature roses can be traced back to a hybrid of a Floribunda with a small Chinese rose, which was originally only available with either white or pink flowers. They make suitable border and hedge plants to define beds of tall roses. Miniature bush roses are also attractive additions to rock gardens. These small roses with their tiny flowers are particularly effective when grown in a slightly raised position, on a wall or on the edge of a terrace.

If sufficient space is available, Hybrid Teas and Floribundas make attractive plants for hedges and provide additional structure in larger gardens. However, achieving the required shape and density of a rose hedge needs careful forethought. Different roses have different growth rates and the type of rose used will determine whether the resulting hedge grows tall or wide. In addition to the roses used in beds and hedges, British gardeners adore climbing roses which evoke the characteristic image of elderly ladies sipping tea under a rose covered pergola – or perhaps the overgrown façade of a half-timbered house behind which lies a traditional village pub.

M.R. = Modern Rose
O.R. = Old Rose

Rosa, M.R., Hybrid Tea, "Loving Memory"

Rosa, M.R., Hybrid Tea, "Can-Can"

Rosa, M.R., Floribunda, "Disco Dancer"

Rosa pimpinellifolia, syn. *Rosa spinosissima*, Wild rose, "Old Yellow Scotch Rose"

Rosa canina, O.R., "June"

Rosa O.R., Gallica "Rosa Mundi," syn. "Versicolor"

Rosa, M.R., Hybrid Tea, "Tequila Sunrise"

Rosa, Canina, Wild rose

Rosa O.R., Moschata

Rosa, M.R., Floribunda, "Old Port"

Rosa O.R., Gallica "Officinalis"

Rosa, O.R., Remontant rose, "Frau Karl Druschki"

Her Majesty's Lawn

No other single component of the English garden has achieved as much fame across the world as has the lawn. We expect this to feature in well-tended gardens, but it is also a characteristic of cricket pitches, bowling greens, and tennis courts. The high esteem in which lawns are held has even found its way into the world of comic books. The book *Asterix in Britain* features an Englishman who staunchly defends his perfectly manicured lawn against the threat of devastation by trampling hordes of Roman soldiers. It is no surprise then, given the time and effort dedicated to creating a beautiful lawn, that the world's best lawn mowers are manufactured in Great Britain.

Based in the Suffolk town of Stowmarket, Atco-Qualcast Ltd have been manufacturing lawn mowers for over 75 years. As is typical in England, they have managed to combine traditional good looks and superb technology. Just one look at the color is enough to make the anglophile's heart beat faster. Elsewhere in Europe canary yellow or crimson are regarded as suitable body-work colors, but in England it has to be green – British racing green. The names given to each of the models also contribute to the make's genteel image: "The Balmoral", "The Windsor", or "The Admiral" are the names of just a few of these substantial grass cutters. The company is understandably proud of its two "Royal Warrants": Atco's lawn mowers trim no lesser lawns than those of the Queen and the Prince of Wales.

There are two different types of lawn mower. The first is the cylinder mower, which uses a rotating, horizontal cylinder to cut the grass. Blades in the cylinder cut the lawn along a base-plate, creating a scissor effect which guarantees an even cut, while the rotating cylinder evenly pushes the grass in one direction, producing an attractively striped pattern on the lawn. A checker pattern is achieved by skillfully changing the direction in which the grass is cut.

The second type of mower is based on a system akin to a propeller, and is known as a rotary mower. Sharp, rotating edges shear the grass like a scythe. Mowers fitted with rotating blades are also suitable for cutting long and wet grass. The results may not be as perfect as those of a cylinder mower, but a heavy-duty rotary mower allows the hobby gardener to trim the lawn with less effort, even when it has been neglected for a while and grown rather wild as a consequence. This type of mower is ideal for less frequently mown large lawns.

Both types of lawn mowers are available in electric and petrol-driven versions. Cordless electric mowers are particularly useful for small lawns or irregularly shaped gardens with narrow strips of lawn running between flower beds where a heavy cable could damage the plants. However practical electric mowers may be, the classic lawn mower is petrol driven. This confers something of the race track to lawn mowing, thereby making it a more palatable chore for the less enthusiastic gardener. Enjoyment is at its peak if the mower in question is a "Royale" ride-on model. A steel roller at the rear of this lawn mower produces an exceedingly even stripe, and can be swapped for a coupe of wheels whenever wet or long grass needs cutting.

Quality has its price. The "Royale" model mentioned above costs around £2,000 (US$2,900). However, this is considered a sacrifice worth making by the many gardeners who will not make do with anything less than a perfect English lawn.

Gardeners with secret Formula One ambitions will relish the "Royale" model. Atco's own advertisements describe it as the king of ride-on mowers.

The "Balmoral" is a classic English lawn mower. The quick exchange system allows easy removal and replacement of the cylinder.

The "Regent" is a larger than usual electric mower with the capacity to tackle large lawns and, most importantly, longer grass.

The "Viscount" model offers a more streamlined design. It features a particularly large grassbox and can tackle even very wet grass.

The flagship among rotary mowers is the "Admiral". This will tame even the wildest and longest grass.

The "Windsor" model is the electric equivalent of the "Balmoral", and its design emulates that of the classic petrol-powered cylinder mower.

The "Club" model offers the highest degree of perfection for the sacred greens of English lawn sport. Fitted with a large tank it can cover large areas without having to stop for refueling.

Spring

Lawns should be cut as frequently as possible during the spring, because mowing promotes thick and even growth. To avoid damaging the grass carpet, the mower should be turned in a different place at each mowing. As the weather becomes warmer, the lawn should not be cut quite as short, otherwise the soil will become susceptible to drought. Lawns should be watered early in the morning or late in the evening during dry spells.

Summer

Lawns should continue to be cut twice a week in summer. This stimulates growth and suppresses weeds. When the weather is dry the lawn can be left a little longer, and grass clippings do not have to be removed. This helps to keep in moisture. Gentle scarifying is good for the lawn, except during very dry spells. Mature lawns can be spiked and scarified as required.

Fall

Young lawns still have to be cut regularly in the fall, but not too short. More mature lawns are mowed less frequently. Fallen leaves must be swept regularly. Where shade has caused damage to the grass, trees and shrubs should be pruned to allow access to the light. The last mowing of the year takes place in November.

Winter

You should avoid walking on the lawn in winter, particularly in frosty or very wet weather. Preparations for sowing new lawns may begin when the coldest of the weather is over. This is also the right time to resume scarifying. The grass can be mown as soon as it begins to grow again, but should not be cut too short. Remove all grass clippings.

The rotary mower's rotating blade cuts the grass.

The rotating shaving head in the cylinder mower trims the grass tips.

The blades should be cleaned after each mowing.

The lawn mower should be lubricated with oil before it is put away for the winter.

Croquet

Most people regard croquet as a frivolous game played at summer garden parties. This kind of croquet has as little in common with the actual sport as checkers has with chess. Croquet rules are quite complex and it is best to learn them by playing the game. The game's principal aim is to win points while preventing the adversary from scoring. There are two versions of croquet. The more sophisticated version is association croquet, and golf croquet is the somewhat easier version to learn.

Association croquet is played by two or – in the case of doubles – four players with four balls. The balls are made of a synthetic material and are colored black, blue, red, and yellow. The court has to be marked out on a completely flat lawn. Its dimensions are 25.8 by 32 meters, and six cast iron hoops are arranged on the court with a peg at the center. The mallets of association and golf croquet are more robust than those used for playing in the garden at home. Lightweight mallets are made of ash or boxwood, while tropical timbers are used for heavier models. The front end is often protected by a layer of plastic, while the striking end sometimes features a covering of brass. The players may choose the form of the mallet's head, although its weight must lie within three pounds and three pounds six ounces – English pounds and ounces that is, so between 1360 and 1530 grams. The shaft of the mallet is made of wood, fiberglass, or metal.

Each player, or team, must strike their balls through the hoops in a particular sequence and direction, whereby the balls have to pass through the hoops both backwards and forwards. Consequently, each player can achieve a maximum of 12 points, to which one point may be added for touching the peg at the center of the court. It follows then that a doubles team can score up to 26 points. Balls can be played directly to the hoops, although they may also bounce off other balls. The tactic of the game lies in achieving as many points as possible with one's own balls while positioning them in such a way that the adversary's point scoring opportunities are minimized. Colored clips indicate the sequence in which the hoops have to be played. Clips are attached to the top of hoops 1 to 6, or on the hoop upright for the second set of six hoops.

The players play alternate turns. The game begins with each player striking his or her ball into the court from one of two baulk-lines. In the case of a doubles match, a decision now has to be made as to which ball is to be played. This decision cannot be reversed during a team's turn. Principally, a turn consists of a single strike, although additional strikes may be won, either by a player running the correct hoop at the first stroke, or by executing a croquet stroke. A croquet stroke is due when a striker hits an adversary's ball (a roquet). The player's ball is positioned next to the adversary's ball and must be struck in such a way as to move the previously touched ball. If successful, it is termed a croquet stroke which is then rewarded with a continuation stroke. A turn ends when a player has played all his or her strokes or when a ball rolls out of the court during a croquet stroke.

If the ball leaves the court after an ordinary stroke, it is returned to its original position. In contrast to the rules of simple garden croquet, there is no point in roqueting the adversary's ball as far away as possible. It is equally impermissible for players to strike balls against their own feet.

The second form is golf croquet. This requires dexterity rather than tactical skills, and is therefore easier to learn than association croquet. Each side has two balls: blue and black against red and yellow.

Each turn consists of one stroke and, unlike association croquet, there are no additional strokes. A coin is tossed at the beginning of the game, and the winner of the toss decides who plays first. The first team to score a hoop is awarded a point, after which the scored hoop is considered dead, and all subsequent strokes are played to the remaining hoops. All strikers play for the same hoop. Even when a player has no chance of getting to the hoop in question before an adversary, he or she may not strike towards the next hoop in the sequence. The aim of the game is to be the first to get the balls through all of the hoops. The sequence of hoops is the same as in association croquet. The winner of the game is the first player or team to score seven points.

As in golf, handicap rules are applied to both these versions of croquet. They characterize the strength of each player, although they also balance differing ability levels. Hence weaker association croquet players are given additional strokes to increase their chances of winning. In golf croquet's handicap system, the handicap number is changed in order to reflect the number of won or lost games.

The serious game of croquet must not be confused with the familiar game played at children's parties. Croquet as played in the British Isles is an extremely sophisticated game of tactics and skill.

PIMM'S – BRITAIN'S FAVORITE SUMMER DRINK

Summer in the United Kingdom's gardens and parks would be incomplete without Pimm's. Pimm's is a kind of punch made by mixing Pimm's with gin, lemonade or ginger ale, ice, cucumber, a slice of either lemon or orange, a few leaves of mint and borage. Some people like to add a few pieces of apple to the mixture. The ingredients are combined in a large jug and then drunk from similarly large glasses.

There are many variations of the basic recipe. Connoisseurs generally insist on the ingredients listed on the back of the bottle: Pimm's, lemonade or ginger ale, ice, a slice of lemon or orange, and cucumber. Real Pimm's aficionados provide their mixture with a bit more kick by adding a shot of gin, which makes the effect of this already rather dangerous drink even more hazardous in the summer heat.

Despite the potency of its ingredients, Pimm's is drunk in vast quantities at almost every outdoor event, whether public or private. Innocent foreigners who have never sampled Pimm's before are in for a big surprise. Unaware of the high alcohol content they may regard Pimm's as a harmless punch, similar to the wine, champagne, and lemonade concoctions served on the continent. Hence a first encounter with Pimm's can often conclude with a nap on an English lawn.

Pimm's was invented by James Pimm of London. In 1841 he opened an oyster bar in the City, where he served "modified" Gin Slings which were instrumental in securing the restaurant's success. In the mid-19th century, a Gin Sling consisted of a large measure of gin, slices of lemon, sugar, and ice or iced water. At least, this is how Mrs Isabella Beaton described it in her *One Shilling Cookery Book*. The drink served by James Pimm contained all the ingredients mentioned above, plus something else. This mysterious drink could only be bought at the oyster bar at first, but about 30 years after it first opened its doors to customers, James' successors began to bottle the drink with the secret recipe and sold it to other bars and restaurants.

Like gin, Pimm's was exported to every corner of the British Empire, where it moistened the throats of thirsty colonial administrators. It is said, for

Still life of a British summer – a glass of Pimm's and a good book are the perfect accompaniments to a hot summer's afternoon.

example, that Lord Kitchener's officers sought refreshment by drinking Pimm's both before and after the legendary Battle of Omdurman. In his *Gin Book*, the gin expert John Doxat speculates that the young Winston Churchill may well have fortified himself with a large glass of Pimm's after participating in the last cavalry charge of British military history. If he didn't, then his fellow officers, who needed to wash down the dust following the infamous carnage of that battle, certainly did. Incidentally, Doxat also confesses not only that he fortifies his Pimm's with gin, but that he flavors it with a dash of Cointreau.

Pimm's on the lawn is many British people's definition of summer. The British season's numerous events held between June and August therefore tend to be events at which Pimm's is served – from the "Fourth of June" at Eton, to Henley, and Goodwood. Pimm's is also a favorite drink at private parties during the warm season. And what does the legendary refreshment taste of? Certainly not of gin. A sip of undiluted Pimm's reveals a slightly bitter, herbal taste reminiscent of Italian aperitifs.

Ingredients for Pimm's: Pimm's No.1, gin, lemonade, fresh mint, cucumber, and lemon.

Ascot, Henley, Wimbledon and last but not least Glyndebourne, the legendary opera festival held 50 miles south of London – these are the key events of the British season, when even the most refined people of society enjoy a picnic out of doors. However, relaxed, open-air meals with friends are not restricted to these events, but can take place almost anywhere on the British Isles.

THE ENGLISH PICNIC

Contrary to all appearances, the picnic is unlikely to have been a British invention. *Picnic* derives from *pique-nique* and it therefore sounds like a French idea. Art history's most famous open-air meal also comes from the other side of the Channel, where it was painted by Edouard Manet. Nevertheless, it is England that immediately springs to mind whenever the word picnic is mentioned. It evokes images of navy blazer and white flannel trouser clad gentlemen, and ladies wearing bright cotton print dresses. And it is undeniable that there are few British outdoor events which do not feature meals eaten on the lawn.

Ascot's legendary horse races, Henley Regatta, a Sunday spent by a lake, or a day in the country – the picnic hamper is a must. This useful item of basket-ware is available in a wide price range, filled or empty, with or without accessories. Frugal people shop at Boots where a starter kit is available for around £35 (US$50). At this price the crockery is made of plastic. Somewhat better quality hampers are available from John Lewis in Oxford Street, where the prices range from £85 to £150 (US$120–200). The most expensive model in the range contains real tableware for four people. If even that is not sufficiently refined, a luxury version can be purchased from Westfield. This contains exquisite china, high-quality cutlery, a stainless steel tea pot, cotton table napkins, and the finest English crystal glasses. This will set a buyer back somewhere between £1,000 (US$1,400) and £1,500

(US$2,100). However, a Westfield hamper is only truly impressive if it comes out of the trunk of a Jaguar, Rolls Royce, or Aston Martin.

People without the time or inclination to prepare their own picnic may opt to have a specialist firm do it for them. Delicatessen shops like Villandry, Bluebird, and Partridge's can supply all the classic ingredients of an English picnic. Alternatively, ready-filled hampers can be ordered from Fortnum & Mason. These contain all the requirements in a meal al fresco: fois gras, fresh brioches, wine, mineral water, as well as porcelain plates, cutlery, table napkins, and glasses. Only the food and drink are included in the price, so the "hardware" has to go back to Fortnum & Mason. People who prefer to trust in their own culinary talents need not bother with any of that, and make do with a simple basket à la Little Red Riding Hood instead of using a special picnic hamper. A pretty table cloth can be used instead of a picnic blanket. A plastic lining protects against damp. The tidbits can then be spread out on the blanket's woolen side, which usually features a tartan pattern – and the authentic English picnic may begin.

Ingredients for a Successful Picnic

Careful planning and organization are needed in order for a picnic to be successful. The host is far from his well-equipped kitchen and the spices, crockery, cutlery, tools, and electric gadgets which help to solve all culinary problems. Disregarding classic hiccups such as broken corkscrews and forgotten cruets, two things must be avoided: a lack of cooling elements for the cool box, and foods that are difficult to eat while sitting on a picnic blanket.

It comes as no surprise to discover that sandwiches are the most popular form of outdoor food. Easy to eat without having to resort to cutlery, the space between two slices of white bread leaves plenty of room for the imagination to run riot. Creations such as prawn and mango chutney, or avocado and lemon sandwiches prove the point. On the other hand, traditionalists may prefer their sandwiches filled with cucumber, smoked salmon, or roast beef. According to culinary legend, sandwiches were invented by John Montagu, the fourth Earl of Sandwich. The Earl's two great passions were playing cards and eating, particularly red meat. The fact that indulgence in one of his favorite activities prevented him for exercising the other was a constant source of frustration, so he asked his cook to invent a meal which he could eat as he played cards. The cook duly sliced some roast beef, laid it between two slices of bread, and the sandwich was born.

A couple of sandwiches with a well-cooled bottle of white wine or Champagne, followed by classic strawberries and cream are all that is needed for a very English picnic. If a more substantial meal is required, the inclusion of a few additional delicacies such as Dorset crab salad (scrape out the crab meat at home and bring the dressing separately), cold chicken (also cut into portions at home), quail's eggs, and a cheese board to finish (taking consideration of the temperature if taking very soft cheeses), fruit, or even a cake will not go amiss. Dishes that can be prepared in advance are ideal. And if the cruet set and an emergency corkscrew are included in the hamper, nothing can go wrong.

Patés of all kinds are perfect for picnics. Fois gras with crusty white bread is particularly sophisticated. Canapés are quick and easy to make at the picnic site itself.

Hard boiled eggs make a fantastic outdoor snack: their packaging is environmentally friendly, they are pre-portioned and they stay fresh. Quail's eggs bring a touch of refinement to a meal.

Cold soups must always be transported in suitable containers, but are well worth the effort. Nothing is more refreshing on a hot day. Serve with plenty of bread.

Probably the most English of all summer desserts is strawberries and cream. This traditional snack is de rigeur at Wimbledon – a heavenly accompaniment to tennis.

Smoked salmon is an essential picnic ingredient. It is particularly delicious served with white bread and a dill vinaigrette, which can be brought along separately.

An English picnic, complete with first and main course, cheese and drinks can be quite a lavish affair, and diners should be given plenty of time to eat. Truly a pleasure when the weather permits.

FINANCIAL TIMES

Tories routed at Scottish polls

Party loses every council it held ■ Labour fends off challenge from nationalists

EU attacks Canada in fishing row

Manufacturing recovery stalls as growth slows

Virgin settles UK 'dirty tricks' dispute with BA

HOME FROM HOME

"Standards Must be Upheld"

The British are a home-loving people. The best place in the world is and always will be home, whether it is large or small, sumptuous, or ramshackle. The English saying "an Englishman's home is his castle" meets with the approval of all the island's inhabitants. Young people like to frequent London's trendier bars and restaurants, but they still regard invitations to private dinner parties as the crown of British hospitality. Meeting friends in restaurants, as is the custom in France, still meets with a certain amount of skepticism, the more so since there may only be a single pub for miles around in some areas. Hence people prefer to stay at home and spoil themselves and their guests with home-cooked delicacies. Classic dishes like lamb chop with mint sauce or the famous roast beef with Yorkshire pudding have enjoyed uninterrupted popularity across all social classes and generations. These specialties are the staples of a basic culinary vocabulary, and awaken a sense of the familiar among invited friends and relatives. The customary after-dinner stilton and port (whereby the decanter is passed counter-clockwise) add the finishing touch to the homey atmosphere.

However, when they cannot avoid leaving their own four walls, British people prefer to frequent places that remind them of home. Whether up north or down south, in the west or the east of the realm – hotel lounges are never cold and sterile waiting rooms furnished with chrome, glass, and black leather sofas, but rather oases of English coziness where high tea is served punctually from three o'clock in the afternoon. The British feel at home wherever brightly colored check cushions await the weary traveler on floral chintz armchairs. Restaurants, clubs, pubs, and stores strive to recreate the drawing room's coziness.

Many of Her Royal Highness' male subjects regard the club as a second home, a place where they need never be deprived of the accouterments familiar from their own studies and smoking rooms. A fire burns, newspapers and smoking materials are conveniently close to hand, as are crystal decanters full of all manner of elixirs (and always include one of port), as well as buttoned leather sofas and comfortable wing chairs. It is a place where one can eat, meet friends, entertain business acquaintances, or simply have some peace and quiet – and best of all, the servants take great care to ensure that the gentlemen have full satisfaction at all times.

The British gentleman's club exudes an air of exclusivity which is reflected in the interiors of other establishments designed with the same type of client in mind. Gentlemen's outfitters, whether in London, Birmingham, Edinburgh, or any other town in the United Kingdom, will endeavor always to have an open fire burning in winter, even if it is only artificial. Antique, or just old, chairs will be provided in the changing rooms, where silver or brass shoe horns hang from hooks on the wall, and buttoned sofas or comfortable wing chairs invite shoppers to take a well-earned rest. The same principle applies to the furnishings in tailors' shops, shoemakers, hatters, and barber's shops. All are designed to mirror the gentleman's club.

Some young gentlemen who have finished school are expected to join the armed forces. Here too, the basic look harks back to the club, at least as far as the higher ranks are concerned, and care is taken to ensure that nobody, and this includes all the ranks, has to make do without their beloved tea and familiar nursery food. Paradoxically, it is precisely because they are members

Having to leave the security of home, of their parents and nanny, in exchange for the cool atmosphere of boarding school may not be a pleasant prospect for all young British people, but this is the unavoidable fate of many. However, boarding school is not all bad, many friendships and contacts are forged here which can last a lifetime – and have definite career advantages.

of the armed forces that many British people find themselves living far from home. Any trial or tribulation one may have to face in a foreign country is countered by a simple yet effective measure: traditional British standards are merely emphasized. People who are stationed abroad with their units do not have to do without a single familiar detail. On the contrary, it is said that British officers' messes in Germany are more British than any on the other side of the channel.

Ultimately, however, men are not the true guardians of traditional style. This is an honor reserved for their wives, girlfriends, mothers, sisters, aunts, and all the female islanders whom we have to thank for never abandoning the dictums of the United Kingdom, even in hard times and on the dustiest of desert roads. With extraordinary determination they have managed to enforce the principle of "home from home" even under the most dire circumstances. The greater the distance from home, the more British life became. Even India's tropical climate did not deter them from taking a hot cup of afternoon tea. The subcontinent's poverty and misery provided these genteel ladies with abundant opportunities for charity work. The remainder of their time was spent playing bridge, dancing, competing in tennis tournaments, and, naturally, attending dinner parties.

Lady diplomats and diplomats' wives also adhered to the rule that "standards must be upheld". Ella Sykes first accompanied her brother Percy on his diplomatic missions in 1915. This lady was of the firm conviction that there had to be ways and means to boil and starch Percy's shirts properly, even in remote outbacks like Kaschgar. There were no compromises at mealtimes either. Caviar on toast, salmon with mayonnaise, and sausages, followed by chicken in jelly, steaks, and Indian curries, topped off by English trifle were no more than was expected. Living in a Chinese oasis on the western edge of the Tarim basin, such feasts required not only magnificent cooking skills, but also a huge talent for organization combined with absolute confidence that this was the only way to do things.

According to the testimonies of female diplomats, they still like to travel with substantial stores of Marmite, Ribena, Christmas pudding, Worcester sauce, Coleman's mustard, and Cooper's Oxford orange marmalade – not to mention all the less important items for personal consumption. Although one may acquire supplies from the Army & Navy stores which operate in almost all corners of the globe, it can take months for goods to be delivered to remote regions. During this period, sticking to the rules and keeping a British home can become exceedingly difficult.

Afternoon tea can be a serious matter of grave social importance, and should be taken in a suitably stylish environment. Yet, however formal the setting, the British never entirely sacrifice their sense of comfort. Even the Dorchester Hotel in London allows people to relax in comfortable arm-chairs and sofas.

An Oxford college refectory may not offer the best of all possible culinary experiences, but as a stylish place to eat it is hard to beat.

BRITISH HOSPITALITY

"Here am I man, I feel it here!" No other sentence such as this quote from the German writer Goethe could better describe British sensibilities with regard to the old-established bastions of British style, be it a hotel, pub, or any other place where standards are steadfastly upheld by a characteristic décor which defies imitation. The gentleman's club is a haven of comfort. Here, a man may retreat from the outside world, take a seat in a Victorian leather armchair, gaze at the flames of the open fire, barely noticing the quiet rustling of newspapers and discreet clink of ice cubes in glasses. This may seem a somewhat tedious way to pass the time given our modern leisure industry, and club members would not disagree. On the contrary, they would also tell you that clubs are the dusty old places of yesterday, the food is insipid, and that even the wines are not what they used to be, not to mention the staff. They would pick their club to pieces. And why? Quite simply because they love their clubs, because they are refuges from work and home, and much too precious to endure the threat of a sudden surge in popularity. The best things in life are best kept to oneself.

The tea rooms of British grand hotels have a similar feel to them. Afternoon tea at Claridge's or Brown's in London, and at all the other elegant establishments around the country, is still a favorite way to pass the time between lunch and dinner, despite the fact that one now has to book a table in advance, and that the enjoyment has to be shared with numerous tourists who raptly devour their sandwiches, scones, and petits fours. There was a time when afternoon tea was the exclusive province of hotel guests and regulars who generally kept to themselves. It was rare for this idyll to be disrupted by the appearance of unexpected guests.

The most popular – and democratic – place for that "home away from home" feeling has to be the pub. Unlike refined hotels, these establishments do not impose dress codes, and during the summer months pubs even welcome people dressed in shorts and sleeveless tops. Ale, lager, and cider are served in the comfortable ambiance of these unpretentious barrooms with their dark carpets, heavy wooden counters, upholstered stools and armchairs, and blazing log fires in winter. Here, people enjoy their drinks in contented solitude, not unlike the peace and quiet enjoyed by the port-quaffing members of the gentleman's club. On entering a city pub at lunchtime, one is faced by a veritable rush of somewhat untypically dressed people: this is the time when men and women in suits temporarily escape from their banks, insurance offices, and law firms for a quick lunch-time pint and a bite to eat. By evening, however, the regular customers are among themselves once more – in their favorite "home from home."

Many Britons regard luxuriously furnished hotels as second homes for use during private or business trips to the city. They prefer to frequent the same establishment over many years, and are often allocated their favorite rooms. A number of traditional London establishments could proudly produce an illustrious and loyal guest list, although discretion prevents them from doing so.

When British people who live in the country go to London on business, many of them like to take their meals and spend the night in their clubs. This dining-room is in the Reform Club, which is housed in a generous classicist 19th-century building on Pall Mall, a stone's throw from other clubs.

Claridge's is among the most refined of venerable London hotels. Established in 1898, the house has continued to be a favorite haunt of the royal family as well as many important foreign guests. The generous entrance hall features fireplaces, tall mirrors, and Art-Deco embellishments.

Even when not within their own four walls, people like to feel at home. Hence the axiom "standards must be upheld" applies even when people are traveling. British taste dictates that even ocean liners have to follow the mandates of interior design, as in this cabin on the Queen Elizabeth II.

The pub is typical of the "home from home" principle. British landlords know that their guests do not in general seek adventurous gastronomy, but would rather meet friends and drink their beer in a homey environment. No customer would voluntarily set off from home unless their pub was carpeted and featured plush sofas and fireplaces.

The Boarding School

Very few continental Europeans have ever set eyes inside a British boarding school – and yet, many like to think they know what goes on within these educational institutions. A widespread misconception is that the idle progeny of the upper classes merely acquire qualifications from uncritical teaching staff. The unenlightened tend to imagine this scenario within an Edwardian or Victorian environment, with pupils in archaic uniforms, and tweed-clad teachers. Such ideas may contain a grain of truth, but this is not an accurate representation of everyday life in the boarding schools of the British Isles.

Most boarding schools in England are what is known as "public schools." However, public schools are anything but accessible to everyone, because in Great Britain the term is used to refer to private schools. This linguistic confusion has an historical explanation. Schools used to be run by the Church, and could only be attended by selected pupils whose intention it was to ordain as priests. Private schools, however, were open to anyone, not just trainee clerics. As today, a certain amount of money had to be paid to attend the public schools, although pupils were (and are) guaranteed an excellent education in return. This is what matters to parents, who rightly expect their not inconsiderable investment to pay off. Schools would not survive if their results were invariably unsatisfactory, and many public schools can look back on a long tradition, priding themselves on an impressive list of successful alumni.

The oldest of these schools is Winchester College, founded in 1382. Eton (1440), St Paul's in London (1509), Shrewsbury School (1552), Westminster in London (1560), Merchant Taylor's (in Crosby 1561 and Northwood 1620), Rugby (1567), Harrow (1571), and Charterhouse in Godalming, Surrey (1611) followed. In 1861, a commission headed by Lord Clarendon awarded these nine schools the distinction of "Great Schools". Radley College in Abingdon, founded in 1847, was later added to this group. As well as age, another criterion used to judge the quality of a school is the headmaster's or headmistress' affiliation to the "Headmaster's Conference" founded in 1869, the "Association of Governing Bodies of Public Schools" founded in 1941, or the "Girls' School Association" established in 1973. Schools that are able to meet both requirements tend to have long waiting lists.

Yet money alone does not guarantee acceptance to a famous school. Contacts are equally ineffectual if a child fails the entrance examination. For this reason there are preparatory or prep schools where 7- to 13-year-old children are prepared for the "Common Entrance Examination". Children who make the grade are considered to have made a great step forward – for both their educational and academic future as well as in social terms, since children at public schools forge lifelong friendships that form the basis of a network of personal relationships, and because these schools help them to adopt a certain lifestyle. State school education may be just as good, but the world of the upper classes is only accessible through the public school.

This aspect of public school education is invaluable, does not form part of the curriculum, and is provided not by the teachers but by the pupils themselves. Their language use, sense of humor, dress sense, and behavior in various social situations – all these factors enable public school boys and public school girls instantly to recognize one another. Furthermore, teachers, whether consciously or unconsciously, nurture their charges' awareness of being recipients of a unique education. Last, but not least, sport is regarded by the headmasters and headmistresses of public schools as a character-building part of the curriculum. The British public school offers pupils a truly broad education. They learn for life, although the ways and means by which they do so has frequently been subject to criticism. However, most of it tends to be based on a lack of understanding of the true nature of this type of school.

Above: The expansive lawns at Stowe offer almost limitless space for the sporting activities that have such an important role to play at public schools.

Left: The pupils of King's College wear stand-up collars as part of their uniform. However, they look no less mischievous than boys dressed in jeans and sweatshirts.

Below: Although these boys look like out of control rugby players, they are in fact involved in the annual "St Andrew's Day Wall Game" at Eton. It is almost impossible to score points in this game, because the opposing team simply throws itself at the wall which serves as a goal.

Private Schools for Boys
Ampleforth College, York, North Yorkshire
Charterhouse, Godalming, Surrey
Eton College, Windsor, Berkshire
Fettes College, Edinburgh
Gordonstoun, Elgin, Moray (Scotland)
Harrow School, Harrow on the Hill, Middlesex
Marlborough College, Marlborough, Wiltshire
Milton Abbey School, Blandford, Dorset
Stowe School, Buckingham, Buckinghamshire
Wellington College, Crowthorne, Berkshire
Winchester College, Winchester, Hampshire

Private Schools for Girls
Benenden, Cranbrook, Kent
Convent of the Sacred Heart, Woldingham, Surrey
Cranborne Chase School, Tisbury, Wiltshire
Downe House, Newbury, Berkshire
Heathfield, Ascot, Berkshire
North Foreland Lodge School, Basingstoke, Hampshire
Roedean, Brighton, Sussex
St Mary's Convent, South Ascot, Berkshire
St Mary's School, Calne, Wiltshire
Stonar School, Atworth, Wiltshire
West Heath School, Sevenoaks, Kent

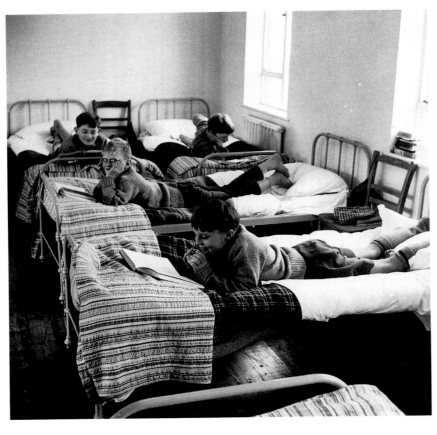

This photograph was taken in 1965, and is a good illustration of how little boarding school life has changed in the intervening years. Perhaps it is this continuity that parents appreciate about this type of educational establishment, which seems to promise that their children will become adults who share their values.

Although a public school education is expensive, the pupils' accommodation seems somewhat modest. The British upper classes firmly believe that unpretentious surroundings promote the development of good character.

Sharing a room would be inconceivable to many continental European school children. But at public schools, this is the rule. Few boarding schools provide single rooms.

The British public school truly provides an education for life or, more accurately, for life at the top, which is where traditional boarding school "old boys" still take their place. State school children are rarely admitted to these ranks.

Eton College is unquestionably the most famous public school of all. A glance at the list of its successful alumni explains why. It reads like a *Who's Who* of British history. Nineteen British prime ministers were Eton boys. Consequently, parents who wish to provide their sons with private education tend to put the institution near Windsor at the top of their wish list. Unless, naturally, they attended a different, though similarly renowned school, and therefore prefer their son (or daughter) to follow in their footsteps. Professional opportunities for those whose school years were spent at Eton abound. However, first they have to pass the Common Entrance Examination. This consists of written tests in English, French, mathematics, history, and a few optional subjects, and can be sat on three occasions each year. Hence, a career at Eton is not determined merely by the financial means available to parents, but above all by the candidates' intelligence and willingness to work.

Contrary to popular belief, Eton is not the first choice of the British royal family. Only one English king, George III, has so far been educated at this institution. Young princes were generally tutored at home, hence the education of the current Queen's father, George VI, was left entirely in the hands of a private tutor. Prince Charles was the first crown prince ever to attend prep school and boarding school. His father, the Duke of Edinburgh, sent him to his old school Gordonstoun – a boarding school founded by Dr Kurt Hahn in 1934. This German educator had previously been the headmaster of the Schloss Salem boarding school in Baden-Württemberg founded in 1919, but Nazi persecution forced him to leave Germany in 1933. In his memoirs, the Prince of Wales expresses little fondness for Gordonstoun, and he subsequently decided not to subject his own sons to the school's harsh teaching methods. Both princes, William and Harry, were therefore sent to Eton.

All Eton pupils, whether aristocratic or plutocratic, are subjected to the same strict daily routine. The alarm clock rings at seven o'clock, breakfast is at eight. Half an hour later, the boys assemble for morning prayers in the school chapel, whose walls are adorned by 15th-century frescos in the Flemish style. This spiritual refreshment is followed by classes from 9 till 1.25 p.m., the only interruption being a break at 11.20 a.m. Their lunch consists of meat and two vegetables followed by a dessert. In the afternoon, sport is on the timetable until 4 p.m. Pupils can (and must, since sport is a compulsory subject) choose between time-honored sports like rowing and cricket, or exercise comparably modern disciplines like soccer. Afterwards, the boys return to their studies until it is time for their evening meal.

The only other public schools whose fame and renown approach that of Eton are Winchester School in Hampshire and Harrow School in Middlesex. Year on year, these three famous schools bring forth the junior members of the elite. The cabinet of Margaret Thatcher's 1979 government, for instance, was made up entirely of public school products, and not much has changed in the interim, even in Tony Blair's Labour government. Perhaps this is because he is a public school boy himself. He attended Fettes College in Edinburgh.

Eton College, founded in 1440 near Windsor, is still considered prime among British public schools. An Eton education provides the best possible preconditions for a successful career in business or politics. Important personal contacts are also forged – the "old boy's" network is very useful both professionally and privately.

The College

In Great Britain, "college" can mean a variety of institutions. A college may be an independent, self-governing, and self-financing educational establishment. Or the term may be used to refer to technical or vocational schools. Other institutions are divided into sub-colleges such as business colleges or art colleges. Finally, the word college is also used to describe secondary schools for boarding pupils.

There are many modern colleges, but the majority of British people and their foreign visitors associate the concept primarily with the ancient and honorable educational establishments of Oxford and Cambridge. There are around 30 colleges in these English citadels of university education, each of which are attended by around 10,000 students. The colleges are entirely independent and have the right to select their students. All applicants are subject to personal interviews during which their level of education and motivation is assessed. This helps colleges to determine whether candidates are suited to a particular course, and prospective students have the opportunity to reconsider their choices. The drop-out rate is correspondingly low.

Each college's highest authority is its director, who is known by a variety of titles. At Christ Church College, Oxford, for example, he is known as the *dean*, whereas he is the *rector* at Exeter College, the *president* at Trinity College, the *provost* at Worcester College, and the *warden* at New College.

An Oxford or Cambridge education cannot easily be compared with a course of study at a modern mass-university. Tutor groups are much smaller, and personal progress is constantly monitored in tutorials. This type of personal dialog also ensures that every student is provided with the optimum amount of support and encouragement to fulfill his or her potential. The colleges are not just centers of academic life. Many students live-in and take their meals there. Sport and leisure activities are also on the program. However, despite excellent study conditions and Oxford's and Cambridge's remarkable scientific reputations, not all graduates necessarily become a credit to academic life. A student's choice of subject and personal ambition determine how well they do. Where one student's aim may be to progress molecular biology, and

Oxford provides students and academic staff with exemplary learning, teaching, and research conditions.

may even justifiably include the hope for a Nobel Prize, another will regard time spent at university as an amusing interlude and springboard to a lucrative career in business or banking. Although selection criteria are becoming ever more onerous, there was a time, not that long ago, when the mere fact of having studied at Oxford or Cambridge was all the qualification anyone needed. It is not unusual for bankers to have degrees in archeology, or for insurance company chairmen to have studied literature. This may be because graduates are often no older than 21 or 23, and therefore young and flexible enough to successfully complete specialized and intensive trainee programs.

Although Oxford and Cambridge are often mentioned in the same breath, the towns differ in several respects. Oxford was a stronghold of Catholicism for centuries, and is now renowned for its humanities. Cambridge on the other hand can look back on a Protestant tradition, and is better known for its sciences. These divergent orientations are still noticeable today. Furthermore, Oxford is regarded as a hotbed of political activity, whereas Cambridge has a reputation for moderation. But in terms of career prospects, there is little to choose between the two universities. Less than five percent of Britain's students attend Oxford and Cambridge, but this minority continues to represent the largest part of the financial, scientific, political, artistic, and cultural elite.

Oxford yesterday: Intellectual greatness on a small scale.

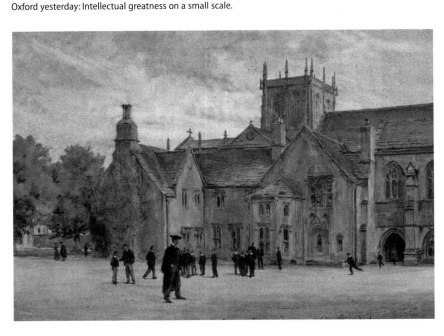

Oxford today: State of the art scientific research within ancient walls.

A selection of Oxford colleges

All Souls College
Founded in 1440 by Henry Chichele, Archbishop of Canterbury

Balliol College
Founded in 1266 and hence one of the oldest colleges

Christ Church
Originally founded in 1523 by Cardinal Wolsey, it was reestablished by Henry VIII in 1546

Corpus Christi College
Founded by Robert Fox in 1517

Jesus College
Founded in 1571 by Elizabeth I for Welsh students

Lincoln College
A seat of study since 1427, the later buildings were constructed in the 17th-century

Magdalen College
Founded in 1485, it is one of Oxford's most famous colleges

Merton College
Thought to have been founded in 1266, which would thereby make it as old as Balliol College

New College
Founded in 1379, this college is anything but new

Queen's College
Established in 1340 and named in honor of King Edward III's wife

St John's College
Established in 1554 to replace St Bernard's College

Trinity College
Founded in 1555 by Thomas Pope

University College
Founded in 1249, University College is now housed in 17th- and 18th-century buildings

Wadham College
The precise year of its foundation is unknown, but is thought to have been in the early 17th century

A selection of Cambridge colleges

Christ's College
Founded in around 1500 by Lady Margaret Beaufort, mother of Henry VII

Clare College
The year of its founding is unknown, but the college was rebuilt after a fire in the 17th century

Emmanuel College
Founded in 1584, it boasts a chapel by Christopher Wren – as does Pembroke College

Gonville and Caius College
Established by Gonville in 1384; John Caius was a patron whose name was added to the institution's name in 1559

Jesus College
Founded in 1496 by the Bishop of Ely within the walls of a convent

King's College
Named after Henry VI, who founded the College in 1441

Magdalen College
Founded in 1428, this college has a namesake in Oxford

Pembroke College
A seat of learning since 1347, its chapel is an early Christopher Wren building and was constructed in 1663

Peterhouse
Founded in 1284, most of its buildings date back to the 17th century

Queen's College
This college was established in 1448; Erasmus of Rotterdam was a famous fellow there

St John's College
Founded in 1511, another college for which we have Lady Margaret Beaufort to thank

Trinity College
Michael House College and King's Hall College were amalgamated in 1546 to make this Cambridge's largest

Trinity Hall
Founded by the Bishop of Norwich in 1350

The attraction of the colleges of Cambridge and Oxford can be ascribed to the historical backdrop they provide, as well as to high academic standards.

A glance at the biographical details of most British notables will confirm the preeminence of Oxford and Cambridge. People at the top of their profession tend to have studied in one of the two university towns. This also applies to politicians of all colors, be it Margaret Thatcher, Michael Heseltine, or Tony Blair, but also to businessmen like Jamie Palumbo and Wafic Said, and to artists and authors like Lord Snowdon and Salman Rushdie. Among leading actors and comedians, there are many who can remember academic years at one of the renowned colleges – but who did not necessarily leave with a degree under their belt. This includes the comedian Rowan Atkinson, best known as Mr Bean, the film star Emma Thompson, comedian Stephen Fry, and Monty Python icon John Cleese. Oxford and Cambridge are justifiably described as elitist institutions, but they are open to all high achievers, regardless of social status – equally, money and titles cannot provide admittance if grades do not come up to scratch.

A recognized advantage of the British college system is the personal supervision provided by tutors.

A *Who's Who* of British degrees

Most other European academics can find it difficult to make sense of the degrees awarded by British universities, although the difference between them and French or German degrees are less extreme than would appear. Principally, there are three levels of degree. The simplest degree, also known as a first degree or undergarduate degree, is a Bachelor. As a rule, this is awarded after a course of study lasting at least three years, although medical students have to study for seven years. The subject's field of study is contained in the full degree title. There are more than 30 Bachelor titles, the best known being the Bachelor of Arts for the humanities, the Bachelor of Science, Bachelor of Divinity for theologians, and the Bachelor of Laws. A Bachelor is more or less equivalent to a German Magister or French licence. The next degree up is the Master. In contrast to the first or undergraduate degree of the Bachelor, a Master is a postgraduate degree. Like Bachelor degrees, Masters are classified as Master of Arts, Master of Science, etc. The next highest postgraduate degree is a Doctor. Unlike on the continent, British Doctor titles do not become a part of a person's name, and a Doctor of Philosophy would put the letters Ph.D. after his name. It seems that British academics pay less importance on the title itself than its providence, which is why they like to add an indication that the degree was gained at Oxford or Cambridge. The magical letters for a Cambridge degree spell "Cantab." (short for Cantabrigiensis, the town's Latin name), and Oxford University degrees bear the letters 'Oxon.' (from Oxoniensis). Degrees are awarded during solemn, traditional ceremonies, during which all the participants have to wear the traditional academic gowns.

The color and attributes of the gown differ according to the wearer's academic degree and the field of study.

Above: The unique architecture of the two cities, and the striking gowns worn by graduates, endow degree ceremonies at both Oxford and Cambridge with an atmosphere all of their own.

From left to right: The colorful academic gowns of Oxford and Cambridge are based on the medieval dress of scholars.

Female graduates can choose to wear a mortar board or the square cap shown here with their academic gown.

The various academic gowns worn at Oxford were first listed in 1636. This rule-book continues to be in use today, and was not subject to revision until 1957.

THE BRITISH MILITARY SYSTEM

The heir to the British throne underwent extensive military training. In 1969 he began his career with the newly formed Royal Regiment of Wales, whose uniform he wore on the occasion of his investiture as Prince of Wales.

Britain's armed forces are entirely made up of professional soldiers nowadays, which is why they are considered one of Europe's most efficient armies. Since general conscription was abolished, the majority of young British people do not experience military service – with the advantages that they enter the world of work when they are still at a very young age.

The armed forces consist of three different branches of service: navy, army, and airforce. The navy is the oldest, hence it is known as the "senior service", although its official title is the Royal Navy, just as the airforce is called the Royal Air Force. The army is the only service which may not use the word "Royal". The reason for this is to be found in British history. After the bloodless "Glorious Revolution" of 1688 and the overthrow of King James II, the "Bill of Rights" was instituted to provide a legal framework for the rule of his successors. This included an injunction against raising an army in peacetime without the agreement of Parliament. Therefore, the standing army is not a royal force but a government service. Regardless of this, some units do include the word "royal" in their names.

Among the army's regiments are the Household Cavalry, infantry regiments such as the Guards Division, the Royal Corps of Signals, and the Intelligence Corps, and regional units such as the Royal Welsh Fusiliers, the Royal Scots, and the Ghurkas.

The Household Cavalry is made up of the Life Guards and the Blues and Royals. The latter were formed in 1969 by amalgamating the Royal Horseguards and the Royal Dragoons. Although the history of army regiments does not date as far back as that of the navy, most army units were founded quite some time ago. One of the most venerable army regiments is the Royal Scots Greys (1678). The Life Guards have been in existence since 1656, and the Royal Horse Guards since 1661.

The Royal Air Force seems rather new in comparison, which is why service in this force is sometimes considered less prestigious. Members of the upper class are primarily attracted to the regiments of the army.

Admittance to one of the more renowned units of the armed forces is not difficult, so long as applicants can show themselves to be physically fit, have good school qualifications and the appropriate social background. There are various options open to new recruits. Successful school leavers are given the opportunity to go to university by applying for one of 40 cadetships offered each year. Trainee officers who opt for this path have to serve in the army before taking up a place at university. After officer training, they enter uni-

Right: The decor of the Wellington Barracks' officers' mess is rational and modern. Only officers are permitted access to this room, where meals are served by orderlies whose presence further enhances a sense of exclusivity.

Far right: The rank and file of the Grenadier Guards take their meals in a vast dining hall, where a self-service system operates.

Right: Grenadier Guards devote a great deal of time to the correct maintenance and care of their uniforms and equipment.

Far right: A soldier's shoes have to be spotless and gleaming before he may come before a superior officer.

Left: Tourists and Londoners are equally attracted to the Grenadier Guards' band as it plays in front of the Wellington Barracks built in 1833.

versity where they receive full pay. Once they have graduated, they must spend a further five years in the army. People with less lofty military ambitions may apply for a bursary. In this case, people complete their university degrees before serving in the army. They receive a small allowance while at university, after which they attend officer's school and commit themselves to serve for three further years. Youngsters who are not sure what they would like to do after leaving school can commit themselves to a three-year short service commission.

Although British officers no longer enjoy quite as much prestige as they did prior to the Second World War, it is still considered a socially acceptable career path, and the variety of English gentleman known as the Guard officer type can still be found on the island. He usually stems from an ancient family, has a more than adequate private income, and spends his free time in the pursuit of sporting activities such as polo or the steeplechase. In town he wears a dark suit, the regimental tie, a bowler hat, and in his hand he holds an efficiently rolled umbrella. Naturally, he is also an excellent soldier — but he is too much of a gentleman to ever speak about that.

Being an officer can clearly be an advantage when pursuing a number of other career paths. This is because the armed forces form part of the network of contacts which critics often describe as the "old boys' network." This system includes former public school boys, Oxford and Cambridge graduates, and the officers of prestigious regiments. Whenever a business or administra-

tion vacancy needs to be filled, a favor asked, or assistance of any kind provided, gentlemen can count on the help of their friends from school, college, or army days. This is the accusation leveled at this particular social group by people who do not form part of the magic circle. Naturally, the old boys themselves vehemently deny giving preferential treatment to their old friends. Nevertheless, it is no disadvantage for a job applicant if the head of personnel at a bank, insurance office, or real estate agency should happen to have been a member of the same regiment. Why — as is so often the logic of the employer — should a position not be given to a candidate whose training is familiar and who probably shares the same basic values? A glance at a British *Who's Who* proves that many former officers are business leaders, politicians, and members of the still influential aristocracy. It seems also that the youngest generation of the royal family intends to preserve this tradition.

From Empire to Commonwealth – the History of British Global Power

The efficiency with which the British would one day pursue expansionist policies was probably not foreseeable when Sir Francis Drake set off on his first circumnavigation of the earth in 1577. His victory over the Spanish Armada in 1588 marks the beginning of British naval supremacy which eventually guaranteed safe passage across all the oceans to the conquerors and colonialists of later centuries. The first settlers arrived in Newfoundland in 1583, and a year later Sir Walter Raleigh made the first attempt to settle English colonizers in Virginia.

The establishment of the East India Company in 1600 was a major factor in the subsequent conquest of India. This period saw the Portuguese lose their Indian trade monopoly to the Dutch, English, and French. In 1612, British traders founded their first staging post in India. The West Africa Company was founded in 1618, and a base established in Gambia. British colonialism was institutionalized with the creation of a Colonial Office.

From 1623 onwards, the English and French pushed forward to the West Indies. The naval war between England and the Netherlands (1652 – 1654), strengthened England's naval and colonial position. In 1655, England took the island of Jamaica from Spain. In 1664 the Dutch conceded New Amsterdam, later known as New York, to the English. In 1689 the English and the French began to fight for supremacy over North America, a struggle which was to drag on until 1763 when France lost this important colony. Canada and the French Indian possessions went to England as a result of the Peace of Paris. England acquired Florida from Spain. The former French possession of Louisiana was split up between England and Spain. 1746 saw the beginning of another war, this time in southern India, which also continued until 1763. Again France lost large territories to England. In 1770, James Cook arrived in Australia, and in 1778, he discovered Hawaii, where he was murdered by the natives a year later. In 1774, Warren Hastings, the Governor General of Bengal, began to extend the British conquest of India. In 1788 Australia became a British penal colony, and the fifth continent had to wait until 1829 before being granted the status of a regular colony.

In 1759, a British expedition corps occupied the Cape of Good Hope, thereby establishing a base for the gradual conquest of the southern Africa. In 1796, the British took over Ceylon (Sri Lanka), thereby further extending their power base in Asia. By 1818, England had become the most important colonial power in India. The decades that followed saw Britain's rule expand to other parts of Asia. In 1841, the English occupied Hong Kong and acquired Amoy, Nongpo, and Shanghai. Britain also consolidated its power in southern Africa by taking over the Boer republic of Natal. In India, the Sikhs held out against the British for a long time, but the warrior people of the Punjab were vanquished in 1849.

The English also advanced into eastern and central Africa, prompting David Livingstone to undertake four research expeditions in the dark continent between 1849 and 1873. The period between 1875 and 1879 saw the British expanding their Cape colony to the Natal coast, and in 1877 they appropriated the Boer Republic of Transvaal. The Cape colony's hinterland was annexed in 1884, Zululand was annexed in 1887, and in 1889 Rhodesia became a British possession. British East Africa was created at the same time. In 1898, after taking Omdurman during the war against the Mahdists, the Sudan came under British rule. The Boer War, which had begun in 1895, finally came to an end in 1902, and the Boer Republic became a British colony.

The expansion of the British Empire was at its peak in the 1920s, but the system was beginning to crumble. In 1931, Canada, New Zealand, Australia, and the Union of South Africa were formally awarded independence. The Empire was replaced by the Commonwealth, a loose association of autonomous nations. However, the real decline of the British Empire did not commence until India, Burma, and Ceylon became independent in 1947 and 1948. The end of British rule on the subcontinent, and thus the demise of the Raj, was a painful blow. It formed the conclusion of a chapter of British history which had begun 371 years earlier when Sir Francis Drake circumnavigated the earth for the first time.

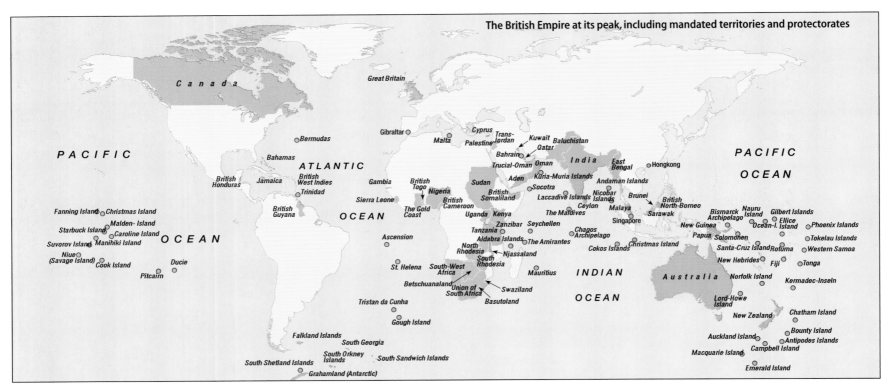

The British Empire at its peak, including mandated territories and protectorates

A Colonial Dictionary

Gingham

The word gingham refers to a particular type of check fabric often use to make shirts. The word originates in the Malay language. Originally gingang or guingan, the term originally meant "striped"

Jodhpur

Jodhpurs are narrow riding trousers. Their name derives from the Indian city of Jodhpur. Jodhpur boots are ankle-high riding boots which can be worn with the trousers.

Khaki

In modern usage, the word khaki refers to an indeterminate color somewhere between brown and green. It is a Hindi word used to describe the color of dust. Colonialists dyed their white cotton uniforms with a mixture of coffee, curry powder, and mulberry juice to produce a color which would camouflage the dust. The result was khaki.

Kedgeree

The British love a hearty breakfast. If eggs, bacon, sausages, and black pudding do not appeal, why not try kedgeree? This dish consists of fish, rice, and eggs. Originally called khichri, it entered the English language as kedgeree.

Mufti

Mufti describes any sort of civilian clothing worn by off-duty British officers – a pinstripe suit and bowler hat, or a tweed jacket and cavalry twill trousers.

Sahib

This word is known to us from the innumerable period movies set in colonial India. Indians addressed Europeans as sahib, while ladies were addressed as memsahib.

Pukka

The spelling of this Hindi word varies, and can also occur as pucka. Whatever the spelling, it means solid, enduring, or authentic. A gentleman would be known as a pukka sahib.

Raj

This word often features in the names of Indian restaurants in London. The "last days of the Raj" refers to the end of British rule. Naturally enough, Indians do not share the sadness felt by the British with regard to those particular days.

Seersucker

Not many people purchasing a seersucker suit will know that it is a Persian word which literally means milk and sugar. Seersucker is a lightweight cotton or cotton-mix summer fabric.

Tandoori

The United Kingdom's culinary landscape would much the poorer without its many Tandoori restaurants. These Indian or Pakistani restaurants bring a breath of oriental opulence to even the most insignificant suburb. They have become indispensable providers of take-away food.

From top left to bottom right:
The popularity of Indian delicacies, including curry powder, is based on the Victorian and Edwardian romance with India.

The Ghurkas are a part of the British land forces, and a symbol of former imperial glory. Their trademark is the kukri knife, a practical tool and deadly weapon.

The game of polo was invented in Persia and not in Britain – and it is more than 2,000 years old. 19th-century British colonialists were taught to play the mounted ball game by Indian Maharajahs.

Rudyard Kipling's Jungle Book is a major work of a period characterized by romantic enthusiasm for the Indian colonial empire.

Sun helmets can still be purchased from the famous hat maker's James Lock and Co. in London's St James Street.

Paisley patterned cashmere scarves came into fashion during the rule of Queen Victoria. The Indian pattern has been a staple of British fashion and textile design ever since.

Opposite page:
The world map of 1945 shows the extent of the former British empire.

THE GENTLEMAN'S CLUB

There was a time when it was inconceivable for a gentleman not to join a club, by which is meant not the local pigeon fanciers' association or motoring club, but the venerable institution of the gentleman's club. Founded in 1695, White's Club is the oldest, but the others equally represent tradition: Athenaeum, Beefsteak, Brook's, Boodle's, Buck's, Carlton Club, Garrick's, Guards and Cavalry Club, In and Out, Reform, and Traveller's, to name but a few.

Clubs started out as places where one could get a cup of coffee. However, a number of clubs dedicated to a variety of causes were established in the 18th and 19th centuries. Quite how seriously these causes were taken is hard to tell, since the chief purpose of these establishments was to provide second homes. In Victorian times there were approximately 860 clubs.

Gentlemen who wish to become members of a club cannot themselves instigate the procedure for admittance. They must wait for someone to

Above: A gentleman's club provides its members with everything required in a metropolis like London: peace, good value meals in familiar surroundings, tea and drinks served at a drop of a hat, washrooms, a bed for the night, and of course, the daily newspapers.

Right: The Reform Club at 104 – 105 Pall Mall was opened in 1832. The club was built in the style of an Italian palazzo, and offers members and guests the impeccable infrastructure of a grand hotels combined with the pleasant atmosphere of well-run private homes.

invite them to join. First of all, two club members have to put forward an applicant's name. The proposer and his seconder enter the name into a book and, if enough members show their support by adding their own signatures, the proposal is put before a committee where the question of whether or not to accept the newcomer is decided. This sounds fairly simple. The snag, however, is that it is considered ungentlemanly to ask a befriended club member to put forward one's name. Either he does it, or he doesn't – and he usually has his reasons for both. Any attempt to bribe the committee is regarded in a very bad light, although there have been instances of applicants finding it impossible to resist the temptation. Only people with a good chance of admission should ever allow themselves to be put forward for membership, since a rejection can prove deeply embarrassing. By the same token, individual club members have to consider carefully whether their candidates are really suitable to join the club. A candidate's rejection reflects badly on the proposer.

Contrary to the general perception, the mysterious world of the gentleman's club is not open only to members. Anyone with the good fortune of being invited by a member may naturally step foot in such an establishment. If asked to meet at the club, a visitor should wait in the hall. It is considered impolite to look into adjacent club rooms. Another important point: do not tip staff. You are in a gentleman's club, not an hotel. The difference between the two is simple but important: anyone with the financial means may enter an hotel, whereas club membership is not for sale. Therefore, an invitation to a gentleman's club should be considered an honor equal to being asked for tea or dinner at his home. After all, the club is his second home.

Lord's Cricket Ground in London's St John's Wood is a Mecca for the many fans of the sport.

THE SPORTING CLUB

The British love sport, although here too tastes vary – as do ideas of what exactly constitutes a sport. For some people it is fox hunting, the steeplechase, or polo, others prefer soccer, rugby, bowling, croquet, hockey, tennis, or golf, and a third group may consider only rowing or sailing as proper sports. Whatever the case, sport is always connected to a club. There are clubs, club houses, and club colors for every imaginable discipline. This is such a vast area, that we can only illustrate a small section of the British enthusiasm for sport and sporting clubs. We therefore begin with a sport which undeniably unites all social class and age groups: cricket. This national sport is utterly incomprehensible to the uninitiated, and was brought to the island by the Saxons. The game was originally called *creag* and was played with a curved bat. The first organized game was played between Kent and All England.

A major objective of the game of cricket is the defense of two small pieces of wood, or bails, which rest on three wooden sticks, the stumps. The batsman uses his bat to defend the bails against attack by the opposing team, whose skillful bowling of the ball is aimed at the bails. An explanation of the complete set of rules would go beyond the limits of this book.

Cricket is still regarded as a British national sport. Here the batsman is defending the wicket from an opponent's ball.

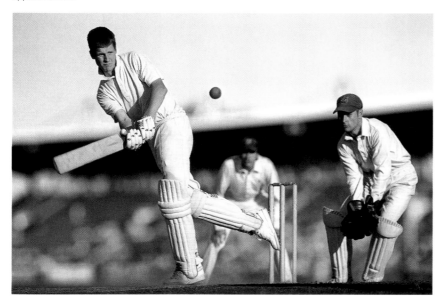

The first club to be established is thought to have been Hambledon Cricket Club in Hampshire, founded in 1750. However, the real Mecca of the global cricket fan congregation is located in London's St John's Wood. Lord's Cricket Ground on St John's Wood Road is probably the most famous playing field. Its club is Marylebone Cricket Club. When Hambledon Cricket Club was disbanded in 1791, the MCC adopted its leading role among clubs. It was given its name after it moved from Islington to Marylebone.

It is quite easy to become an MCC member. One's name has to be put forward by a proposer, with a seconder to support the application for membership. Members are allowed to wear the famous club tie, but they may also visit the Long Room where there is an exhibition of diverse memorabilia to make the heart of any cricket enthusiast beat faster. There is also an MCC Museum, founded in memory of club members who died in the First World War. In addition to numerous devotional articles, this is where the legendary "ashes" – literally the ashes of two bails – are kept. Ashes and urn make up the trophy over which England and Australia compete every two years. Regardless of who wins, the ashes always remain at Lord's Cricket Ground – to the delight of the many visitors who make the pilgrimage to this cricket reliquary in London.

A Nation of Shopkeepers

People in the 20th century tend to assume that their forebears were quite free of the plague of consumerism. It may be true to say that the mass production of all kinds of goods only became possible with the industrial revolution, but that is not to say that people did not like to shop even before then. A peep inside the young Samuel Pepys' diaries reveals that many prosperous 17th-century city dwellers also spent a great deal of time shopping for clothes and luxury articles.

London has always been a particularly stimulating place for people interested in acquiring beautiful things. Everything the heart desires and more could be bought. Groceries, on the other hand, were almost never purchased by the upper classes themselves. This was the province of their servants. Ladies and gentlemen only ever mingled with the people buying meat and vegetables at the market in emergency situations, or under cover of darkness. However, these restrictions imposed by etiquette found compensation in other areas such as the procurement of clothing or furniture. These items were not purchases as such, but commissions, since some time could elapse before the latest hat was ready for Ascot or new side tables could be delivered.

People liked to acquire articles made especially for them, rather than mass-produced goods.

A huge number of specialized tradesmen and retailers worked to meet the demand for these goods. Naturally, the majority of these businesses has disappeared since the 17th century, either because the specialized services or goods became surplus to requirement, or as a result of larger stores driving smaller outlets out of business. Nevertheless, there are still parts of London which have been dominated by specific trades ever since the 17th century. Hence Mayfair and St James's are favored addresses for luxury items, and it is worth considering a visit to Fortnum & Mason not just for its wide selection of goods, but also as a journey into history. This establishment has supplied the good and the great of politics, business, and the arts with groceries, clothing, toiletries, and accessories since the 18th century. The purchase of a box of tea or a jar of jam can, therefore, justifiably be regarded as a way of preserving tradition, as does buying a book at Hatchard's, a bottle of wine at Berry Brothers & Rudd, or a hat at James Lock & Co. Shopping is a cultural pursuit – an experience one may only enjoy in one of London's old-established stores.

Londoners as well as foreign bibliophiles have been making the pilgrimage to Hatchard's Bookshop at 187 Piccadilly since 1797.

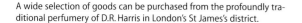

The saddlers of Swaine Adeney was founded in 1750. In 1943 they went into partnership with Brigg & Sons, an umbrella manufacturer which began business in 1836.

Lock's, Bate's, or Herbert Johnson in St James's Street are the places to buy hats in London.

The shirt-maker and gentleman's outfitter Turnbull & Asser is worth a visit for its splendid interior alone.

A wide selection of goods can be purchased from the profoundly traditional perfumery of D.R. Harris in London's St James's district.

Skin and hair-care products as well as perfumes are for sale in the old-fashioned apothecary atmosphere of D.R. Harris.

If plastic supermarket toothbrushes seem too profane for your dental care, you will find a superior version in London.

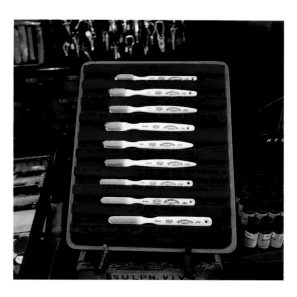

The distinction between a really old-established store and one that merely tries to awaken an impression of age with an old-fashioned façade or a dusty interior can often be made by looking out for the presence of a "Royal Warrant". These small coats of arms have become familiar from a variety of British products. The desirable emblems identify manufacturers as suppliers to the royal court. Since the first days of the monarchy, the court has made use of the best merchants and craftsmen to meet its enormous requirements – a tradition that lives on to this day. However, the daily deliveries of goods and services to the Palaces do not ensure the smooth running of general palace business alone, they also encompass everything required for the everyday life of the royal family and their closest attendants in a never-ending procession of delivery vans. This explains why there is a court supplier for every imaginable product and every possible service. "Royal Warrants", therefore, are not awarded only to manufacturers and purveyors of luxury goods – the majority adorn ordinary stores and businesses.

The oldest "Royal Warrant" was awarded to a weaving mill in 1155 by the then King Henry II. However, until the reign of Queen Victoria, the number of official court suppliers was kept within limits. No more than 25 businesses were to be found within this illustrious circle, including a "golffe club

maker", an "operator for the teeth" and a "royal mole taker". Under the long-lived Queen, the number of entries on the list of suppliers shot up dramatically. Over three dozen companies take care of the current Queen's requirements, added to which are the companies which supply Queen Elizabeth the Queen Mother, the Duke of Edinburgh, and the Prince of Wales. The Queen's favored suppliers include ordinary tradesmen such as a piano tuner, dry cleaners, and a handbag store. Some of the entries on the list on the other hand may be less useful to ordinary citizens, for example, the bagpipe maker.

A "Royal Warrant" is not awarded in perpetuity, but only for five years at a time. The order of rank among warranted companies is therefore determined by the number of "warrants" they have received in uninterrupted sequence, and by how many members of the Royal Family have awarded them with the honor.

THE BRITISH PUB

One aspect which unites all north-western Europeans is a love of beer. In this respect the traditional British pub differs less from Dutch, German, or Belgian bars than many anglophiles would admit. However, this by no means lessens its attraction.

In addition to the fundamental parallels that can be drawn between bars and pubs, there are indeed some major differences, as, for example, on the matter of payment. In Germany, the tab is added up on a piece of paper or beer mat until the guest is ready to leave and pays. As a regular patron, he will be given credit if unable to pay. Pubs expect payment to be made as soon as the drink is passed across the bar. Opening times are equally unusual. Most pubs still close at 11 p.m. This means that, about half an hour before closing time, "Last orders!" is called, at which point very thirsty drinkers buy themselves several beers at one go, which they gulp down at speed. The legal limitations on drinking times may have contributed to the somewhat coarse drinking habits which seem common throughout Great Britain. On the other hand, the local ale or bitter is not as strong as continental beers and can therefore be consumed in larger quantities.

As quickly as a glass is emptied it is filled once more. The view that slow pouring improves a beer's flavor is not common on the island. The beer rushes out of the tap like lemonade, and everyone is served in a matter of minutes, which is considered a definite advantage. Brews like ale or bitter are not subjected to compressed air, but are mechanically drawn from the barrel to the tap. Consequently the beer has less fizz.

Continental tastes are catered for with lager. It is similar to a Pilsener or Export beer. The British do not make a great distinction between lager and blond, foreign beer which is served on tap or by the bottle. It could be Holsten Pilsener or Holsten Export, DAB pilsener or even Beck's – it is always referred to as lager. This type of beer has become increasingly popular since the 1970s and now makes up half the British beer consumtion. The remaining 50 percent have remained faithful to their ale, the traditional English beer.

From spring until the fall, the slightest ray of sunshine lures British people to sit outside their pubs.

Ale is a top-fermented type of beer, and a number of varieties are available. These are pale ale, light ale, bitter, brown ale, mild, barley wine, and stout. Devotees of this, allegedly, lukewarm beer bravely defend their British libation against the influx of continental, bottom-fermented beers. A special initiative, the "Campaign for Real Ale", CAMRA for short, has even been established for precisely this purpose. It publishes pamphlets and books such as the "Good Beer Guide" and, after many long years of battle, this organization can now boast some success. More and more British people are returning to their incomparably aromatic traditional brew.

Non-beer drinkers who would nevertheless enjoy a visit to the cozy pub around the corner, will find a large selection of alternative beverages on offer. Cider, for example, is similar to French or Hessian apple wine. Cider tastes a little bit like sparkling apple juice and, like beer, it is served in pint or half pint glasses. However, caution is advisable: it may go down like lemonade, but cider has a high alcohol content. Beer and cider are drunk at lunch-times and in the evenings. Alternatively, a mixture of beer and lemonade, known as "shandy", is a particularly popular drink among young women. Gin and tonic is a common pre-dinner drink, closely followed by vodka and tonic or vodka and bitter lemon.

Pubs specialize in traditional beverages. Naturally, this includes whisky, without which pubs would be inconceivable. Particularly in Scotland and Ireland, whisky is the second classic ingredient of the pub scene. Incidentally, to experience the authentic atmosphere of a British pub, it is best to go to a village pub in the countryside. With a little luck, a traditional establishment complete with hand-painted sign, a small selection of local ales and home-cooked pub food may still be found. Here it is possible to enjoy the extremely pleasant illusion that England is still the idyllic land of our dreams – at least for as long as it takes to drink one or two glasses of ale.

Left: In the British Isles the pub is still the favorite place to end the day with a measure of peace and quiet.

Right: There is no class differentiation in the pub. With a pint glass in their hands, all Brits are equal.

Famous Pubs

The Grenadier
18 Wilton Row, London SW1X 7NR

Ye Olde Cheshire Cheese
145 Fleet Street, London EC4

Ye Grapes
16 Shepherd Market, London W1

The George Inn
77 Borough High Street, London SE1

The Lamb & Flag
33 Rose Street, London WC2

Prospect of Whitby
57 Wapping Wall, London E1

The Anchor
34 Park Street, Bankside, London SE1

Eating Out in St James's

A true paradise for sophisticated shopping enthusiasts is found in London's district of St James's, where the stores stock everything a heart could possibly desire. Situated between Piccadilly, Regent Street, Pall Mall, and St James's Street, shirt-makers and bespoke tailors, antiques and art dealers offer their merchandise and services. Restaurants, cafés, wine merchants, delicatessens, and tobacconists provide tired shoppers with both physical and spiritual refreshment.

A welcoming haven of hospitality can be found in Green's Restaurant at 36 Duke Street. Every morsel of food consumed in this establishment will be sure to expel any remaining prejudices regarding English cooking, and the wine list is equally satisfactory. With its green leather, mahogany, and brass dominated interior, the restaurant is a favorite lunch-time meeting place for elegant men and women. Food can be taken in the bar, at the oyster bar, or in the dining-rooms at ground and basement levels. The menu features an interesting mixture of international dishes, modern cuisine, and old English classics. A typical lunch may consist of half a dozen oysters, a portion of fish and chips with mushy peas, and a bread and butter pudding for desert. A glass of champagne before the meal could be followed by some Chablis and a bottle of thirst-quenching Scottish spring water. If this seems too much for lunch, it is quite acceptable to restrict oneself to just a light starter. Refreshed, the shoppers can then resume their expedition. They may wish to wander up Duke Street in the direction of Piccadilly to the Royal Academy of Arts, or through

The oysters are a recommended prelude to lunch or dinner at Green's. They are best washed down with a glass of chilled house champagne.

the Burlington Arcade toward Bond Street or Savile Row. In the evening, it is time once more to visit Green's – dinner provides a welcome opportunity to sample some more of the delicious items on the menu.

The legendary department store Fortnum & Mason is also located in this select neighborhood. As mentioned in all the guide books, the male members of staff really do wear morning suits. The term "shop assistant" suits them well since they can frequently be observed patiently following elderly customers from shelf to shelf in the ground floor grocery department, while they fill the shopping baskets with mustard, wine, vinegar, or quail's eggs. Naturally, Fortnum's also stocks cheese, but it is much more fun to purchase cheddar or brie from Paxton & Whitfield a few doors along. Since 1797, gourmets have patronized this store which stocks an unequaled selection of predominantly English and French cheeses. Should you require liquid refreshment to go with your stilton, the finest port wines can be found at the back of the store. After thus whetting your appetite, you may confidently enter one of the many local restaurants.

Caricatures adorn the wall of Green's Restaurant and provide entertainment should one need to wait for a lunch-time table.

Green's Restaurant is only ever this peaceful and empty early in the day, when preparations are underway for the turbulent lunch-time session.

One of the Oldest Wine Merchants in the World

People whose interest lies in the history of specialist retailers will find London a perfect place to deepen their studies. Some stores have been in the same location for hundreds of years, and some are still owned by the families that founded them. Berry Brothers & Rudd of 3 St James's Street is a prime example of this ancient retailing aristocracy. In 1696, the widow Bourne opened a grocery on this site, which became the wine merchant Berry Brothers & Rudd during the 18th century. The store quickly established itself as a favorite haunt of London's gourmets and wine lovers. In 1765, another, very special service was offered to the store's genteel clientele. Patrons could take a seat on a weighing machine and have their weight measured. The results were diligently entered in a book for the information of future generations. The legendary dandy George Bryan Brummel features in this record, as do six generations of England and France's royal families along with innumerable other celebrities. Fortunately, the weighing wine merchant still looks after the welfare of Londoners. They deliver champagne to the city's best addresses, and are equally happy to serve customers in search of a moderately priced white wine. And nobody is forced to reveal their weight.

The first thing to strike anyone entering Berry Brothers & Rudd wine merchants, is the small number of bottles on display. The process of buying and selling is done the old fashioned way: the customer must ask for the desired item before one of the highly trained sales assistants goes into the cellar to fetch it. Whisky aficionados also appreciate Berry Brothers, since the house label is Cutty Sark, one of the best blends on the market.

English wine? Yes, English wine. The Romans introduced vines to parts of the island, including today's county of Gloucestershire, where the climate proved ideal for the grapes. Monks maintained the tradition of viniculture during the Middle Ages and, had the Reformation not intervened, this part of the British Isles may have become a respected wine region. However, since history took its own course regardless of the fate of wine, modern vintners had to start from scratch. Among these thriving businesses is the Three Choirs Vineyard in Newent, established in 1973. It all started as an experiment, but the micro-climate in this part of England, with its slightly higher temperatures and lower rainfall, had a positive effect on the grapes. The gentle slopes and sandstone soil secured good harvests. Their continued success seems to have proven the Gloucestershire vintners right, because their annual production of around 250,000 bottles sells well, and even wine experts are beginning to take note of Three Choirs. This is due in no small measure to the fact that nearly every year the British win prizes at the major wine fairs. At Vinexpo 93, for example, they were awarded the first ever gold medal to be won by an English wine. Visitors are warmly welcomed: vineyards and cellars are open to the public, and the excellent restaurant has recently been complemented by the addition of a small, comfortable hotel.

The Luxury Hotel

Visitors to Great Britain who cannot stay in a private home and have to rely on hotel accommodation will immediately feel cocooned as if in a very comfortable home – as long as they avoid the large chains with their cold entrance halls and standardized rooms, and opt instead for traditionally British establishments. These tend to be lovingly furnished and professionally run places, where no detail has been overlooked. This is because they do not cater solely for European or overseas guests, but also aim to provide their compatriot with a refuge should they ever – voluntarily or otherwise – need to stay away from home. For example, home refurbishments may require one to stay in hotels for several weeks, or even months. This is an obvious solution, since English hotels are a prime example of the "home from home" principle.

It goes without saying that British people, who expect pleasant hotel surroundings when away on business, or even when merely escaping the chaos of building works at home, must be treated in accordance with British standards. This means not only that they are served their accustomed breakfast in the dining-room, but – in compliance with the English tradition of service – that it is taken to the guest's own room without a murmur of dissent. However, of far greater importance is the decor awaiting the guests. People whose homes reflect the British style of combining different fabrics, antiques, and a sense for symmetry, and who have also grown up with an unshakable belief that this represents a traditional – and therefore unassailable – decorative scheme, will always feel comfortable in such surroundings. Consequently, hotels make every effort to satisfy precisely these requirements. British hoteliers are aware that this atmosphere cannot be created merely by hard work and goodwill. A hotel either has it, or it has not. And British hotels are also aware that many of their guests live in beautiful houses or even palaces. Providing these people with that "home from home" feeling is a constant challenge.

Helpful doormen stand outside the Savoy to help guests with their luggage or call a taxi.

There is a wonderful institution that caters for the many British and non-British people who will make do with nothing but the very best: the British luxury hotel. Notwithstanding the prophets of doom, the best establishments in London and in the countryside have no shortage of guests. We would like to mention just four representatives here, although there are many more which are in no way inferior to those named.

When the Savoy opened its doors in 1889, it outranked its competitors in a number of respects. First, by its seven stories, and second by its up-to-date technology. Hence, the Savoy was the first public building in the world with electric lighting throughout. The power required for this was produced by an in-house generator, just as the running water in its 70 bathrooms came from its own waterworks. The water pressure produced by this system is higher than usual – making a shower in the Savoy a truly special experience. Furthermore, the Savoy could boast of elevators, known at the time as "ascending rooms". A peerless kitchen staff under the direction of legendary head chef Auguste Escoffier ensured that even the most sophisticated culinary requirements were more than adequately met.

A few years later, on May 24, 1906, the Ritz opened to the public. Just as the Savoy embodied the transition from the 19th to the 20th century, the Ritz was the perfect expression of the Edwardian era. Although its Louis Seize decor seems a little overdone to modern tastes, contemporary society loved it. Nearly all the legendary greats of the time were guests at the renowned establishment, including Winston Churchill, Aristotle Onassis, Charlie Chaplin, Noel Coward, and the Duke and Duchess of Windsor. Located in London's tourist center, the area around the Ritz tends to be busy nowadays.

Claridge's on the other hand, stands aloof in Brook Street. The Art Deco oasis of British hotels continues to enjoy the patronage of crowned heads. It is not unusual to see screens being erected around the entrance area for a few

Left: Guests are provided with every imaginable comfort in London's hotels, provided they are willing to part with a great deal of money. Other than that, there are no obstacles to a luxurious stay in genteel surroundings.

Above: Truly excellent service should be forthcoming at any time of day or night, and should combine a pleasant demeanor with distance and discretion – as in the Lanesborough Hotel.

Right: Claridge's legendary entrance hall welcomes visitors with the simple elegance which distinguishes it from the heavy pomposity of other hotel foyers.

minutes to permit the Prince of Wales to exit discreetly. The Cadogan is an altogether more intimate establishment. This Edwardian establishment is located at 75 Sloane Street, an ideal address for anyone wishing to explore South Kensington, Knightsbridge, and Belgravia. This hotel, which is rich in tradition, is situated within walking distance of museums like the Natural History Museum or the Victoria and Albert Museum, as well as department stores like Harrods and Harvey Nichols, or even Sloane Square and surrounding streets. The interior is reminiscent of the grand, turn of the century country houses, providing guests with the feel of a feudal country seat in the middle of London.

LUXURY ON THE OCEAN WAVES – THE QE2

According to a famous quote, the British and the Americans are two peoples separated by a common language. However, they are also separated by something else: the Atlantic Ocean. Since the early 19th century, numerous ship owners and seafarers have had as their goal to cross the ocean as rapidly, comfortably, and safely as possible. The first steamship ran the distance in 1819 – albeit with the assistance of its sails – but regular crossings between Great Britain and the USA were not established until 1840. The ship that undertook these regular journeys between America and Europe was the Cunard Line's Britannia. Today, more than 160 years later, the first is also one of the last, because Cunard's Queen Elizabeth II is one of the few ships that still makes the journey between Europe and North America. This project began in 1960 when the British government granted Cunard a loan of £18 million. After a construction period lasting seven years, the successor to the legendary Queen Elizabeth was launched on September 20, 1967. The liner was consciously designed to be smaller and leaner than the ocean giants of previous decades, since her purpose was not merely to sail between North America and Great Britain, but also to serve as a vessel for leisurely cruises. Technical delays and industrial action delayed the final completion of the ship, and two years passed between her launch and her maiden voyage.

Although we now regard the QE2 as the luxury cruise liner *par excellence*, she cannot compare with her predecessors. One of these unforgettable ships was the Queen Mary. She was built in Clydeside between 1930 and 1934. The depression temporarily threatened progress on the works, but the government granted Cunard a loan on condition that they went into partnership with their competitor White Star. The naming of the ship took place in pouring rain on September 26, 1934. King George V's wife gave the ship her name: Queen Mary. On May 27,1936, the liner left Southampton for her maiden voyage, and in August of the same year she was awarded the much sought after Blue Ribbon for the fastest Atlantic crossing. Furnished in the Art Deco style, the Queen Mary made the journey in precisely three days, 20 hours and 42 minutes, and thus became the first to do so in less than four days.

Between 1939 and 1945, the Queen Mary and her sister ship Queen Elizabeth served as troopships in the war against Hitler, transporting thousands of soldiers from America to Europe faster then any warship. Their service for King and Country came to an end in the final days of September 1946. Following a thorough overhaul, both ships resumed their familiar duties. The Queen Mary until 1967 and the Queen Elizabeth until 1968. Thus the QE2 arrived at the precise moment when the two ships whose tradition she was intended to continue were put out of commission. However, even Cunard's second Queen Elizabeth was to see war service. In 1982, she transported 3,000 British soldiers to the Falkland Islands. Today, a refurbished QE2 is ready to take passengers across the Atlantic with renewed splendor and every comfort, but above all, in style.

The Queen Elizabeth II, also known as the QE2, was launched on September 20, 1967, and began her maiden voyage on September 18, 1969. Since planning for the ship began at a time when passenger shipping between Europe and the USA was declining rapidly, she was purposely kept smaller in scale. 293 meters long and weighing 65,000 gross register tons, she was somewhat lighter and slimmer than her predecessors. Hence she could pass through the Suez- and Panama Canals, making her suitable as a cruise ship. As it turned out, this was exactly the right way to proceed, and the versatile QE2 is still in service today.

In 1953, the Royal Yacht Britannia was christened by the newly crowned Queen Elizabeth, and did not leave royal service for another 44 years. A crew of 275 men and women looked after the well-being of the royal family and their guests on their many journeys around the globe. Starting in the 1960s, the private vessel's mounting costs became the subject of growing criticism. In the late 1990s, when the only way to keep the Britannia going was to subject her to expensive refurbishment works, Buckingham Palace finally gave in to public pressure and had her taken out of commission.

When the Royal Yacht Britannia was taken out of commission in 1997, the Queen was seen to shed a few uncharacteristic tears in public. This was understandable, since the monarch had spent many happy hours with her family on board this ship, far away from the inquisitive eyes of the press.

Right: Sun loungers on the deck of the QE2 – a positive invitation to cross the Atlantic by ocean liner. However, most travelers prefer to fly from London to New York, probably because the journey takes too long by sea.

Acknowledgements

Stuart and Heidi Ahrens
Charles Alford
Colin and Carol Arnold
Laura Ashley Ltd. London
Asprey's and Garrard, London
Atco-Qualcast Ltd. Suffolk
Jasper Bagshawe
Balliol College, Oxford (Dr. Jones)
Bernadette
Berry Bros. & Rudd Ltd. London
Justin Bird and Jo
Lucy and Peter Boutwood
Brintons Fine Carpet (Sylvia Herbert), Kidderminster, Worcestershire
Buckingham Palace, The Press Office (Dickie Arbiter), London
Rhu Callender
Jasmin Cameron Antique Decanters, London
Fiona Campbell Interior Design Ltd. (Fiona and Giorgina, thank you), London
Chesney's Antique Fireplace Warehouse Ltd. London
The Claridges, The Savoy Group, London
Cloakrooms, Traditional Wooden Furnishings (John Crellin), Kingsbridge, Devon
Cunard Line, London
Michael and Sue Cunningham
Davidoff, London
Drummonds Architectural Antiques Ltd. Hindhead, Surrey
The Duke and Duchess of Devonshire, Chatsworth House
Duresta (Darren Paul Nicholson), Nottingham
Encyclopaedia Britannica (Jane Reynolds), London
Rose Fane
Julia Hall
D.R. Harris, Chemists and Parfumiers, London
Hypnos Ltd. (Ruth Simmons), Buckinghamshire
Gainsborough's Silk Weaving (Diane Sargent), Suffolk
Green's Restaurant, London
Countess Le Grelle
Francesca Hanbury-Tenison
Merlin Hanbury-Tenison
Robin and Louella Hanbury-Tenison
Erika Hellmuth Public Relations (Wedgwood, Waterford Crystal), Hamburg
The Historic Houses Association, Letchworth, Hertfordshire
Anthony and Sylvia Hopkinson
Inchbald School of Design, London
Marcus Kemp Estates, London
Rob and Carolyn Kempthorne
Lady Victoria Leatham, Burghley House
Sammie Leslie and Sir Jack Leslie, Castle Leslie, Co. Monaghan, Republic of Ireland
Evan Lewis
David Linley Furniture Ltd. (Susanna Wass), London
Angus and Claire Macwatt
Johnny and Lucy Madden, Hilton Park, Co. Monaghan, Republic of Ireland
Mickey Madden
John Morgan, London

The National Trust, London
Jeremy Nichols and the Stowe School, Northamptonshire
The Duke of Northumberland, Alnwick Castle and Syon Park
Kerry O'Connell
Olive Coffee-shop, Fulham, London
Richard Pailthorpe
Parker Hobart Associates (Caroline Wolfenden), London
William and Meredith Proby
Henry Poole & Co. (Angus Cundey), London
Jo Potter
Purdey, Gun and Rifle Makers, London
The Reform Club, London
Brigadier Sebastian Roberts
Robinson & Cornish OHG (Petra Schönfeld), Espelkamp
Sigrid and Prof. Dr. Ing. Wilfried Roetzel, Sülfeld
Rolls Royce and Bentley Motors Cars, Crewe (and Annette Koch from the Press and Information Office, Germany)
Hector Russel Kiltmakers, Inverness
Peter Sinclair
Ivor Spencer School for British Butlers and Administrators, London
Moyses Stevens, London
St Austell Ales Brewery
St James's Palace (Amanda Neville), London
St Kew Inn, Cornwall
Polly Shillington
Capel Tenison
Jack Tenison
Lucien Thynne
Turnbull & Asser (Ken Williams), London
The Victoria & Albert Museum, London
James Webster
Welsh Guards, Wellington Barracks, London
Des and Ginny Weston
Richard Wilkin
Brigadier Gage Williams
Christopher Wray Lighting, London and Birmingham

We hope we haven't forgotten anybody!

The publishers would also like to thank the many committed helpers, who by word or deed have assisted in the completion of the book.

Robin Bastian
Waltraud Düber
Tanja Godlewsky
Sabine Hesemann
Andreas Jeßberger
Holz Konkret, Schreinerei Wachhelder und Moritz GmbH
Horst Kraus
Andreas Mann
Antje Mehners
Ruth Pauli
Angelika Peters
Dr. Johannes Röll
Antje Schwesig-Simac

De Britse Eilanden

Shetland Islands

Orkney Islands

Wick

SCHOTLAND

Inverness *Moray*

Highland

Aberdeen-shire

Ben Nevis 1344m • Braemar • Aberdeen

Perthshire and Kinross *Angus* • Dundee

Argyll and Bute *Stirling* *Fife*

Glasgow Edinburgh

East Lothian

North Ayrshire Berwick-upon-Tweed

South Lanark-shire • Peebles *Holy Island*

East Ayrshire *Scottish Borders* • Rothbury

South Ayrshire

ATLANTISCHE

OCEAAN

Dumfries and Galloway • Morpeth Newcastle upon Tyne

Northumberland *Tyne and Wear*

NOORD-ZEE

Donegal • Londonderry

North Channel

Carlisle • Durham

NOORD-IERLAND *Cumbria* *Cleveland*

Belfast *Middlesbrough*

ENGELAND

Sligo *North Yorkshire*

Mayo *Leitrim* *Monaghan*

Roscommon *Cavan*

Isle of Man *Lancashire* Leeds

Longford Dundalk *West Yorkshire* *Humberside*

REPUBLIEK *West Meath* *Louth* *Meath*

Galway *I e r s e* Liverpool Manchester *South Yorkshire*

Z e e *Merseyside*

Offaly Fingal *Anglesey* *Cheshire* Sheffield • Worksop

IERLAND *Kildare* Dublin *Derby-shire* *Notting-ham-shire* *Lincolnshire*

Clare *Laois* Bray *Stafford-shire*

Wicklow *Gwynedd* Nottingham

Limerick *Tipperary* *Leicestershire*

Carlow *Kilkenny* *Shropshire* *Northampton-shire* *Cambridge-shire* *Norfolk*

Kerry *Wexford* **WALES** Birmingham Northampton Norwich

Waterford *Ceredigion* *Powys* *Hereford and Worcester* *Warwick-shire* • Lode *Suffolk*

Cork Rosslare • Builth Wells *Bedford-shire* Cambridge • Bury St. Edmunds

St. George's Channel *Pembroke-shire* *Carmarthen-shire* *Gloucester-shire* *Oxford-shire* *Bucking-ham-shire* *Hertford-shire* Ipswich

• Llyswen *Essex*

Swansea Cardiff Oxford London

Chippen-ham Dorchester Maidenhead Taplow

Avon Berkshire • Eton *Theems* • Borough Green

Wiltshire Windsor *Surrey* Ide Hill Seven-oaks *Kent*

Devon *Somerset* Salisbury *Hampshire* Bramdean oaks • Folkstone

Exeter • Axminster Southampton *West Sussex* *East Sussex* *Straat van Dover*

Cornwall Shute *Dorset* Portsmouth Brighton

Marldon *Isle of Wight*

Plymouth Paignton

Land's End

Het Kanaal

Kanaal-eilanden

Guernsey

Jersey

NEDER-LAND

Rotterdam

BELGIË

Brussel

FRANKRIJK

Paris

100 km

Chronological Table

Tudor and Jacobean style (1485–1625)

The monarchs

- Henry VII (1485–1509), Henry VIII (1509–1547), Edward VI (1547–1553), Mary I (1553–1558), Elizabeth I (1558–1603), James I (1603–1625)

Portrait of Henry VIII by Hans Holbein (1497–1543) around 1536/1537, oak, 28 x 20 cm Foundation Colección Thyssen-Bornemisza, Madrid

Historical events

- 1534 Reformation and separation of the church from Rome under Henry VIII, the English king becomes head of the Church of England
- 1588 Sir Francis Drake defeats the Spanish Armada with his fleet. The beginning of English maritime power
- 1600 The East India Company is founded and trade with the Orient begins
- 1605 The attempt by a group of Roman Catholic fanatics to assassinate King James I – the Gunpowder Plot – fails and Guy Fawkes, the hired assassin, and his hirers are executed

1649, Execution of Charles I in Whitehall

Art & culture

- 1516 Thomas More writes Utopia, one of the first humanist visions of the future
- 1536 Hans Holbein the younger becomes court painter of Henry VIII and introduces the genre of the portrait as one of the most important forms of painting
- 1593 Death of Christopher Marlowe, dramatist and contemporary of Shakespeare
- 1599 The Globe Theatre in Southwark, where Shakespeare performed his plays, is founded

Science & technology

- 1530 The use of the spinning wheel spreads over the whole of Europe

William Shakespeare (1564–1616) is probably the most famous British dramatist and poet. Title page of the first folio edition of Shakespeare's plays with an engraving of the playwright, colored by Martin Droeshout, London, 1623

Architecture & design

- 1466–1515 Building of King's College Chapel in Cambridge by Henry VI
- 1502–1509 Erection of Henry VII's chapel in Westminster Abbey
- 1515 Building of Hampton Court Palace begins
- 1531 Building of St James's Palace
- 1616–1635 The architect Inigo Jones builds the Queen's House in Greenwich and in so doing introduces classicism to England

Hampton Court is considered one of the most important buildings of the Tudor period. In 1689 the palace was remodeled in the Baroque style by Sir Christopher Wren.

World events

- Around 1450 invention of printing by Johannes Gutenberg
- 1492 Christopher Columbus goes on his first voyage around the world and discovers Cuba, the Bahamas, and Haiti
- 1498 Vasco da Gama discovers the sea route to India
- 1534 Foundation of the order of Jesuits by Ignatius of Loyola
- 1572 2,000 Huguenots are murdered in Paris on St Bartholomew's night
- 1614 The Blue Mosque in Istanbul is completed

Baroque (1625–1714)

- Charles I (1625–1649), Charles II (1660–1685), James II (1685–1688), William III and Mary II (1689–1694, William III alone until 1702), Anne (1702–1714)

Portrait of Princess Anne of England, later Queen of England, Scotland, and Ireland, by Sir Godfrey Kneller (1647–1723), around 1700, oils on canvas, 76 x 64 cm, Schleswig-Holsteinisches Landesmuseum, Schleswig

- 1642 Beginning of the Civil War between the Royalists and Oliver Cromwell
- 1649 Execution of King Charles I in Whitehall
- 1649–1660 Establishment of the Commonwealth, rule of Oliver Cromwell
- 1660 Restoration under Charles II
- 1665 The plague rages in London
- 1666 The first London newspaper appears
- 1666 London is devastated by the biggest fire in its history. It rages for three days in the capital and in the City destroys 13,000 houses, 87 churches, the bulk of the public buildings, and St Paul's Cathedral
- 1685 Many Huguenots flee from France to Britain
- 1689 The "Bill of Rights" restricts the power of the monarch and strengthens the Parliament

- 1667 John Milton publishes his verse epic Paradise Lost, a Protestant re-telling of the Creation, the Fall, and Redemption
- 1678 John Bunyan publishes his allegory The Pilgrim's Progress
- 1658–1695 Henry Purcell is England's best-known composer
- 1660 The King permits the re-opening of theaters in Covent Garden, after the years of Puritanism under Cromwell

- 1645 The Royal Society is founded
- 1675 The Observatory in Greenwich begins its work

- From 1630 onward The Covent Garden Piazza in London is built
- 1730–1748 William Kent develops English landscape gardening
- 1660 Design of Bloomsbury Square, London's first square
- 1666 Beginning of the rebuilding of St Paul's Cathedral and the churches in the City of London under the direction of · Sir Christopher Wren
- 1705–1724 Building of Blenheim Palace

St Paul's Cathedral, built between 1675 and 1709, is considered the masterpiece of the English Baroque. Its architect, Sir Christopher Wren, was a professor of astronomy and also studied geometry. He came to architecture via his interest in geometry and became one of the typical British gentlemen architects of the Baroque period, who first pursued the art of architecture as a hobby and then adopted it as a profession.

- 1618–1648 Thirty Years War
- 1682 William Penn establishes a Quaker colony in North America
- 1689–1725 Reign of Tsar Peter the Great, beginning of the Europeanization of Russia
- 1713 The Peace of Utrecht ends the War of the Spanish Succession and the war between England and France over the North American colonies

Early Georgian style (1714–1765)

- George I (1714–1727), George II (1727–1760)

- 1721–1742 Robert Walpole governs as Prime Minister
- 1757–1761 William Pitt the elder is Prime Minister
- 1739 Beginning of the War of Jenkin's Ear between England and Spain in the North American colonies

Equestrian portrait of George I, King of Great Britain, at the same time Elector of Hanover and Osnabrück, by Sir Godfrey Kneller (1646–1723), oils on canvas, 120 x 100 cm, Handel's House, Halle

Contemporary representation of the devastating fire of London in 1666. People tried to escape from the fire, which raged in London for three days, by crossing the Thames in overloaded boats. It was a miracle that only nine people died in the flames.

- 1719 Daniel Defoe publishes Robinson Crusoe
- 1719 George Frideric Handel becomes leader of the Haymarket Opera in London
- 1726 Jonathan Swift publishes Gulliver's Travels, a satirical view of contemporary England
- 1741 George Frideric Handel composes The Messiah
- 1753 Establishment of the British Museum

- 1727 Death of Isaac Newton, the English physicist and mathematician

The Wilton violin bookcase was created around 1763 and is one of the few pieces of furniture which can be directly attributed to the hand of the cabinet-maker Thomas Chippendale. This mahogany bookcase with its graceful Rococo lines is an outstanding example of Chippendale's technical artistry and style.

- 1729 John Wood the elder builds Queen's Square in Bath
- 1739–47 Construction of Westminster Bridge by Charles Laa Belye
- 1767–1775 Building of the Royal Crescent by John Wood the younger
- 1730–1795 With Queen's Ware and Jasper, Joshua Wedgwood develops important raw materials for the ceramics industry
- 1754 Thomas Chippendale publishes The Gentleman and Cabinet Maker's Director, a book of designs for cabinet-makers

This sumptuously upholstered armchair in the Neo-classical style was created in Chippendale's workshop in 1765 from a design by Robert Adam, the Scottish architect and designer. It is the only one of Adam's furniture designs which was with certainty carried out by Chippendale.

- 1715 The British East India Company begins trade with China
- 1741–1748 Maria Theresa declares herself in the Austrian War of Succession
- 1756 Outbreak of the Seven Years War

Late Georgian style (1765–1811)

Regency and early 19th century (1811–1837)

The monarchs

- George III (1760–1820)

- George III (1760–1820), George IV (1811–1820 as Prince Regent and 1820–1830 as King), William IV (1830–1837)

Portrait of George IV, King of Great Britain and Hanover, by Thomas Gainsborough (1727–1788), 1781, oils on canvas, 76.5 x 63.5 cm, Nationalmuseum der Schönen Künste, Berlin

Historical events

- 1783–1801 William Pitt the younger governs as English Prime Minister
- 1801 Union of Ireland with Great Britain to form the United Kingdom
- 1803 The British occupy Delhi
- 1805 Battle of Trafalgar, Admiral Nelson falls in battle
- 1807 Britain prohibits the slave trade

Regal portrait of George III, King of Great Britain and Hanover, by Allan Ramsay (1713–1784), Guildhall Art Gallery, London

- 1825 Formation of the first legal labor union by William Cobbett
- 1832 Reform Bill, the members of the middle classes receive the right to vote
- 1833 Factory Act for the textile industry, restriction of work done by children and juveniles
- 1837 Release of Hanover from England following the death of King William IV

The ideas of industrialization and progress in the 19th century are reflected in the painting Rain, Steam and Speed by William Turner (1775–1851), 1844, oils on canvas, 91 x 122 cm, National Gallery, London

Art & culture

- 1727–1788 Thomas Gainsborough, landscape painter and most important portrait painter in England in the 18th century
- 1763–1804 George Morland, the great painter of outdoor sport
- 1724–1806 George Stubbs, important painter of horses
- 1768 Foundation of the Royal Academy by leading artists, sculptors, and architects
- 1785 Establishment of The Times newspaper.

- 1775–1851 William Turner, landscape painter and forerunner of Impressionism
- 1771–1832 Sir Walter Scott, Scottish poet
- 1824 Inauguration of the National Gallery

Science & technology

- 1768 James Watt constructs the steam engine
- 1768 James Cook begins his voyages of discovery
- 1768 The Encyclopaedia Britannica appears for the first time
- 1784 Cartwright develops the mechanical weaving loom
- 1796 First vaccination against smallpox by the country doctor Edward Jenner

In this workshop James Watt developed the design for his revolutionary invention, the steam engine.

- 1814 George Stephenson builds the first working locomotive
- 1818 Samuel Clegg develops gasworks engineering to the point that gas lighting can be introduced
- 1828 Foundation of the non-ecclesiastical University College
- 1830 The Royal Geographical Society is founded
- 1831 The decidedly clerical King's College is founded as a reaction to University College

Architecture & design

- Robert Adam (1728–1792) is the most successful architect of the second half of the 18th century and one of the advocates of Classicism in England
- 1788 Two years after the death of the cabinet-maker George Hepplewhite, The Cabinet Maker and Upholsterer's Guide is published
- 1791 Thomas Sheraton first publishes The Cabinet Maker and Upholsterer's Drawing-Book, followed later by two further books

This upholstered chair in mahogany was produced in the workshop of George Hepplewhite, the London cabinet-maker, in about 1780. The delicate filigree work is typical of Hepplewhite's style.

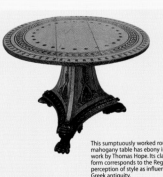

Symbol for the ideals of the French Revolution: the painting, Liberty Leading the People by Eugene Delacroix (1798–1863), 1830, oils on canvas, 260 x 325 cm, Musée du Louvre, Paris

- 1812 Design and building of Regent Street by John Nash
- 1823–1847 Building begins on the new building for the British Museum

This sumptuously worked round mahogany table has ebony inlay work by Thomas Hope. Its classical form corresponds to the Regency perception of style as influenced by Greek antiquity.

The Carlton House writing table was designed for George IV when he was still the Prince of Wales. It is a good example of the elegant classical style of the Regency Period.

World events

- 1762–1796 Catherine the Great is Empress of Russia
- 1763 End of the Seven Years War
- 1775–1783 American War of Independence
- 1789 Beginning of the French Revolution
- 1804 Napoleon crowns himself Emperor

- 1813 Beginning of the German War of Liberation against Napoleon
- 1814–1815 Congress of Vienna
- 1815 Return of Napoleon from exile on Elba, he is beaten decisively by Prussia and England at Waterloo
- 1830 July revolution in France, Louis Philippe becomes King

Victorian (1837–1901)

- Victoria (1837–1901)

This early photograph of Queen Victoria, Queen of Great Britain and Ireland and Empress of India, and her Prince Consort Albert of Saxe-Coburg-Gotha was taken in 1854 by Roger Frenton.

- 1848 Karl Marx and Friedrich Engels publish the Communist Manifesto in London
- 1849 Beginning of British rule over the whole of India
- Wave of emigration from Ireland reaches its peak, 830,000 people go overseas
- 1854–1856 Crimean War
- 1859 Palmerston becomes Prime Minister for the second time
- 1860 Introduction of horse-drawn trams
- 1867 Second Reform Bill, extension of the franchise to further sections of the population
- 1884 Third Reform Bill, extension of the franchise to the rural population

- 1812–1870 Charles Dickens, author of realistic novels highlighting social problems, e.g. Oliver Twist
- 1853 Foundation of the Victoria & Albert Museum
- 1856 Beginning of additional museum buildings in South Kensington
- 1896 The London Daily Mail appears for the first time

The theories presented in Charles Darwin's work The Origin of Species which appeared in 1859 caused an outcry of indignation in Victorian society. Darwin's theory of evolution is caricatured on the title page of this edition of the satirical journal Punch that appeared in 1862.

- 1851 Great Exhibition in Hyde Park
- 1859 Charles Darwin publishes The Origin of Species
- 1881 Electric light burns for the first time in private houses in Great Britain

- 1837–1867 Building of the Houses of Parliament
- 1863 Beginning of the building of the London Underground
- 1894 Opening of Tower Bridge
- William Morris (1834–1896) sets up various workshops, producing everything for the Victorian interior: furniture, textiles, wallpapers, accessories, etc – with his Arts and Crafts Movement he becomes one of the forerunners of art nouveau.

The exterior of the Houses of Parliament was created in the Perpendicular style by the London architect Sir Charles Barry (1795–1860), who gave England a landmark known throughout the world.

- 1840–1842 England's Opium War against China
- 1848 Revolutionary movements all over Europe
- 1870–1871 Franco–Prussian War, victory of Germany
- 1900 Boxer Rebellion in China

Edwardian (1901–1914)

- Edward VII (1901–1910), George V (1910–1936)

- 1903 Beginning of the Women's Suffrage Movement
- 1905 Foundation of the nationalist Sinn Fein movement in Ireland
- 1912 Miners strike resulting in the Minimum Wage Act
- 1911 National insurance first introduced for workers in Great Britain against illness and unemployment

This photograph of Edward VII, King of Great Britain and Ireland, was taken in about 1906.

- 1909 Completion of building work on the museums in South Kensington begun under Queen Victoria
- 1912 Ezra Pound founds the literary school of imaginism in London

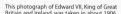

- 1902 Robert Falcon Scott discovers King Edward VII Land in the Antarctic

Captain Robert Falcon Scott led two expeditions to the Antarctic. The first attempt in 1902 failed 150 miles away from their goal. The expedition ship proved useless in spite of its much-vaunted equipment. The second expedition reached the Pole in 1912, just four weeks after the Norwegian Roald Amundsen, the first man to reach the South Pole.

- 1898 In his book Tomorrow: A Peaceful Path to Rural Reform Ebenezer Howard develops the concept of the garden city and thereby provides an important impulse for the course of housing development in the 20th century
  - 1890–1910 Development of Modern Style, the Anglo Saxon manifestation of art nouveau

This photo of Ned Parfitt the paperboy, taken on April 14, 1912, achieved sad notoriety. The headline announces the sinking of the Titanic, in which over 1,500 people lost their lives on April 12, 1912.

- 1911 China becomes a republic
- 1912 Sinking of the Titanic
- 1914 Opening of the Panama Canal
- 1914–1918 First World War

Glossary

Adam, Robert (1728–1792)
Scottish architect and designer in the Neo-classical style. With his brothers James and John, Adam established the extremely popular Adam style between 1760 and 1780.

Aga
Kitchen range combining fireplace, oven, and boiler invented by the Swedish scientist Nils Gustav Dalén. An indispensable item in any country kitchen since the 1930s.

Art Nouveau
A Europe-wide trend in architecture, design, and art in the late 19th and early 20th centuries, known as Jugendstil in Germany. Its stylized organic forms were particularly popular on the Continent; the best-known British advocate of the art nouveau movement, which overlapped with the Arts and Crafts Movement in Great Britain, was the Scot Charles Rennie Mackintosh (1868–1928).

Arts and Crafts Movement
Movement in architecture and arts and crafts founded by John Ruskin (1819–1900) and William Morris (1834–1896), which originated in the last third of the 19th century from a rejection of mass-produced products. Unlike the similarly motivated art nouveau, the adherents of the Arts and Crafts Movement took their inspiration from the techniques and esthetics of past epochs.

Axminster carpet
Woven, velvety floor covering named after the factory set up in 1755 in Axminster, Devon by Thomas Witty.

Baroque
A style trend in art, architecture, fashion, and music originating in Rome in the late 16th century; popular in England in a more austere form from the 17th century. Besides Italian and French elements of style, Dutch influences are also found in the late 17th century. Blenheim Palace in Oxfordshire, built by J. Vanbrugh, is considered one of the most important houses of this period.

Billiards
Billiards has been played in England since at least the 17th century, but the exact origin of this popular pastime is unknown. The oldest existing billiard table stands in Boughton House, Northamptonshire, and dates from before 1670. From the early 18th century the billiard room comes as standard in the country house. An early example of such a room can be found in Southill (built from 1767 to 1803) in Bedfordshire.

Bloomsbury Group
Literary circle of English publishers, poets, artists, and authors who met regularly between about 1907 and 1930. They met at the home of Virginia Woolf in the London district of Bloomsbury, hence the name of the group. Besides Virginia Woolf, Vita Sackville-West, David Garnett, Adrian Stephen, Clive Bell, and others belonged to the group. From 1909 to 1919 the members of the Bloomsbury Group met at the weekend at Durbins, Roger Fry's country house in Guildford, Surrey.

Brown, Lancelot "Capability" (1716–1783)
Landscape gardener and architect, known chiefly as a garden designer. The list of parks he created contains the names of more than 200 properties, including Alnwick Castle, Holkham Hall, and Wrest Park.

Bureau
Writing desk with angled top, which forms a writing surface, and drawers for stationery and writing materials.

Bureau bookcase
Writing desk with bookcase on top.

Butler
The word "butler" comes from the French bouteiller. At first only responsible for the bottles, his tasks, and hence also his influence, expanded constantly until into the 19th century. In the Edwardian period the butler often managed enormous households and commanded an army of staff. Today butlers function more as personal assistants to their employers, often with extensive logistical and administrative responsibility.

Butler's tray
A tray with fixed or collapsible legs, frequently also with a separate lower shelf. Originally it served as a mobile table, for the tea service, for instance. Popular today as a sofa table or occasional table.

Cabinet-maker
Skilled joiner in the 18th century who made furniture to his own designs or from design books.

Cabriole leg
S-shaped curved leg of tables, chairs, and other pieces of furniture, typical of furniture in the Queen Anne and Chippendale styles.

Canterbury
Wooden stand, originally for storing sheet music. Apparently the cabinet-maker Thomas Sheraton first described a piece of furniture of this type in his design book in 1803, made for the Archbishop of Canterbury, hence the name.

Carlton House writing table
Style of writing table from the Georgian epoch with a small super-structure of drawers and compartments around an open middle part, originating in around 1785.

Chaise longue
Modern armchair from 1780 onward, with or without an armrest and an elongated seat for resting the legs on.

Chesterfield
Sofa with deep buttoned upholstery in which the arm and back rests are the same height. Leather is the typical covering, but all kinds of fabric are used.

Chintz
Printed cotton fabric, a popular material for upholstery and decoration in Great Britain since the 18th century.

Chippendale
Synonym for furniture by Thomas Chippendale (1718–1779), England's most important cabinet-maker. His fame rests both on the pieces originating from his workshop and on his design books. Thomas Chippendale the younger (1749–1822) continued his father's work. Work offered under the Chippendale label today has little to do with the cabinet-maker or his workshop.

Coffee table
Living-room table for drinking coffee or tea and as a place for decorative items and, especially, books.

Conservatory
Winter garden or greenhouse developing from the orangeries of the late 18th century. Unlike the orangery, however, the conservatory served the additional useful purpose of raising plants and protecting them from the cold, as well as being a pleasant place to spend time between house and garden.

Conservator
Specialist in cleaning and maintaining paintings and drawings.

Cottage
Blanket term for rural houses which originally provided accommodation for the common people.

Country house
House in the country, according to age and size originally the dwelling of a farmer, craftsman, or member of the landed gentry, from the 18th century onward often also a second home in addition to a town house. At the end of the 19th and beginning of the 20th century the country house increasingly came to be a status symbol and weekend cottage for the upper and middle classes.

Country life
Living in the county, not so much as the working rural population experienced it, but romantically glorified and idealized. Often also equated with the pursuits of the landed gentry, such as hunting, for example.

Country sports
In the terminology of the upper classes, these include hunting, shooting, and fishing.

Croquet
Croquet can be traced back to a French game called paille-maille that has been played since at least the 13th century in Languedoc. The modern form is said to have originated in Ireland in about 1834 and came to England in 1852. Croquet was one of the first outdoor games in which men and women could play against each other.

Cylinder desk
Small desk with a drawer section which could be closed by a cylindrical curved cover. This variant of the bureau, which came into fashion in the 18th century, enjoyed a revival in the Victorian period as a desk with a curved cover.

Damask
Fabric of wool, cotton, silk, or linen in which the pattern and texture are not printed, but woven. Named after Damascus, its original place of origin.

Davenport
Small writing-desk of the Regency epoch. Similar to a standing desk with a sloping writing surface, but lower so as to facilitate work sitting down. The drawers pull out at the side.

Dresser
Often also called a "Welsh dresser." Rustic sideboard consisting of a table or chest of drawers with cupboards and shelves above for the decorative presentation of attractive crockery.

Dumb waiter
Table with several shelves, suitable for holding plates, fruit, or candy depending on size. The dumb waiter was used particularly for intimate suppers: the servants put all the prepared dishes on the dumb waiter and then withdrew so that the master and mistress could dine undisturbed.

East India Company
Trading company incorporated on December 31, 1600 which deputized for the British government in India from the 18th century onward. There were attempts to limit the power of the East India Company as early as the 18th century, but it was not until 1858 that it was taken over by the state India Office and completely wound up in 1873.

Edwardian
Style epoch named after the reign of Edward VII, who occupied the throne from 1901 to 1910. Stylistically this era also includes the closing years of the 19th century; the outbreak of the First World War in 1914 marks its end. This period is important not so much for great innovation in furniture design as for the craftsmanship of its very high-quality reproductions.

Esquire
Originally the page of a knight, later designation and form of address for a landowner, not a title of nobility. Today, a polite form of address when addressing a letter.

Fourposter bed
The fourposter bed is a bed with a canopy attached to the four extended bed posts.

Georgian
Depending on various sources and interpretations, the Georgian period is considered to be approximately from the first decade of the 18th century to the first decade of the 19th century. If it is based on the reigns of George I, George II, and George III, the epoch lasts from 1714 to 1811. The reign of George IV is included in the Regency period. Georgian style draws its inspiration from the art and architecture of Italy.

Gothic
Gothic architecture is characterized by pointed arches. The pointed arch developed in the 12th century out of the round arch of Romanesque and Norman origin. The eastern end of Canterbury Cathedral is considered the first example of Gothic architecture in England. According to Thomas Rickman (1776–1841), English Gothic is divided into early English, decorated, and perpendicular. The Tudor period is also considered as the Late Gothic period.

Half-tester Bed
A "halved" form of the fourposter bed. In the half-tester the canopy or tester is supported by the extended posts at the head end, and therefore only reaches to about the middle of the bed. Half-tester beds came into fashion in the second half of the 18th century.

Hepplewhite, George
London cabinet-maker of the 18th century, who died in 1786. He is known exclusively from the three editions of his design book, the designs of which were made up by countless cabinet-makers. No furniture from his workshop has been preserved. Hepplewhite's classical furniture is lighter and more delicate than that of Chippendale; a typical feature of his style is the shield-shaped backs of his chairs.

Interior designer
An interior designer or interior decorator plans the decoration or design of room interiors and pieces of furniture, often in collaboration with an architect.

Jacobean
The style of the reign of James I, who occupied the English throne from 1603 to 1625.

Kent, William (1684–1748)
Artist, landscape gardener, and architect, born in East Yorkshire. After studying in Italy he first made a name for himself as an artist and garden designer, and then in the middle of the 18th century also as an architect. Besides numerous country houses together with their interiors and gardens, he also designed urban architecture, an example of which is the Horse Guards building in London's administrative district of Whitehall.

Landed gentry
Lower land-owning aristocracy. Old land-owning families without titles are often classed as landed gentry.

Liberty's
London department store established in 1865, mainly known today for its decoratively printed textiles. At the end of the 19th century furniture, glass, and ceramics in the art nouveau style were also sold.

Lutyens, Sir Edwin (1869–1944)
English architect influenced at first by the Arts and Crafts Movement, who later developed a more eclectic style. Well-known houses from this phase are Lindisfarne Castle and Castle Drogo. Also made a name for himself in town planning, for example in New Delhi.

Marquetry
Decoration of furniture by combining different colored veneers, ivory, or mother of pearl to produce pictures or designs. The technique came to England from continental Europe in the 17th century.

Morris, William (1834–1896)
English craftsman, designer, and author; he inspired the Arts and Crafts Movement. Morris advocated the improvement of man through the beautification of his environment. To this end he counteracted mass-produced products with objects made by craftsmen.

Muthesius, Hermann (1861–1927)
Initially a German architect, Muthesius became acquainted with the English style of house-building while cultural attaché in London, and on his return to Germany he concentrated on building large country and town villas according to the model of English vernacular architecture. His influence on residential architecture in Germany was strengthened by the publication of the three-volume work Das englische Haus (The English House) in 1904. He made a name for himself as a founder member of the Deutscher Werkbund (German Craft Work Association).

Nanny
Affectionate name for the British nursery nurse. Until very recently in many well-to-do families she took charge of the children's upbringing in place of the mother.

Nash, John (1752–1835)
Most important English architect of the Regency period, besides his country houses he is mainly known for his marked influence on the cityscape of London. His designs include Regent's Street, Carlton House Terrace, St James's Park, Trafalgar Square, and Marble Arch, and the Royal Pavilion in Brighton.

Orangery
Protective building for growing citrus fruit known in Great Britain since the middle of the 16th century. Orangeries were the forerunners of the conservatory.

Palace
Seat of residence and/or government of secular and ecclesiastical leaders, other nobility, and rich commoners. Unlike the castle, the palace is designed purely with grandeur in mind. In the 15th and 16th centuries the origin of the palace in the medieval castle could still be recognized. In the Renaissance four-winged structures appeared, which were replaced in the Baroque by extensive three-winged structures, open to town or country. The Rococo brought single structures, and in the Neo-classical period palace-building diminished in importance.

Palladio, Andrea (1508–1580)
Italian architect of the High Renaissance. Both his country villas and town houses in the Veneto and his writings inspired such architects as Inigo Jones in the early 17th century. In the 18th century there was a Palladio revival which led to numerous buildings and renovations in the Classical style.

Pedestal desk
Simple form of desk consisting of two pedestals with drawers and a writing surface.

Pele tower
Defensive tower originating in defensive buildings with ditches and protective ramparts of wood and earth in use in Scotland in the 14th century.

Piano nobile
The "noble" floor, the floor with the reception and state rooms, usually situated on the second floor.

Pier table
Narrow table between two windows, usually intended as a decorative surface for displaying ornaments.

Public school
The English term for a private school, a fee-paying educational establishment. The name "public" is a reminder that these schools are not supported by the Church.

Queen Anne style
English manifestation of Baroque style, named after Queen Anne, who reigned from 1702 to 1714. This style is characterized by the use of brick for the masonry and contrasting pediments, cornices, and window frames in light natural stone.

Refectory table
Long narrow table usually from the dining-room or refectory of a monastery or convent. Popular for kitchens and rustic dining-rooms.

Regency
Style epoque of the early 19th century named after the period when King George IV was Prince Regent from 1811 to 1820.

Repton, Humphry (1752–1818)
English garden designer who took the potential already present in a landscape and emphasized and accentuated it through his design. To this purely landscaped garden Repton added more formal gardens near the house.

Restorer
In contrast to the conservator, the restorer is not concerned with merely cleaning and preserving works of art, but also repairs them and replaces damaged parts.

Sash window
Windows that are opened by pushing up the frame. Typical of British houses since the 18th century.

Secretaire bookcase
Writing desk with drawers, with bookcase on top.

Secretaire chest of drawers
Unlike the bureau, the compartments and drawers are concealed behind a false drawer which lets down as a writing surface. When closed the secretaire chest of drawers looks like a chest of drawers.

Sheraton, Thomas
Sheraton, presumed to have been born in 1751 and to have died in 1806, is one of the big four of English cabinet-making, although it is not clear whether he ever made his living as a cabinet-maker. He became known from his books about cabinet-making, which influenced furniture design in England, Europe, and America until into the early 19th century.

Soane, Sir John (1753–1837)
English architect of Neo-classicism, noted buildings are his house in Lincoln's Inn Fields in London and the Dulwich Picture Gallery.

Sofa table
Occasional table, frequently with folding side sections and drawers. In contrast to the coffee table it is placed behind the sofa and not in front of it. The sofa table appeared at the end of the 18th century.

Tallboy
Consists of two chests of drawers placed on top of each other, or one chest of drawers on legs, popular at the end of the 17th and the early 18th centuries.

Tapestries
Handwoven textile fabrics with pictures or designs, the main decoration in the house in the 14th and 15th centuries. The most coveted examples came from Arras, Bruges, Brussels, and Tournai in present-day Belgium. The first English tapestries date from the 16th century. Tapestries enjoyed a revival through the Arts and Crafts Movement in the late 19th century.

Terracotta
Fired but unglazed clay with a characteristic reddish color, frequently used as flooring material, architectural decoration, or for plant containers.

Tudor style
Historically the reign of the Tudor dynasty from 1485 to 1603, stylistically the term describes the transition from the Middle Ages to the Renaissance. The reign of Elizabeth I (1558–1603) is often treated as a separate style epoch.

Vanbrugh, Sir John (1664–1726)
English dramatist, soldier, and architect, one of the main exponents of the Baroque style. Since he had no special architectural knowledge he worked in conjunction with Nicholas Hawksmoor in the implementation of his designs. Vanbrugh's best-known building is Blenheim Palace, the completion of which he did not witness, since he quarreled with the Duchess of Marlborough, the wife of his employer, before it was finished.

Vernacular architecture
Rural residential architecture with a regional flavor, dependent on the locally available building materials and local social structures, encountered in very many houses built between 1350 and 1800. With the beginning of the 19th century and the increased possibilities for transporting building materials, regional differences became less marked and vernacular architecture slowly disappeared.

Victorian style
The style of the Victorian period, the reign of Queen Victoria from 1837 to 1901, is characterized by the revival and mixing of past style periods, and incipient industrialization in the manufacture of furniture and commodities.

Windsor chair
Rustic chair with curved wooden seat, turned legs, and a semi-circular back with upright rods. Probably originating in Buckinghamshire, from about 1700 onward it spread throughout Great Britain. A popular chair until the present time, especially for the kitchen or country dining-room.

Wren, Sir Christopher (1632–1723)
English scientist and important architect who created some of the most significant buildings of the English Baroque. After London had been devastated by the fire of 1666 he headed the rebuilding of the City. He had a hand in, among other things, the design of 51 churches. St Paul's Cathedral is his masterpiece. In addition, Wren designed numerous secular buildings, including the Royal Hospital in Chelsea.

Bibliography

Adburgham, Alison: *Shopping in Style* Over Wallop, Hampshire 1979
Astaire, Lesley, et al.: *Living in Scotland* London 1987
Barley, Maurice: *Houses and History* London 1986
Boyle, Philip: *Englische Möbel* Munich 1998
Bridge, Mark: *Schreibtische* Cologne 1996
Brown, Craig, Lesley Cunliffe: *The Book of Royal Trivia* London 1982
Brown, Michèle: *Prince Charles and Princess Diana* London 1984
Busack, Walter: *Das neue Hundebuch* Niedernhausen/Ts 1994
Calloway, Stephen (Ed.): *The Elements of Style* New York 1996
Chambers, James: *The English House* London 1985
Chambers, James: *Georgian London* London 1991
Collins, Wilkie: *The Woman in White* London 1860
Connolly, Sybil (Ed.): *In an Irish House* London 1988
Cowley, Robert: *Die Herrscher Britanniens* Munich 1983
Crook, J Mordaunt: *Victorian Architecture* New York 1971
Durant, David N.: *Life in the Country House* London 1996
Garnett, Oliver: *Country House Pastimes* London 1998
Fischer, Paul, Geoffrey Burwell P.: *Kleines England-Lexikon* Munich 1991
Fox, Robert: *Liners* Cologne 1999
Franklin, Jill: *The Gentleman's Country House and it's Plan* London 1981
Gibbs, Jenny: *The Country House* London 1997
Hardyment, Christina: *Behind the Scenes* London 1997
Hardyment, Christina: *A Slice of Life* London 1995
Harling, Robert, et al.: *The House & Garden Book of Drawing-Rooms and Sitting-Rooms* London 1991
Hartley, Dorothy: *Food in England* London 1996
The House & Garden Book of Essential Addresses London 1997
Jackson-Stops, Gervase, James Pipkin: *The English Country House, a Grand Tour* London 1993
Jennings, Charles: *People Like Us* London 1998
Jones, Richard: *Walking Haunted London* London 1999
Kamm, Anthony, Claude Poulet: *Britain and her People* Godalming, Surrey 1990
King, Constance: *Sofas* Cologne 1996
Kravchenko, Chrissie: *Collector's Lot* London 1998
Linley, David: *Classical Furniture* London 1993
Lord, Graham: *James Herriot* London 1998
Macaulay, Rose: *Life among the English* London 1996
Matthews, Rupert O.: *Großbritannien* Erlangen 1991
Matz, Klaus-Jürgen: *Europa-Chronik* Munich 1999
Montgomery-Massingberd, Hugh, Simon Sykes: *Great Houses of England and Wales* London 1994
Montgomery-Massingberd, Hugh, Simon Sykes: *Great Houses of Scotland* London 1997
Morgan, John: *Debrett's New Guide to Etiquette and Modern Manners* London 1996
Moynahan, Brian: *Das Jahrhundert Englands* Munich 1997
Muthesius, Hermann: *Das englische Haus, Entwicklung, Bedingungen, Anlage, Aufbau, Einrichtung und Innenraum* 3 vols Berlin 1904-1905
Nicolson, Nigel: *Portrait of a Mariage* New York 1973
Plumptre, George: *The Garden Makers* London 1993.
Prince Charles and the Architectural Debate, in: *Architectural Design* Vol 59, Nos 5-6, 1989

Quiney, Anthony: *House and Home, A History of the Small English House* London 1986

Service, Alistair: *London 1900* St Albans and London 1979
Smith, J.T.: *The English House 1200–1800* London 1992
Somerset Fry, Plantagenet: *Kings and Queens* London 1990
Spencer-Churchill, Henrietta: *Classic Fabrics* London 1996
Strong, Roy: *Country Life 1897-1997, The English Arcadia* London 1999
Summerson, John: *Architecture in Britain 1530-1830* London 1991
Trembath, Geraldine: *The Connoisseur's Guide to English Style* Honiton, Devon 1996
Watkin, David: *English Architecture, A Concise History* London 1979
Way of Plean, George, Romilly Squire: *Clans and Tartans* Glasgow 1995
Westland, Pamela, Marjie Lambert: *Blumenschmuck* Cologne 1997
Which? Way to Buy, Sell and Move House London 1998
Wigan, Felicity: *The English Dog at Home* Massachusetts 1987
Willes, Margaret: *And So to Bed* London 1998
Yapp, Nick; Rupert Tenison: *London* Cologne 1999
Yates, Simon, *Tische* Cologne 1996
Young, Geoffrey: *Walking London's Parks and Gardens* London 1998
Zeutschner, Michael: *England* Erlangen 1995

Text credits

The following authors have written contributions on various subjects for *Traditional Style*:

Till Busse: "From cottage to cottage ornée", (p 61), "The Arts and Crafts Movement", (pp 152f)
Waltraud Düber: "The fruits of the plant hunters" (pp 286f)
Sabine Hesemann: "The discovery of the landscape" (pp 282-285)
Uta Kornmeier: "The development of castle building" (pp 34-37), "From castle to palace" (p 42), "The golden age of the country house" (pp 50f), "The Palladian Movement or Palladianism in country house architecture" (pp 56-58), "The business of the lease" (p65), "The English house – model for the modern" (pp 72f), "Guests at Durbins – the Bloomsbury Group" (p 74), "The development of the town house" (p 87), "The Prince's principles" (p 100), "Inventor of the modern flush toilet – Thomas Crapper" (p 230), "Sissinghurst Castle Garden" (p 281).

Picture Credits

Authors and publisher have all made intensive efforts, right up to going to press, to locate all owners of rights to illustrations. Any persons or institutions who may not have been reached and who assert rights to illustrations are asked to contact the publisher immediately.

l. = left; r. = right; c. = center; t. = top; b. = bottom

All photographs © Könemann Verlagsgesellschaft mbH, Cologne/photo: Rupert Tenison.

With the exception of:

Abode, Macclesfield: 6 c. b. 133 t.c.r. 133 c.r. 134 b. 149, 162 t. 162 b.l. 194/195, 198, 199 b.r. 202 b.l. 202 b.c.., 260 t.

Andes Press Agency, London/photo: Carlos Reyes-Manzo: 309 b.c. 315 t. 318 t.

Arcaid, Kingston-upon-Thames/photo: Richard Byrant: 81 b. (Clarence House), 281 t. 281 b.l. 329 r.c.b.

Archiv für Kunst und Geschichte, Berlin: 72 t. 118 t. 209 b.c. 240 b. 243 c.l. 328 l.t. 328 r.b. 329 l.t. 329 r.t. 330 l.t. 330 r.t. 331 l.t. 331 r.t.

Atco-Qualcast Ltd. Stowmarket: 290, 291

Franz Baghi, Weil der Stadt: 219 t. 219 c.

John Bethell/by courtesy of Marquess of Zetland/photo: Eduard Noack: 329 r.b.

Bildarchiv Foto Marburg: 73

Bildarchiv Monheim, Meerbusch

Bilderberg, Hamburg/photo: Popperfoto: 118 c.r. 303 b.r.; Walter Schmitz: 305

The Bridgeman Art Library, London: 152, 153, 285 t.

Brintons Ltd. Kidderminster: 159

British Library Board, London: 247 b.

Cinetext, Frankfurt: 71 t.r. (film still)

Cloakrooms, Kingsbridge/Devon: 115 l. 115 r.c.t.

© House & Garden/The Condé Nast Publication Ltd. London/photo: Simon Brown: 133 b.c.l. 135 t.c.; Andreas von Einsiedel: 148 t.

Deutsche Presse-Agentur dpa, Frankfurt: 174, 241, 254 b.l. 324 b.r.

Duresta Upholstery Ltd. Nottingham: 136

Edifice, London/photo: Darley: 50 b.r. 83, 86 b.l. 86 b.r. 95, 279 t. 280 t. 281 b.c. 281 b.r. 283 b.; Lewis: 48, 96 b.r. 161 t.c.l. 161 b.c.l. 282 t.; Ryle-Hodges: 55 t. 58 l.; Sayer: 40 t.

English Heritage Photographic Library, London: 56 b.r.

Das Fotoarchiv, Essen/photo: Ernst Horwath: 260 b. 261 b.; Knut Müller: 299 b. 306 b.r. 307; SVT-Bild: 209 t.r.; Jochen Tack: 7 b. 79 t. 296/297, 300, 319, 322 t.

Gainsborough Silk Weaving Company, Sudbury: 20, 21 t.

Richard Greenhill, © Sally + Richard Greenhill, London: 309 c. 309 b.l. 309 b.r.

Hamley's, London: 259 b.r. 262 t.l. 262 t.c.l. 263 b.

Heather Angel, Farnham: 286/287 (except 287 b.r.), 288, 289

Markus Hilbich, Berlin: 72 b.

The Hulton Getty Picture Library, London: 74 t. 176 t. 208 t. 209 t.l. 209 b.l. 209 b.r. 237 t.r. 237 b.l. 259 t. 328 t.r. 329 r.c.t. 330 l.c.t. 331 l.c. 331 c.r. 331 r.b.

Hypnos, Bucks: 204, 205 (except r.)

The Interior Archive, London/photo: Simon Brown: 202 t.; Chris Drake: 268 b.; Fritz von der Schulenburg: 242 r. 243 t.r. 248 b.l.; Christopher Simon Sykes: 185 b.r. 238 t. 242 l. 243 t.l. 243 t.C. 248 b.c. 248 b.r.

Kartenstudio Maiwald, Norderstedt: 90/91, 312, 327

Barbara Klemm/Frankfurter Allgemeine Zeitung (16.1.99): 74 b. 75

© Könemann Verlagsgesellschaft mbH, Cologne/photo: Günter Beer: 143 b. 193 (Barsch); Christoph Büschel: 193 (perch, tench, carp, eel); Elsner/Schulzki: 213 l.; Eduard Noack: 24/25 (except oak, walnut, mahogany, cherry, sycamore); Ruprecht Stempell: 193 (trout)

Helga Lade Fotoagentur, Frankfurt/photo: 261 t.; Paul Steeger: 206 b.c.l.

laif, Cologne/photo: Peter Bialobrzeski: 218, 219 b.; Heiko Specht: 78 b. 93 t.; Tophoven: 78 t.; Fulvio Zanettini: 79 b.l.

David Linley & Co Ltd. London/Press Office: 244, 245

James Lock, London: 313 b.c.

Look, Munich/photo: Ingolf Pompe: 249 t. 303 l. 309 t.

Mallet & Sons (Antiques) Ltd. London/photo: Eduard Noack: 330 l.c.b.

Mary Evans Picture Library, London/photo: 306 b.l.; Henry Grant: 304 t.l.

Bildarchiv Monheim, Meerbusch: 50 b.l. 60 t. 80 b. (Kensington Palace), 86 t. 87, 282 b. 283 t. 331 l.b.

National Gallery Picture Library, London/photo: Eduard Noack: 330 l.c.t.

National Trust Photographic Library/photo: 71 b.(Compton Castle); Matthew Antrobus: 57, 112 t.c. 237 t.l.; Oliver Benn: 56 t.; John Blake: 46 b.r. 47 b.l.; Andrew Butler: 44, 71 t.l. (Claydon House); Peter Cook: 47 t.r.; Andreas von Einsiedel: 182 r. 189 t.r. 189 b. 192 t.l. 192 b. 243 c.r. 243 b.; Mark Fiennes: 59; Geoffrey Frosh: 238 b.; Andrew Haslam: 193 t. (lake); Nadia MacKenzie: 109 t.re, 124, 170 t.; Rob Matheson: 51 b. 189 t.l.; Nick Meers: 45 b. 52 t. 53; Alasdair Ogilvie: 34 b.r.; Stephen Robson: 33 t.l. 46 t. 192 t.r.; David Sellman: 46 b.l.; Ian Shaw: 45 t.; Rupert Truman: 47 c.l. 47 c.r. 47 b.r. 52 b. 71 t.r. (Dyrham); Mike Williams: 47 t.l. 229 b.r.

Okapia, Frankfurt/photo: Renee Lynn/NAS: 119 (beagle); Klein & Hubert/BIOS: 119 (bloodhound)

Picture Press, Hamburg/photo: Camera Press/Clive Arrowsmith: 118 b.l.; Corbis/Bettman: 68 t. 118 c.l. 237 b.r. 254 t. 310 t.

Henry Poole & Co. London: 175 t. 175 b.l.

James Purdy & Sons, London: 220 t. 221

Robinson & Cornish, London: 6 c.t. 180, 183, 186, 187, 190 t.r. 193 b.l. 269

Rolls-Royce Press and Information Office, Germany: 165

Ronald Grant Archive, London: 70 t. 71 t.l. (film still), 71 b. (film still), 208 b.

The Royal Collection © HM Queen Elizabeth II/photo: 265, 325 t.; David Cripps: 264

Scala, Antella/Florence: 330 l.b.

Science Museum, London/Science & Society Picture Library: 138 t.

Sipa Press, Paris/photo: 80 (Princess Alexandra), 81 (Queen Elizabeth II & Prince Philip), 145 t.l. 240 t.; Steve Butler: 81 (Queen Mother); Cherrnauld: 80 (Princess Diana); Gamble: 145 b.l. 145 b.c.r.; Gunther: 81 (Prince Andrew); Thomas Haley: 217 216t; Harvey: 118 b.r.; Anwar Hussein: 80 (Princess Margaret), 145 t.c.r.; Steve Lemere: 80 (Prince of Wales, Prince William, Prince Harry), 81 (Prince Edward & Sophie Rhys-Jones); Mark Lloyd: 205 t.r.; Mantel: 324 b.l. 325 b.; Schneider: 80 (Princess Anne)

Spode, Stoke-on-Trent: 146/147

Three Choirs Vineyards, Newent: 321 b.

Tony Stone Images, Munich: 315 b.

V&A Picture Library, London/photo: 173 r.; Courtesy of Trustees of the V&A, London/photo: Eduard Noack: 330 r.c.b. 330 r.b.

Georg Valerius, Cologne: 249 b.

Erika Hellmuth PR, Hamburg/photo: The Wedgwood Museum: 144, 145 t.c. l. 145 t.r. 145 b.c.l. 145 b.r. 178 b.l. 299 t.

from: **Architectural Design** – Prince Charles and the Architectural Debate, Vol. 59, Nos. 5/6, London 1989/photo: Eduard Noack: 100 b.

from: **Architecture in Britain** 1330-1830, John Summerson, Penguin Books Ltd. London 1991/photo: Eduard Noack: 50 t. 41 b.

from: **English Architecture**, David Watkin, revised edition, Thames and Hudson Ltd. London 2000: 34 b.l.

from: **A Guide to Architecture** – The Architecture of London, Edward Jones/Christopher Woodward, Weidenfeld & Nicolson, London 1983: 56 b.l.

from: **House and Home** – A History of the Small English House, Anthony Quiney, British Broadcasting Corporation, London 1986: 60 b.

from: **London 1900**, Alistair Service, Granata: 94 b.

from: **Town Houses** – Evolution and Innovation in 800 years of Urban Domestic Architecture, Marcus Binney, Reed Consumer Books Ltd. London 1998: 82 r.

Index